# THE
# ENGLISH
# DAIRY FARMER
# 1500—1900

# The English Dairy Farmer

## 1500—1900

### G. E. FUSSELL

FRANK CASS & CO. LTD.

1966

Published in 1966 by
FRANK CASS & CO., LTD.
10 Woburn Walk, London, W.C.1.

Printed in Northern Ireland by
W. & G. Baird, Ltd., Belfast.

"We rob her of her children that
we may rob her of her milk"

# INTRODUCTION

The only one good reason for presenting yet another book to the public in these days of massive book production is that a subject has not already been discussed in detail. I think that reason holds good for this book. Although the importance of dairy products in human diet is now realised as never before, no attempt has so far been made to write the history of the English dairy farmer and his business.

The Dairy Farmer was always a man who did his job in the best way he knew and who was willing to change his methods if a new way seemed good to him. Dairy farming is the work of human beings, and its development was the result of human action, not the result of the blind forces of nature, nor of impersonal economic forces. All history is, in fact, the story of what men and women did, and it is the development of one group of human actions through four centuries that I have tried to describe here.

Like all branches of farming the subject is complex. Its elements necessarily interlock, and splitting them up for discussion is a matter of some difficulty. Some repetition is unavoidable, but this is less than it must have been if the story was told in periods of time. Change was slow in the earlier days, and I am sure readers would find tedious the repeated details of very similar practices in Tudor times, and under each subsequent dynasty until the end of the nineteenth century. The story has therefore been broken up into the various branches of the subject, and the developments that took place throughout the whole period discussed in separate chapters. Where it was necessary I have tried to show the bearing of each upon the others and so to make a significant whole. The effect of external influences outside the farmer's control have been treated in the same way.

The farmer's cow is, of course, the centre round which all

dairy farming must revolve. Despite the numerous books on the individual breeds and Mr. Trow-Smith's recent work 'British livestock husbandry to 1700' the cow must therefore take pride of place here, but strictly as a milk producer.

Much of the greater well-being of present day dairy cattle is due to better feeding. The improvement of grassland was something the old-time farmer gave thought to, but it is a development that has largely taken place in the last half century, and is therefore outside the scope of the present study. The efforts to improve the sustenance of the cow however clearly deserve the second place in the discussion. Also we must consider the comfort of the cow, another important factor in encouraging its productivity, which can only be secured if it has a pleasant home to live in when it is not grazing in the fields.

After the cow has been cared for, fed, housed and milked the milk has to be processed. In modern times this is a simple operation because most milk is sold liquid and has only to be cooled and put in the transport churn for collection. Until 1850 this was a minor department of the dairy farmer's business as most of the milk produced was made into butter and cheese, both commodities that would keep longer and were more easily transported in good condition than milk, even had there been a sufficient demand for it. The dairy itself was an important place and a good deal of thought was given to its construction, and though the utensils used in processing milk were simple, they became complex as time passed and invention flourished.

When the milk, butter and cheese had been produced, they had to be sold, at a profit if possible. It seems to me however that it is not of very great service to include dairy farmer's accounts of different dates. The value of money has changed so much in the period as to render financial comparisons of various times of very little significance: so I have confined myself to describing the marketing and transport systems by means of which dairy produce passed from the producer to the consumer.

This rough outline of the dairy farmer's business from

cowkeeping to the sale of the produce has only been given because it shows why I have planned the book as I have. No doubt the story could have been arranged in other ways; all have disadvantages as they have advantages. The best is difficult to choose. The one selected seemed to me preferable for in some ways it is based on the cow like the business itself.

To compile the story it has been necessary to range widely. The main source of information is, of course, the numerous farming textbooks that were published during the period. Although most are general works, they do contain something about dairy farming. It was only towards the end of the eighteenth century that specialist dairy textbooks were first published. The number rapidly increased. Topographical descriptions of counties and of districts and traveller's tales of their tours in England often contain descriptions of the local dairy industry. Country people's diaries and occasional accounts throw light on this or that part of the subject. Fiction and poetry, as well as local superstition, proverbs and sayings, supply human touches, sometimes flavoured with bucolic humour and wit. While for the last century and a half there are the proceedings of local and national agricultural societies, and there is some primary and secondary material in the publications of learned societies, again both local and national. Doubtless too there is other material in the county record offices, but these are now so numerous that it has not been possible to visit them. I hope that nothing significant has been missed for this reason.

Finally I must add that this work has been made possible by a grant from the Milk Marketing Board, and that I owe a considerable debt to officials of that Board for their valuable help in collecting statistical material at the Public Record Office and elsewhere. Without that help the research would have been much more arduous, and unduly prolonged. My wife, too, relieved me of much tedious work, of which there is always so much to be done.

The courtesy of Librarians is proverbial. The resources of my own library, which are comparatively limited, are quite inadequate to the purpose of this book. Those of the British

Museum are almost inexhaustible, but the specialist libraries have also their advantages. The Royal Agricultural Society Library is invaluable, and Miss R. Watson has given me great help. For modern works the library of the Ministry of Agriculture is unsurpassed, and it has also an excellent collection of sources. The School of Agriculture library at Cambridge is also most useful, and, of course, the University Library, both within reasonable distance of my home.

I wish to thank the following, who have been kind enough to read and offer helpful criticism of chapters of the work. Mr. E. Capstick of the United Dairy Co., Ltd., and Hon. Editor of the British Dairy Farmer's Association Journal, read Chapter I; Mr. A. R. Beddows of the Welsh Plant Breeding Station, Chapter II; Miss Cheke and Miss Sheppard of the Dairy Department, Reading University, Chapter IV; and Mr. Norman Ashworth of the Express Dairy Co. Ltd., Chapter VI. The original draft has certainly been improved as a result, but I must nevertheless take full responsibility for all that is said, and ask the reader to bear with any mistakes of detail that I may have perpetrated and for any expressions of opinion with which he may disagree.

Some material published in serial form in the Dairyman (now Dairy Engineering), and other periodicals has been used here and due acknowledgements are made.

G. E. Fussell

*Sudbury, Suffolk*
*1966*

# CONTENTS

# LIST OF ILLUSTRATIONS

# CHAPTER I

## Dairy Cattle

### (i). The farmer's herd

All over the world and at all times the ambitious small-holder has made it his aim to possess a cow, and then to progress to the ownership of another, until he had a small herd.

Our Tudor ancestors were mainly small farmers. Many working tiny holdings in the arable fields, had some rights to a measure of grazing, and every one of them must have aspired to this ideal. All who could kept a cow or so, as its produce was so important to the daily diet. Milk, butter, buttermilk, cheese, curds and whey were extremely useful at home; and in those parts of the country where dairy farming predominated, formed important elements of nutrition as well as the main cash crop. In other districts any surplus over household requirements could be sold to bring in a little money.

So the struggling peasant who lost his cow from disease, accident or poverty, suffered a major disaster, as a supply of wholesome food vanished and the minute income as well. The seriousness of such a misfortune was known to everyone, even London playwrights in Elizabethan England. Death or accident was natural and could be accepted, but when Alcon lost his cow to the usurer his bitter words must have found an echo in many hearts.

'No cow, Sir! alas that word "no cow" goes as cold to my heart as a draught of small drink on a frosty morning. No cow, Sir! why alas master Usurer what shall become of me, my wife and my poor child?'[1]

Though there were many poor husbandmen and cottagers whose indigence prevented them from keeping even one cow, the farmers, gentlemen, yeomen and husbandmen alike, owned livestock according to their financial ability or the fortunes of inheritance. Usually the Tudor farmer's herd was less than that of his modern descendant, but the number of beasts on one man's farm varied then as now, and there were even then some sizeable herds. In Kent, religious houses had large scale undertakings, but all over the country they must have had to keep larger than average flocks and herds to provide their own necessities, as well as to produce for sale. St. Mary's Hospital, Dover, had three milch cows for the house in 1529. In addition they had 35 kine, 45 bullocks of various ages and 15 calves, as well as cattle in Romney Marsh, nearly 1,000 sheep and a herd of swine. Similarly Minster Priory, Sheppey, in 1531 owned a large herd, comprised of 5 'contre' and 4 western oxen 'fatt' in March, 38 kine and heifers, 12 two year old steers, 28 yearlings and 26 cattle (of that year). This Priory also had a very large flock, a herd of pigs and bred horses.

Other religious houses went in for livestock on a similar or even larger scale. Fountains Abbey had 738 cows, plus steers, calves, bulls and oxen forming a total of about 2,500 head. Some, though, owned much smaller herds only equal to the average of a well-to-do gentleman or farmer, as in the case of the Priory of St. Martin, Dover.

Private gentlemen occasionally farmed equally great enterprises in the sixteenth century. Sir John Gage of West Firle, Sussex was one. His herd was equal in number of any of those of the larger farmers of the nineteenth century, and he must have been engaged in breeding as well as dairying. The nucleus of his dairy herd was the 48 milch kine. There were also 34 fattening oxen, 4 fattening barren cows, possibly indicating complete replacement of the dairy herd over twelve years, 1 fattening bull, 24 working oxen, 4 three year old stores, 23 three year olds, 14 two year, 9 heifers, 2 three year bulls, 2 one year, 1 bulcher, 18 weaners. Unfortunately the sex of the young stock is not given, but the indications are that Sir John went in largely for dairying in spite of the poor name Sussex cows have always had as milkers. Other animals on this farm were a large flock of sheep and a herd of swine.[1b]

In the sixteenth century a comparatively rich Buckingham-shire farmer died owning 2 bulls, 22 cows, 12 three years olds, 10 two year olds and 7 yearlings, besides 10 draught oxen and 140 sheep. A Berkshire farmer of this time was more ordinary. He had only two cows; and 1 heifer, 2 four year olds, 2 bullocks, and 2 calves, probably the produce of his two cows; 4 sheep and 2 lambs, 2 hog shoots and a few poultry. On a Gloucester manor there were 16 cows and 1 bull, 3 young heifers and steers and 16 draught oxen. Here there were only 11 store sheep. A few pigs (various) 5 cart horses, a mare and foal and a few poultry complete the list. A Lancashire holding carried about the same stock as the Gloucestershire manor. A Salopian cleric had a cow, a calf and two heifers; a farmer in the same county had 4 oxen and five more beasts, 3 cows and 3 calves, 17 pigs, 33 sheep and lambs and 4 horses. About the same stock was owned by other farmers in Hants., Lincoln, Salop, Stafford, Suffolk and Surrey. There was not much difference in the Northern counties, though many Tudor farmers there usually, but not always, had more sheep than farmers elsewhere in the country. Dairy herds in Lincoln were sometimes large, and some were becoming more numerous, but the average was not.[2]

Cheshire was always a dairy county, but I have only seen one inventory of a Cheshire farmer, that of Richard Wishall of Leighs. In 1604 he owned 16 cattle, 2 oxen, 2 steers, 4 kine, 2 bullocks, 1 cow stirk, 1 heifer and 3 calves, which evidently included a small dairy herd. He had a few other livestock as well. Another member of the family, Alexander Wishall, possibly his successor, died about a decade later, and his inventory, made in 1618, included 4 cows, 2 heifers, and 3 calves, a rather smaller dairy, and only 1 hog and 1 shoot.[3] However some Cheshire dairies must have been larger than this for in 1618 they were compared with the larger butter dairies in Suffolk where farmers often owned 40 or 50, or even 60 head of milch kine.[4] The Suffolk dairy farmer's herds were individually larger than those of the Fen farmers of Cambridge-shire, but not always than those of Leicestershire. Latimer's mother milked 30 kine on the family farm at Thurcaston, not

3

far from Leicester, and these, with a bull, if young Latimer had one, must have made up a substantial herd. This holding has been estimated at about 150 acres, plus some additional pasture, but if it was only this size there must have been substantial rights of common grazing as well. The richest yeoman in this county was Thomas Bradgate of Peatling Parva. Though he went in largely for sheep, he had 16 kine with 8 smaller beasts, 30 steers and 30 yearling calves. Besides being an extensive arable and sheep farmer he was evidently a breeder and grazier with a large dairy herd. Later his son Richard increased the family holdings and sheep, but did not make any great addition to the cattle. However some Leicestershire husbandmen, doubtless like many elsewhere, owned no cows in the sixteenth century; while others owned a few head ranging up to 13 in John Palmer's herd, and 27 in Robert Bakewell's.[5]

The majority of Essex farmers of the Stuart age did not own many cows. Over 60 per cent. possessed only 1 to 3, and nearly 21 per cent. only 4 to 6. The balance had mainly between 7 and 12, with not quite five farmers the comparatively large number of 13 to 18.[6]

The yeomen of Bedford were dairy farmers to some extent, some of them having herds of from 20 to 30 animals, or even more. Many husbandmen and labourers had from one to six or seven cows, and some light is thrown upon the part time nature of the occupation of village tradesmen by a large collection of inventories of about 1619 in the County Record office. Village smiths, wheelwrights, carpenters, weavers, shoemakers, all owned one or more cows, and some widows continued to run their husband's farms though these were usually on the small side.[7]

At about the same date Nicholas Toke, gentleman, flourished at Godinton and Milstead, Kent. He had a large estate and owned some 1,600 sheep, as well as large herds of cows and oxen. There were 73 oxen, steers and heifers at Godinton in 1624—approximately as many as the Leicestershire yeoman owned in 1588.[8]

There is little doubt that enterprises of this size were very

4

much in the minority. The little man was preponderant then as he has always been.

Similar numbers were common throughout the seventeenth century, and there is no real reason why they should have varied widely. Holdings were on the same scale, and so far as there is any statistical guide, continued to be, except in those parts of the country where the great works of reclamation were carried out from the seventeenth century onwards, and where perhaps the larger farm predominated. The herd of cattle, which lived on grass, hay and straw, could not be enlarged on a holding of a given size because the farmer could not provide more food to keep additional cows.[9]

On the mixed but mainly arable farms of the Midlands, which were for the day highly cultivated, the number of cattle was further restricted by the social organisation which often stinted the number of animals each farmer could turn out on the common grazing. Naturally there were often disputes about these grazing rights. One occurred in Leicester in 1624 when it was decreed that 'allsuch leyes and other greensward which hathe been plowed up within the South fields at any time within XVIII yeares last past, shall be layed to grass again'. Here farmers were restricted to 2 kine and 30 sheep per yardland.[10] The principle of stinting is well known. It was an integral part of open field farming and the manorial courts all over the country were accustomed to decide the number of animals which the occupier of each holding might turn out on the common grazing. Though there were unstinted commons in some places the system was generally an effectual bar to enterprising farmers who wished to increase the number of their livestock, which was only possible if they owned or occupied enclosed grassland.

Both these problems had begun to be solved by the end of the seventeenth century but it was not until the large scale enclosure and redistribution of open arable field and waste made in the eighteenth century that farmers could segregate their cows from the village herd. Only then could they either improve their stock or increase the number kept. The large scale reclamation of land previously only used for summer

5

grazing, like the Fens and Sedgemoor, and wide areas of land previously lying waste and desolate, like Lincoln Heath and the Yorkshire Wolds, brought more land into cultivation and enabled farmers who from the first occupied these lands in severalty to play their part in improving and increasing the national herd.

During this time new fodder crops were introduced and grown in ever expanding areas by leading landowners and farmers. They also made the first elementary steps in the improvement of grassland. Progress here was very slow owing partly, no doubt, to lack of scientific information, but very largely to the acceptance of grass as a natural rather than a cultivated product, an attitude of mind still not unknown. Artificial flooding of riparian meadows was one way of stimulating the growth of grass in favoured places. Consequently the cows could be better fed as well as more carefully bred.

Enterprise too, was able to find an outlet. Population was increasing at an unusual rate and there was the novel situation that the larger number of people in the land were not employed in farming. New industries were being developed and old ones expanded, often in parts of the country where few people had formerly lived. All had to eat, however sparely, and their main source of supply was the native farmer. Only after the 1770's did imports of grain exceed exports. Dairy produce was as yet far from being in the same situation, giving the dairy farmer every reason for doing his utmost to increase his output.

Naturally any increase in the size of herds that was achieved took place in those areas where dairy farming was the principal enterprise. Such figures as remain are therefore likely to be overweighted on the side of the larger herds, and this is particularly evident in the total figures collected by Arthur Young over the large part of the country he travelled when making his Northern Tour. Omitting draught and fattening animals his figures, in 1770, show on 250 farms average herds of 24 or 25 cows and young animals, the last probably including steers and bulls. This is no doubt much above the national average. Just before he concludes that the general run of farmers in Essex owned from 20 to 30 animals. He revised this estimate in 1805 when he reported that Essex farmers thought a herd of 25 cows was large.[11]

Cheshire farmers were reputed to keep vast herds of cattle, and in 1784 they were recorded as often keeping as many as 100, while in the neighbouring counties of Stafford, Leicester and Derby they kept from 20 to 40. These figures can be corrected by the accounts of some contemporary Cheshire farmers. Thomas Furber entered the family farm at Austerson Hall, near Nantwich, in 1767. He bought 20 cows and a bull, 6 two year olds and 4 yearlings as dairy stock with other livestock. Ralph Basford, of Stowford Farm, Weston, near Crewe, (120 acres) fed a herd of 20 cows here from his marriage till 1804. Then he moved to Church Farm, Barthomley, and increased his dairy herd to 25 cows. William Williams farmed some 200 acres on the Cheshire Staffordshire borders from 1812 to 1829 and his land carried a herd of 30-40 milch kine. Thomas Leech, Brine Pitts Farm, Nantwich (about 200 acres) kept between 26 and 30 cows from 1828 to 1854. An American visitor at that time recorded that Cheshire farmers usually kept from 15 to 20 cows on a hundred acre farm. Leech's farm was taken over by his nephew Thomas Furber who farmed it in the same way until the 1880's, though he had suffered like others from the cattle plague in 1866 losing in all 43 females in that year, and it was only slowly that he rebuilt the herd after that disaster.[12] An outstanding dairy farmer toward the end of the nineteenth century was John Lea of Stapleford Hall near Tarvin, who won the R.A.S.E. prize in 1877, and again in 1885. His herd was 91 Shorthorn cows, and it is recorded that in the previous year he had 85 cows in milk. Thomas Farton of Chorlton Farm, Weston, near Crewe, had a herd of almost equal size; but these were exceptions, though there may have been others. On smaller farms of the best type (below 100 acres) about 30 milch cows and followers were carried. Much the same conditions ruled until 1910.[13]

The dairy industry flourished on the land adjacent to Cheshire in the neighbouring counties, but there is no similar detailed information about the size of herds the farmers maintained.

In 1871 John Clay of Kinsale, Oswestry, kept 52 milking cows, 38 followers and 3 bulls on a Shropshire holding of 328 acres, but he was another "Royal" prizewinner and perhaps exceptional. An average of from 25 to 50 or more cattle was, however, kept by the best farmers in 1884, showing that the dairy farms of Shropshire were fairly large in the late nineteenth century, possibly larger than they had been at an earlier date.[14]

Staffordshire farmers owned about the same herds as those of Cheshire. William Pitt estimated the range was 10 to 40 cows in 1808; a few rose to 70. Sixty years later there was at least one large farm with 61 milk cows and 62 followers. At that time Lord Ferrars of Chartley milked 32 graded Shorthorns in his modern cowshed in 1869. These were a great contrast to the wild herd kept at this seat.[15]

The Suffolk dairy industry, which had then been substantial for at least two centuries, was founded on herds that ranged up to a 100 cattle in 1784, but twenty years later Arthur Young found that it was less vigorous. One thousand less cows were then kept in the neighbourhood of Debenham than ten years before. This decrease became progressive until the mid-nineteenth century, but it is difficult to find any reason for this if it was in fact so.[16]

Across the country in Somerset the famous Cheddar cheese was made, though here nothing much is known about the size of herds in early times. In 1790 one herd was of 32 cows on 100 acres and there were 20 on another. This is no more than an indication. Acland estimated that 30-60 animals was the average number on South Mendip farms in 1851. Cambridge, Hants and Berkshire were about the same, but the Dorset dairy herds were somewhat larger. Kent and Cornwall at the turn of the century were less engaged in dairy farming, having only small herds of 6 to 8 cows. Yorkshire farms had from 11 to 30 cows in 1883.

Figures of this kind are not susceptible to statistical treatment especially those relating to the later dates. All that they can be used for is to gain an impression, and that impression may have to be greatly changed when more figures can be obtained from more farms and at more dates. What can be gathered is that possibly herds in the sixteenth century were generally similar to the scale of farming—on the small side. Many people whose main occupation was that of village tradesman kept a cow or two as well as doing a little farming, both in Tudor and in Stuart days. At the opposite end of the scale there were scattered enterprises of large dimensions, the religious houses and hospitals before the dissolution of the monasteries, and those of landowners and yeomen thereafter. It is however, abundantly clear, and indeed has perhaps never been in question, that the majority of dairy herds were of small numbers. Many remained small, but the proportion of larger enterprises steadily increased as time passed and progress was made in breeding and feeding, and in the production of fodder crops. The increase in the number of cows kept by individual farmers was naturally more noticeable in the areas where dairying predominated.

Today the average of the national herd is 16 cows per farm. Herds of 60 or more are not uncommon. The figures I have been able to collect for earlier times cannot be so precisely analysed. All together they do not make up a sufficient sample at any particular point in time, nor are they well enough distributed over the country as a whole. In some degree the evidence confirms the natural conclusion that herds are generally larger today than in former times. Few Tudor farmers had more than half a dozen cows, many had less. The same can be said of those who lived in early Stuart days. Gradually thereafter the dairy and stock farmers were able to expand, and the proportion of larger herds became greater, especially in the counties of Cheshire and its neighbourhood, in Somerset, Suffolk, Essex and Cambridgeshire. Gloucestershire, Wiltshire and Dorset may have expanded in the same way, but any precise account of this development remains impossible and may perhaps always be impossible. With a large measure of evidence I suggest that the change between say, 1550 and 1950, may have been from average herds of 6 or maybe less,

9

to an average of 16. This is highly speculative, and is founded more upon an impression than upon the scanty evidence. The figure for the early date may be far too high, but this is as much as can be said.


## (ii). His choice of a cow


The Tudor dairy farmer had little choice in the type of cow he could acquire as in most parts of the country he could do nothing to improve types. Scientific knowledge of breeding was only to be gained at a much later date. He was handicapped, too, by the physical composition of his holding, and it is likely that he only knew the livestock of his own locality. These were usually called breeds and named after the county in which they were born.

The main distinctions between the breeds were shape of horns, colour and size, but there is some truth in Dr. Cooper's contention that at a much later date 'in Bakewell's day there were no breeds as we know them, but just local races of cattle, sheep and pigs which had some distinguishing character attributed, either to their local environment, or to their source. Where the Danes had settled there would be polled cattle, while in the Anglo-Saxon districts the cattle would be predominantly red. 'All would be long in the leg and the carcase have a high proportion of bone. The hindquarters would be poorly developed relative to the forequarters and head. Genetic differences would be masked through poor feeding tending to bring all stock to the common level.'[1] Contemporary pictures, though few, go far to confirm this impression.

Most modern historians seem to have oversimplified this subject. They are moreover, chiefly interested in the production of beef animals. Carrier reduced the variation in the sixteenth century to two main breeds, longhorn and shorthorn, but allowed some differentiation in these two breeds; and later immigrations such as the importation of Friesians and

Low Country cattle during and after that century were to bring about a general increase in size. There is, of course, a constant rumour of the import of Dutch cattle, but substantial as the evidence may be, and I must return to the subject in later pages, I have so far been unable to find any exact record of landings.[2]

Nothing very much was said about dairy cattle in Ernle's sketch of the distribution of breeds in the seventeenth and eighteenth centuries. For the first he relied upon Gervase Markham's *Cheape and Good Husbandry*, 1631 and John Mortimer's *The Whole Art of Husbandry* 1707, and wrote,

> 'Among cattle, the best breeds for meat were the long-horned cattle of Yorkshire, Derbyshire, Lancashire and Staffordshire. The tall long-legged Lincolns, generally pied with more white than any other colour, were reckoned the best for labour and draught. Those in Somerset and Gloucestershire are generally of a blood red colour in all shapes like unto the Lincoln-shire, and fittest for their uses. So far Markham. Mortimer adds other breeds. The best breed for milking in his opinion was the long-legged, short-horned Cow of the *Dutch* breed chiefly found in Lincolnshire and Kent.'

No very different distributions or improvements had taken place by 1786. Ernle's estimate was,

> In cattle . . . no true standard of shape was recognised. Size was the only criterion of merit . . . The pail and the plough set the standard; the butcher was ignored. Each breeding county however, had its native varieties, classified into Middle-horns, prevailing in the South and West of England, in Wales and in Scotland; Longhorns in the North-west . . .; Yorkshire and Durham; Shorthorns in the North-east. Stock breeding, as applied to both cattle and sheep was the haphazard union of nobody's son with everybody's daughter.

All this is based on George Culley. His immediate followers have much the same sort of thing to say despite the efforts of the highly successful breeders of the late eighteenth century. Omitting the Scots there were then about ten recognised

11

breeds. These were the Devons, Herefords, Sussex, the Holderness or Dutch, the Lancashire long-horn, the Leicester, the Alderney, Welsh of two sorts, Suffolk Duns and Northern or Yorkshire polls. Slightly different classifications were adopted by the various writers, but these deviations are not significant because they include what may be regarded as slight variations on the main types.[3]

To return to an earlier day. Tudor farmers producing butter and cheese for sale must have had some concern for their cattle. They must have noticed the cow that gave most milk, that produced the best calf and that gave the best return for the rations. They would have been great fools if they did not. It may have been that in the Midland Plain and elsewhere among the open fields the necessity for common grazing before the manor cowherd prevented them from doing anything about it. But they were not the specialists of the dairy districts and kept cows for their own supply, anything over going to market. Many of the dairy farmers occupied enclosed pasture and so could control their breeding. They worked under many handicaps, more particularly a shortage of winter keep, but I have no doubt some of them were a little choice in the selection of cows to breed from and the bulls they used.

Confirmation of this not unreasonable supposition is hard to find. The textbooks suggest points whereby a good bull or cow or ox could be recognised, but many were of little real value. The writers, in the circumstances of their time, did not suspect this, nor did the readers who sought their guidance.

Fitzherbert was not very specific on the purchase of replacements. He had no elaborate list of points, expecting the farmer to rely mainly on experience and commonsense. Anyone buying a cow for the pail must see that she was young and good to milk and keep her calves well. The only thing that he was to look for was that she should have a deep navel. She should be bought out of poorer ground than that of the farm she was to go to—a notion repeated for centuries and regarded as applicable to all kinds of livestock and crop seed alike. Nearly a hundred years later Markham advised his readers that the red cow giveth the best milk, and the black cow bringeth forth the goodliest calf. The young cow is best for breed yet the indifferent old one is not to be refused. The cow that giveth milk longest is best for both purposes (a glimpse of the obvious) for she which goeth long dry loseth half her profit and is less fit for teeming' (breeding).

He did not indicate how to judge these characters except in the result, but another work advised that the larger the cow the better she is, for when age or accident comes she can be made fit for the shambles. She must however have all the signs of plenty of milk. These were a crumpled horn, a thin neck, hairy dewlap, and a very large udder with four teats long, thick and sharp at the ends, for the most part either all white, or of what colour so ever the cow be, or at least the forepart thereof, and if it be well haired before and behind and smooth at the bottom it was a good sign.

With pardonable pride he added that all our cows were good, yet, understandably enough, some were better than others. A cheese dairy ought to be made up of black cattle from Cheshire, Lancashire, Yorkshire and Derby, i.e., Longhorns, of red cattle from Gloucester, Somerset and parts of Wiltshire, i.e., Middle horns, or pied Lincolnshire animals, a kind of Shorthorn. The farmer should be careful to have all his cows of one breed. Markham had the excuse of local patriotism in praising the native cows; his enthusiasm was shared by at least one foreigner, Rathgeb, who described the beautiful English oxen and cows with horns usually black. They were not as large as Burgundy cattle, but were low and heavy. Harrison asked where anyone could find cows more commodious for the pail. Cows should be beetlebrowed and stern of look, said an unidentified writer cited by Miss Seebohm.

Another list of the good points of a cow was of continental origin. Hartlib thought the advice contained in the English translation 'not squared for us in England'. This must have been prejudice. Hartlib was not himself an Englishman and ideas had been of international currency long before he wrote. The good cow, according to this authority, was of mean stature, long body, large flank, four or five years old, of a parti-black colour, or spotted black and white, her bagge great, a great belly, broad between the brows, a black eye and great horns not turning in towards one another, nor yet short and small, but bright black, ears very hairy, etc., etc.[4] Some of these points have little relation to the breeding quality or yield capacity of the animal. Similar advice with modifications continued to be offered, and no doubt the visual character-istics of a good cow gradually came to be recognised. Much of this kind of thing was really of very little use, although it may have had a selection value of a sort. Some modern points are little better, but the existence of opinions of this kind, if only vaguely useful, indicates that as early as the reign of Henry VIII, some farmers were discussing the best type of beast to use for their purposes, and the signs which indicated it.

Their choice was based upon experience. If a cow gave a high yield of milk and dropped healthy calves, she was a good cow, and the owner must have argued that her appearance reflected her good qualities. If he could secure other cows that looked the same their performance would be the same the reasoning must have run. Not yet was the influence of the bull to be taken into account.

Men who thought as far as this could not have been numer-ous. A contributor to Hartlib's *Legacie* stated quite categori-cally—with or without authority—that cattle breeding in Lancashire and some Northern Counties was not studied. No attempt was made to improve the best breeds for milking or for fattening. Dairying needed attention. English butter was not all it might be, and the cheese was inferior to some foreign products. It was probably as true as it is today that some foreign cheeses, mostly rather fancy, are and were more tasty than the ordinary farmhouse product.

John Worlidge, who lived at Petersfield in 1666, and was an observant man, unfortunately thought he need record little about the form, nature and choice of cows because every countryman ought to be able to understand how to deal

for them. He was a protagonist of the large Dutch cow that
brought two calves at a birth, and gave two gallons of milk at
a meal. These cows were much like an ox with ill-shaped
heads and horns. Their twinning capacity was repeated by
Richard Blome, and, as Ernle has said, by John Mortimer.
The last thought the Dutch cows tender, and that they required very good keeping. They were kept mainly in Kent
and Lincolnshire, two counties in close touch with the continent.[5]

Nobody criticised Markham's ideas during the second half
of the seventeenth century. It was still regarded as an excellent
principle to buy a cow with a great navel for then it is likely
to be well tallowed. It was still fruitless to buy animals that
had been bred on better ground than one's own farm. However one feature emerged at this date that most modern farmers would agree with. The udder, preferably white, should
have four teats and no more. That the cow should be chosen
of 'the same countrey' (or breed) as the bull is another good
principle. She should not be fleshy, but lean and lank, her
belly should be round and large, and her forehead broad and
smooth with well spread horns. Such a one would prove good
for the pail, according to Richard Blome. Mortimer added
that they should have black eyes, a long and thin neck, thick
thighs, round legs and short joints. The red cow was still
reckoned the best for milk. A notable Leicestershire dairywoman told Edward Lisle, who owned estates in the county
at the end of the seventeenth century, that cows with slender
horns always gave the best milk.[6] Most people agreed that a
young cow was the best, though not everyone thought this. At
Halsall in Lancashire the farmers chose for breeding a cow
about six years old bulled by a large broad headed bull of
about the same age. The cow should be equally broad headed,
with small and slender horns, and a tail reaching to the back
knee. The calves that were begotten were bulled at two years
old by a three year old bull, because a great bull would spoil
such young ones.[7] What this amounts to is that the animals
used for breeding should be about the same age. It would
have been grotesque in those days, or at any other time, to

keep a cow until she was six years old before breeding from her.

The natural interest which any farmer must have in the quality of his cattle was already being emphasised in the early eighteenth century. No pain or charge was too great to obtain a good breed, says one; the best choice that can possibly be got, says another, is essential to the man who is furnishing a dairy. Though opportunity for doing very much to breed better and more productive animals was not very frequent or general, the farmers were, no doubt, alive to what there was.

Preference for a large, big-boned cow remained, for the excellent reason that when she was old—ten or twelve years old or more—she could be made to put on flesh before sale to the butcher. A crumpled lean neck, hairy dewlap, and very large udder with only four teats, and all white were signs usually looked for during the first half of the eighteenth century. If the udder was well haired before and behind and smooth at the bottom all the better. Most opinion, too, confirmed that of earlier times in the certainty that no crossing between breeds should be practised. The local breed, which was likely to be best in its own area, was the best and the bull must not be a foreigner, but of one country, shape and colour with the cow. For example, Bradley thought that mixing red and white cattle had produced the pied kind which were fairly frequent in 1726, and that this had brought the more lusty race to a degeneracy.[8]

Markham's broad classification of breeds was repeated by several early eighteenth century writers, but the Rev. John Laurence of Bishop Wearmouth, Durham, remarked the growing preference, especially in the north, for the Dutch breed that had short horns and long necks in spite of their price which was often as much as £20. He did not agree with the farmers who liked these cows, maintaining that English kinds, if carefully chosen, were just as good. It has been said that, about 1700, the owner of Fountains Abbey and its cattle, which were descended from the white, bought bulls from Holland, red, or red and white in colour, to mate with his cows. Evidently he did not subscribe to the no-foreigner theory, though the imported bulls and native cattle may have been kindred strains. The offspring of his cross were generally roan.[9]

The importation of Dutch or Flanders cattle, related by contemporaries, was another sign of the growing interest in the breeding of higher yielding and more remunerative cattle that was soon to flower in the work of Bakewell, the Collings Brothers and others. William Ellis of Little Gaddesden, Hertfordshire, was a strong supporter of the Holderness breed with which the red cattle, so popular in the West, could not compare, and he too favoured 'these great Dutch or Flanders cows' that bred well if crossed. He once had a heifer bred from a Dutch white cow that proved the best milk cow in the country, and speaks highly of another. Welsh cows crossed with an English bull were, in his opinion, likely to be profitable. He also distinguished the Suffolk dun as a separate breed, and also the blue cows seen in Norfolk. In the main he used the accepted appearance of a good cow, but he is perhaps the first to mention the importance of feeling to see if her milk vein is large.[10]

About 1750 the importance of the sire began to be recognised. Farmers began to be dissatisfied with the haphazard mating of their promising cows with 'everybody's son' on the common wastes, or with the parish or manor bull. John Laurence had suggested in 1726 that a good breed could be obtained by selecting a good bull. A Country Gentleman, who may have been a Grub Street hack, or what he signed himself, put the matter in a nutshell. 'As the males of all creatures are the principal in the breed and generation' great care ought to be taken in the choice of a bull. He set out the points to be looked for, but a Somersetshire grazier, Robert Brown, evidently a practical man, is better worth quoting. The bull should be of sharp, quick countenance, his forehead broad and curled, his eyes black and large, his horns long, his neck fleshy as against the lean neck of the cow, his belly long and large, his hair smooth like velvet, his breast big, his back straight and flat, his buttocks square, his thighs round, his legs straight, and his joints short. This sort of bull was the

17

best for breed.[11] The Country Gentleman's story that a gentleman took white cattle from Lincolnshire to Surrey as a curiosity and so originated the white cows of that county may be true, but it is a little doubtful whether white cows were really numerous there.

By the middle of the eighteenth century the distinctive characters of modern breeds were beginning to emerge, or perhaps I should say were beginning to be more closely noted by the writers of farming textbooks. All have something to say about the advantages of the breeds they distinguished, but it is fairly clear that they preferred the Longhorn for most qualities. That is perhaps one of the reasons why the first of our renowned breeders, Robert Bakewell, based his experiments on this breed. Ernle has concisely described their results.

> 'It was his material not his system which failed. He endeavoured to found his typical race on the Lancashires or Craven Longhorns which were the favourite cattle in Leicestershire, and, in his opinion, the best breed in England.'

This opinion was general at the time. Nearly all the contemporary topographers considered the Lancashires and the Somersets the best breeds, and some added the Lincolns. Bakewell

> 'based his improvements on the labours of two of his predecessors. Sir Thomas Gresley of Drakelow, near Burton-on-Trent began about 1720 the formation of a herd of Longhorns. On the Drakelow blood Webster of Canley, near Coventry, worked, and to his breed all the improved Longhorns traced their descent. Bakewell founded his experiments on a Westmorland bull and two heifers from the Canley breed. To them he applied the same principles that he followed in sheep breeding, and with great success. As grazier's stock the breed was greatly improved, but as milkers (unfortunately for the West Midland dairy farmers) the new Longhorns were deteriorated by their propensity to fatness. In a county like Leicestershire which depended not only upon feeding stock but

upon dairy produce, the poverty of milking was a fatal objection. Even in his Longhorns Bakewell did not long retain the lead. It soon passed away from him to Fowler of Rollright, Oxfordshire. But the breed was beaten by one which possessed superior natural qualities. Almost throughout England (a picturesque exaggeration) the Durham Shorthorns, founded on the Holderness and Teeswater cattle, jumped into first place, as the best rent payers, both as milkers and meat producers. The Ketton herd of Charles Colling became to cattle breeders what Bakewell's Dishley flock was to sheepmasters. A hundred years later Bakewell's favourite breed was almost extinct.'[12]

In his enthusiasm for the great improvers Ernle said that Bakewell's success raised a host of imitators, and gave the impression that practically all breeders adopted the new methods. This implication is of very doubtful validity, especially in the light of the main purpose of eighteenth century enclosure, which was to afford an opportunity for improved arable farming. He also accepts as a criterion of the improvement in the general cattle of the kingdom the average weight of carcases sold at Smithfield in 1710 and 1795 as supplied by Sir John Sinclair, with the reservation that Sir John is not always a reliable witness. These figures have however now been questioned, and even if they were a true statement of the carcase weights at the Smithfield Market, they need not necessarily reflect a general development, nor indeed an increase in the size and productivity of dairy cattle. The average weights may indeed have been influenced by the comparatively high number of large dairy Shorthorns fattened by the London cowkeepers when their yield declined, and sold as meat in the Metropolis.[13]

These dairy Shorthorns were obtained by the London cowkeepers from Yorkshire where Arthur Young saw them on Cleveland farms in 1770. These cows he said were improperly called Holderness, but were really the Dutch sort. They fed to a vast weight, but Charles Turner of Kirkleatham, was one experimental gentleman who did not like them. He thought them less profitable for the breeder, the grazier and the dairy than the true Lancashire breed. He made two trials to prove this and showed that while the Shorthorns gave more milk it did not work up into as much cheese or butter. Naturally he decided to go in for Lancashire Longhorns. This he found difficult and expensive for the breed was in great repute, and the genuine breed much sought after 'among the capital breeders of stock.' Pedigrees were examined as closely as those of racehorses. Turner's first bull was given to him by Sir William Lowther, and he bought fifteen cows at twenty guineas each. Success followed, and was marked by an offer from the famous Bakewell of sixty guineas for two of the cows.[14]

This was only one of the many attempts then being made to improve cattle and to put more productive breeds at the choice of the farmer. Some people were inclined to be cynical, and to regard the strongly sustained preferences of noted breeders as a matter of fashion. James Anderson was amongst these, and he was certainly right in one respect.

'At one time', he wrote, 'the large Dutch breed of cows was much in vogue, and were more valued than any other kind. But in a few years it was discovered that they did not possess all the qualities claimed, and fell into disesteem. They were succeeded by the Yorkshire . . . in turn by the Lancashire breed, which is at present more esteemed than any other sort, and will probably continue to be so for a few years when they in their turn will be neglected, and give place to some other favoured breed . . . In this manner things will go on till mankind shall become so sober-minded as to be firmly persuaded that perhaps no one breed of cattle is possessed of all the different qualities that could be desired on different occasions.'

He mentions the Alderney for richness of milk, and Young's contention that the Suffolk gave more milk for their size than the Longhorn,[15] showing that there was some disagreement about breeds already.

Practical or fashionable as they may have been, the efforts

of the breeders were hampered by visitations of grave disorders and misfortunes amongst the livestock. Disease was rife in the early years of the eighteenth century, but died down by 1714, only to break out again in 1740, when many cattle perished in Cheshire, Wales and Devon. It was also prevalent in London in 1744 and an order to slaughter the diseased beasts was issued in December, 1745. The ruin caused by this outbreak was compared to that of 1711-1713, and one lady recorded that nothing but mutton could be bought in the Metropolis. An outbreak at Hull in 1748 was so severe that the market for horned beasts at Pontefract was closed and not re-opend until 8 May, 1756. The disease was murrain, but some of the symptoms were those of anthrax according to Youatt. He examined the contemporary literature carefully and did his best to diagnose the 'distemper' but was rather uncertain what it precisely was.[16]

In addition to the devastation caused by these sporadic outbreaks of disease, handicaps were imposed by the occurrence of bad seasons. There were cattle losses in 1741 due to the failure of the hay harvest, and again in 1762. A further shortage in the meat supply, and presumably in the stock of dairy cows resulted from frosts and floods which destroyed the fodder and turnips in the winter of 1770-1771; drought in the following summer spoiled the hay harvest again. There was another drought in 1785 when the cattle had to be sold whether they were fat or lean.[17]

Nevertheless progress was being made, and the distinctive characteristics of the modern breeds were beginning to emerge. The broad general classification originally made by Markham continued to be repeated, but some additions and modifications were introduced, and these must have been acceptable to farmers, or they would not have read the books. The Suffolk cow was praised, the white cow for which Surrey was famous had evidently become more or less standard there. The rich milk of the Alderney, and the poor conformation of the Wiltshire dairy cow are all remarked. The points to be looked for in choosing an animal likely to be productive remained much as they had been, and as set out above.[18]

The influence of Dutch cattle on the Shorthorn is emphasised by George Culley, who stated quite categorically that he remembered a gentleman of the county of Durham, a Mr. Michael Dobison, who went in the early part of his life to Holland to buy bulls. He and his neighbours were noted for the best breed of Shorthorns in 1786, and sold bulls and heifers at high prices. Less knowledgeable people, in imitation, bought poorer types of Dutch cattle, though very large, and introduced lyery or black fleshed animals to the dismay of the Tees-side breeders. This was also found in the Holderness cattle, again as a result of a Dutch cross.[19] Some twenty-five years after Culley, Richard Parkinson related that his grandfather had some experience with the so-called Dutch breed, though he had some doubts whether the cattle called Dutch were imported, or were a breed of England. His grandfather had a bull of the kind from the Duke of Northumberland's steward (the Duke was another reputed importer), but it had very bad effects. One cow died in calving and calves that survived birth died young. Black or lyery flesh was also produced in the progeny that survived. His grandfather's herd, very like Hereford to look at, generally red with white faces, appeared to be well and healthy but could never be made fat. In this connection there is a tradition, so far unsupported by records, that Lord Scudamore had imported Dutch cattle to improve Herefords in the late seventeenth century. The Dutch were very thick in the flesh of the thigh, and clumsy about the breeches, but not to be compared to the true Yorkshire breed. Parkinson's final opinion does not emerge very clearly from his rather confused argument, though he thought that the largest cows gave the most milk. Consequently none could compare with or equal the Teeswater, or Yorkshire cow. The Longhorn looked well in a gentleman's park, but was rarely a deep milker.[20]

The business of droving Welsh and Scottish cattle increased during the eighteenth century, and not all these cattle were brought in for slaughter. Many Scots mixed their blood with the local breeds from Cumberland down through the Midlands and to Norfolk. Many Welsh did the same through

Salop and across country, in Somerset and the southern counties even to Kent. Eager breeders throughout the country bought both Longhorn and Shorthorn to improve their own stock. Some Channel Island were imported, especially in the counties across the narrow seas, but possibly most of these were bought by the gentry to adorn their parks and supply their kitchens with milk and cream. The majority of farmers may have been impressed by all this, but many of them went along stolidly, more or less in the traditional way, not altogether because they wanted to, but because they could do nothing else. The high prices charged for first class animals were not only outside the capacity of their pockets, but also, to their minds, outside the range of possible profit.

All this is made abundantly clear in the enormous literature that appeared between about 1784 and 1818. Arthur Young made his most extensive tours about 1770, but his frequent shorter journeys are described in the *Annals of Agriculture* he began to publish in 1784. Other people followed his good example of travelling to look at distant farms and writing up their impressions. The number of textbooks printed rose yearly. William Marshall began farming and his one-man survey of the nation's agriculture. The Board of Agriculture, established in 1793, immediately initiated a national survey of farming, county by county. Its reports in two or more editions, not always written by the most appropriate people, appeared in a stream between 1793 and 1816.

In many parts of the country, including some where dairy farming was the chief occupation, farmers did not confine themselves to any one breed for replacements either of their own breeding or purchased, though most Sussex, Somerset and Devon men remained loyal to their red cattle. An experienced farmer relied upon his judgment of the size and shape of udder, the importance of which character had been recognised for centuries. It was taken into greater consideration by Cheshire farmers than the 'figure and bulk' of the beast itself and they bought Lancashire Longhorns, Yorkshire and Holderness Shorthorns, Longhorns from the adjoining counties, Irish, Scotch and New Leicester cattle indiscriminately

C

at the beginning of the nineteenth century. They had not changed much fifty years later when they still had these mixed herds, though the Longhorn element was not noticed, having probably vanished. Shorthorns, Ayrshire and Welsh cattle were kept in Cheshire then, and the farmers bred many of their replacements. By the end of the century there was a general preference for the Shorthorn.[21]

The Longhorn was the general choice of the Staffordshire farmers at this time, but in 1790 Marshall thought them too gaunt to be eligible either as dairy or grazing stock, though there were some good cows. There were several fine breeders in the county, including Princep of Croxhall on the borders of Derby, Lord Fisherwick, Lord Bagot, and Sir Edward Littleton, and many local farmers are recorded as keeping fine and large cows in 1808. The Longhorn was indeed still generally preferred throughout Lancashire and the north-west Midlands to Leicester and Northampton, and there were, in Marshall's words, 'many fine breeders besides Bakewell'. The farmers of eastern England from Northumberland southwards to Lincoln favoured the Shorthorn of various quality, ranging between the outstanding animals produced by the Collings Brothers, Booth and Bates and the lyery fleshed animals so much condemned for their admixture of Dutch blood. In Yorkshire some West Riding farmers bred Longhorns or Cravens, and some in Nidderdale a cross between the two. Elsewhere, as in Lancashire, one or two individuals were experimenting with breeds different from those of their neighbours.[22]

Little dairying was done by Norfolk farmers except in the west of the county. Their stock may have been Norfolk Red Polls, but is more likely to have been a mixture. Suffolk, always famous for its dairy produce, and the Suffolk Duns, were gaining a great reputation towards the end of the century and the true Suffolk Polled cows were considered by Young to be the finest in England in 1784, an opinion he repeated in 1797. Unfortunately the number kept began to decline owing partly to the high price of corn in the Wars, and partly to the innumerable cases of the poor losing their cows after enclosure.[23]

Essex and Cambridge dairies were both famous, but not because the farmers were particularly choice in selecting the breed of cows. Those in Essex had generally the 'broad-horned' Derbyshire, but they were not particular. Some had Suffolk Polls, others Welsh. Lord Braybrooke of Audley End kept a herd of Yorkshire Polls; Lord Western had a mixed herd of Devons, Suffolks and Shorthorns. Mr. Conyers of Copt Hall made a trial of Devons for a few years before 1801 with some success,[24] in spite of their reputation of being primarily beef cattle. Coke of Norfolk had carried out a successful fattening trial with them.

Vast herds of dairy cows were kept at this time in the parts of Middlesex and Surrey close to London, and in the city itself. Many of these were Longhorns bought by drovers in the North of England, Lancashire and Stafford. Some cowkeepers preferred them to Holderness which were not so tender, but since large milk yield was the point of importance Holderness were also bought in large numbers at the fairs at Islington where they were brought by other drovers at three or four years old. Here again the cowkeepers did not confine their choice to any one breed, though there is however little doubt that the Holderness or Shorthorn steadily gained favour with them.[25] Gentlemen's families in Surrey kept Jersey, Alderney and Suffolk cows for domestic supply. Sussex dairies were small, but the Sussex Red was the most usual cow, long established and naturally preferred in its native county. In Kent, where the dairies were likewise small, the herds were very mixed, and there was a long standing tradition of the use of imported Dutch cows. Neither Hampshire nor the Isle of Wight had a large reputation for dairy produce, but proximity to France had enabled farmers to obtain imported Norman and Channel Island cattle with which to improve the richness of their milk.

There was a large dairying area in the Vale of Aylesbury, and in the western end of the Vale of White Horse. The favourite dairy cow in Buckingham was the Shorthorn, although a minority preferred Leicester Longhorns and a few farmers Suffolks, while some gentlemen kept Alderneys. Besides these Devons and Welsh were kept in the Vale of White Horse. The dairies in the Vale of Gloucester, the Vale of Berkeley, and North Wiltshire had at one time all been stocked with the old Red Gloucester, an animal that greatly resembled the old Red Glamorgan, but in the last half of the eighteenth century, the North Country cow—Longhorn—became popular. Marshall did not altogether like this as the old Gloucester breed had raised the Gloucester dairy to its greatest height, being very good dairy cows. The farmers evidently did not agree, or they would not have turned over to Longhorns, even such good ones as the Fowler and Bakewell strains. Far away from Suffolk as this was a few gentlemen had imported Suffolk Duns, and some of the farmers used Devons. They were more concerned that any cow bought should have a large, thin-skinned bag, and superstitiously *a large tail,* a factor that could have had little influence on milk yield. Welsh and Hereford cows were also to be seen on these farms. Some dairy farmers in Wiltshire had tried to substitute Devons for the Longhorns that Marshall thought had been in the area from time immemorial, and as fully established as in Leicester. They were bought at Highworth Fair from drovers, but were also bred on the farms. There were one or two outstanding herds. Baydon of Dayhouse, near Swindon, had 60-80 fine-bred cows; Beames of Avon, near Chippenham, the foremost dairy farmer in the district had 40 home-bred cows as fine as any the Midlands could produce, but he was careful to hire good bulls from the Midlands.

The Dorset farmers did not choose a select breed, but the dairy cows on the chalk and in the south east of the county were Longhorns, rather short in the leg with white backs and bellies, and dark spotted or brindled sides. Near the coast some Norman and Channel Island cattle had been introduced, and in the west and in the Vale of Blakemoor Devons were in the majority, as they were in Devonshire, except in the South Hams. In Cornwall there was a mixture. Many farmers kept Devons, some kept the old, small Cornish cow, and others had, if not complete herds of Jersey and Guernsey cows, some of these kinds on their farms. Shorthorns were to be seen in the north-east of Somerset, but the popular cow of that county was a rather larger animal of the same type as the Devon.[26]

This rapid survey demonstrates that the farmers of the different areas where dairying was practised had not at the end of the eighteenth century made many changes in their choice of a cow. Most were content to stick to the local breed. The predominance of the Longhorn in the western counties was being challenged. The Shorthorn was slowly spreading over a wider area. Breeds formerly intensely local, like the Suffolk Dun and the Red Devon, were being carried by interested gentlemen and farmers into other districts. Drovers' cattle from Wales and Scotland too must have played some part, especially those from the improved districts of Ayrshire. Channel Island cows were slowly penetrating further inland than the coastal counties. Multitudes of cattle had made long journeys through the country since Markham wrote two centuries before. Some of them had stopped on the way at different places for a year or more, perhaps to make a contribution to local herds, as well as to prepare for the next stage of their travels. But broadly speaking what he said about the distribution of breeds still applied, though it was, of course, being speckled here and there by penetrations from outside the locality, either casual or purposeful. There was still a strong body of opinion that believed the Longhorn was the best dairy cow,[27] and this was an opinion that was repeated, possibly parrot fashion, until at least 1850.

Authority does not agree. By 1833 the Longhorn had entirely disappeared from Dishley Grange and its locality. The Shorthorn was being introduced into Westmorland, the original home, it is said, of the Longhorn, but many Scots were also grazed in that county. In South Lancashire the breed was rarely seen in a pure state, and the town cow-keepers kept the Yorkshire milch cow. Many Lancashire gentlemen had taken up breeding Shorthorns though a few remained loyal to the native breed. The Shorthorn had penetrated into Cheshire dairy country with variable advantage, the old mixed breed Cheshire cow being well adapted to its environment. All across the Midlands William Youatt reported that the old Longhorns had disappeared, and their place taken by the all conquering Shorthorns. Wiltshire dairy farmers had adopted a cross between the two, but its productive capacity had to be kept up by frequent infusions of Shorthorn blood. Farmers were no doubt encouraged in their favourable opinion of the Shorthorn as a dairy cow by the publication of Coates' Herdbook in 1822, the first of all our herdbooks, but David Low found the most varied types of all sorts of different origin, that is amongst our native cattle, in the dairy districts in 1843. He had no very high opinion of the native livestock as a whole. A 'large part of the cattle of Britain consists of a mixture of races, having no uniformity of character, and generally defective in some important points'. Celebrated races did not, sometimes, come up to expectation. Sir George Head was disappointed in the cows he saw in Holderness when he passed through the country in 1835. Its reputation had prepared him for such beautiful cattle as he had rarely seen, but he 'never saw a handsome beast all the time he was there'. Here the native cattle were being displaced by Scotch and Irish stores of a lighter type, and kept for grazing only. Charles Hillyard thought two or three herds of Longhorns kept near Warwick about the same date worthy of remark as high yielders.[28]

The choice of a cow did not become simpler, and little was added to the long established ideas of what constituted a good animal. Not only did breeds vary in different parts of the country, and become modified when taken to new homes, but individuals of the same breed were frequently unlike each other in yield and figure. In a good dairy cow beauty of form was not important, but the first care should be taken to select young and promising stock, and there were certain indications by which the quality of a good milch cow could be recognised —irrespective of breed. These were much the same as they had always been: head small and fine, eye bright and full,

neck deep and thin, shoulder and breast narrow but projecting, light in the fore-quarter with little dewlap, ribs flat,
rump broad and tapering down to the knee joint, udder large
and round with four teats, well formed and tapering to the
end, skin thin to the touch, with a large subcutaneous or milk
vein. She should be of a quiet and gentle temperament.[29] Emphatic as everyone was about the importance of a correct
selection of the dairy cow very few people had given much
consideration to the choice of a bull before 1800. Any bull
was used except by the famous breeders. The majority of
farmers were condemned for this by the more penetrating
critic in 1851. He gives praise to the dairymen for their care
in selecting cows. The bull was too often a matter of convenience, not choice. 'They know he is a bull, that is all'.
What his parents were or his offspring likely to be was not
considered.[30]

The importance of their cattle to the Channel Islanders
made them good breeders. About 1835 a scale of points was
laid down for both bulls and cows of the Jersey breed to guide
the judges of cattle at the shows of the Jersey Agricultural
Society. This had an excellent effect upon conformity, and
perhaps on yield, though the older ill-formed animal produced much rich milk. The points set out are much the same
as those recommended by writers of textbooks, but, no doubt,
coupled with the requirements demanded for the entry of
Shorthorns in Coates' Herdbook, they provoked discussion
and ideas.[31]

A new element in the choice of milk cows was introduced
by the publication of Guenon's escutcheon theory, though
exactly what relation the placing of the hair on the udder
had to milk secretion it is now difficult to understand.
Guenon's idea was that it was possible to judge a cow's probable standard of production by what he called the 'escutcheon'. This was the udder and the parts above it between
the thighs and hips as seen from the rear, special attention
being given to the direction of the growth of the small hairs
occurring on those parts. Guenon is said to have made protracted observations and comparisons over a period of years,

29

until despite some conflicting results he arrived at the conclusion that there was a relation between the shapes of curls and upward or downward growth of hair, and the productive capacity of a cow. If his conclusions were correct, they were probably coincidental rather than consequential. He suggested that other points should be taken into consideration as well, particularly conformation; his ideas on this subject were the same as those so frequently repeated by other writers.

The 'escutcheon' theory became immediately popular, and was enthusiastically subscribed to by the highest contemporary authority. Guenon's book was translated into several languages, and must have been widely read by advanced farmers who would have been on the look-out for any novel way to judge cows advantageously. Gamgee declared it 'the most valuable of all the methods to determine the milking qualities of a cow'. It was recommended by J. H. Magne, and continued to be regarded until well into the twentieth century. Parmalee Prentice dismisses it as ridiculous, and perhaps like all judgments based upon visible signs it may have been somewhat uncertain. Nevertheless centuries of experience had taught farmers that a cow of a certain appearance was likely to be a good yielder, and in their eyes it was not altogether fantastic to lay particular emphasis on the part of a cow closest to the milk producing glands.[32]

All sensible men believed that the purchaser of dairy stock should be able to judge from outward appearance whether a cow was likely to be a good milker. Many farmers were remarkably clever in this way as many still are, being able to guess (it can be little more) which of a bunch of animals offered are likely to be 'good doers'. By 1866 the Shorthorn had come into such general favour that it had obtained a strong footing in all the dairy counties. In the Midland counties there was still a variety of Longhorn, which had been so long inured to the soil and climate that it suited dairy farming there better than more improved breeds; it was often, as it had been for half a century, crossed with a Shorthorn, a process that increased its bulk, but reduced its yield of butter and cheese. Only the local breeds of exceptional merit were able to withstand the pressure of Shorthorn popularity, e.g., the Suffolk, Ayrshire and Channel Islands. The small Kerry cow, too, had some adherents.

The dairy farmers of Bucks, Derby, Salop, and the West of England, who were not selective, but who did a good deal of crossing, were getting rather more careful than anyone had formerly been in choosing a bull. Many were still content to accept any bull, but some were already beginning to look for an animal that came from a good milking family. A bull of this descent would soon improve a dairy herd if the heifer calves were reared for replacements, a remarkably modern idea. 'On dairy farms a good bull is an article of strict economy', wrote John Coleman.[33]

The dairy Shorthorn undoubtedly became the most numerous of any breed of dairy cows during the second half of the last century. The other breeds remained in the same order of preference though Ayrshires were being sought by some dairy farmers, and were sometimes used for crossing with the Shorthorn in an attempt to improve the richness of the milk. The Alderney or Channel Island cow came to be called the country house or family cow. The Norfolk Red Polls were well regarded, and the Suffolk Duns well liked in their own habitat; the Suffolk Red Polls are possibly the result of careful crossing between these. There was little change in Somerset and Devon or in Sussex. By some it was said that the Longhorns, formerly the cows mainly seen in Cheshire, Derby, Nottingham, Stafford, Oxford and Wilts had so been changed by crosses that they had developed their own character. These and other Midland counties were however able to offer dairy Shorthorns of a very high milking type in 1889. Judging probable productive capacity by visual signs was the farmer's stand-by as it had always been, and the signs he looked for were much those that had always been recommended. Different people used a slightly different set with minor variations, but all agreed upon the importance of the milk vein and udder shape, softness and so on. Colour was thought important. The Guenon theory was applied by some, but had

31

now passed out of use. Visual and tactual points of much the same kind are still discussed today,[34] although modern choice can be made by reference to records of performance of both cows and bulls that serve them.

Though there was not apparently much change in the appearance of a cow chosen by the dairy farmer, and little in the factors that caused him to prefer one cow to another there had been more than is at once apparent. For one thing the dairy Shorthorn that had so largely replaced the old Longhorn was a bigger animal yielding more milk. Other animals, too, were larger and more productive than their ancestors because of selective breeding and better feeding. Measurement of these things is difficult, if not impossible, but clearly they existed. The modern cow has a size, sleekness and well-being that would have been incredible to the Tudor farmer, just as his animals would look like dwarf bags of bones, misshapen through ill-feeding and casual breeding, ridden with disease, and wholly unacceptable to us.

## (iii). Management

The dairy farmer must feed his cows and his bull if he has one. The Tudor dairy farmer did not find any difficulty in supplying the needs of his cattle during spring and summer. The feed they got in these good weather months was not all that a modern farmer would want to give his beasts, but it sufficed for the poorish, small animals that were all that the sixteenth century farmer could breed and maintain. From late autumn and through the winter a sufficient supply of feed was more difficult to provide. 'Grass does not grow for five months of the year', and no one cultivated roots or 'artificial' grass.

It has been repeatedly said that the amount of keep available determined the number of cattle that survived the winter until the following spring. Many beasts were slaughtered at the beginning of winter because there would be nothing to feed them on in the Lenten Months at the end of winter.

'The problem of the dairyman and the grazier of the Tudor and Stuart period was predominantly one of feed. Pasture conservation therefore became a prime question . . . he was forced to work out a careful use of his grassland . . . and a careful apportioning of garnered hay and straw to see the animals through the winter . . . these were the matters that kept the stock growers busy.'[1]

I am however, gradually coming to the conclusion that the specialist dairy stock farmer was not so desperately short of feed as has been supposed. One example at least has been recorded. John Johnston

'was one of the fortunate farmers who had pasture in plenty. He sometimes wintered cattle for his neighbours charging them for the "hay of pasture" the animals consumed'.

He also took in horses to graze until in good condition. Some of his own horses too, were turned out to fend for themselves during the winter in closes or 'even in the woods where they could be recaptured in the spring'.[2]

The mixed farmer working in an open arable field village was worse off. He could do little but go with the tide. The common pastures, often in a state of nature except for the modifications induced by the grazing animal, were the only grass that many of them had for their beasts. These grazed in common under the control of the village herdsman. Every morning he gathered the village cows belonging to those farmers who had common rights, drove them to the grass, or cow leaze, and brought them home at night.[3] In such plain champian (unenclosed) country the cows and calves, if any, had to be kept on dry feed in the house during the winter, though wise men held that they would do better lying without in a little close where a trifle of grass could be picked up, and the animals foddered on straw. But he who had no pasture must do as he may.[4] At some places there were other patches of grass beside the common waste. At Laxton, for

example, the waste had been narrowed down by new cultivation as population grew, but there were

> 'the odds and ends of grass beside the green roads that
> led to the open Fields; there was the aftermath of the
> common meadows; there were the sikes, baulks, road-
> sides and stubbles of the Open Fields themselves,'

but the relics of the commons and the roadside wastes only
amounted to 108 acres.[5] Many other open field villages in the
Midlands must have repeated this pattern. Indeed I have
seen tethered cows grazing on roadside wastes in recent times,
and Robert Loder sometimes left a strip of his arable land at
Harwell, Berks, unploughed. On the weeds and grasses he
hitched animals to graze.[6] Other farmers who housed their
cows in cold weather let them out once a day for exercise and
to drink. The animals 'were fed on all sorts of straws beginning with rye the least appetising, and coming last to hay'. By
January supplies might be getting short and Tusser advised
that 'browse' (leaves and twigs of trees) be cut for food. The
cows had their tongues rubbed with salt then and were given
a drench of verjuice.[7] Culls were not milked after the end of
August but were fattened for sale or domestic consumpion,
possibly as salt or dried beef in the winter months.

The management of the common Fen grazing of a Cambridgeshire parish is disclosed by contemporary documents.
The fen was about four miles from east to west, and one mile
wide. Articles of agreement were entered into between the
Lord and the tenants in 1596 and several interests were
extinguished by alloting closes, while twenty customary
tenants were to be chosen as 'ordermakers'. Their orders,
which were not always obeyed, reveal the system. Sheep were
allowed open grazing during the three winter months, but
after that the pasture was shut up to allow the grass to grow
ready for the weanling calves and their mothers on May 1st.
These and the regulation number of bulls, were grazed until
after harvest, being brought home in the evening for milking,
and being milked again in the morning before being taken
out. Another section of the fen was closed from February 20th
until May 1st to provide summer feed for the working oxen,

34

yearlings and sick bullocks. This was probably inferior pasture. The horses and swine were each grazed in separate allotments, the former in a definite enclosure, and the latter along the drove ways, getting the major part of their food from waste dairy products. In the winter months the feed was hay, and the straw threshed out from the corn crops. It was understood that animals fed upon straw should have first rye, then wheat and last peas straw. The problem of feeding became acute for the couple of months before the pasture was opened to grazing again.[8] Unfortunately it

'was no one's business to root out the whins and brushwood or to improve the commons in any way; the cutting of turf was sometimes reckless and wasteful, and the commons through neglect went to rack and ruin.'[9]

No very different system could be adopted elsewhere by the dairy farmer and grazier whether his farm was several (enclosed) or champion (open field), or whether the grazing lands were fen or dry like those in Cheshire, Stafford, Gloucester, or the Vale of White Horse. The circumstances of all farmers were so similar that they must all have been obliged to act in very much the same way. Their support was home-grown fodder, and this was limited to grass, hay, straw, and pulse, so that the dairy farmer's feeding methods cannot have varied very widely. Indeed a modern farmer deprived of concentrates and roots would be forced into the same system.

Actual examples of feeding are difficult to find and the only one I know of is that of Robert Loder of Harwell, Berkshire. In the summer his cows, like most others, lived on grass. For winter sustenance he estimated three loads of straw for each beast, and draws no distinction between wheat and barley straw. Of other sorts he had none because he did not grow the crops. His cattle had to overwinter on this ration of straw and what herbage they could graze. Perhaps they had some hay because Loder did on one occasion at least sell hay. In one season however seven beasts ate nothing but straw after Candlemas Day, (February 2nd) presumably until the new grass was ready.

Such rations, which were those used commonly and of

necessity, were bulky and fibrous, (browse even more so), but were low in true feeding value i.e., starch equivalent. Although they had the effect of filling the animal's belly,

> 'they supplied very little actual digestible nutrient for maintenance, that is, of keeping the vital metabolism going normally and maintaining the health of the animals, or production in which are included milk production or live weight increase'.

Indeed milk production, or live weight increase on such scanty winter rations of poor roughage was usually out of the question. They rarely supplied enough starch equivalent for maintenance alone. The result was that such animals as were kept over the winter found it necessary to draw upon their bodily reserves of fat, which they had stored on the pasture during the summer, for maintenance of bodily warmth and for providing energy for muscular activity. Naturally at the end of the winter they were in poor condition.[6]

There was need to beware of keeping the cows too well in the winter as it was when they were at grass in the summer. The farmers were warned, and doubtless accepted the warning, if not already familiar with the necessity, that

> 'A milch cow may have too much meate: for if she wax fat she will rather take the bull and give less milk for the fatnesse stoppeth the pores and the veines that should bring the milk to the paps'.

Mean grass was the best to keep her in a mean state. Fitzherbert was convinced, too, that if the grass in a close had got away the cows would feed the worse. They would bite the top and no more because that was the sweetest and most appetising. The rest rotted on the ground, and the horse was the only animal that would eat it in the winter. Mascall repeated that warning a century later in almost the same words, but advised cowkeepers that they must have a care to provide proper feed in due season. Stalls must be kept clean, and all sorts of poultry kept out because their cast feathers and dung were unwholesome for the cows. Some people then thought that these things caused murrain.[10] No doubt these were the opinions generally held by the dairy farmers of the sixteenth century.

Of course it was more convenient to have enclosed grassland than to have to send the cows out to feed on the cow leaze or common waste, where no control over feeding could be exercised. A farmer who had an enclosed pasture for his cows and another for his calves and water in them both was in a happy position. He could both breed and rear good animals cheaply. Fitzherbert's ideal was to have a number of closes and pastures, well quick setted, ditched and hedged to keep the strongest and weakest cattle apart, especially in wintei when they were foddered. A farmer who held his land for twenty years could, he estimated, afford to spend the equivalent of three years' expenses of the livestock on enclosing. During the balance of the term they could be kept at one-tenth of the former cost of having them go before the herdsman. He suggested that landlords and tenants should agree with each other to exchange lands so that they could make enclosures. One quarter the hay fed in a pasture would go as far as four times as much in the house.[11]

General ideas of feeding and management did not materially change during the seventeenth century in spite of the publication of a great deal of advanced farming literature, and the introduction of clover and turnips as new crops. Both Joseph Blagrave and Richard Blome repeated Fitzherbert's advice at the end of the century as Leonard Mascall had at the beginning. It evidently remained acceptable to the farmers who bothered to read farming textbooks, and most probably reflected the practice of those who did not or could not.[12]

Recent investigation has disclosed that turnips were grown in High Suffolk at a much earlier date than formerly thought. The fine Suffolk Duns, so much praised by Reyce and others, flourished and turnip husbandry was 'established as ordinary practice between 1646 and 1656'. The turnips were partly drawn in autumn and stored in sheds for immediate use and partly left in the ground to be lifted as wanted. They were fed with straw and hay to milch cows in sheds or houses so that milk production could go on uninterruptedly throughout the winter. The last of them were not pulled until some time in March, a proportion being left for seed. While some bullocks were winter fattened on turnips, they were grown mainly for the production of winter butter. The Suffolk dairy farmers were, if this was so, far in advance of those in other parts of the country. Already they were accustomed to the idea of feeding animals on roots, for a coastal part of the county about Orford had long been renowned for its unusual and magnificent crops of carrots, part of which were exported to London and part fed to animals, mainly horses. This process must have made their minds very responsive to the idea of growing turnips on the fallow and using them to feed dairy cows.[13]

Essex dairy farmers had another idea. Cow parsley, now regarded as a weed to be got rid of, grew freely there in the spring. The cattle were fed on it at the beginning of the year and ate it well. It must however have contained a high proportion of fibre though having succulent parts. Some farmers thought winter feeding should be with straw in racks in the yards. If the cows were let out into the fields to graze at will they spoiled a great deal of ground by poaching, and were inclined to run up and down which could overheat them. Good drinking water was important and thought to affect the milk. Observation had shown that some cows drinking from a pond on the Kentish chalk gave rich milk and others poor milk. This result was attributed to one side of the pond being on the chalk were a good deal of trefoil grew; the other side was dug out of gravel where only couch grass grew. This led to the conclusion that the difference in the milk was the result of drinking water containing variable soluble matter.[14]

Ideas about feeding were very mixed at the end of the seventeenth century. Some good sense was mixed with a good deal of superstition or nonsense. If 'milk was nought' the cattle should be allowed to feed in short clover for a while, and be given cummin seed and black oats in their dry provender. Barren cows should be fed in a field where broom was growing. It is reasonable to suppose that higher feeding would increase milk, but whether cummin seed would help

A Seventeenth Century Cow

Tudor Cowherd and Shepherd

Milking Time about 1800

to increase milk or broom fertility is another question. Edward Lisle reasonably remarked that a cow well summered was half wintered, and some of his farmer friends estimated that a milch cow would eat as much hay in the winter as a fattening ox. In 1714 spring was late, and he tried putting the cows on French grass (sainfoin), but did not find it as good as broad clover. Grains, cabbage leaves and bean shells were fed by some farmers near Crux Easton in Queen Anne's reign, but the milk would taste of the last. Farmer Stephens of Pomeroy, Wiltshire, grew vetches for cows that calved in winter or early spring. Cows in a hill country were let go dry just before winter by the best farmers, and foddered in a close for the benefit of the 'rowet' (aftermath). It was the way to keep them in case all the winter. Cows tied in a cowhouse never looked so well as those foddered in a back side, and in-calf animals fed on straw all the cold months were inclined to go pot-bellied. It was not advisable to keep them for the dairy after six years old.

An increased area under turnips had already made it easier for the farmers who cultivated them to overwinter their cattle, but some still clung to the opinion that in hard frosts nothing agreed with them so well as browse, an idea possibly connected with the continental practice of feeding vine leaves and waste grapes which were more nutritious than browse cut from elm and beech. It was mistaken policy to let cows feed on the new grass on hedge banks and other such places in January as they took a dislike to their dry feed if they did.[15]

Fitzherbert's idea that it was a good thing to have several closes had been expanded by this time, and the new forage crops, grasses, legumes and roots which had been steadily, though slowly, growing in favour during the seventeenth century, helped it forward. Small closes of two or three acres, it was said, enabled the farmer to freshen his pasture as he pleased. Cows should not be allowed to roam about from pasture to pasture. This idea led to the occasional practice of a system which, with the help of modern artificial fertilisers was revived in the late 1920's as 'Rotational Grazing'. It is today strongly supported by informed opinion as the best use

D

for carefully treated grassland. Though the system was primarily recommended for fattening cattle it was equally applicable to grazing dairy cows. In 1739 Samuel Trowell told his readers that

'It is a great advantage to the Feeder to have several grounds to shift often, which brings cattle forward very fast; and in three Weeks or a Month's time those Grounds will be ready again to receive them; which does very much add to the fatting of them'.

Hale repeated this advice because moving the cattle from close to close would give the beasts a change of food, and would also allow the grass to spring, the cattle preferring new growth. James Anderson was even more modern in 1775 when he suggested dividing the pasture and grazing off each portion in rotation. This can easily be done today by using electric fencing, but must have been difficult then unless done with hurdles or temporary pole fences. After the turn of the century a Leicestershire grazier recommended heavy stocking and frequent change of pasture as the best method of bringing on the cattle quickly.[16] Dairy cows, of course, flourish if treated in the same way. Long grass fed well and produced a good flow of milk, but the product was not so rich as when the cows fed on short grass,[17] something every modern farmer knows.

So late in the season as April it was still considered necessary to fill the racks with hay at night, especially if the common grazing was distant from the village. Hay would help the cow to keep warm at night, and would correct any ill effects of eating too much wet grass and drinking too much water in the wet places on the commons. In May the oxen were kept separate from the cows because the oxen became somewhat gamesome at that time. No good farmer would allow his cow to be tantalized by an ox.

W. Waller, who had a West Country farm of £200 rent in the 1720's was a thoughtful man. There must have been many others. There was about 20 acres of enclosed pasture on the farm, and some rights of common attached to it. Besides that he had the advantage of some turnips for winter feed—a modest way of saying that he had been sensible enough to grow some of this new crop. By this means he was able to keep nine cows, and could have kept two more. He sold off his cows as their milk declined, and replaced them, thus obtaining a full yield all the year. This was also the practice of the London cowkeepers, except that they fattened off their cows and sold them to the butchers. They fed early and late rank grass, hay, turnips and brewer's grains, and so kept their cows at the highest point of yield, and fattening at the same time. The dairymen at Over, Cambridgeshire, did the same to maintain supplies for the colleges throughout the year.[18]

Though these new feeds were being used by a few people, the ordinary farmer continued to turn out the cows that were still in milk into the rowens (aftermath) from September until snow fell or hard frosts occurred. Straw was good enough for those that gave little milk, but a bushel a week of malt dust mash helped. This had been tried early in the seventeenth century by Robert Loder, and was again experimented with in 1763 by a Berkshire farmer, who lived near Abingdon. He had the idea from a relation living in Hertfordshire who had used the material for many years. It proved very successful, as the London cowkeepers knew, increasing the milk yield and making it of better quality without giving it a bad taste. By 1750 some Suffolk farmers, who were growing rye grass which comes early in spring, were cutting it green for their cows. They did the same thing with clover throughout the summer. In Gaddesden, Hertfordshire, old and sterile cows were culled this month, and sold to the Vale of Aylesbury graziers for fattening.[19]

Another fodder crop, that may have been introduced by the Dutch who had come over with Vermuijden to drain the fens, was cole or rape. The leaves were used in that area as winter feed, and had been found excellent for keeping the cows in heart and strength at a time when feed was scarce. In Yorkshire cabbages were much esteemed as fodder, and looked upon as only second in value to turnips. Oilcake from rape was also used as feed, though sometimes wastefully burnt as fuel.[20]

Bad seasons occurred then as now. The winter of 1740 and spring of 1741 followed a bad year for hay and Cheshire hay sold for half a guinea a cwt. Stover (straw and haulm) was so scarce—there was no great area of ploughland in the county —that five or six cows had been seen lying dead in a farm-yard. In Devon, too, large numbers of cows died of starvation. The farmers themselves were hard put. Many who had never done so before were forced to eat barley bread, and amongst the poor there were deaths from starvation.[21]

By the mid-eighteenth century there was 'dairy farming of a primitive kind' on the south coast of Cornwall, where the pastures were the most fertile in the county. In the parish of Constantine, for example, 1,000 milch cows were kept. They were let to dairymen at 48s. a year each including the calf. The owner provided summer grazing, and about Michaelmas turned them into winter grazing, which had been kept for the purpose. The system of keeping separate pastures for summer and winter grazing was a relic of transhumance. Formerly the cows had been summered on the high moor and brought to lower ground in the winter. The number of cows kept in Constantine in 1754 greatly overstocked the grass, but no hay was given in the winter, and the beasts survived as best they could, if they did. This system continued in an attenuated form until 1812, possibly a little later.[22]

It was a poor way of keeping cows but probably very ancient. The animals were better off in the comparatively warm climate of Cornwall; farmers elsewhere preferred to house their cows in the winter. If they were kept out-of-doors they were always wet and cold, and generally in a very wretched condition by the spring. Housed cattle ate rather more, but if kept well and in good condition they would be all the more productive in spring and summer. Thoughtful farmers realised that winter grass had lost its genuine juices, was 'in a state of corruption', and must be the worst food that could be given. Moreover the man who let his cows eat off his winter grass was not only giving them poor material, but also eating off his crop of hay or early bite for the following year. Some thought that it was wasteful to give hay in the meadows, often being trodden, and spoiled by rain and dung. When the animals were kept in stalls they were taken out to water at a pond near the cowhouse while the dung was removed and the racks filled with hay. It a few days the cows learned to go out to drink and to return quite naturally. Some thought it did not matter or hurt the cows if the water was dirty, others that it was preferable for them to have it clean. There was however no danger of their overfeeding, for when nature was satisfied they would simply lie down and chew the cud.

Some Yorkshire dairy farmers, perhaps influenced by the summer stall feeding practised in the Low Countries and parts of Germany, kept their cows in the house all the summer as well. They gave grass fresh cut, and as one piece was mown, watered it with the urine to which they added dung in the winter. This process allowed five cuts a year, and the cows had fresh green food for a longer time than they could if grazed. One man declared that he had kept 10 cows on four acres of grass throughout the year by adding £4 worth of grains each. Another kept 13 cows through the winter on turnips and oat straw. A warm stable was essential, and currying them like horses pleased them and caused them to give more milk. If the cows were kept in the pasture in summer there should be trees to provide a cool shade during the heat of the day because great heat caused diseases. A prophylactic was to give each animal a raw egg and some salt dissolved in a pint of wine or ale about once a week. To this mixture bruised garlic, vervain and rue might be added.

There was never complete agreement about the best way to keep cows over the winter, and practice varied widely. Those who did not like winter housing protested that the want of air made the cows unhealthy. Many of the late eighteenth century writers promised great things from the cultivation of the new crops. If cowkeepers would cultivate a few acres of burnet, lucern, cabbage, turnips and carrots, they would have a constant succession of green crops, thus saving the cost of purchased hay, and thereby keeping their cows at a cheaper rate; so wrote Richard Weston in 1773. He also advised eradicating crowfoot from pastures as the cows did not like it. James Anderson, a great authority, quoted well into the nineteenth century, added trefoil, sainfoin, angelica. 'About the walls of houses and on insides of hedges lavage should be sown,' he said. In another place he reported a common belief that chickweed caused a large flow of milk, and the Dutch used spurrey with success although it was a very pernicious weed. He wondered why some pastures gave richer milk than others. One vulgar prejudice was that yellow flowers made yellow butter, which was assumed to be the best. He was not sure about this and many other questions to which there was no certain answer.[24] More exact information based upon accurate tests was urgently needed. Feeding for milk was at that time partly a matter of what was available, partly empiricism—no bad guide—and partly guesswork, especially where the new crops and feeds were concerned. It could have been no more on grassland because so little was known of the relative feeding value of the different plants, and no more about the botanical composition of the pastures. This was already recognised by the most advanced thinkers. Twamley said plainly that pastures were the result of chance. Yet it was winter feeding that was still the greatest problem. In the summer, provided there was a cool place for them either under trees or in a rough open fronted shed, possibly roofed with brushwood or thatched, the cows did well enough to satisfy their owners on the natural grass of the meadows, be it good or bad. Everyone agreed that good natural grass was the best feed for dairy cows then, and the same thing was said on the radio on April 11th, 1957. Anderson had arrived at the conclusion, on what grounds he did not say, that a cow should never experience cold below 50 degrees, F., or heat about 70, something that it must have been difficult to ensure in the circumstances of the day. He and others also emphasised the necessity for ample supplies of fresh, clean water, and some maintained that cows should not be allowed to step into ponds.

Opinions differed as to the value of cabbages as winter feed. Many held the view that they caused a taint in the milk and prevented it by feeding dry hay with the cabbages. This was not Arthur Young's opinion. Anderson and Willich recommended crushed or bruised furze, gorse or whins, which would keep the animals in high fettle. It was used well into the nineteenth century as the many examples of crushing machines to be seen in agricultural museums and the literature of the period demonstrate. Anderson thought it would be a good idea to grow furze for ten years for this purpose, but he had never heard of anyone doing it. Besides cabbages, carrots, oilcake, turnips, potatoes and burnet were all considered good winter feeds as well as the other artificial grasses. Brewer's and distiller's grains were extensively used all the year round by town cowkeepers in London, Liverpool, Leeds and elsewhere. But Dickson (1802) said very correctly that experiments had not yet been made on the best yield from cows of different sorts for the food provided, and Twamley (1816) warned farmers that unless they kept some kind of records they might spend for many years without any real return.[23]

Contemporary estimates of the food consumed by cows are few, but are not very different from later ones. In Cheshire about two acres of pasture was thought to suffice to keep a cow the year round; but the usual dry foods, straw and crushed oats, were used in addition. Some farmers had adopted soiling and stall feeding. Somerset farmers thought that three to four acres of grass were necessary. In winter they gave $1\frac{3}{4}$ cwt. of hay a week to in-calf cows, or 200 turnips, or 150 cabbages every twenty-four hours. Ringsted estimated 40 lb. hay daily, 'but 50 lb. turnips will be a necessary and increasing quantity for them before calving'. About $1\frac{1}{2}$ to 2 acres of grass from May Day till the aftermath was ready was allowed by Midland farmers for summer grazing. Cut turnips were thrown on the autumn grazing. Mr. Conyers of Copt Hall, Essex, summered 31 cows on 48 acres from 10th May till the end of September, then turned them into a 'lawn' of 100 acres for four weeks. They went into 36 acres of rowen next, and with $1\frac{1}{2}$ loads of hay each, the produce of 1 acre, carried them over the winter. Ordinarily two prime acres of pasture were allowed to a cow in this county. In Hants. the south-western system of letting dairy cows was followed, and keep allowed at 2-2¼ acres per annum, the animals being kept on an unspecified quantity of hay in yards during the winter. Some farmers however had found this unprofitable, Mr. T. Bernard for one, and were giving up the system in favour of feeding young stock. In 1784 he had let a dairy of 20 cows and allowed 35 acres of meadow for summer feed with 26 acres of aftergrass. During the winter these cows ate the straw of 120 qrs. of barley and 27 qrs. of oats. Bernard found he lost money as he only received £5 a head rent. As much as £7 or £9 was sometimes paid. In Dorset two acres of summer grass and one of eigrass (aftermath) was allowed on this system. Berkshire farmers found that 90 acres would carry 20 cows.

The dairy farmers of High Suffolk had evolved a system of open air feeding by about 1770 if not earlier. They tied their cows up in the fields without any cover over them. With rails and stakes they made a rough manger, and the cows were fastened to stakes about three feet from each. A screen of faggots was formed at their heads. Litter was regularly supplied, and the dung piled in a wall behind them. This procedure was considered better than allowing them to range at will. The cows were sheltered from cold winds and kept warm. Cabbages were then cultivated for feed as well as the long established turnips. It was somewhat doubtful whether this practice was profitable, though it probably was in competent hands. For example at Bedingfield Hall, a farm of 290 acres, only 40 cows were kept when it was all in grass, but in 1785 the same herd was maintained, 70 acres having been ploughed out for cropping. Some farmers were careless in feeding cabbages, scattering them over wet pastures for the cows to pick up. Arthur Young condemned this though he approved open air feeding.[26]

When at free range, either in enclosed fields or on the common, pasture cows often injured each other, probably more frequently when all the village cows grazed together. John Lawrence may have exaggerated when he said that in 1800 it was a common and shameful sight to see cows gored and wounded in a dozen places because the owner had neglected to tip their horns. He would certainly have been a strong supporter of the modern practice of dehorning. In his opinion the weaker animals should be fed separately, and the master animals tied up in yards. Another bad habit was the drinking of their own milk. Willich advised rubbing the teats with the most foetid cheese available to prevent this. This was one of the many oddities habitual to our ancestors. Few modern farmers would agree to treat a cow with a gangrenous udder by cutting off her dugs, and immediately driving her about until she bled heartily, then annointing the wound with hog's lard, a proceeding William Ellis advised in 1732. He said she would do well after this somewhat drastic treatment, but only if she was to be fattened as quickly as possible. I wonder if anyone ever did such a thing? To my mind it is unlikely, but then I probably think differently from an eighteenth century farmer. They were steeped in thoughts we regard as superstition.

During the first half of the nineteenth century there was little change in the estimates of the area of grassland required to keep a cow, nor was there any great change in methods of feeding. Farmers generally held to the accepted ideas, and kept their cows indoors or outdoors as they thought fit. Times were unpropitious for twenty years after the French wars and did not get really better until the accession of Queen Victoria. Sticking to the old ways and grimly carrying on has always been thought best in similar circumstances, and some neglect of maintenance to save expenditure occurred. The town cow-keepers were probably in a better position than the dairy farmers, but the population was growing, and people had to have butter, cheese, and milk, though the per capita consumption of milk was very low. Town cows continued to be fed highly on grains and other rich food to stimulate a large production of milk, often complained of as being of a poor, watery quality. The country cow got more natural if not more wholesome food.

There was a large measure of agreement that grazing was best. Soiling was economical but did not always produce such good milk. If it was practised the kind of feed was changed frequently in order to tempt the appetite. The more variety the less waste was the slogan, and many plants that would have been neglected in the fields were eagerly consumed in the stall. Grass cut for soiling was always young, a factor of importance. Alexander Taylor estimated that about 75 lb. of green clover was sufficient for one beast. He made no other estimates, but a Mr. Bordley, with whom he was acquainted, had suggested that each feed should be weighed, and recorded and the results noted. This practice would have the tendency to teach farm servants to observe method. Only the quantity that was cleared up completely should be given at one helping. Whether they kept their cows in stall, summered in the field and stalled in winter, or outdoors through the year all sensible farmers recognised that it was fatal to let their in-calf or milch cows fall into poor condition in winter. Some may have had little or no option even yet, but these were certainly becoming fewer in number as the new resources in fodder crops were developed. Everybody realised that if cows got low in the winter it was impossible to secure a good milk yield even by bringing them into first rate condition in the summer. It was important to treat cows kindly, even to avoid harshness of language, and they should certainly not be hunted with dogs, beaten or frightened.[27]

In both Somerset and Cheshire it had been found that yields were not being kept up, presumably because of the continual abstraction of phosphates from the pastures as milk. In Cheshire some attempt to combat this was made by using bone manure. Somerset farmers were advised in 1851 as they had been in 1797 to combine arable and dairy, growing roots and artificial grasses to feed their cows. They shared a fairly general opinion that three acres of pasture were necessary to keep a cow, i.e., $1\frac{1}{2}$ acres of good land for the summer, and 2 tons of hay each for the winter as well as aftermath grazing. Some found that turnips were inclined to taint the milk, but that mangolds proved a good spring feed. Already there was a feeling abroad that more exact feeding methods were necessary. C. W. Johnson emphasised the need for chemical research. Good wholesome food at regular times and in small portions that would be completely consumed was proper when the cows were in the house or in the yard, and cleanliness in both was essential. Wholesome grassland was equally important and must be properly drained to get rid of all stagnant water thus preventing the cows drinking it. This was a counsel of perfection. Though the milk producing breeds were believed to be more widely distributed than any other, the bulk of dairy cows were kept on the poor grass growing on clay soil, the slopes of uplands, and on poor sandy lands.

Johnson quoted the Rev. W. L. Rham, who in turn had, I imagine, his data from Albrecht Thaer, that a cow required 3% of her weight per diem in food to keep her in health. He adopted Thaer's standard of 100 lb. of good hay, a somewhat insubstantial and variable basis for calculating the values of other foods. For example, clover hay in blossom equalled 90 when the hay was 100; mangold 339; linseed cake, 69; rye and barley chaff, 179; and so on.[28] This was the dawn of the scientific feeding of livestock. Most of the early work was done on the continent, and the importance of the mineral constituents of the soil and their assimilation by plants, and so by the grazing animal, was already appreciated before Liebig's great work was published. Sprengel, for example, realised that clover grown upon a marly soil was more nutritious than that on a loam. Boussingault, the Dutchman Mulder, and Liebig were all contemporaries and their works were speedily translated into other languages. Boussingault was translated into English by an American in 1845. He made analyses of the food taken in by dairy cows and their excreta to determine whether nitrogen was taken in from the atmosphere. Mulder's book was translated and published at Edinburgh between 1845 and 1849, Liebig's in 1840, and his *Researches in the Chemistry of Food* in 1847.[29] Rothamsted was founded in 1843, and from this time onwards the chemistry of animal nutrition was studied by Lawes and Gilbert, Voelcker, and many others with close attention and increasing exactness. All kinds of feeding stuffs were analysed and

49

valued according to their composition, and many suggestions were made for the rationing of livestock including the increasingly important dairy cow. The results obtained were published in such periodicals as the *Journal of the Bath and West of England Society*, the *Royal Agricultural Society Journal*, and reprinted in popular papers like the *Farmers' Magazine* and many others. No doubt they were discussed by many smaller and more local clubs and societies of farmers. The material found its way into textbooks both of the recondite and popular sorts. From all these sources farmers could learn of the progress made in the novel science of rationing their animals with the food that would do them the most good, and so make them profitable. Those whose farms were large and extensive, and who were highly educated and wealthy men, or a proportion of them tried out the new methods and often recorded the results of their experience in print, or in some discussion group. How many did so and how far down the scale the knowledge sank is impossible to say. It is unlikely that a man who owned a few cows would either be greatly impressed by all this literature, or indeed whether he would have the capital to enable him to practice its precepts. The gentleman who kept a cow or two to provide dairy produce for family consumption may have insisted on his cowman trying out the new ideas. This is only speculation, but nothing more is possible. What appears certain is that a great many dairy farmers managed their cattle in very much the same way after 1850 as they had done before, though their feeding was helped by the increasing use of oil cake, linseed and imported maize.

The Shorthorn became more and more popular with the dairy farmer as the century advanced. William Marshall noticed that the dairy cattle of Gloucestershire were deficient in chine and too long in the leg in 1788. The dairymen then raised their own cows, but some bought replacements in Gloucester market. By 1850 part of the grass formerly used for dairy cattle in the Vales of Evesham and Berkeley was being used for grazing and fattening, though Berkeley still retained its reputation for butter and cheese. Formerly the cows kept both here and in North Wiltshire were Gloucester and Longhorns, but in both counties the Shorthorn was replacing them. Some farmers crossed Shorthorns with the few remaining Longhorns; others preferred a cross with the Hereford. By 1883 the county had become famous for pedigree dairy Shorthorns; the tenants had followed the lead of the Earl of Sherborne. Carrington in Stafford, too, had bred Shorthorns famous as milkers, and Tisdale of Holland Park, London, had selected the best dairy Shorthorns from all parts of the kingdom. Unfortunately this herd was dispersed about 1882. The general situation in Gloucester at this date was that about 25 cows were kept on 100 acres of grass with followers reared to maintain the herd. Young cows were preferred as old ones ate more hay in the winter, and did not give a proportionate increase in yield. If they did not rear the farmers bought in-calf three-year old heifers. Keep was estimated at $1\frac{1}{2}$ acres grass from May to December with $2\frac{1}{2}$ tons of hay each, the produce of $1\frac{1}{2}$ acres, for the winter and spring months. Cut barley straw was sometimes fed to dry cows; grains and roots were rarely used. The cows were not housed in winter, but kept in the warmest and most convenient pasture and fed hay. This was a great waste of feed, and more was necessary to maintain body heat than if they had been housed, especially in wet and snowy weather. In summer they were turned into a new pasture every ten or fourteen days— an exemplary procedure.[30]

There had been some improvement in the keeping capacity of Somerset dairy farms by 1860. Earlier in the century about 150 acres, i.e., 110 acres grass and 40 acres arable, was necessary to carry a herd of 30 cows and 5 or 6 heifers for replacements, but this area would then keep 50 cows. Most of the arable was under grass or roots, corn only being grown 'in the decay of grass'. This gain had been obtained by the efforts of informed and intelligent dairy farmers, who had had less help from the agricultural societies than the corn or meat producers. This was the opinion of Joseph Harding of Marksbury, one of the outstanding Somerset dairy farmers of that date. Fifteen years later his daughter, Mrs. Gibbons of

Tunley Farm, near Bath, had a herd of 38 useful Shorthorns with a pedigree bull, and at Oubley Farm, near Bristol 48 dairy Shorthorns with 8 two-year old heifers were kept on 24 acres of arable with 156 of pasture which goes far to confirm his opinion. Cheese remained the chief product of the Somerset dairy until the end of the century and only a small proportion of liquid milk was sold. The Shorthorn was the chief breed kept, but there were many others, including Devons, Herefords, Jersey, Guernsey and Kerry.[31]

Elihu Burritt, that indefatigable American pedestrian, was highly impressed by the standards of dairy farming in widely separated parts of the country in the 1860's. Naturally the Queen's dairy at Windsor was outstanding 'a little marble temple polished after the similitude of a palace'. Burritt thought some of the more expensive details unnecessary or rather not essential to the conduct of the dairy. However, the herd of 10 Alderneys and graded Shorthorns was very productive. Similarly there were fine graded Shorthorns in Lord Ferrar's dairy at Chartley, Staffordshire, and on his way from Shaftesbury to Bridport, Dorset, he saw the fine dairy cattle in the Blakemoor Vale. These were kept almost entirely on straw in the winter to which he took some exception.[32] This was, though Burritt perhaps did not know it, common form on many farms. Practice was various as it has always been when new ideas are being preached.

The number of papers published on the chemical composition of feeding stuffs was rapidly increasing, and very numerous experiments were being made, but some writers, like Pringle and Professor Murray, felt that no clear guidance was being given to the farmer. Test tubes and reports did not, they thought, have the same effect as living stomachs. Many farmers and their advisers preferred practical empiricism. The new feeds were more extensively used as time passed though their purity was often in question. Rape cake was frequently adulterated. Palm kernel cake was introduced in the 1870's and with bean meal and brewer's grains, where available, began to be used as concentrates in many parts of the country especially where the cows were housed in winter, as in Cheshire, Yorkshire, Lancashire and Stafford, or on those farms where summer stall feeding was practised. Towards the end of the century supplements were fed even in such favoured counties as Cornwall, where a large proportion of cereal food was used in winter, e.g., maize meal, crushed oats, barley meal and crushed wheat, although the cows were out in the fields all day and often all night. Generally speaking practical wisdom dictated that the proper treatment of a cow was simply to give suitable food and water at regular times, allow sufficient exercise for health, and keep the animal clean and warm.[33]

The disasters of the 1870's culminating in 1879, and thereafter the rapidly growing imports of farm produce inaugurated a period of change for most English farmers. Many failed to weather the storm, but the graziers and dairy farmers did best. Once again a great deal of arable all over the country fell down to grass, and farmers who had never thought of doing so turned to dairying. The heavy clays of Essex, for example, had tumbled down and were colonised by Scottish farmers and others as milk producing farms. In 1893 they were making a living. The West of England, from Cumberland to Cornwall, too, suffered less severely than the more arable country in the East. Milk and butter fell in price, but grain was cheap, so low as to ruin corn farmers; it made excellent feed. Similarly in Wiltshire much land fell down. In the hamlet of Medbourne, near Badbury, the land, formerly all tilled, was allowed to fall down to grass. In 1913 the farmer kept some 80 cows. Milk was also produced at Coate where Richard Jefferies was born, and the Vale of Pewsey was largely devoted to the production of milk for London in 1912. The cows here were largely fed on arable crops, but some land had been laid down. The same thing happened at Corsley.[34] These are widely separated examples of what was taking place all over the country.

Some people believed that soiling cattle (feeding cut green crops in stall) was on the increase at this time. If the cows were kept in stall they must be let out into a small pasture daily for fresh air and exercise. A frequent change of pasture was strongly recommended. Great interest was aroused in the preparation and preservation of ensilage and the British Dairy Farmer's Association formed a Committee on this subject. Various crops were tried and various shaped containers were designed, but the process did not catch on very extensively. Large numbers of patents in connection with it were taken out, no less than 49 applications being made in 1884. Its great weakness is its variability of quality, resulting not only from the variety of material, mixture of grasses and so on, but also from the knowledge and care with which it is made. If the cows were fed in stall the milk yield was thought to increase, especially on a farm where this method was combined with judicious cropping to produce the maximum of home grown food.[35] This may or may not have been an economy. It probably meant, if no more, that there were less bills to pay at the end of the year, because the men's wages had been paid weekly, and the horses' keep was largely provided on the farm. On a farm of 100 acres one quarter of the area under crop, growing tares or Italian rye grass, as catch crops, would provide the essential supplementary feed. Cabbages and roots must also be grown, and it was advisable not to repeat a crop on the same ground in less than eight years. A judicious mixture of feeds for dairy cows, including decorticated cotton cake, linseed, bean, pea and wheat meal with an equal proportion of Smith's palm nut meal mixed with straw and hay chaff, and a few pulped roots, was recommended by Gilbert Murray in 1880. This mixture was to be boiled or steamed, and given with an addition of lukewarm water. The animal should be fed in this way two or three times a day. This was not a new principle though the ingredients were. A warm mash of mixed ingredients, hay tea and boiled potatoes had been discussed, if not extensively used, for at least half a century.

The necessity for grooming and washing cows was steadily becoming more widely appreciated, together with regular times for feeding, milking, always taking the cows in the same rota, and putting them always in the same stall. All these helped to keep the cows calm and satisfied. For cows have a

THE COW HOUSE ABOUT 1800

A NINETEENTH CENTURY COW HOUSE

A Farmhouse Dairy about 1880

The Dairy about 1830

great appreciation of a standard routine and like to be in clean surroundings. It is therefore important to remove the dirty and supply clean litter in stalls as well as keeping the animals clean. Modern dairy farmers are sometimes criticised on this score.[36]

No regular principles of feeding had yet been established. In 1874 the German, Emil von Wolff had stated that the requirements of a 1,000 lb. milch cow giving 20 lb. were 2·5 lb. digestible protein, 0·4 lb. digestible fat, and 12·5 lb. digestible carbohydrate, but his book was not translated into English until 1905. The necessity for a production as well as a maintenance ration had been recognised by Professor Julius Kuhn in 1887, but it was not until Oscar Kellner published his book in 1905 that the modern method of assessing feeding stuffs by starch equivalent was devised.

Consequently the dairy farmer had to feed his cows by rule of thumb, by wisdom gathered from his own and other people's experience, right up to the end of the century. He was told that if milk was wanted for cheese he must give plenty of flesh forming food e.g., peas and beans and water, and other 'carbonaceous' feed; for cream and butter, rich oily food, such as linseed and other cake; for high yield of milk, liberal supplies of watery food, swedes and brewer's grains. Again in buying concentrates he must compare price and feeding value: some were charged much too high. Feeds that tainted the milk must be avoided. The more common (i.e., cheap and poor) meals and cake were liable to do this, and some people still did not like using cabbages, mangolds and turnips. Another point to be taken into account was the condition of the animal. Meals made of legume seeds for example, were costive, which could be corrected by bran, an excellent thing for stimulating milk yield. Some farmers over-fed in the hope of doing this. Opinion, possibly determined by the local climate, differed about the need for housing cows in winter or at least after Christmas. In the warmer southwest it was, and is, practicable to leave the animals out during the whole of the winter. They did not suffer much from the relatively small change of temperature. On the

E

other side of the country and in the north it was necessary to house them. The best farmers gave a feed of hay, green fodder or concentrates at milking.[37]

By the end of the nineteenth century dairy farming was becoming a more and more important branch of English farming. Over large parts of the dairy districts the farmers had a preference for the dairy Shorthorn cow, or a cross between the Shorthorn and some local animal. The Ayrshire breed had been developed in the late eighteenth century, and many farmers found it profitable. The Suffolk Red Poll retained its hold on its native countryside as did the Devons and the Sussex. Polled Galloways were found on some farms in the north and northwest. The number of milch cows kept in the country was perhaps larger than it had ever been.

Systems of management differed, practice often being determined by climate, elevation, and whether arable crops were cultivated. New feeding stuffs, both crops that could be grown by the farmer, and imported or waste products like the oil cakes, had become generally available. Careful selection and good feeding had vastly changed the appearance of our dairy cattle, and consolidated the characters of the different breeds. Knowledge of the best use of the new resources was spreading. The Tudor farmer would have been astounded at the high average of the dairy cows of 1900, especially the best; he would have felt little surprise had he seen the poor stock, miserably housed, ineffectively maintained that had not yet been wholly eliminated; they would have seemed to him the familiar cows of his own day, except that so many of his were Longhorns.

## (iv). Breeding replacements and calf rearing

Breeding must be combined with dairying. The cow must have a calf before it can give milk. In the sixteenth century men used or disposed of the calves according to custom, to their prejudice, or as opportunity offered. Fitzherbert thought it was 'convenient' for farmers to rear calves, especially those dropped between Candlemas (February 2nd, old style) and May, because milk could best be spared at that season, and by the time of weaning there would be grass enough into which to put the calf. This is a little odd because all modern historians have commented on the difficulty of carrying live-stock through the winter owing to the shortage of feed, and the young spring grass could not have been ready for grazing much before April. Fitzherbert does not mention this diffi-culty. He apparently saw none in a cow carrying a calf successfully through the winter, and dropping it in February or March so that it would be nourished on its mother's milk for a couple of months before being weaned. How was the cow's health and strength kept up at this time when keep was at its scantiest? I am equally puzzled by the existence of fat cattle in January among the possessions of a Kentish priory, though that may have been due to the high feeding quality of Romney Marsh.[1]

The early spring calf would be big enough by winter to be put with the other beasts at that season, and its dam would bull again in time to bring another calf at the same time of year as before. A calf that came after May would still be weak when winter came. Its mother would not bull again and would often go barren. No breeder should keep a calf born after Michaelmas. Such a one should be sold as it would be costly to keep through the winter, and would use milk wanted in the house. The cow, too, would more readily take the bull if the calf was removed. Fitzherbert objected to wean-ing calves on hay, a necessity then for late autumn or winter calves. It swelled them up, gave them great bellies, and made them prone to rot when they came to grass. The more mature spring dropped calves were able to take hay in winter with-out harm, especially if it was given them at night in a house by themselves. They could be put in a good pasture by day. Treatment like this made them much better to handle when cows or oxen.[2]

Markham did not agree with him, though he thought the

best time for cows to calve down was the end of March or April—when the grass began to spring to its perfect goodness. It would occasion a great spring of milk, as everyone knew. One good early cow would, he said, countervaile two later. Yet he did not think spring calves should be reared. Those that fell in October or November, or any time in the depth of winter, might well be reared up for breed because the main profit of the dairy was then spent. He was writing a century after Fitzherbert, and perhaps this contradictory opinion was a sign of the times. Fitzherbert did not like keeping winter calves because they consumed milk that was wanted for domestic use, apart from not developing well on a dry feed like hay; Markham, who was looking for profit from sales of dairy produce, preferred to breed up the autumn or winter calves because milk yield was low then, and the calves were welcome to what there was.[3]

In the general opinion it was unwise to put the cow to the bull until she was three years old. The young cow was the best for breed, yet the indifferent old one ought not to be refused. If, however, she was too young, she would bring forth weak calves; she would do the same if too old. The maximum limit of age for breeding everybody did not agree upon. Some thought twelve years or even ten enough; others that only after fifteen would she wax feeble and weary. The best months for bulling were May, June and July when the grass was most flourishing. She would calve nine months later when there would again be fresh grass, and the calf could be better fed. The cow should be kept bare and lean before bulling, but the bull must be fat and strong and 'well meated' and ought to be fed with barley and vetches for a couple of months beforehand. Farmers must watch over the in-calf cows and prevent them from leaping hedges or bushes in case they slipped the calf. The wise man fed her with good provender in a cowhouse or yard adjoining it for a few weeks before calving, and did not milk her at all during that time. He must not milk for butter or cheese for at least two months, letting the calf have its natural food for that period, after which it could go to pasture if it had a little milk night and morning.[4]

Practice in caring for in-calf cows and rearing calves could not have changed very much between the reigns of Henry VIII and Charles II, because Joseph Blagrave reprinted much of Fitzherbert leaving the fact quite open by using Black Letter type for the portions copied. Once again opinion, if Markham's advice reflected opinion, had returned to the idea of rearing spring rather than winter calves. This indeed must always have been more usual. The author of *Dictionarium rusticum* 1717, more or less agreed with both. It was not advisable to overfeed the in-calf cow. A fat cow would rather take the bull, and give less milk 'for the fatness stoppeth the pores and veines that should bring the milk to the paps'. Furthermore, a fat cow calved at great hazard, and her calf was usually small. It was therefore best to keep her in mean grass in a low state.

At Halsall in Lancashire the breeders chose a cow about six years served by a bull of about the same age for breeding. They were willing to pay good prices for young bulls to keep up the breed, and they fed the calves on whole milk. After a month they put the calf with another to an old cow in a good pasture where there was some good, clear water. The animals were left out until the end of August, but always in the edish or youngest short grass on the farm. Since the Lancashire farmers cut hay from Midsummer to Michaelmas they always had a fresh spring of grass. After August the calves were taken away from the cows, and a herd of them put in the best young pasture as long as there was any in sheltered warm ground. When the grass was gone the calves were fed on a mixture of hay and oat straw, because oat straw was considered more tender than any other kind. This may, in fact, have been too bulky for real efficiency in feed, but it was how the calves were kept until they were two years old. When that age the heifer was covered by a young bull of three years old—a great bull would have spoiled such young ones. A little before Christmas, or earlier if the weather made it necessary, the heifers were tethered in the cowhouse at night with a manger full of food before them.

The wisdom of the Lancashire methods was reflected in the reputation of their cattle, some of which were sold as in-calf cows to farmers in Leicestershire. The latter were inclined to be economical in feeding calves. After a month on new milk they gave their calves only skimmed milk and whey. The result was that the Lancashire breed deteriorated in Leicester, and some of the farmers found breeding horses and fattening stores more profitable than dairy cows.

In 1718 Edward Lisle of Crux Easton, Hants., weaned twenty calves. The summer was wet, and there was a heavy crop of grass. In the winter they ate straw and picked up what they could running in the wood. These did well, but the following summer was dry, and Lisle's calves were pinched for grass. Eleven did badly, because they would not eat the briar leaves in the wood, five died, and six had to be given hay in February. Farmer Chivers, a friend or tenant of Lisle's, told him that a cow just calved ate twice as much if being milked as well, and other farmers agreed with him. Though the Lancashire farmers let the calves run with an old cow all the summer this was not general. Most weaned their calves at from two months to ten weeks old, and probably did as the Leicester men, giving skim milk and whey for part of this time. In the Isle of Wight the heifer dropping her first calf was not milked. The calf had it all for its keep. The time of bulling was limited by some to the month between 10th May and 10th June, but Chivers and Stephens, the latter another friend of Lisle, thought it unwise to have calves dropped at Candlemas unless the keeping was good, and they highly disapproved of those who were foolish enough to let yearling heifers take the bull.[5]

It was not really argued about, but the question whether it was most advantageous to have calves dropped in spring or autumn for breeding continued to be ventilated throughout the eighteenth century, and there was no complete agreement about the earliest age at which a cow might be bulled. Richard Bradley put it higher than most people; not less than three years old. He struck a new note, too, in suggesting that an attempt should be made to secure an all the year round supply of milk by letting the kine go to bull from the spring to the winter whereby the farmer might always milk some. If a man had a good store of pasture he could let his cows go to bull every year, but should see to it that a bull did not serve more than two a day. Twenty cows were usually allowed to one bull. This was, of course, impossible in those places where the town had a common bull that ran with the cows on common grazing. Marshall saw this system still in operation in the western chalk hills of Southern England in 1798 as he did in the Cotswolds in 1789. Sir George Head remarked the common grazing of the cows on the town meadows at Newcastle-on-Tyne as late as 1834.

Spring calves should not, Bradley thought, be allowed to have milk, an opinion no one else expressed, but the autumn calves could—the milk then not being fit for the dairy. Such calves would be hardened against distempers and thrive by the nourishing food of the following spring. Ellis's principle was to feed straw in winter to spring calving cows. If given hay a month or so before calving they gave milk for a longer time thus making it profitable to do this; and in a good season it was best to let the cow calve in a yard or in the field.[6]

John Mills emphasised the necessity for taking great care of in-calf cows. They should not be allowed to work or jump about, advice with a reminiscent flavour. They should be put into the richest pasture, provided it was not too moist and fenny, and fed generously for six or eight weeks before calving, given summer grass in the house, or, during the winter, bran, lucern, sainfoin, burnet, etc., the last being a theoretical idea rather than a practical method on most farms in 1776 or even today. For ten days after calving they ought to be given ground beans, corn or oatmeal diluted with water in which salt had been dissolved in addition to the green feeds mentioned. Ordinarily hay and turnips were fed before and after calving. Some cows did not give any milk for a month or so before calving, but he thought that those which had milk at calving made the best mothers and the best nurses. The

61

calf should have all the milk, suckling in a pasture for the first two months of its life.[7]

Thomas Crook of Wiltshire, a rather vague identification, had adopted a system of rearing calves without milk, which he thought brought them on quicker than those of his neighbours who raised them on the cow. In 1787 he weaned 17 calves, in 1788, 23, and in 1789, 15. He fed them on linseed of which he bought three sacks in 1787. He boiled 1 quart of linseed in 6 quarts of water for ten minutes, and made it into a good jelly. This he mixed with a small quantity of the tea of the best hay steeped in boiling water. His calves were dropped at different times of the year, and he fed them the jelly and hay tea three times a day. He could not or did not keep an exact account, but 'at the last' he had better than two bushels of linseed in hand. His calves were kept in a good growing state, and did not fall off when they came to grass like his neighbours' milk fed calves. A slight modification of this system, or rather a combination of the two systems was adopted by some farmers twenty years later. Their calves had milk for one month, and then hay tea with linseed jelly in milk.

A good deal of the finest and best hay could be wasted by feeding it to calves. Some thought it necessary, especially those who had large herds, to have a calf house for their cows to calve in. Cheshire farmers when rearing calves for replacement kept the calves for three weeks on their mother in February or March. After that time they gave whey, oatmeal gruel, buttermilk, etc. They aimed at calving in March or April though some of their calves were dropped from Christmas to February. At calving time the cowman or the farmer was often up two or three times a night, an experience common enough today.[8]

In spite of these innovations there was a strong feeling that the best calves were those brought up on their mother's milk. It was indeed the usual practice to bring them up in this way in the Weald of Sussex, where the calves ran loose with the cows in the farmyards during the early summer months, and generally also in the Midlands. Here, as soon as cheese-making began, they were sold to the butchers for the manufacturing towns and the Staffordshire collieries after being fattened with wheat balls about the size of a walnut made into a paste with gin. Three or four of these were fed a quarter of an hour before each meal. It kept the calves quiet, as one may easily believe.[9]

Selling calves for veal was, of course, no new thing. Essex farmers had done this in the seventeenth century, and probably earlier. Thomas Fuller had declared they produced calves of the fattest, finest and fairest veal in England. He modestly added 'consequently in all Europe'. William Ellis praised the Essex men no less. They were allowed to be the richest and best calf sucklers of all in the early and mid-eighteenth century. They maintained this reputation. About 1800 they generally sold their calves, but if they reared them they were taken from the dam at about a week old about Christmas, and had skim milk, being given a 'lock' of hay after a while, and when they began to eat, water mixed with milk. In the North Riding and Lancashire replacements only were brought up, the rest being sold to butchers, or to feeders who raised them as stores. The West Norfolk dairy farmers sold their calves to the graziers of East Norfolk, and those in Buckingham to sucklers at from four to twelve days old. Calves fattened by suckling in North Wiltshire were sent to London dead, and cut up into quarters. Cows were brought in rather than bred here. The Vale of Gloucester dairymen reared their own replacements for the excellent reason that they knew what they bred, but could only guess at what they bought. The calves from the dairies of East Devon and even Dorset were bought by graziers on the borders of Dartmoor while those born in West Devon were either reared or fattened for veal.[10]

Although the Suffolk farmers did not wean the first calf, and the Suffolk Duns had so fine a reputation, they were in the habit of breeding with a two year old bull on a two year old cow. This was criticised as making for small size, the animals seldom weighing over 50 stone, but despite all that could be said against Suffolk methods of maintenance and breeding, a fine and productive breed of cows was kept up. The Somerset farmers bulled their heifers at eighteen months, but only kept enough of the heifer calves for replacements. Their bull-chins were mostly sold; cows were kept till ten or twelve years old. Arthur Young, a Suffolk farmer himself, thought that bulls were used too young there, but James Adam did not agree. Adam advised that the bull should be well fed and kept from coition till his second, if not his third year. If so, his vigour would last for two years. Heifers, in his opinion, should not be bulled till their fourth year, and their third, fourth and fifth calves would be the most robust and best to breed from. Parkinson thought heifers old enough at two years or thirty months.[11]

All these differences in opinion and practice persisted throughout the whole of the nineteenth century. There were, in fact, wider variations in that century than ever before, because of the increasing demand for liquid milk, as a result of larger population, improvement in transport facilities, and changes in dietetic habits. Most people however still preferred their cows to calve down between January and March, and even in 1920 Fream considered that calves born late in the year did not do so well as those of the early months. Some calves were taken from the cow at birth, and fed on whole milk for periods of a week or two up to three months, and thereafter on skim milk, linseed jelly and so on. Others were allowed to run with the cow. A rather vague piece of advice was to feed them from the first on food that tended to increase milk secretion. One method was to take the calf from the cow at a week old, and then to give it two quarts of whole milk every morning and evening for one month, one quart of milk with $\frac{1}{2}$ lb. meal for six weeks, after which they were turned out to grass. Replacements where this was done were estimated at 25%, the farmers either rearing their own, or buying in-calf three year old heifers. Others thought replacements necessary every five years. In Staffordshire the best farmers raised their calves in pens till May, but some liked to have calves dropped all the year round in the 1850's. James Long preferred rearing calves to buying when it was done with skill and H. M. Upton considered that by carefully breeding from the deepest milkers in the herd, and keeping only calves of the best cows the productive capacity of a herd would be raised. The bull, he said, is half the herd, an opinion that was shared by more and more farmers. If a cow was fed on rich foods that stimulated the formation of milk the farmer then intensified in the offspring the tendency already existing in the parent. Another advantage of breeding was that there was less chance of importing diseases as might be done when replacements were bought. When a calf sucked it was important that it should be made to suck all four teats, otherwise the cow might lose a quarter.[12]

Fundamentally much of the practice was sound in spite of its variety, as the centuries of experience behind it made certain. So long as the calf was kept in a state of continuous growth and well-being—especially in its first year of life—all was well. From one year until in-calf the heifer had to be kept healthy and in good condition, but it is still thought a bad thing to make her too fat. For a while before calving more generous feeding is necessary, as so many writers have said for so long. During the nineteenth century concentrates came on the market, and some expenditure on these, prior to calving, is amply repaid when the heifer becomes a milking cow. This had been realised by knowledgeable dairy farmers for a very long time. The problem today is much the same as it always was. A recent authority has confirmed ancient practice. It is logical for the cow to calve in spring to coincide with the flush of grass. The mother then gets enough good feed to make her a good nurse, and as the grass falls off so do her requirements. She can be dried in autumn. This was largely the simple system of our forefathers. It does not provide for winter milk. When that is wanted, the cow must calve in the autumn, and an adequate supply of winter feed makes growing some arable crops essential. This too was realised by our ancestors, although they have only been able to supply it since such things as seeds, hay, roots and the brassica have been cultivated.[13]

## NOTES TO CHAPTER I (i)

1 Thomas Lodge and Robert Greene. *A Looking Glass for London and England*, 1594. Reprinted in J. Churton Collins. *The Plays and Poems of Robert Greene*, 2 vol. 1905.

1a *Archaelogia Cantiana.* vol. 7, pp. 279, 287, 302.

1b *Sussex Arch. Collec.* xlv (1902) p. 126 ff.

2 Fussell and Atwater. *Farmers' goods and chattels, 1500–1800.* History. XX Dec., 1935 and the authorities there cited.

3 James Wishaw. *A history of the Wishaw family*, 1935. pp. 23, 35, 61.

4 Robert Reyce. *Suffolk in the 17th century.* 1618. With notes by Lord Francis Hervey. 1902. p. 38.

5 W. G. Hoskins. *The Leicestershire farmer in the 16th century.* Trans. Leics. Arch. Soc. 1942. pp. 22–30.

6 Francis W. Steer. *Farm and cottage inventories of mid-Essex, 1635–1749.* 1950. pp. 53–55.

7 F. G. Emmison. *Jacobean household inventories.* Pubns. of the Bedfordshire Histl. Record Soc. XX. 1938.

8 Eleanor C. Lodge (ed.) *An account book of a Kentish estate, 1616–1704.* 1927. *passim.*

9 The mid-Essex inventories printed in Steer—note 6—confirm this conclusion as do the following:—1612. John Aridge of Ifold, 16 cattle. *Sussex Arch. Collec.* XXIX (1879) p. 132; 1637. John Potter, Surrey. 4 cattle. *Surrey Arch. Collec.* XXIII. (1910) p. 80 ff; 1646. Sir Thomas Whitmore, Bart., Apley Hall, Salop. 12 cattle. *Trans. Shropshire Arch. Soc.* 4 ser. (1914) p. 305; 1676. Robert Marples, Barlborough, Derby. 19 cattle. *Derbys. Arch. Jour.* IX (1879) 31 ff.; 1677. James Stillwell, Surrey. 41 cattle, *Surrey Arch, Collec.* LI (1908) p. 115 ff.; 1697. Cornelius Humphrey, Newhaven. 16 cattle. *Sussex Arch. Collec.* VI (1853) p. 190 ff.

10 *Records of the borough of Leicester, 1608–1688.* ed. by Helen Stocks. 1923. p. xxxvii. C. J. Billson. *The open fields of Leicester.* Leics. Arch. Soc. 14 (1925–6). pp. 23, 214.

11 Arthur Young. *Six weeks tour.* 1769. pp. 79, 83. *ibid. General view of . . . Essex.* 1805. pp. 270, 276.

12 W. B. Mercer. *Two centuries of Cheshire cheese farming.* Jour. R.A.S.E. 1937 *passim.* See also my *Four centuries of Cheshire farming systems.* Trans. Historic Soc. of Lancs. & Ches. 106 (1954). Fred Law Olmstead. *Walks and talks of an American farmer in England.* 1852. p. 173.

13 Samuel D. Sherriff. *Report on Liverpool prize farms.* J.R.A.S.E. 1877. J. A. Clarke. *Report on laying down . . . ibid.* 1875. J. Chalmers Morton. *Report on the dairy and stock farm competition. ibid.* 1886. James Edwards. *Report on the farm prize competition of 1885. ibid.* 1885. J. Bowen Jones. *Typical farms in Cheshire and North Wales. ibid.* 1893. Wm. H. Hogg *Farm prize competition. ibid.* 1910.

14 *Report on prize farms.* J.R.A.S.E. 1871. *The farm prize competition of 1884. ibid.* 1884.

15 Wm. Pitt. *General view of . . . Stafford.* 1808. p. 175. H. Evershed. *The agriculture of Stafford.* J.R.A.S.E. 1869. p. 278. Elihu Burritt. *Walks in the Black country and its green borderland* 1869. p. 339.

16 *Annals of Agriculture.* II (1784) p. 151. Arthur Young. *General view of Suffolk.* 1803. Wm. & Hugh Raynbird. *On the agriculture of Suffolk.* 1849. p. 97.

[17] *Letters & communications to the Bath and West Soc.* V. (1790) pp. 222–224.
Sir Thos. Dyke Acland. *On the farming of Somersetshire.* 1851. p. 134.
*Annals of Agric.* XVI (1791) p. 492. *ibid.* IV. (1785) p. 240. Wm. Maver,
*General view of Berkshire.* 1813. p. 377. *The Berkshire farm prize competition,* 1882. J.R.A.S.E. 1882. pp. 545, 552. Wm. Stevenson. *General view of Dorset.* 1815. Elihu Burritt. *A walk from London to Lands' End and back.*
1868. p. 126. John Boys. *General view of Kent.* 1796. p. 147. G. B. Worgan
*General view of . . . Cornwall.* 1811. p. 144. *The Yorkshire farm prize competition,* 1883. J.R.A.S.E. 1883. pp. 520, 555, 579.

## NOTES TO CHAPTER I (ii)

[1] M.McG. Cooper. *Competitive farming.* 1956. p. 49.
[2] E. H. Carrier. *The pastoral heritage of Britain.* 1936. p. 91.
[3] Ernle. *English farming, past and present.* 6th Edition 1961 pp. 137–138, 188.
John Mortimer's statement was copied by Society of Gentlemen. *The complete farmer.* 4th ed. 1793. c.f. Robert Brown. *The compleat farmer.* 1759.
p. 19. John Mills. *A treatise on cattle.* 1776. p. 295. George Culley. *Observations on livestock.* 1786. pp. 40–83. George Garrard. *A description of the different varieties of oxen common in the British Isles.* 1800. John Lawrence.
*A general treatise on cattle.* 1805. p. 34. William Bingley. *Memoirs of British quadrupeds.* 1809. p. 398. Richard Parkinson. *Treatise on the breeding and management of livestock.* 1810. pp. 105–138. W. H. R. Curtler. *A short history of English agriculture.* 1909. pp. 176–168. see also my *Size of English cattle in the 18th century.* Agric. Hist. (U.S.A.) III. 4. Oct. 1929 & *Animal husbandry in 18th century England.* ibid. XI. April & July, 1937.
[4] *Fitzherbert's Husbandry,* 1523 in *Certain antient tracts,* 1767. pp. 44, 45. Gervase Markham. *Cheape and good husbandry.* 8th ed. 1653 (1st. 1614) p. 90. idem. *The English housewife,* 1653 (1614) pp. 140, 141. Richard Surflet. *The countrey ferme* translated from the French of Estienne & Liebault. 1600. p. 89 Hartlib. *Legacie.* 1655 (1651). p. 90.
[5] John Worlidge. *Systema agriculturae.* 1666. p. 161. Richard Blome. *The gentleman's recreation.* 1686. p. 256. John Mortimer. *Whole art of husbandry.* 4th ed. 1716. I. p. 222.
[6] J. B., Gent., *Epitome of the art of husbandry.* 1675. pp. 67, 68. Blome. *op. cit.* p. 256. Edward Lisle. *Observations in husbandry.* 1756. (relates to period 1690–1712) p. 273. Mortimer. *op. cit.* I. p. 228.
[7] John Houghton. *Collection of letters for the improvement of husbandry and trade.* 1681–1683. II. pp. 154, 155.
[8] Anon. *Dictionarium rusticum.* 1717. R. Bradley. *General treatise on husbandry.* 1726. I. p. 79. T. Hale. *Compleat body of husbandry.* 1756. May. p. 26. Country Gentleman. *Complete grazier.* 1767. pp. 2–6.
[9] John Laurence. *New system of agriculture.* 1726. p. 130. Carrier. *op. cit.* p. 98.
[10] William Ellis. *Modern husbandry.* 1750. I. May. p. 95. June. pp. 143, 144, 147, 148.
[11] Robert Brown. *Compleat Farmer.* 1759. p. 20.
[12] Ernle. *English Farming.* pp. 187–188. H. Evershed. *Agriculture of Staffordshire.* J.R.A.S.E. 1869. p. 270.

[13] See my *Size of English cattle in the 18th century.* Agric. Hist. (U.S.A.) III. 4 Oct. 1929 and the authorities cited therein pp. 160–181.

[14] Arthur Young. *A six month's tour through the north of England.* 2nd ed. 1771. II. pp. 126–127.

[15] James Anderson. *Essays relating to agriculture.* 4th ed. 1797 (1773) II. pp. 128, 132.

[16] Richard Brocklesby. *An essay concerning the mortality now prevailing among the horned cattle . . . about London.* 1746. William Ellis. *Modern husbandman.* 1750. III. pp 131–133. D. P. Layard. *Essay on the nature of the contagious distemper among the horned cattle in these kingdoms.* 1757. p. 12. E. F. D. Osborn (ed.) *Political and social letters of a lady of the 18th century, 1721–1727.* 1891. p. 87. Malcolm Flemyng. *Proposal in order to diminish the progress of the distemper amongst the horned cattle.* 1754. *Family history begun by James Fretwell. Yorkshire diaries & autobiographies in the 17th & 18th centuries.* Surtees Soc. Publns. 1875. vol. 65. p. 238.

[17] Ellis. *Mod. Husb.* IV. p. 106. Powell. *A view of real grievances; with remedies proposed for redressing them.* 1772. p. 237. *House of Commons Jour.* 1764. vol. 29. p. 1046. William Marshall. *Rural Econ. of Yorkshire.* 1788. II. p. 210 & *Rural Econ. of Midland Counties.* 1790. II. pp. 100, 293–294. & *Rural Econ. of Norfolk.* 1787. II. pp. 327.

[18] John Mills. *Treatise on cattle.* 1776. pp. 295, 309–310. George Culley. *Observations on livestock.* 1786. *passim.* Josiah Ringsted. *The farmer.* n.d., c. 1796. p. 79. A. F. M. Willich. *Domestic encyclopaedia* 1802. cf. Russell M. Garnier. *History of English landed interest.* 1893. II. p. 263.

[19] Culley. *op. cit.* pp. 29–30, 35. cf. M.Mc. Cooper. *Competitive farming.* 1956. pp. 50–52. Sir Walter Gilbey. *Farm stock 100 years ago.* 1910. pp. 67, 70.

[20] Richard Parkinson. *Treatise on livestock.* 1810. I. pp. 9, 11, 102, 103, 107.

[21] Henry Holland. *General view of . . . Cheshire,* 1801. pp. 249–251. L. F. Olmstead. *Walks and talks of an American farmer . . .*1852. p. 173. A. D. Hall. *Pilgrimage of English farming.* 1913. p. 212.

[22] See the Board of Agriculture reports on the various counties—and Marshall. *Midland counties.* 1790 I. pp. 315, 341–343.

[23] Marshall. *Norfolk.* 1787. I. p. 328. Naomi Riches. *Agricultural revolution in Norfolk.* 1937. p. 99. *Annals of Agric.* II. (1784) p. 151. Arthur Young. *General view of . . . Norfolk.* 1797. p. 179. *idem.* Select Committee House of Commons. *Report relating to the Corn Laws.* 1814. p. 86. *Annals of Agric.* XXXVI (1801). pp. 456, 510, 511.

[24] *Annals of agric.* XI (1789). p. 125. XXXVII (1801) p. 43 ff. cf. Sir Walter Gilbey. *op. cit.* p. 75. Young. *Essex.* II. (1805) pp. 270, 273, 275, 276.

[25] *Annals of agric.* XXI (793) p. 113. John Middleton. *Middlesex.* 1798. pp. 327, 328.

[26] See Marshall and the county reports for each of the counties.

[27] John Lawrence. *New farmer's calendar.* 4th ed. 1802. pp. 492, 493. R.W. Dickson. *Practical agriculture.* 1804. pp. 1118–1124. John Lawrence. *General treatise on cattle.* 1805. p. 135 notes Shorthorn are beginning to replace Longhorn. Twamley. *Essays in management of dairy.* 1816. p. 32.

[28] William Youatt. *Cattle.* 1834. Chap. VI. Sir George Head. *A home tour . . . in 1835.* 1836. p. 259. C. Hillyard. *Practical farming and grazing* 3rd ed. 1840. p. 82. David Low. *Practical agriculture.* 4th ed. 1843. pp. 608–613, 622. *idem. Domesticated animals of the British Isles.* 1845. pp. 330–389.

29 A. Lawson. *Modern farrier*. 8th ed. 1825. p. 384. *Baxters' Library of agricultural & horticultural knowledge*. 3rd ed. 1836. pp. 141, 160. James Jackson. *Treatise of agriculture and dairy husbandry*. 1840. p. 105. John Sherer. *Rural life*. n.d., c. 1850. pp. 662, 663.

30 M. M. Milburn. *The cow: dairy husbandry & cattle breeding*. c. 1851. p. 49.

31 Colonel le Couteur. *On the Jersey, misnamed Alderney cow*. J.R.A.S.E. V. (1845) pp. 43–49.

32 François Guenon. *Traité des vaches laitières*. 1839. J. H. Magne. *How to choose a good dairy cow*. 1853. pp. 177–184. John Gamgee, *Dairy stock*. 1861. p. 50. Willis P. Hazard. *Guenon's system of selecting cows by the escutcheon*. J.R.A.S.E. 1885. Robert Wallace & J. A. Scott Watson. *Farm livestock of Great Britain*. 1923. p. 352. E. Parmalee Prentice. *American dairy cattle*. 1942. pp. 385, 432.

33 J. C. Morton. *Handbook of dairy husbandry*. 1860. pp. 31–33. J. Donaldson. *British agriculture*, 1860. II. pp. 400–441. John Coleman. *The cross-breeding of cattle*. J.R.A.S.E. 1861. pp. 351, 352. R. O. Pringle & Prof. Murray. *Practical farming: stock*. n.d., c. 1865. pp. 3–11. This book is based on J. H. Magne. *Choix des vaches laitières* & P. A. Tier. *La laitèrie*. Samuel Copland. *Agriculture, ancient and modern*. 1866. I. p. 745. H. Evershed. *Agric. of Staffs*. J.R.A.S.E. 1869. p. 269.

34 D. F. G. Macdonald. *Cattle, sheep and deer*. 2nd ed. 1872. pp. 55, 75, 143. H. Epstein. *Domestication features in animals as functions of human society*. Agric. Hist. (U.S.A.) 29.4. p. 138. Arthur Roland. *Farming for pleasure and profit: dairy farming*. 1879. pp. 31–38. *Ward and Lock's Book of farm management*. n.d., c. 1880 pp. 287–295. John J. Pilling. *Scientific agriculture*. 1881. p. 212. R. Scott Burn. *Directory for the improvement of landed property*. 1881. pp. 462–464. Joseph Darby. *Pedigree cattle in dairy herds*. Jour. Bath & West Soc. 3rd ser. 15. (1883–4) John Walker. *The cow and the calf*. 1886. pp. 5–14. James Long. *Dairy farm*. 1889. pp. 39–49. Robert Wallace. *Farm livestock of Great Britain*. 1889. pp. 28–61. J. P. Sheldon. *The farm and the dairy*. 1889. pp. 8–15. Robert Bruce. *The influence of locality on breeds of cattle*. Jour. Farmers' Club. Dec. 1895. p. 23. Ernest Matthews. *Economics in dairy farming*. 1903. p. 15. E. R. Cochrane. *The milch cow in England*. 1946. p. 46.

## NOTES TO CHAPTER I (iii)

1 Mildred Campbell. *The English yeoman under Elizabeth and the early Stuarts*. 1942. p. 204.

2 Barbara Winchester. *Tudor family portrait*. 1955. pp. 181–182.

3 Ernle. *English farming* . . . p. 27.

4 *Fitzherbert's Husbandry*. 1523. p. 51.

5 C. S. & C. S. Orwin. *The open fields*. 2nd ed. 1954. p. 132.

6 *Robert Loder's farm accounts, 1610–1620*. Camden Soc. 3rd ser. LIII. 1936.

7 M. E. Seebohm. *Evolution of the English farm*. 1952. p. 205.

8 W. Cunningham. *Common rights at Cottenham and Stretton in Cambridgeshire*. Camden Misc. 3rd ser. XVIII (1910) pp. 169–287. J. E. Foster (ed.). *The diary of Samuel Newton, Alderman of Cambridge*. Pubns. of Cambridge Antiq. Soc. XXIII (1890) p. 40. cf. F. J. C. Hearnshaw. *Leet jurisdiction in England*. Southampton Record Soc. 1908. p. 207.

[9] W. Cunningham. *Cambridgeshire materials for the history of agriculture.* Proc. Cambs. Antiq. Soc. XX (1917) pp. 50–51.

[10] *Fitzherbert's husbandry.* (ed. 1767) p. 56. Leonard Mascall. *Gouvernment of cattell.* 1627. pp. 69, 70, 51.

[11] Fitzherbert. pp. 51, 70.

[12] J. B., Gent. *Epitome of the whole art of husbandry.* 1675. p. 66. Richd. Blome. *Gentleman's recreation.* 1686. p. 257.

[13] Eric Kerridge. *Turnip husbandry in High Suffolk.* Econ. Hist. Rev. 2nd ser. VIII (April, 1956) pp. 391–392. John Norden. *Surveyor's dialogue.* 3rd ed. 1608 (1617). cf. Soc. of Gentlemen. *Complete farmer.* 1766 art. Carrots. Robert Billing. *Account of the culture . . . of carrots.* 1765.

[14] *Samuel Hartlib his legacie.* 1655. pp. 87–88, 170.

[15] A. S., Gent. (Adolphus Speed) *Husbandman, farmer and grazier's complete instructor.* 1697. p. 53. Edward Lisle. *Observations in husbandry.* 1757. p. 277 (refers to period 1690–1712). Anon. *Tusser redivivus.* 1710. Jan. pp. 6, 7.

[16] *Tusser redivivus.* Feb. p. 13. Samuel Trowell. *New treatise of husbandry.* 1739. p. 47. Thomas Hale. *Compleat body of husbandry.* 1756 vol. 2. p. 38. James Anderson. *Essays relating to agriculture & rural affairs.* 1775. pp. 443–450. William Pitt. *General view of . . . Leicester.* 1809. p. 161.

[17] Richard Bradley. *Gentleman and farmer's guide.* 1729. p. 136.

[18] idem. *General treatise of husbandry.* 1726. I. pp. 68, 74. John Laurence. *New system of agriculture.* 1726. p. 130. William Ellis. *Modern husbandman.* 1750. III July, p. 161. Country Gentleman. *Complete grazier,* 1767. p. 83.

[19] John Mortimer. *Whole art of husbandry.* 4th ed. 1716. I. pp. 233, 234. *Museum rusticum et commerciale.* 3rd ed. I (1763) p. 113. Ellis. *op. cit.* I. May. p. 103, 108, but cf. p. 126. Richard Weston. *Tracts on practical agriculture.* 1773. p. 270.

[20] Hale. *Compleat body.* 1756. p. 511. Thomas Comber. *Real improvements in agriculture.* 1772. pp. 48–51, 71. Charles Varlo. *New system of husbandry.* 1774. III. pp. 191 ff., 125. John Randall. *Semi-Virgilian husbandry.* 1764. pp. 315–325.

[21] Ellis. *Mod. husb.* 1750. II. May. p. 158. June. p. 106.

[22] A. K. Hamilton-Jenkin. *Cornwall and its people.* 1945. pp. 380, 381 citing *Notes from a journal made during a 16 day riding tour in Cornwall in 1754.* Penzance Nat. Hist. & Antiq. Soc. 1888–92. p. 283. etc.

[23] Thomas Comber of East Newton. *Museum rusticum.* V. (1765) pp. 125–128, 130. John Mills. *Treatise on cattle.* 1776. p. 317. *Annals of Agric.* XXII (1794). p. 414 ff. *ibid.* XXIV (1795). p. 463. Young *Northern tour.* 1771. II. p. 138.

[24] Richard Weston. *Tracts.* 1773. pp. 195, 271–273. James Anderson. *Essays.* 4th ed. 1797 (1773). II. p. 60–68. Idem. *Practical essays on agriculture.* 1787. II. p. 477. Russell M. Garnier. *History of English landed interest.* 1893. II. p. 264.

[25] Josiah Ringsted. *The farmer.* 2nd ed., n.d., c. 1800. p. 83. James Anderson. *Recreations in agriculture.* 1800. pp. 241–247. A. F. M. Willich. *Domestic encyclopaedia.* 1802. John Lawrence. *New farmer's calendar.* 4th ed. 1802. pp. 107, 108, 183, 414. R. W. Dickson. *Practical Agric.* 1804. II. p. 968–994. Arthur Young. *Farmers' calendar.* new ed. 1804 passim. Twamley. *Essays in management of dairy.* 1816. (1784). pp. 34, 39–46. L. W. Moffitt. *England on the eve of Industrial Revolution, 1740–1760.* 1925 p. 69 cf. the relative county reports issued between 1794 & 1816.

[26] *Annals of agric.* II. (1784). p. 151. *Ibid.* V. pp. 193–203. Arthur Young. *General view of . . . Suffolk.* 1797. pp. 182, 183.

[27] Alexander Taylor. *A farmers's guide.* 1829. pp. 210–216. Baxters' *Library of agricultural & horticultural knowledge.* 3rd ed. 1836. pp. 160, 161. James Jackson. *Treatise of agric. & dairy husbandry.* 1840. p. 106. David Low. *Practical agric.* 4th ed. 1843. pp. 650, 651. George Nicholls. *The farmer.* 1844. p. 179.

[28] C. W. Johnson. *Modern dairy & cowkeeper.* 1850. pp. 21, 24, 34. M. M. Milburn *The cow: dairy husbandry . . . c.* 1851. pp. 16, 98. Thomas Dyke Acland & Wiliam Sturge. *Farming of Somersetshire.* 1851. pp. 52, 135, 138, 139.

[29] Charles A. Browne. *Source book of agricultural chemistry.* 1944. Chronica Botanica. Vol. 8. no. 1. pp. 231 ff.

[30] John Bravender. *Farming of Gloucester.* J.R.A.S.E. 1850. pp. 147–151. Edward Little. *Farming of Wilts. ibid.* 1845. p. 175. Joseph Darby. *Pedigree cattle in herds.* Jour. Bath & West Soc. 3rd ser. XV (1883–4) p. 107. J. C. Buckmaster & J. J. Willis. *Elementary principles of scientifi agric.* n.d., c. 1883. pp. 167–168.

[31] Joseph Harding. *Recent improvements in dairy practice.* J.R.A.S.E. 1860. pp. 82, 83. cf. his articles in Jour. Bath & West Soc. 1857 & 1861. J. Bowen Jones. *Somerset prize farm competition.* J.R.A.S.E. 1875. p. 538. George Gibbons. *Dairy industry of Somerset.* Jour. Brit. Dairy Farmers' Assoc. VIII. (1893). p. 75.

[32] Elihu Burritt. *Walk from London to Lands' End.* 1868. pp. 126–128, 339–343. idem. *Walks in the Black Country . . .* 1869. p. 339.

[33] J. C. Morton. *Handbook of dairy husbandry.* 1860. pp. 13–23, 36. Samuel Copland. *Agric., ancient & modern.* 1866. I. p. 752. R. O. Pringle & Prof. Murray. *Practical farming; stock.* 1865. p. 59. D. F. G. Macdonald. *Cattle, sheep & deer.* 2nd ed. 1872. pp. 144, 145. John Coleman. *Cattle, sheep & pigs of Great Britain.* 2nd ed. 1887. pp. 82 & many articles in periodicals.

[34] Ernle. *English farming.* 1961. pp. 379–381. Alfred Williams. *Villages of the White Horse.* 1913. pp. 122, 123. A. D. Hall. *Pilgrimage of English farming.* 1913. p. 161. Maude F. Davies. *Life in an English village.* 1909. pp. 87, 108.

[35] *Ward & Locks' Book of farm management.* n.d., c. 1880. p. 298 ff. R. Scott Burn. *Directory . . .* 1881. p. 468.

[36] Gilbert Murray. *Notes on dairy farming.* n.d., c. 1880. pp. 10–13. H. M. Upton. *Profitable dairy farming.* 1888. pp. 34, 61. Prof. Muir. *Management of dairy cows.* Jour. Bath & West Soc. 4th ser. V. (1895) pp. 57–61. C. G. Freer Thonger. *Some essentials of successful dairy farming. ibid.* XIII. (1903). p. 78.

[37] Cyril Tyler. *Development of feeding standards for livestock.* Agric. Hist. Rev. IV (1956). pp. 97–107. Frank H. Garner. *British dairying,* 1948. p. 23.

[38] John J. Pilley. *Scientific agric.* 1881. p. 229. Robert Wallace. *Farm livestock of Great Britain.* 1889. pp. 148, 149. J. Sutcliffe Hurndall. *The management of dairy stock.* Jour. Farmers' Club. Apl. 1896. p. 48. F. Punchard. *Dairy farming of Cumbld. & Westld.* Jour. B.D.F.A. VII. (1892) pp. 111, 115. John B. Spearing. *Management of dairy cows.* J.R.A.S.E. 1892. pp. 169–172. Henry J. Webb. *Advanced agric.* 1894. pp. 183–509. C. G. Freer-Thonger. *op. cit.* note 36. pp. 78, 82. Ernest Matthews. *Economics in dairy farming.* 1903. p. 38. A. D. Hall. *Pilgrimage of English farming.* 1913. *passim.* H. I. Moore. *Science and practice of grassland farming.* 1949. p. 21. E. R. Cochrane. *Milch cow in England.* 1946. p. 50.

## NOTES TO CHAPTER I (iv)

1 *Archaelogia Cantiana.* Vol. 7. pp. 279, 287, 302.

2 Fitzherbert. *op. cit.* p. 51.

3 Gervase Markham. *English housewife.* ed. of 1653. (1615). p. 142.

4 Markham. *Cheape and good husbandry.* 1653. (1616). p. 90. Richard Surflet. *Countrey ferme.* 1600. p. 86. Leonard Mascall. *Gouvernment of cattell.* 1627. pp. 52, 53.

5 J. B., Gent. *Epitome of the whole art of husbandry.* 1675. pp. 68–72. John Houghton. *Collection of letters for the improvement of husbandry and trade.* 1681–1683. II. pp. 154, 155. A. S., Gent. *Husbandman, farmer & graziers complete instructor.* 1697. pp. 2, 3 Edward Lisle. *Observations in husbandry.* 1757. pp. 273–275, 279, 280.

6 Richard Bradley. *Gentleman & farmers guide.* 1729. pp. 131–133. *idem. General treatise of husbandry.* 1726. I. p. 84. William Ellis. *Practical farmer.* 2nd ed. 1732. p. 109. T. Hale. *Compleat body of Husbandry.* 1756. p. 556. Country gentleman. *Complete grazier.* 1767. pp. 5–7.

7 John Mills. *Treatise on cattle.* 1776. pp. 311, 312. Josiah Ringsted *The farmer.* 2nd ed. n.d., c. 1796. p. 83.

8 *Land Agents' Record.* 31 July, 1943. p. 248. Richard Parkinson. *Treatise on livestock.* 1810. pp. 19, 22, 27. Henry Holland. *General view . . . of Cheshire.* 1808. pp. 253, 257, 259. R. W. Dickson. *Practical agric.* 1804. II. p. 998. John Lawrence. *New Farmers' calendar.* 4th ed. 1802. p. 488.

9 Marshall. *Rural econ. of southern counties.* 1798. II. p. 146. *idem.* Midlands. 1790. I. p. 350.

10 Thomas Fuller. *History of the worthies of England.* 1662. new ed. ed. by P. Austin Nuttall. 1840. I. p. 497. *Annals of agric.* XI (1789) p. 127. Arthur Young. *General view of . . . Essex.* 1805. II. pp. 273, 278. John Tuke. *General view . . . N. R. York,* 1800. p. 249. John Holt. *General view . . . Lancashire.* 1795. p. 149. Marshall. *Norfolk.* 1787. I. p. 328. Rev. St. John Priest. *General view . . . Bucks.* 1813. p. 302. Thomas Davis. *General view . . . Wilts.* 1811. p. 206. Marshall. *Gloucester,* 1796. I. pp. 215, 216. II. p. 160. *Idem. West of England.* 1796. I. p. 248. II. p. 149.

11 *Annals of agric.* V. p. 213. John Billingsley. *General view . . . Somerset.* 1797. p. 145. Young. *General view . . . Suffolk.* 1797. p. 183. James Adam. *Practical essays on agric.* 1787. II. p. 477. Richard Parkinson. *op. cit.* p. 99.

12 James Jackson. *Treatise on agric. & dairy husbandry.* 1840. p. 105. David Low. *Practical agric.* 4th ed. 1843. p. 622. Samuel Copland. *Agric., ancient & modern.* 1866. I. p. 748. John Coleman. *Cattle, sheep and pigs of Great Britain.* 1887. (1875). p. 84. Henry Stephens. *Book of the farm.* 3rd ed. 1887. I. p. 5. Arthur Roland. *Farming for pleasure and profit.* 1879. pp. 137–147. James Long. *Dairy farm.* 1889. p. 51. J. P. Sheldon. *Dairy farming.* n.d., c. 1883. p. 59 ff. H. M. Upton. *Profitable dairy farming.* 1888. p. 112. John J. Pilley. *Scientific agric.* 1881. p. 212. Robert Wallace. *Farm livestock of Great Britain* 1889. pp. 140, 152. Henry J. Webb. *Advanced agric.* 1894. p. 485.

13 William Lawson. *Reflections on milk production.* Sussex Agric. Jour. Nov.–Jan. 1955–56. p. 5. H. I. Moore. *Science & practice of grassland farming.* 1949. pp. 21, 22.

# CHAPTER II

## *Grassland and fodder crops*

### (i). Natural grass: permanent pasture and meadow

Except rough grazing, mountains, moors and downs, there are no longer in England wide areas of wild grass, uncultivated but not undisturbed by animals and man, which were once the unenclosed waste of the manor. There were in the sixteenth century. Most of these wastes have been made enclosed arable, pasture and meadow, and have now been under individual control for generations. The arable always received most attention, and in spite of all the recent research and propaganda, many modern farmers regard grass as a gift from heaven, not as a crop to be managed as carefully as their arable crops if it is to be fully productive.[1] This complaint is not new. It is almost as perennial as the literature of farming.

Modern conditions vary all over the country as all farming necessarily does, but they do throw some light on earlier times. Grassland today is of fairly stable botanical composition, dependent upon soil and management in cultivation and stocking. On good bodied loams heavy grazing throughout the season induces a sward mainly perennial rye grass and wild white clover. The same treatment on poorer soils produces an agrostis-wild white clover combination. Climate does not materially affect the type of grassland. Where the rainfall is highest there is more grass, but lowlands with a higher temperature have a longer growing season: excellent swards of rye grass, cocksfoot and white clover can be found in the drier parts of England, e.g., East Anglia, and exactly the same type at over 1,000 feet in Yorkshire, Wales and Scotland. There is also a difference in the length of the grazing season, which lasts from March to October in East Anglia, but is restricted

73

to the end of April until mid-September in the hills. From these considerations Professor Moore deduces that the influence of management is more important than either soil or climate. On the other hand Gordon Manley places some emphasis on the influence of rainfall though slope and soil are important. Hay is sometimes cut in the Lake District valleys, which drain relatively quickly, in seasons when 100 inches of rain fall, but in the Pennines generally old reclaimed intakes are today abandoned when rainfall approaches 55 inches. He thinks these enclosures were probably made in the late seventeenth or early eighteenth centuries when the rainfall may have been for a decade or so less than at present. Also he considers that East Anglia is only suitable for arable, the closing of meadows for hay being unprofitable in most seasons. The regional differences in agricultural practice are still largely dependent upon climatic factors.[2]

A large number of species and varieties of grasses is indigenous to this country. Of these only a small percentage is really useful to farmers, a maximum of twenty of which about twelve are very valuable and commonly sown. About the same number are weeds, the balance being neither useful nor harmful. This is to put it at its lowest figure. In permanent pasture the longevity or persistence of the plant is its most valuable character combined with its ability to flourish despite the treading of the grazing animal. Perennial rye grass, smooth stalked meadow grass, *Agrostis Stolonifera* and *Holcus lanatus* possess this capacity as does wild white clover. *Poa pratensis* has stems buried in the ground, but *Poa trivialis* with its stems on the surface is easily damaged. The value of the grasses depends upon their environment, the purpose for which they are to be used, and their treatment. Questions of palatibility, chemical composition and digestibility are, of course, involved. As to environment Armstrong says persistence is relatively greater on poor land, e.g., red clover on poor upland, bird's foot trefoil on wet land.[3]

The most useful grasses recommended to the modern farmer are rye grass, cocksfoot, timothy and meadow fescue, and the legumes, red and white clover, lucern and sainfoin.

Of these cocksfoot will develop tufts of stringy grass unless stocked heavily enough to leave no uneaten material. Meadow fescue is quickly suppressed by rye grass unless the same precaution is taken. Timothy flourishes in good moist land, as does Tall fescue. This last can support drought, and makes early grazing on rich land and is another grass inclined to grow in tufts. But the list is long, and sufficient has been said to indicate that a great deal is known today about the growing habits and value of the different indigenous grasses, knowledge that was by no means available to our ancestors.[4]

On the best modern grazing lands perennial rye grass with white clover forms the basis of the pasture, but as the proportion of rye grass decreases agrostis (bent grass) takes its place as the main plant on lower grade pastures. On a still lower class of grassland agrostis is the main constituent. In other places red fescue will oust agrostis and become dominant. The last is less valuable, and will not carry as many stock as the agrostis. The fescue pasture shows its greatest development on unimproved downs. This must therefore have been the grazing of the Wiltshire dairy cows centuries ago.

The composition of some modern dairy pastures show variation. Some 3,840 acres in the Faddily district of Cheshire were divided into 9% agrostis pastures without rye grass, 42% agrostis dominant with some rye grass, and 37% good rye grass with a few fields of the highest standard. An area of the same size in the Winslow, Swanbourne district of Buckingham showed 8% of rye grass rather better on the average than that of Cheshire, and only $3\frac{1}{2}$% agrostis with no rye grass; 40% had a large proportion of agrostis with some rye grass, and there was 41% of good rye grass.[5]

Though it would be impossible to question Professor Moore's dictum that grass is the cheapest food for herbivorous animals, and that by far the cheapest way of feeding it to them is to let them help themselves, animals often demonstate a craving for plants with a greater mineral content than grass. These include weeds and herbs such as ribwort plantain and knapweed, both of which have a comparatively high content of phosphoric acid, lime and potash, all much higher than wild white clover or Italian rye grass. In a grazing test made at Nottingham University in 1950 forty dairy short-horns showed a marked liking for ribwort plantain. Other plants higher in content of these minerals are the rather despised daisy, dandelion and yarrow, so that the early writers who recommended these were not so greatly in error as might be supposed.

Cows, too, need a largish measure of dry matter in their diet just as human beings require bulk as well as quality. The instinct of the animal leads it to seek hard fibrous herbage when its main diet is too succulent, and natural appetite will lead it to choose its feed—if there is a choice—so as to make the best of what is offered.

Modern knowledge forms a criterion of the value of the grazing available to our ancestors, and of the methods, such as they were, which they adopted to improve it. In the sixteenth century the grassland consisted largely of common waste and meadows, the latter often being low-lying grounds on the banks of some stream or river. The waste was never mown, though turves were cut from it for fuel, and the gorse bushes with other brushwood cropped for the same purpose. The meadows were closed to grazing at some agreed date, and the crop retained for hay. Otherwise the waste was left in its natural state except as it was affected by the grazing animal, and by the activities of the turf and furze cutters. Bedford Franklin thinks that the grazing in the Highland sheilings was improved by heavy stocking. 'Hard grazing and summer stocking produced a change of dominance from heather and blaeberry to wavy hairgrass, bent-fescue, and bird's foot tre-foil pasture which were of more value to feeding sheep or cattle'. It is unlikely that either the waste lands or the cow leazes of England were sufficiently stocked in the sixteenth century to produce a similar result.[6]

In the hilly and mountain districts there were immense tracts that had not yet been brought under cultivation. These provided grazing of a kind for the ubiquitous sheep and semi-wild cattle. A little of this land here and there was sometimes enclosed and ploughed for a few years. Often it was sown with oats for these years, and then let fall down to wild grass, a system that may be called convertible husbandry. This was done in the south-west, in Cannock Chase, and in the north-west—possibly in other places. The legal arrangements permitting it varied. The downland of Kent and Sussex, the Berkshire downs and the Cotswolds, indeed the chalk hills from Bedford to Wiltshire and Dorset, the wild moors of Somerset Devon and Cornwall were in a state of nature. Again there were areas of great feeding value like Romney Marsh.

The value of the grazing on the waste must have varied with its elevation, state of natural drainage, and climate, but it is now almost, if not quite, impossible to say what its herbage consisted of, though it is perhaps permissible to suggest that the less palatable grasses would predominate, because the animals ate them last, and thus gave them the best chance to survive.

Ernle described it in his picturesque manner.

'The common pasture was pimpled with mole heaps and anthills, and from want of drainage, pitted with wet patches where nothing grew but rushes.'

Where it was everybody's business to improve the pastures it was nobody's business, and furze and bramble flourished except so far as they were cut for fuel. Some gorse may have been cut and chopped or crushed for feed. Indeed in some parts of Wales gorse was actually grown for feed and used in the same way. No doubt there were patches of nettles, thriving colonies of thistles and docks, but there must have been the perennial indigenous grasses as well.

On the chalk land sheep's and other fescue with crested dog's tail provided dry and wholesome sheep pasture. Burnet and other nutritious grasses and herbs grew there, some of which came into great prominence at a later date. There was probably a larger number of brambles, whitethorn and scrub timber trees on the downs than there is today. On the lowland wastes there was no doubt a great deal of cocksfoot, which later was used with rye grass and clover to make grazing leys, but which is not in itself very appetising to cattle. Meadow

77

fescue flourished in the Vales of Aylesbury and Berkeley. Foxtail is very common, and probably always was. Rye grass, clover and other less valuable plants are indigenous to England and these must have flourished in favourable situations, but most of the grazing in the waste could have supplied only a poor sort of nutriment to cattle, though being better in some places than others.[7]

One of the features of the late fifteenth and sixteenth centuries was the enclosure of arable for sheep grazing. The area affected has yet to be precisely assessed, in spite of contemporary enquiries, and a recent controversy amongst historians. It must have been substantial in some places, but whether the movement really affected more than a small proportion of the total area of the country is to seek. Also whether land enclosed for this purpose ever received any treatment to make it into pasture is not clear. The probability is that any extensive area was just allowed to fall down to grass and weeds as farmers were quite accustomed to grazing their cattle and sheep on the stubble and weeds of the fallow. Smaller areas may have been given the same treatment as the meadows.

Aside from the enclosure of former arable land for sheep, which was undertaken from different motives, the desirability of enclosed pastures for cattle had for long been recognised by the astute. They could be given more attention than was possible on the waste, the weaker animals could be kept apart from the stronger if a man had several closes, labour was saved and the beasts could not wander in the corn. An optimistic estimate was that one quarter the amount of hay would maintain beasts in an enclosed pasture as well as four times the amount given in the house. If however the pasture became mossy, Fitzherbert thought it should be ploughed out and cropped for a few years; after that it might be let fall down to grass again. Treated so it yielded much better grass for ten or twelve years. Bushes must be stocked (dug) out of the pastures, and if there was an old marl pit, a new one must be dug. Marl was used for treating grassland as it had been time out of mind in Cheshire, and some other counties. Elsewhere marling may have gone out of use until revived on the advice of the Tudor textbooks.[8]

Surflet warns the lazy-minded that they who say there is no work about meadows are foolish. The good farmer must not neglect his meadow ground. He must re-sow as often as necessary, especially if it was grazed by horned beasts. In autumn or winter he must pull out bushes and thorns, and great, high-stalked herbs by the roots and gather and remove stones so that the haymaker's scythe might not be blunted or broken. The best manure he could use was fine earth mixed with dung which was better than cowhouse dung. If he collected the dust from frequented highways he could make a compost with house sweepings and filth, and all sorts of animal droppings. Fitzherbert thought molehills should be spread in April with a bush harrow; Tusser advised the farmer to do it in November. Whenever he did it, this was a good job done.[9]

In villages like Cottenham, Cambridgeshire, farmers made some attempt to keep up the quality of the herbage on the common fen; but the continued use of the pasture, when the only manure was the excreta of the grazing animal, may have been exhausting in spite of their efforts. If, however, the Tudor and early Stuart farmers' methods were along the same careful lines as the modern treatment of the grazing land in the Welland valley, any deterioration of the summer grass was minute. The nutrients supplied by the winter grass and feed were everywhere inadequate. Grazing farmers were then advised to consider this point, and, if the pasture was barren or short of nutritious plants like clover, dandelion, honeysuckle and cowslips, to obtain hayseeds and sweepings from haylofts in the fruitful countries to amend it. It is perhaps unlikely that the order-makers of an open village would take this advice, but some heed may have been given to it by the owners of several closes.[10]

Many, perhaps most, meadows, except uplands, were waterside meadows. Nature was a great fertiliser of these, and the value of the winter flooding was clearly recognised by landowners in Cheshire, Sussex and elsewhere. Fitzherbert advised that if there was any running water or land flood that could be made to flow over the meadows from the end of mowing through autumn and winter to the beginning of May it would be a good thing to do, especially if the water came from a town, and was thoroughly impregnated and polluted by urban waste products. Surflet agreed and so do other contemporaries. For this reason interference with the flooding of the river Dee was opposed in 1616. A century later the undertakers for the Itchen navigation were obliged to arrange for the watering of the meadows on the banks of that river during the winter. The Weaver navigation was opposed because the meadows would be deprived of water.[11]

Continuous mowing of the meadows, in spite of some grazing of the aftermath, made it necessary to restore the plant food removed with the crop, just as it was on the arable land. Meadows overflowed by water were sufficiently recompensed by the 'fatness' the water left behind, and rich and dry enclosed grassland may have been improved by the dunging of the animals, if it were spread and harrowed in at appropriate times, but the hay meadows could become mossy and less valuable. When the meadows deteriorated the best method to restore them was to plough out, and grow cereals, letting them down to grass again after a few years. The final crop was oats, 'a great breeder of grass', if assisted with hayseeds collected in the hayloft and cast upon the ground before the harrow.[12]

Sowing hayloft seeds was the usual way of renewing depreciated meadows. Some men were choice, and only used the finest seeds from their best hay, which included 'Clauer grasse or the grasse honysuckle'. These were mixed with fine earth and sown broadcast. Meadow clover was called in some places 'sops-in-wine' because of its colour, though Miss Rohde believed sops-in-wine to have been a carnation. Shakespeare refers to clover as a pasture grass in two plays. It was indeed said to be a herbage plant made much of in former times, and sown by itself like vetches. Snail clover (sainfoin), gallion or petty muggalt, wild fitch and haver (oat) grass were all recommended as profitable forage, but what the second was I do not know. The small wild mallow was not amiss, nor little crowfoote, a plant much liked by Fitzherbert. Plantain, wild carrot, laughing smallage, small rampions, and others, some of which would be classified as weeds now, though thought to be useful sources of minerals, were commended. Carpenter's wort balm was said to mend meadows, and raise milk in kine —as was butterwort; but all were agreed on the value of clover or trefoil. There was no better fodder, said Googe, but he was not very clear about its identity. It was that 'which people of old time called Trefoile, the Frenchmen Grand Trefle, and the Spaniards Alfalfa'. These are now recognised as distinct plants, i.e., nonsuch clover, sainfoin and lucern. This confusion makes it all the more difficult to understand exactly whether the Tudor advisers were as well informed as they so confidently assume.[13]

The herbalists were possibly more knowledgeable, though much of the writing is derivative. Gerard was aware of a meadow trefoil sown in the Low Countries, Italy and elsewhere, which both fattened cattle and increased milk yield. Indigenous clover was recorded in Belgian pastures in 1550; and it was also certainly present then in some midland pastures as some field names indicate, though this was spontaneous or perhaps due to the grazing animal. William Turner in the 16th century had sown three kinds of 'medic fother' in his botanic garden, 'the leste kinde, the grete and smoothe kinde, and the grete rough kinds'. Raven therefore concluded that he introduced lucern as a forage crop to English agriculture, but I have been unable to find any evidence of its cultivation as a field crop before the eighteenth century. In 1650 Gow recorded wild varieties of sainfoin, tares and clover, but Russell M. Garnier's conclusion that Gerard, half a century earlier (1597), knew that most of them were already used here as forage crops is a very doubtful assumption. Tares were, but not the other two.[14]

All these things were for the future, when they were collectively known as the artificial grasses. The only fodder crop of the Tudor farmer was grass, cut from the meadows and made into hay, or cereal straw or haulm of peas, beans and vetches, perhaps a trifle of the grain if it could be spared. He had no true cultivated ley, short or long. The arable enclosed for sheep pasture was not seeded down so far as can be judged, but allowed to fall down. The only grassland he looked after at all was the hay meadow, although people who had enclosed pastures may have done something to keep them in heart. Supplies of animal manure were very scarce, and all that could be collected was wanted for the arable land. Any compost that was made (Furse of Morshead, Devon had a sandhill) was added to the dung. A few farmers may have taken the advice to use ashwood ash on their meadows, but how many did so cannot be determined. Few, if any, I suggest. Perhaps some farmers cut grips or gutters to drain wet places, and followed the advice to weed, pick up stones, and spread anthills and molehills, but it is an open question whether these activities figured as much in the fields as they did in the books. It is pretty certain that the wild grass pasture of the waste was never treated in any way. There was for example, no means of controlling the grazing when the livestock wandered at will under the control of the village herdsman. Markham indeed went so far as to say that there was rarely any good pasture except the water meadows, a highly controversial statement. Unless the most careful judgment was exercised in controlling the flooding, drowning or floating, it would produce 'a coarse sowre herbage'.[15]

Hartlib, who was by no means openhanded in praise, recognised that by Commonwealth days there were 'good husbands' who cared for their meadows and pasture lands in all the accepted ways. Ash destroyed moss, and salt killed worms, something perhaps not always desirable. Stock and dairy farmers were stimulated to attend to their grassland both by their own needs, and by the growing volume of advice. Hartlib already thought that the stock of meadows was of greater value than cornland, and that England had more pasture than other countries.[16]

Grassland deserved more attention than it has ever received, but a few of the more enterprising farmers in the second half of the seventeenth century began to treat grass as a crop. The first species to be isolated and used was Rey, Ray or Rye grass (Lolium perenne), but none of the early seventeenth century writers mention it. Robert Plot makes the earliest reference to it in 1686. He had been told that it was sown in the Chiltern part of Oxfordshire, whence it had been brought nearer Oxford by Mr. Eustace, an ingenious husbandman of Islip. Naturally Eustace was thought a trifle pedantic by his neighbours, but they soon became convinced, and this grass began to take precedence of all others. Farmers realised that it would thrive on a variety of soils, though it was not in such vogue as sainfoin. It was sometimes sown by itself on heavy clay soils, and sometimes mixed with clover in 1700. Mr. Lawrence of Upcern, Dorset, grew 18 acres at about that date for seed, which he sold profitably; and the hay, after the seed was threshed out, proved more palatable to his stock than oat straw. At least one other farmer agreed with him as to its feeding value, estimating that it would keep as many cattle as hop clover. Mortimer thought it would last seven or eight years, and that it ought to be kept grazed short.[17]

Besides watering and draining, the importance of which was more and more emphasised as the seventeenth century drew to its close, it was considered advisable to burn off the coarse grass that flourished, as a result of the preference of the grazing animal, and sow hayseeds, spreading some mould out of ditches to bury it. When cold clay grass land had been allowed to deteriorate, the best method was to pare the turf and burn it. In the following spring such land should be ploughed out and resown with hay dust or corn and haydust together. Some manure ought to be spread in January or February so that the rains might wash 'to the roots of the grass the fatness of the soil before the sun drieth it away'. Wood ash, peat turf, and sand were good for 'cold, spewy, rushy and mossy land'. Pigeon and poultry dung was also recommended. Lime, chalk, marl, or any fossil soil on dry, sandy land was advantageous. The value of eating down close was recognised. Tim. Nourse told his readers in 1700 that 'the better the pasturage the better the Return', which they doubtless realised well enough. If land was overgrown with couch or fog, it ought to be eaten down by hardy, hungry cattle in winter. When the young grass began to show in spring, as he was sure it would because it had been kept warm by the couch and other growths, cattle and horses would eat it off, and would pluck up the dead and withered grass with it. Sheep could then eat it bare, and so produce a fine, sweet turf. Upland meadows too required close grazing, though these should not be mowed as it impoverished them. Moving the herd to fresh grass every two or three weeks in summer was a good way to keep them in good condition and productive—as the modern advocates of rotational grazing have been saying for the past thirty years. Much more detailed understanding of the meadow and pasture grasses was necessary, in Lisle's opinion, if the husbandman was to make the best use of them.[18] This necessity was emphasised by many writers during the eighteenth century, but there was, and could be, little change in the general treatment of grassland during that era.

Some recommended a mixture of dung and mould as the best manure, or the bottom of hay mows or hay stacks 'upon account of the mould 'tis composed of and the hay seed 'tis mingled with'. Ellis was a trifle more explicit, but his advice was always more advanced than his practice. The Hertfordshire farmers in his neighbourhood bought London soot for use on their grassland; coal soot being better than wood soot in his opinion. However if soaked in urine to a sufficient extent wood ash was good. Applied in January it killed moss, but was apt to embitter the hay the first summer. It was in the choice of grass seed, or at least the desire to select it, that most progress was made, and Ellis was a leader in the propaganda to this end. For renovating a meadow or making a pasture, the right sort of natural grasses must be chosen; for example, true honeysuckle seed (honeysuckle was a common term for all the clovers), Lady Finger seed, Tyne or wild thetch, wild cinquefoil and other best sorts. Care taken in collecting seed—I do not gather he suggested buying it—would make a meadow worth two of that sown with dock seed, plantain, penny or rattle grass and yarrow. He could not know that Robert Elliott of Clifton Park would discover in the 1890's that plantain and yarrow were useful. Ellis offered to collect clean seeds for any one who wanted them, warning his readers that rye grass, excellent for providing an early bite for milch cows, must be kept down by heavy grazing, or it would grow away, and become fit for nothing after June.[19]

The fact that rye grass was being grown for seed, and that there was a general ferment in the farming world, led Ellis to make his offer to collect clean seed. This idea was the forerunner, if not the genesis, of a plan made by the Society for the Encouragement of the Arts, founded in 1754, to do just that, and on a scale sufficient to make it possible to grow on supplies for the national market. Richard North, who liked the practice of using hayloft seeds no better than any other sensible man, repeated in 1759 the advice to obtain hay seed from some upland meadow, harvested when pretty near ripe. This would, of course, supply a mixture of indigenous grasses liable to some variation, and to include herbs and weeds, and perhaps not likely to succeed so well on lowland soils. The harvest should be spread to dry, and threshed upon cloths in a field or barn. It should also be cleaned by sifting, and put up in sacks ready for sowing. Thus saved, farmers would find these seeds of great value.[20]

It was really desirable to be rather more selective. Benjamin Stillingfleet accordingly produced his *Observations on Grasses* in the same year as North's work appeared. Stillingfleet claims to have tested several species of grasses in experimental plots on the estate of Mr. Price, Foxley, Herefordshire, and in the second edition of his work first proposed the English, or as he said, the trivial names first used for our more common grasses, probably the names adopted by rustic people. Ernle held a very high opinion of Stillingfleet. He had distinguished good and bad herbage by excellent illustrations of the kinds of grasses best calculated to produce the richest hay and finest pasture. Contemporaries were not so certain. Some of the selected grasses were reputed rare, but could be identified from specimens exhibited at the Society's offices, from his own illustrations, or from those in John Mills' *Practical Treatise on Husbandry*, 1762. These were vernal, meadow foxtail, sheeps fescue, crested dogstail and common poa, but it seems hardly likely that they were so rare as all that. Later the Society offered a gold medal for collecting and growing on 2 lb. each of meadow fescue, yellow oat grass and annual poa. There was a good deal of contemporary criticism of the scheme. The short-lived periodical *Museum Rusticum* printed a lot of it as well as descriptions and some plates of the plants because identification of the growing plants was difficult. Nevertheless the Society believed that it had encouraged the collection of clean seed of the different varieties, its cultivation and careful harvesting, and the production of commercial quantities that could be grown separately or in judicious mixtures.

The Society overestimated its work. It was a failure, or at least had not sufficient momentum to develop. The great difficulty was identification. Many very similar grasses had been given different names, and the average farmer found them indistinguishable. Even the botanists were hard put to it to sort them. William Curtis was satisfied that no pure strains of grass seed were yet on sale in 1790, and that the country's pastures were pretty much in a state of nature, except where rye grass and clover had been sown. He set out to remedy this state of affairs and produced a pamphlet illustrated with coloured plates. He recommended six of the natural grasses that constituted the best of our uncultivated pastures. To this theoretical effort he added the practical one of offering to sell 'the packet of seeds recommended in this pamphlet' for half a guinea, together with instructions how to use them. His mixture, the components of which must be carefully grown on by the purchaser, was:

1 pint each of meadow foxtail and meadow fescue
$\frac{1}{2}$ pint each of smooth and rough stalked meadow grass
$\frac{1}{4}$ pint each of sweet scented vernal and crested dogstail
$\frac{1}{2}$ pint each of Dutch clover and wild red clover or in place of the latter the broad clover of the shops.

The mixture does Curtis credit. The first two components are both valuable pasture grasses liked by cattle, meadow foxtail growing on any soil and yielding rich hay, while the fescue flourishes on drained clay land. Of the two kinds of meadow grass one prefers good dry soil, and the other strong moist soil, the latter forming a large part of the natural turf in valleys between mountains. Sweet scented vernal is very hardy, flowers early, and continues growing until the late autumn, but though it has a pleasant aroma has not perhaps equal feeding value. Crested dogstail is useful in permanent pasture, but is too dry and hard for hay as is clearly shown by the ripe stems being used in the 1880's to manufacture the then fashionable ladies Leghorn hats. As Gustavus Harrison had already said, the number of grasses suitable for the farmer's use is small. The trouble of collecting them was therefore also small. Few took the trouble. Nathaniel Kent thought the best grasses could be collected at too great an expense. Few incurred any expense!

Curtis was perhaps the first to collect turves from various Hampshire and Sussex commons, and to analyse them botanically. William Marshall, however, in his sojourns in different parts of the country made some notes of the species he saw growing in the pastures. The Rev. G. Swayne, a contemporary of Curtis, produced an even more elaborate book on grasses. In it he inserted actual specimens of each grass carefully mounted. He was intensley practical, and demanded experimental feeding tests before he would express an opinion on the value of the different species. A large quantity of separate seeds must, he said, be collected, sown and tried for some time in feeding the different classes of livestock. This would establish the feeding value of each, and then judicious mixtures could be made from the best and most productive sward, an opinion that was shared by George Sinclair.[20]

The contemporary enthusiasm for pure strains of grass seed aroused Coke's interest. He is said to have made a success of teaching his tenant's children to collect the seeds, and to have awakened their father's desire to improve their grassland, which, as Kent, another Norfolk man, had noticed, was more often neglected than arable. He did no experimental work to determine feeding values, but some trials almost on the lines desired by Swayne, had been made by Bramston of Woburn in 1770. Arthur Young recorded them but they had no result, and were not applied in practice. Bramston tried prickly edged Medica; purple fescue; barren brome grass; annual dwarf poa, a shabby, beggarly plant; great oat; bird grass; meadow fescue; crested dogstail; and some lucern.[21]

William Marshall took a different line. He examined the herbage of the grasslands he saw when gathering material for his 'Rural Economy' series, and estimated their feeding value from his own and their occupier's experience. He did not, like Curtis, actually cut turves and examine them. In the Vale of Berkeley the grass on rich soils consisted almost entirely of dogstail, ray grass and white trefoil. This herbage, he thought, might be some centuries old. It may have been too heavily dunged, but the dairy farmers skimmed off the weeds and stale grass once or twice during each summer, 'a practice which cannot be too strongly recommended'. Even if centuries old this pasture was by no means in a state of nature, and its excellent botanical composition must be attributed to human action. Both the Vale of Gloucester and the dairy district of North Wiltshire, with grassland probably just as ancient, were composed largely of the same herbage, and were treated in the same way. The only difference was found in the Wiltshire water meadows where turf drains were cut. There was little long or short ley in Gloucester there being enough grass and hay without. Permanent leys sown on old broken up pasture, cropped out, were a failure. Incidentally, he remarks that the Vale of Pickering had been successfully seeded down after enclosure. The local Gloucester farmers contended that rye grass was 'ruinous to the Vale lands', but actually it was the predominant herbage in the old grasslands.

The Devon farmers did not manage their water meadows well, but they did the aftermath of the meadows. Marshall does not record the composition. Some Midland pastures were centuries old and many were overrun with anthills like a forest and as rough, as well as other encumbrances. The out wintering of the cattle here led to the dung being dropped near the hedges. It was collected in spring and spread but Marshall thought this bad as the grassland was saturated with this kind of dung, which ought to have been saved for the arable land.[22]

Valuable as Marshall's comments are, the long lists of plants he found in the different localities are instructive only in botany. For the feeding value of the pastures all he could offer was his own estimate. The desire for experiment leading to exact knowledge was however becoming more intense. James Anderson, a voluminous writer and reader of the same period, said farmers ought to know the qualities of any kind of grass. They believed that old pasture was better than new, but he was not so sure. The opinion is still held. Meadow grass was thought the best feed for dairy cows, but little was known of the value of the different species in feeding. Rye grass was the only species sufficiently cultivated to admit of its quality being definitely known, but he declared it to be generally thought very indifferent because it became hard and unpalatable early in the season. Richard Bradley had recognised this fact half a century before. The poa grasses formed the richest pasture, but the seeds could not be separated for supply to the common farmer. The Festuca tribe, which could be, were not generally cultivated as a crop. The dairy meadows were, in fact, of accidental composition.

John Lawrence supported Anderson. The farmers were not skilled in grasses, their meadows and pastures being very much neglected, 'committed to the custody of nature and blind chance', although they were not altogether to blame. Grass seed, selected for species, was almost impossible to obtain unless harvested by the farmer himself. Seed bought of London merchants was not to be depended upon. Messrs. Gibbs of Piccadilly were exceptional. They had taken great pains to collect seed by hand, and recommended meadow foxtail, meadow fescue, crested dogstail, common meadow grass, great meadow grass, rough cocksfoot, and sweet vernal, as well as a new variety of rye grass, the same as that which had acquired such a high character in Gloucestershire.

Anderson's discontent with rye grass (it was not consistent) was shared by others, but there was no general agreement about it. Bedford Franklin suggests that it had fallen into some disrepute because of bad management and that it was too often cut for hay, and so died out. The plant, as had already been said, needs close grazing to keep it from running away, becoming tough, unpalatable and less nutritious. Well managed it made fine grazing for fat cattle. When grown with clover it was usually successful, but alone it was a doubtful speculation. Some part of this may have been the result of using impure seed sold by unscrupulous, or even unwitting, merchants.

An ingenious farmer, Peacey or Pacey, of Northleach, Gloucestershire, stepped into the breach, perhaps knowing of the Society of Arts' plan. This is mere speculation, but Peacey collected rye grass seed from the finest meadows in the Cotswold valleys, and by repeated sowings grew sufficient to supply his neighbours. His strain, which was a late flowering, a more leafy and more persistent form than others, became renowned, and was sold commercially all over the country for nearly a century. It was continually recommended by nineteenth century writers as an ingredient in seeds mixtures. Other strains were later cultivated by Russell and by Whitworth, but did not achieve the same reputation as Peacey's.[23]

Some years before this, seed Timothy Hanson is said to have taken from North Carolina to Virginia, was brought to this country. The Society of Arts distributed it for growing on. Bartholomew Rocque tried some, as did the Rev. Dr. Elliott, but James Adam did not think it had made any name for itself after twenty-five years. This, he said, must always be the fate of foreign plants when competing with the native products of the soil, where earth, air and climate are more congenial to them. It was not however a true importation any more than cocksfoot which was also re-imported at about the same time. It was *Phleum pratense,* a plant indigenous to this country and Northern Europe, which gained great popularity in the nineteenth century.[24]

In his efforts to popularise fiorin grass William Richardson did not have the same success as Peacey. He was an enthusiast but not a good scientist and published half a dozen essays in the first two decades of the nineteenth century on the subject. This grass, *Agrostis stolonifera,* was dismissed by Lowe as of no agricultural use. It spreads vigorously and produces a matted growth, but is slow to mature and difficult to harvest. It is nothing more than the famous long grass that grew at Maddingley in Wiltshire, sometimes known as Orcheston grass. This had first been remarked by Hartlib in 1650, who was followed by Worlidge, and references to it crop up in numerous later textbooks, but its feeding value is almost negligible.

The majority of ordinary farmers are not likely to have taken much notice of this sort of thing. They continued to manage their grassland as their forefathers had done for centuries, that is, if they managed it at all. Doubtless most of their attention was given to the meadow. They drained it by open or covered drains, and repaired gates and fences early in the year. They spread droppings, molehills and anthills. They picked up stones, wood and other rubbish that would have impeded the scythe. Some weeded docks and thistles, and stubbed out young thorns. Some of the more enterprising limed and manured, and some may even have scattered some renovating seeds. Some selected them judiciously; others went on using the traditional hayloft sweepings, either their own or obtained from a neighbour.[25]

Towards the end of the eighteenth century there was a new development in manuring grassland. Waste from the knife handle industry of Sheffield, scraps of horn and bone, began to be used in the neighbourhood. The practice spread rather quickly, particularly to the dairy farms of Cheshire, where bones began to take the place of the marling that had been done for centuries, as it had in Sussex and Kent. The advantages were marked. Bone manure is slow acting, but it replaces the phosphoric acid removed in the milk and the bony structure of the grazing animal. Farmers bought crushed bones, mills for crushing bones, and later sulphuric acid for making dissolved bones. The provision of bone manure became a large industry, and Liebig, in 1840, accused us of scouring the ancient battlefields of Europe in a disgusting attempt to find human bones for the purpose, or so it is said. Bone manure was still used in 1910.[26] Parkinson preferred a compost of dung, lime, whale oil waste, ground bones, decayed fish and other wastes mixed with good soil, brush harrowed in and then rolled.

Two other new fertilisers came on the market slowly, but in increasing volume from the 1820's. They were Peruvian guano and Chilean nitrate. Both were used for improving pasture later in the nineteenth century.

One oddity was introduced by Bloomfield of Warham in 1812, which enjoyed a degree of popularity for a few decades. It was known as inoculation. Turves were cut from old pastures, and placed in rows on land prepared for laying down as permanent pasture. They were rolled to press them in, and together with a scattering of clover seed broadcast by hand. It was a slow process, and could not have been very satisfactory or economic. It abstracted from good old pastures, and added only a fraction to the new, as a later writer pointed out.

George Sinclair proceeded along sounder lines. He did what the Society of Arts had attempted, and William Curtis and others had preached. He was in a favourable position to do so—gardener to the Duke of Bedford. He collected the seed of many grasses, and grew them on at Woburn in plots four feet square. He attempted to assess the feeding value of each. He pointed out that some 130 varieties of grasses were indigenous whereas farmers had supposed that the herbage of permanent pastures and meadows consisted of only eight varieties of grasses and clovers. Practice had shown that it was not possible to create permanent pasture of the best quality with rye grass and clover plus hayloft sweepings. The mixtures he recommended are consequently generous. For 'best land' eighteen varieties were to be used; for light, sandy soils, twelve. Bedford Franklin thinks that Sinclair's work had little direct effect upon farming practice, and he is probably right, but it encouraged seeds men to provide clean and reliable seed, more particularly firms like Peter Lawson and Sons of Edinburgh. Lawson's book, *Agrostographia, or a treatise on the cultivated grasses,* became a standard work much used by later writers. Amongst other grasses they offered no less than eleven types of rye grass, and they were the first importers of

Italian rye grass about 1831. The original sample is said to have been obtained by Thomson of Banchory at Munich.[27]

From the 1840's the care and cultivation of grassland received more and more attention in the textbooks, and more and more attention on some farms. Nevertheless most grassland was criticised as lying in a state of nature, and very much neglected. Many estimates were made of the value of the different varieties of the soils in which they ought to be grown, and of the purposes for which they should be used. For example, David Low, after discussing several grasses, pointed out that the best native grasses 'of permanent duration and best suited to culture' were meadow foxtail; meadow catstail, i.e., timothy; meadow fescue; rough stalked meadow grass; cocksfoot and rye grass. He recommended a slight addition of indigenous grass seed to the clover and rye grass then normally sown in the tillage course, and a rather larger quantity for a longer ley.[28] By this time the use of clover and other 'artificial' grasses had become so involved in the sowing and renovation of grassland as well as being used in the alternate or 4-course husbandry that further developments cannot be described except in conjunction with those in the following section.

Clearly the practical management of grassland, and the lines of enquiry into the sciences that underlay it, had been laid down by the middle of the nineteenth century. New means of land drainage had been devised. The mole plough had been known for more than half a century, and the invention of a process for making tubular drain pipes had simplified the construction of effective underground drains. New manures were coming on the market. New implements facilitated the mechanical treatment of the land, making it less laborious to level mole and anthills, spread the droppings and aerate the soil.

The chemistry of the living plant and of the soil became gradually more exact. The work of Lawes and Gilbert at Rothamsted, with their carefully controlled experiments, disclosed to the farmer the best use of the new manures. The botanical composition of the pastures was more precisely determined by the work of Buckland, Voelcker and Fream.

As the century advanced economic and other conditions made the cultivation and effective use of grassland more and more important. Some results were not advantageous. These were simply the neglect of the land, and its decline to poor, natural self-sown grass and weeds. Laying down land to grass became a commonplace in the last fifty years, and a vast literature describing methods, criticising them, and giving advice was produced. Rye grass was condemned by some people, notably Faunce de Laune, and defended by others, but this controversy declined as quickly as it arose. Very extravagant seeds mixtures were often used, containing as many as twenty ingredients. One enthusiast went so far as to consider the number of plants necessary fully to cover an acre with a productive sward, and to count the number of seeds of the different species that would be necessary. From this data he compiled suitable combinations of seed that would, provided they all germinated, supply the required number of plants. Such an investigation demonstrates that the importance of the cultivation and careful management of grassland had at last been fully realised, even if not everywhere practised. Modern methods are however an achievement of the twentieth century.

## (ii). The artificial grasses and other fodder crops

Few incidents in the history of farming are better known than the introduction of the one year clover ley, and the cultivation of turnips as a field crop. It was, of course, the major development between 1600 and 1750, and became known later as the Norfolk 4-course system. It may well be called the alternate husbandry. Grain crops alternate with roots or ley. It is very different from the convertible husbandry of some parts of the country where a few years of cereals were grown, and the land then let fall down to grass for several years.

During the same period other so-called artificial grasses were experimented with and became normal crops in some districts, or failed to secure general recognition and dropped out of consideration. Amongst these one of the earliest to be cultivated was sainfoin. No definite date can be given to its introduction, but it was grown in Wiltshire in 1649 on poor land, and twenty years later had, according to Worlidge, obtained the preference over clover in many parts of England because it lasted longer. Primarily grown for sheep feed, it could be grazed by cows in the third year, and would cause them to give a higher yield of milk than ordinary grass. It is not certain precisely what plant was meant by the term sainfoin or holy hay because it was also known as Medick Fodder, Spanish Trefoil, and Snail or Horned clover. 'Cinque-foil', wrote Aubrey in 1685, was 'much used' on the stone brash soils by that date, having been first introduced by Nicholas Hall of North Wraxall, a farmer who came from Somerset about 1650. Thirty acres of this crop was grown experimentally by a gentleman of Surrey in 1659, if the evidence can be trusted.[1] Sainfoin culture was taken up by the farmers of the chalk downs of Berkshire, Oxfordshire, Wiltshire and Hampshire, and also those on the same strata so far as Bedford and Essex. The plant flourishes on this type of soil, but how long it took to reach all these places, where modern farmers still appreciate it, is difficult to say. It has the disadvantage that when it begins to fail after several years, weeds begin to flourish, and the land becomes very foul if the sainfoin is not ploughed out at a well chosen date.[2] Sainfoin therefore was probably the first crop to be grown as a long ley in this country, but the early Stuart writers of farming textbooks were most enthusiastic about clover as a crop to increase the supply of forage. The later Stuart writers were more expansive, and recommended not only sainfoin, but lucern and particularly rye grass.

John Norden in James I's reign had some very sound ideas about the management of grassland. He advised farmers to look for bare patches of the meadows in spring, and to reseed them with 'some hay seede, especially the seede of the Clauer grasse, or the grasse honey-suckle, and other seedes that fall out of the finest and purest hay; and in the sowing of it mingle it with some good earth. But sow not the honey-suckle grass in too moist a grounde for it liketh it not, therefore you must drain the place before you sow it'.

This was only advice. Norden nowhere mentions a farmer who was doing it. As much or as little can be said about Barnaby Googe, whose opinion in 1577 was that 'the best herbe for pasture or meadow is the trefoil or clover'. In spite of his continental travels Googe had not learned to distinguish between Nonsuch clover, sainfoin and lucern, though his suggestion for the use of the plant was in accordance with the continental system of a clover ley—that is, mow the first year, feed off with sheep the second, and graze with cattle the third.[4]

Many Englishmen serving with Elizabeth's armies, as well as business men, botanists and scholars must have seen the Flemish method of growing clover and using it for cattle fodder before Sir Richard Weston recorded it in 1644. In 1597 Gerard had praised the crop as useful in fattening beasts and increasing the flow of milk, and Dodoens had recorded it in 1550, but there is no native description of the process. Weston's is the earliest known description of clover cultivation in Belgium.[5]

The rotation which Weston saw in Flanders and preached in England was flax, turnips, oats, with clover seed bush harrowed in and grazed from after oat harvest till Christmas, mowed three times the following year, and then left down as a long ley for four or five years until exhausted. He tried out this system on his own land at Worplesdon, Surrey, and the crops were cultivated at his instance in St. Leonards' Forest. Other people were soon interested, but there is some suspicion that the idea was not even then altogether new in England.[6] There had been a great influx of refugees to Kent, Essex and East Anglia during the late sixteenth century, and it has been said that the Dutch introduced the growing of root crops to Norwich in 1575. This 'became general in the early part of the seventeenth century together with the knowledge of various manures, the cultivation of artificial grasses, and methods of treating the soil. This was not a little furthered by English agricultural writers, who insisted upon following the example of Flanders and imitating the methods employed there'.[7]

The first recorded importation of clover seed from Holland to Norfolk was in 1620, and by the 1650's it could readily be bought in London, where it was on sale 'at the shop of James Long at the Barge in Billingsgate'. Another seed merchant was Thomas Browne at the Red Lyon, Soper Lane. By 1653 the trade was well established. Walter Blith in the third edition of his *English Improver Improv'd* wrote in that year,

'There are so many sorts of Claver as would fill a volume, I shall only speak of the Great Claver or Trefoyl we fetch from Flanders, called by Clusius, *Trefolium majus tertium,* which bears the great red Honysuckle, whose leaf and branches far exceeds our naturall Meadow Claver'.

In the last year of the seventeenth century no less than 346 cwt. of clover seed was brought in from Holland and Flanders. By this time, too, a return trade had developed, because 9 cwt. of clover seed were exported to Holland though it is not clear from what port it was sent.[8]

Weston's experiments with turnips were either very quickly imitated, or were not the first in Surrey. Some farmers must have been growing the root on a field scale by 1650. A tithing table of the impropriate parsonage or rectory of Godalming of that date mentions a tithe of roots, and this, except for the unlikely possibility that they were a garden crop, must mean that they were grown in the field there. Sir Richard Weston's house, Sutton Place, is not ten miles distant, but these farmers, if they learned from him, did so surprisingly quickly. The fact may even confirm Garnier's belief in Gerard.

One of the greatest difficulties that confronted a farmer who wanted to grow a clover ley was the poor quality of the 'Dutch' seed. Every body thought it essential to use imported seed, not only in the mid-seventeenth century, but for long thereafter. Unfortunately there was no guarantee with the seed. Blith used some and it failed to germinate. In his opinion this was either because the Dutch did not want us to learn the proper use of the crop and so overdried the seed and destroyed its life, or because the London shopkeepers had been obliged to carry over stock from one year to the next. In order not to lose money they mixed the old seed with the new, and so made the lot virtually valueless. Blith advised sending an experienced man to the Low Countries to examine stocks of seed there, and buy a good sample. When a first crop had been raised from imported seed, then, he maintained, its seed was the best for future use, 'if you can ripen it kindly, get it dry and preserve it'. The method of getting it out of the husk was so far a mystery to the English farmer. The best he could do was to thresh it out of the straw, and polt or faulter it, that is, beat it out again in the husk, and remove as much of the refuse as possible by separating it with a narrow toothed rake. It was then dried in hot sun, and the seed rubbed out.

Hartlib subscribed to this method, which was practised by a great husbandman of clover in Kent. A Mr. Stoughton, who lived in Norfolk, had for many years since used the husbandry of clover. He had either designed or owned a kind of mill to shell the husk from the seed. This very greatly economised the work of preparing it.

When clover was grown it was usually under a nurse crop of barley or oats. The seed was bush-harrowed in. It was necessary to sow when there was little or no wind because the seed was hand broadcast. Clover could also be sown, or so we are informed, on any land intended for grazing, on any bare places in a meadow, or on highways trodden or 'pocked' (poached). The last refers, I imagine, to green verges as the highways were normally unmetalled dirt tracks. But the recommended way was under a nurse crop, at the end of March or beginning of April. All agreed that clover would fatten cattle quickly and increase milk yield, Blith estimating that it might keep two cows to an acre—a conservative figure for his times.[9]

Despite all the difficulties, Andrew Yarranton of Ashley, Worcestershire, declared that soon after Weston's book[10] was published there was some clover grown in most counties in England, and the established trade in imported seed, referred to by Blith, confirms this. Yarranton himself brought clover seed to Ross in Hereford, and popularised growing it in Worcestershire and the adjoining counties between 1653 and 1677. Sir John Winford had no less than sixty acres under the crop, a result of Yarranton's propaganda, and Mr. Thomas Hill, a grazier, who frequented the fairs of Worcester, Stafford and Shropshire, also cultivated it. Yarranton does not supply the names of other farmers then growing clover, but admits that some were not successful with it. This is not surprising with a novel crop, and in addition a modern authority believes that the early leys based on broad red clover are liable to rapid deterioration. The farmers used them in a wholly haphazard way, and the ley was not in any sense a pivotal crop in the rotation.

'Townshend', he says, 'introduced the 4-course system in 1730, but it was long after that date before either the long term or short duration ley came to be regarded as the foundation of any well recognised farming system'.

Meantime Yarranton agreed with the common practice of sowing clover under a nurse crop of barley. The first crop, he suggested, might be grazed when the barley was off, but cattle should only be allowed in the clover for a short time every day to avoid blowing them. The second crop might be mowed in June and again in August, a heavy yield coming from each cutting. This was similar to Low Country practice. In his opinion 6 acres of clover were equal to 30 acres of natural grass—perhaps not an over optimistic claim when we consider the amount of wild grass in his day. He recommended the use of lime to stimulate the growth of clover in meadows, a correct treatment, and his method of making clover hay was, in fact, used for many years.

On the other side of the country Nicholas Toke, a landowner in Kent, bought clover seed in 1653, and from that year his accounts show that clover was a usual crop on his land. On

other land near Ashford both red and white clover were cultivated at about the same time. Critenden of Tonbridge had
four acres of clover before 1653, and threshing clover was already practised then. In 1678 Toke paid the cost of pulling
two acres of turnips. Kent had always been a county of highly
diversified farming, and must have been in constant touch
with the continent. Perhaps that was why farmers there were
not opposed to new ideas, and were quick to adopt the cultivation of new crops. It is difficult to believe that such men
were the only ones in their respective counties who had been
intelligent enough to learn by precept.

This evidence rather confirms the views expressed by
William Stevenson and William Marshall at the end of the
eighteenth century. The former suggested that turnip cultivation originated in Surrey, and that 'Turnip' Townshend
did no more than give it useful publicity: the latter that
clover had been grown at an earlier date in Kent than in
Norfolk. Mr. Kerridge has however now discovered evidence
that turnips were cultivated in Suffolk between 1646 and
1656. They were sowed on one ploughing in mid-August after
corn harvest, and well mucked and hoed at regular intervals.
Some were drawn in autumn and stored in sheds for immediate use, the remainder being left in the ground to be lifted
as required.[11] Colonel Walpole, father of the renowned Sir
Robert, grew both turnips and clover at Houghton in the
1670's, and bought seed for a good many other people too.[12]
W. Upton of Northampton sowed some clover of his own
growing with his hayseeds about 1655. He believed his own
as good as Dutch seed.

At Beenham, Berkshire, a tithing table of 1670 included in
its list of crops to be paid for, beans, peas, hemp, flax, vetches,
hops, clover, potatoes and parsnips: tithes of turnips if they
were not drawn but were fed to 'unprofitable' cattle, became
an agistment tithe calculated on the improved value of the
cattle.

Besides raising clover and turnips as new crops for feeding
livestock it must, of course, be kept in mind that the farmers
had always grown peas and beans at least partly for the same

purpose, vetches and tares wholly for it. Both men and beasts could eat peas and beans and animals vetches and tares. Dr. Hoskins has shown how important peas were amongst the crops of the sixteenth century Leicestershire farmer. The importance of cattle in the Sussex weald in Elizabethan days is indicated by the comparatively large area devoted to peas and oats, while vetches and tares here were sown both as fodder crops, and to recruit the land after cereal crops. Robert Loder of Harwell, Berkshire, grew 'fitches' on the hitch (uncultivated strips of open field land lying amongst the corn crops). The cultivation of these crops was indeed an integral part of contemporary farming.[13]

The second half of the seventeenth century was, it seems, the time when rye grass began to be mixed with clover seed for short leys. John Franklin of Cosgrove, Northamptonshire, who used this mixture on his enclosed farm about 1670, was but one example of what other farmers may have been doing. About the end of the seventeenth century Edward Lisle, who lived at Crux Easton in Hampshire, near where the three counties of Berkshire, Hampshire and Wiltshire abut on one another, noted that clover and rye grass had been grown on the downs in the neighbourhood for at least fifty years. He himself preferred rye grass alone to a mixture with clover. His tenants in the Isle of Wight had the same preference. Clover, vetches and rye grass were, he noted grown there about 1700. Lisle often mentions a farmer who was doing something special. For example, Farmer Iles of Holt got a good crop of red clover on a cold springy clay soil in 1716: Farmer Lavington grew it equally well on black, sandy, mellow land. Lisle was at a loss to account for the success or failure of this crop. Sainfoin was also extensively grown in this area and about this date Jethro Tull had his famous dispute with his labourers when he tried to make them drill sainfoin seed with his newly invented drill machine.

Another of Lisle's friends, Webb of Mountain Farley, got seeds of wild white clover from Sussex, and found that 'it holds the ground and decays not'. A systematic practice had been worked out in Sussex, and the old wheat and bean course abandoned in favour of a rotation of two corn crops, followed by clover and rye grass for a 3-year ley. The seeds were sown under either barley or oats, but occasionally under wheat. English seed was considered best, and a mixture of 10-12 lb. clover and 8 lb. rye grass was sown. This type of soil would not bear a natural grass after being cropped unless it was let lie for a great many years, but the sown seeds did well. The first crop of clover hay was cut in May, and the plant was then left until after it had seeded, when cattle were turned in to graze. The feeding value of an acre of this aftermath was reckoned equal to five-sixths of an acre of natural grass. The clover land was heavily marled or limed, and this treatment had been used on the grassland of Sussex and of Kent for at least a century before 1707; the use of rye grass and clover together may not have been so old. 'Marling' on the heavy clay of the Weald may often have meant treatment with a local subsoil containing a large proportion of calcium carbonate. The term 'marling' was very loosely used, covering a number of systems of mixing subsoil with the surface soil. In the Isle of Wight it meant chalking, and may sometimes have been applied to the same process in the Weald. Lisle thought that 'marls' were not fertilisers in the ordinary sense, but that they helped to cure acidity and to provide a good mechanical condition of the soil; a piece of excellent observation.

John Mortimer, who had an estate in the county, noted that some Essex farmers sowed a pound or two of clover seed per acre as a catch crop, and fed it off in the spring before they fallowed their land. He did not say how long established or widespread the practice was. Clover was certainly grown at Cambridge at an early date. Farmers at Maddingley sowed small quantities of seed before 1662. In some places it was mowed twice in the year; in others the crop 'saved the common field till midsummer', i.e., was used for grazing until the weeds and rough grass of the fallows provided a full bite, or what passed for it.[14]

Oxfordshire farmers, too, improved heavy clay in 1676 by sowing it with peas and vetches, and laying it down to rye grass usually accompanied by Nonsuch or Melilot Trefoil.

They were criticised because they cropped their land repeatedly until it was fit only for rye grass and trefoil. Dorset had always been famous for its sheep, and before the end of the seventeenth century the new grasses were being sown, stimulated as the farmers must have been by the need for winter keep. One of them, Mr. Ryalls, told Lisle that the aftermath of rye grass made excellent manure, and his manner suggests that the crop was common. According to Lennard, too, clover seed was being sold as far west as Exeter soon after the Restoration, and was sown for ley under oats when land went back to grass after several years of cropping.[15]

There were plenty of farmers in seventeenth century England who were willing to grow a new crop. Besides sainfoin, rye grass, clover and turnips, some followed the example of the drainers who came with Vermuijden to the Fenlands. So early as 1639 riots in Lincolnshire caused damage to the 'great crops of rape, coleseed, corn and other grain' already flourishing on the reclaimed land. Many Walloons and French speaking Hollanders from Picardy and North Flanders settled in Thorney after its drainage by Francis, Duke of Bedford in Charles I's reign. They were expert in the cultivation of colza from which they extracted oil.

This new crop (if it were new) immediately found its way into the textbooks. Both Blith and Hartlib came down heavily in favour of it. The first discussed it both generally and particularly. Cole was most useful on marsh and fen lands newly recovered from the sea, or any lands flat and rank. It should be sowed about Midsummer, after the surface had been pared and burned, thoroughly ploughed and ridged up. This advice was based on practical work that had already been done. Vermuijden reported in 1652 that 40,000 acres of the South Level had been planted with cole, seed wheat and other grain. In the Bedford Level 'a small quantity of about 28,000 acres' had been cultivated.[16] Hartlib optimistically estimated that 380,000 acres of the great fen of Lincoln, Cambridge and Huntingdon had been reclaimed by 1655. Land formerly worth scarcely 12d. an acre acquired a high value and a friend offered a mark an acre for 900 acres on which to sow rape.

By the end of the seventeenth century a large area of rape was cultivated. In 1657 this crop was sown between Ely and Southery; by 1696 there were great areas between Spalding and Crowland. It was grown in Kent almost as early as in the Fens, and may have been grown in Essex in the first decade of the century. By 1716 home-grown seed was reputed nearly as good as that imported from Holland, but was not perhaps so plentiful. As the crop became more familiar, its use as green fodder, and the residue of the oil process as dry feed was recognised. In Holland rape was used for feeding oxen in winter, and English farmers followed this example by using it in January, February and March 'when other food is wanting'.[17]

It is clear that many farmers had adopted the new forage grasses and crops by the end of the seventeenth century. Indeed one writer then was fearful that the new grasses and grass and legume mixtures were gaining ground so rapidly, especially in Hereford, Worcester, and some neighbouring places, that he suggested that these ought to be prohibited by Parliament. Otherwise, he argued, the rent of natural meadows would be unfairly depressed. It had already fallen by at least 15%[18] The argument may have been economically correct, but it was politically quite impossible.

The innovators may have been owner-occupiers or gentleman farmers, but it is difficult to believe Tull's complaint that farmers advised to buy clover would reply that it was a gentleman's fancy, and would not pay rent. A good many farmers not far from Prosperous Farm were already growing it, and had long done so. Nor is is easy to accept Richard Bradley's complaint that it was a long time before clover emerged 'from the fields of gentlemen to common use'. It may indeed, as Ernle says, not have penetrated into Suffolk villages as a crop until the eighteenth century, but the Elizabethan herbalist, Turner, records that he saw *Melilot arvensis* in Suffolk meadows. This may have been indigenous, but the Suffolk farmers had been quick to cultivate the turnip as a useful fodder crop.[19]

Soon the rate of progress became more rapid, possibly owing

to propaganda by the renowned 'Turnip' Townshend, and the example of his advanced farming in Norfolk. Early in the eighteenth century squires in the remote north were buying seeds and experimenting with them. Blundell bought 230 lb. of grass seed from London, sowed them on his own land in Lancashire, and sold some to his tenants in 1712. He even tried maize as a crop, not very successfully. Cotesworth of Durham did the same in 1718, but then, as later, some farmers were conservative and objected, both in Yorkshire and Northumberland.[20]

All the textbooks continued the praise of these crops. The anonymous author of *Tusser redivivus,* 1710, speculated whether they were known to Thomas Tusser, and suggested that his poem indicates that there was some sort of artificial fodder in his day, probably 'ray' grass. Switzer praised French grass—he meant either sainfoin or lucern—for increasing herbage on gravelly soils, and repeated the old slogan that one acre of clover would feed as many cows as six acres of common grass. He advised sowing under a nurse crop, and said that this was usual in many parts of England.[21] Ellis thought Lady finger grass, the Nonsuch clover, was very effective, especially if mixed with red clover. He declared that there was no reason at all 'to be searching after foreign spurrey seed' something advocated by Hartlib and his successors in the seventeenth century. It is one thing in which Ellis is right. He remarked that in the late seventeenth century farmers in the Vale of Aylesbury had tried to prevent the introduction of clover in the Chiltern country, but a law case they brought, failed.[22]

William Ellis's offer to collect clean grass seed was, as mentioned above, the precursor of the Society of Arts scheme to do just that. A Somersetshire farmer, Jonathan James of Chilcompton, near Wells, had already shown what could be done in that direction. He told Richard North that his father noticed that Perennial Red Clover grew wild on his farm, in particular where the land had been marled. He let some of it stand for seed, and grew it on, gradually increasing his own acreage, and supplying his neighbours and others with seed.

He called the plant Marl Grass. By 1759 this crop was widely grown in Somerset, Gloucester and the adjoining counties. The seed had been sold in Bristol and other west country market towns, and for a few years past in London at a high price as Perennial Red flowering Clover. North suggested various seed mixtures for short leys. One that was very usual was 10 lb. broad clover and 10 lb. rye grass. Others were 5-6 lb. clover with 3 pecks black grass, meaning hayloft seeds; 8 lb. nonsuch trefoil and 8 lb. clover for pasture or hay; (2-3 pecks) sainfoin with 6 lb. nonsuch for a first crop of hay. So recently as 1901 'brown hayseed', principally loft sweepings, was on sale in Ireland as was ' white hay seed' which was chiefly *Holcus lanatus* (Yorkshire Fog).

About this time Bartholomew Rocque persuaded the Society of Arts to add burnet to the list of plants for which it offered premiums. Several people took it up, some cultivating as much as 30 or 40 acres, but after the first enthusiasm had passed, opinion of its value was very divided. This plant has never been extensively grown by itself though it has certain merits.

The Rev. Walter Harte published his *Essays on Husbandry* in 1764, discussing at length the methods of growing lucern. It was grown in a few places but never became a popular crop like sainfoin. Tull thought this lack of success was due to improper cultivation. Many experiments were made with it all over the country, but in the eastern counties Mr. Ramsey found in 1771 the soil near Yarmouth produced a much greater weight of clover. He had tried it both broadcast and transplanted from his garden.[23] In other parts the experiments were sometimes most successful, but never sufficiently to establish the crop. A measure of its popularity is that 21 cwt. of seed was imported in the year ending Christmas, 1740, and 19½ cwt. in that ending Christmas, 1780. It has never been grown on a really large scale in this country. In the year ended Christmas, 1780, nearly 9,000 cwt. of clover seed came in and nearly 44,000 cwt. during 1800, enough to plant nearly 500,000 acres if used at 10 lb. an acre. If it was all used for short leys there were at that date no less than 2,000,000 acres cultivated on the 4-course system, but some may have been used for renovating meadows, and laying down land to permanent pasture. In addition there were supplies of home-grown seed, but of these and any possible exports there is no measure. The growth of wild white clover was promoted by liming as had been experienced on the barren commons near Buxton, Derbyshire. Richard Parkinson indeed believed that the earth had been impregnated with its seed from the Creation as any kind of land when manured would produce it.

In the 1770's cabbages began to be written about as winter fodder for milch cows and other cattle. John Wynne Baker, who carried out a longish series of experiments (we should call them demonstrations) with various crops in Ireland, claimed to have introduced this crop to the field. Arthur Young criticised him somewhat cursorily for neglecting the turnip and clover husbandry, and at the same time John Randall, author of the *Semi-Virgilian Husbandry*, 1764, had recommended the large Scotch cabbage for the purpose. The matter is further complicated because Baker in the introduction to an abridged edition of Young's *Tours* refers to 'the cabbage culture of Yorkshire', and Randall certainly lived in that county. The probability is that using cabbage for the purpose was not new when these men wrote about it. The crop may have been a novelty to them, but it was not to Young, and twenty years later James Adam was able to say that 'the kinds of cabbage formerly most cultivated in the field for cattle were the large colewort or borecale, and perennial colewort'. These kinds were given up by 1787. A farmer, Ilbert of Devon, had grown one acre of the green Scotch cabbage, and obtained a yield of 35 tons. The plant had been unknown in South Devon five years before, but was then adopted by the best farmers. Tugwell was growing them in Gloucestershire, and the turnip cabbage was being widely discussed.[24]

In 1787 Dr. John Coakley Lettsom introduced the mangold, or 'root of scarcity' as he preferred to call it. Nobody remembers, and nobody has ever called him 'Mangold' Lettsom, but he had a clear right to the title. Seed was brought from France by Sir Richard Jebb, and presented to the Society of Arts for distribution to members. Lettsom was given some. He imported a large quantity after a trial, but it was not at first accepted, partly because the seedsmen objected to him cutting across their market, and partly for more obscure reasons. After some vicissitudes it came gradually into favour during the 1820's, and was widely grown during the nineteenth century. The swede was also introduced towards the end of the eighteenth century and quickly became popular in Cheshire, gaining resounding plaudits from Cobbett in his *Rural Rides* and elsewhere. Like the mangold it became an integral part of nineteenth century mixed farming.

It was fortunate that the brassica, cabbages, rape or cole, were more widely grown. Clover sickness had already made its appearance in some places where the 4-course system had been too strictly adhered to. It was not understood, and the only remedy then suggested was leaving longer intervals between taking the crop. Instead of using it once in a 4-course rotation, farmers whose land was affected grew clover only once in eight or twelve years, other crops such as beans and peas being sown in its place. Clover sickness developed in Norfolk, Suffolk, and other places, but was so trying on the newly reclaimed lands of the Yorkshire Wolds, that a Committee of the Yorkshire Agricultural Society investigated it. The Rev. W. Thorp followed up their enquiry by what is probably the earliest attempt to discover the scientific reason for the failure.[25]

In spite of all these novelties and of the great volume of propaganda that had appeared during the previous two centuries report after report that was made to the Board of Agriculture between 1793 and 1815 complained that the grassland of the county dealt with was only the result of natural selection. Even in Cheshire the species of grass met with were generally such as nature offers, or arose from seed sown without any regard for selection. Rye grass was grown and some short leys on the tillage. Vetches and tares provided spring feed. The old grazing pastures of Durham were mainly composed of cocksfoot, ryegrass, dogstail, foxtail, hard fescue, poa, yellow oat, brome, wooly holcus, ribwort, plantain, red and white clover, yarrow and bush vetch. This was probably much the sort of composition of this kind of grazing two or three centuries before. Burnet flourished in great abundance in moist loams. Timothy was found and other species. Norfolk meadows were overrun with rubbish, bushes, briars, rushes, water, anthills, altogether in a state of nature. Ray grass, known as bents, was used as an auxiliary to small seeds in Bedfordshire. Buckingham meadows were infested by anthills, some a yard long, two feet in breadth and a foot high. Pacey's rye grass was cultivated in Berkshire. Mr Tull of West Ilsley found it fourteen to twenty-one days earlier than the other sorts. The natural grass of the Vale of White Horse was well managed and manured, but there were many anthills. Chalk was used as a top dressing near the Downs, but Mavor did not agree with the tendency to plough out the Downs, take a few years crops, and then reseed with a rye grass mixture. It was rarely possible to restore them to their former state of excellence. Sainfoin was a popular crop in the county; spurrey was indigenous. The grazing land of Sussex was neglected, overrun with rubbish, and wet through lack of draining. The usual kinds of meadow grass were found. Yet clover, trefoil and ray grass were in the highest request as well as other artificial grasses. 'No branch of the art of agriculture', wrote the Rev. Arthur Young, 'is less understood than a right knowledge of our grasses, and the soil congenial to each'. The natural grasses of Cambridge were vernal, foxtail, creeping bent grass, broom grass, dogstail, *Nardus stricta, Festuca,* and *Holcus.* Examples could be multiplied but would add little. It is of interest that Northampton farmers who experimented with timothy declared it to be too coarse to be worth cultivating.[26]

On heavy soils where the alternate husbandry was followed common clover was sometimes sown alone at 10-15 lb. an acre under spring wheat or barley, but a mixture was better. One recommended in 1802 was 12 lb. common clover, 4 lb.

white clover, 2 lb. rib grass and 1 bushel ray grass. This was an expansion of the clover-rye grass mixture that had been used so long, and gave longer life to the grazing. Rib grass was very well liked, especially in Yorkshire, and Haller, the botanist, had said that it was very good for dairy cows in the Alps. The mangold was gradually becoming popular as dairy cow feed too. In Northumberland where a 3-year or longer ley was not unusual, the mixture used was slightly different. It was 8 lb. red and 4 lb. white clover, $\frac{1}{2}$ bushel ray grass, sometimes with 3 or 4 lb. rib grass and hop medic. Soft brome grass had formerly been sown, but had been found to be inferior to ray grass. Much the same mixture was used in the West Riding. In Cumberland, Philip Howard of Corby had been the first to sow a field with clover in 1752. Ray grass there had few advocates.[27]

High prices for cereals during the French Wars had caused a great deal of old grassland to be ploughed out and cropped. Much of this grass needed ploughing, but it would probably not have been touched—it could not have been profitably— except under the stimulus of quite exceptional prices. When these prices fell after Waterloo, no profit could be gained by continuing to cultivate this land, and much of it was allowed to go back to grass without any attempt to seed it down. There is no real measure of this nor is there any criterion of the distress in agriculture that lasted till 1836 or later. It is probable that some land that had been tillage for many years before the wars also went out of cultivation. On the other hand there were broad acres under the most careful management when Cobbett made his *Rural Rides,* for example, in Lincolnshire and Northumberland. In counties such as these the short ley and the root crop played a major part, but were on the whole mainly devoted to feeding store cattle and arable sheep. These spirited farmers were able to face the depression better than some in the less advanced counties, but in the circumstances it is not surprising that some of the best and most productive pastures were being neglected more than usual. Sir George Head found Holderness overrun with coarse 'tore' grass, in many places blotchy and covered with thistles. Formerly a large quantity of lime had been used here as manure, and kept the grassland in heart. The dairy districts did not perhaps suffer so much from the depression, which persisted with brief periods of recovery until the 1850's, as the arable stock farms: but they were not unaffected.[28]

Many farmers adopted economies in management that brought no advantage, but decreased output, and sank them deeper into the mire. Others tried to overcome the difficulties in various ways. Amongst these was careful consideration of the feeding value of different crops including the grasses. Sinclair repeated his recommendation of seeds mixtures containing so many as eighteen items for heavy soil, and twelve items for light sandy soil in Baxters' *Library of Agricultural Knowledge* 1836. The underlying idea was, of course, to secure continuous growth throughout the season. Turnips, cabbages, kohl rabi, and other forage crops ought also to be grown where they could. Another contributor estimated that a cow required 100 lb. green food every twenty four hours. Consequently it was most profitable to grow plants yielding the greatest quantity of green food for summer, and roots for winter feeding.

David Low, John Donaldson and G. H. Andrews all discussed forage crops at length. The first suggested a mixture for one year ley of 17 lb. rye grass, 3 lb meadow catstail, 8 lb. red and 2 lb. white clover; and for long ley 3¾ lb. meadow foxtail, ½ lb. catstail, 5 lb. rough cocksfoot, 2 lb. meadow fescue, ⅜ lb. rough stalked meadow grass, 12 lb. rye grass, 2 lb. red or hybrid clover, 6 lb. white clover, 2 lb. bush vetch, or other legume, making a total of 34 lb. seed per acre. He had a high opinion of cocksfoot, but it was more nourishing in spring than in autumn, and ought always to be sown in mixtures. Like Donaldson he thought well of vetches or tares for clay land.

A much simpler mixture was used by a practical farmer in Yorkshire, James Lamplough. In 1840 he used trefoil 1 stone, white clover 7 lb., rib grass 4 lb., parsley 3 lb. Despite the arguments in favour of complex mixtures, which continued to be used for many years, the old one of clover and rye grass occupied a prominent place, and was esteemed as nutritive and wholesome herbage. All these mixtures were ordinarily sown after being mixed together, but Alexander Taylor regarded this as bad practice. He thought it better to sow each sort separately at the expense of going over the ground several times. This would secure more even distribution of the various species. His plan was not adopted. Yet another mixture was suggested by Henry Evershed in 1856. It was 8-10 lb. cow grass, 2 lb. alsike, 2 lb. trefoil, 1 lb. rib grass, 2 lb. Pacey's rye grass and 1 gallon timothy. This was commonly used in Warwickshire.[29]

Many of the seeds mixtures used or advised during the first half of the nineteenth century are similar to, but often more complex than those used today. The 4-course system with its one year ley, and one year root break was firmly established by the accession of Queen Victoria. It was the basis of the high farming that flourished between say, 1850 and 1875, and continued to be practised until the outbreak of the first World War. It was not strictly followed by every arable farmer. The ley was often left down for two years or longer, and catch crops introduced. The sequence of crops too varied in different parts of the country, but it was the foundation of all the courses of arable husbandry. John Donaldson in 1842 like Walter Blith in 1653, and some writers between them, was an apostle of taking the plough round the farm, but few farmers did this in the mid-nineteenth century. The same sort of seeds mixtures were recommended for laying down land permanently or for long periods. A great deal of grassland then as now, and for long before would have been all the better for being ploughed, cropped and reseeded, but the proverbial wisdom of the day was antagonistic. It was generally held that it was impossible to restore a valuable old pasture—there was particular virtue in aged pasture—once it had been ploughed. Yet Donaldson was able to say that many inferior lands and even good soils are now (1842) producing a crop of weeds regularly pastured and made into hay without any assistance whatever from cultivation, something that had often been said before. Twamley had blamed farmers for failing to remove noxious weeds, a list of which he provided in 1784, and Benjamin Axford considered henbane, hemlock, aconite, and several species of dropwort to be poisonous. The cows would not eat them and other noxious plants if there was plenty of pasture, but all too often there was not. Lovage, agrimony, carraway and cummin should be planted in their place, besides the usual clovers. Real experiments on the management of grassland were lacking, and it was still left to its natural development. The eradication of such obvious nuisances as weeds, thistles, nettles, rushes, hassocks and moss was all too often neglected, and the use of the newly available artificials, guano, nitrate of soda, uncommon.

Bones were in fairly general use. Gypsum, too, had its advocates as it had since the beginning of the century. C. W. Johnson found that four plants, lucern, sainfoin, red clover and turnips contained it as a constituent and argued that it was a good fertiliser. It was well known to the sainfoin growers of Berkshire and Hampshire, and was used as a top dressing by the lucern growers of Essex and Middlesex: but many soils under grass had, he thought, enough sulphate of lime already. Peat ashes used near the Kennet in Berkshire, and coal ashes on clover, sainfoin and lucern were in his opinion beneficial, because they contained gypsum, but this material was later superseded by superphosphate of lime, the Lawes and Gilbert product.[30]

The method of analysing plants to discover their chemical composition and so to determine the kind of nutrition they required, as Johnson discovered the value of gypsum, was the normal method employed throughout the nineteenth century. It was some sort of answer to Horsfall's complaint (he was a prominent Yorkshire dairy farmer) that in 1865 the chemical investigation of our natural and other grasses had hitherto scarcely had the attention it deserved.[31]

The grasslands of Devon were no more carefully managed than those of other counties, but the leases of land in the South Hams had the peculiar feature of constraining the farmers to apply all or most of their farmyard manure to the grass. It was common to apply twenty to thirty two-horse loads of dung per acre. Some grassland in other counties did get an occasional application of dung, but it is fairly certain that most of it was applied to the arable where, of course, the ley and the root break benefited. Great play, too, was made from about 1850 to 1890 with the value of town sewage for producing large crops of rye grass. It had been used for a long time on the Craigentinny meadows outside Edinburgh. A good many experimental plants were set up, usually by the expanding towns that had to find a sanitary method of disposing of their waste. This process however failed to develop into a major branch of farming, and new methods of sewage disposal absorbed the material.[32]

Outwintering cows on the pastures had long been known to spoil them, yet in the 1840's it was still usual in counties so far apart as Lancashire and Cornwall. In the former Lawrence Rawstone could not find a really good grass field in the whole county, to be compared with those to be seen between Leicester and Harborough. By allowing the stock to graze the whole winter the gateways were mired, and land poached, water laid in the footprints, rushes grew, and the pasture steadily deteriorated. The cows were miserable, wet and up to their knees in mire. In Cornwall the grass was often stocked and grazed all the autumn and winter, often right up to the end of April when shut up for mowing. 'The value of the keep at this time cannot be equal to one-hundredth part of the injury occasioned', said Henry Badcock. These meadows were stocked all too often till the end of May thus causing a scarcity of hay; late cutting meant that it was too fibrous, and the value of the aftermath was decreased.[33] Nothing too bad could be said of this practice, which can hardly have been confined to these two counties.

In Buckingham the pastures were not spoiled in this way. There cows were fed on hay, about two tons through the winter, and one oilcake a day, getting a few swedes, mangolds, turnips, or cabbages if and when hay became scarce. Staffordshire cows were tied up from November to May. Cabbages were grown in Sussex for the cows' winter green food in the

1860's.[34] These crops fed in the house saved the grass from winter damage.

The stubborn idea that old pasture was the best did not prevent some farmers laying land down to grass, but the process did not reach its greatest development until after the disasters of the 1870's. It had however become sufficiently marked by 1875 for the Royal Agricultural Society to institute an enquiry in that year. The report shows that some land in almost every county had been laid down. Martin Sutton set out the best methods in 1861. If the land was not clean a crop of turnips or other roots should be grown, manured in the ordinary way. If fed off no other manure was required; otherwise a top dressing of 2 cwt. of guano or nitrate of soda should be applied. The grass seed should be sown on a still, dry spring day, bush harrowed in and rolled. On wet land the seeding should be deferred until August or September without a cover crop, but there was no objection to sowing under wheat in February in clean land. His seeds mixture included twenty-one varieties in small quantities of each, and he strongly opposed the prevalent practice of sowing hayloft seeds as so many had done before him. They were mostly composed of Holcus and Broom, the only grasses ripe when the hay was cut. When the new grass was about three inches high it ought to be rolled again, and any spots where the plant had missed resown. The new grass ought not to be grazed until autumn, but two cuts could be made in the first season, the first as early as possible. This checked the stronger grasses, encouraged tillering, and formed a close sward. A heavy harrow should be run over in the following spring to open the soil, and a top dressing applied. Draining of wet places was something that could not be avoided or neglected. The Royal Agricultural Society report disclosed that most farmers relied upon the usual seedmen's mixtures according to the soil, and that heavier seeding than formerly was general. At Woburn Abbey a mixture of 2 pecks perennial rye grass, 2 lb. cocksfoot, 2 lb. timothy, 7 lb. white and 2 lb. red clover was used. The three important factors were draining, the mechanical preparation of the soil, and manure applied to the seed bed.[35]

Experiments carried out by Lawes and Gilbert demonstrated that upon the whole dung was better than artificials to restore the constituents removed in the hay crop, but was comparatively slow in action. The herbage developed by it was more complex and superior in quality to that produced by the more active artificial fertilisers. In their experiments 14 tons of dung were put on each acre, but it was found that growth was often increased by the direct application of phosphatic manures such as guano or superphosphate of lime. The different manures had however very different effects. Minerals alone diminished grasses and weeds and increased the proportion of legumes, red clover and meadow vetchling. Ammonia salts increased the amount of grasses per acre, produced leafy stem and seeds, and reduced legumes and seeds.

James Buckman thought that clover sickness might be due to getting clover seed from warmer climates and perhaps richer soil, but principally to sowing it under barley and forcing it for the first year into a weak and spindling plant. The mischief was augmented in the second year by the growth of weeds. Clover seed had often been received by the farmer in a shamefully dirty condition, but cleaner supplies were delivered in 1866. A couple of years later he discussed peas and beans, vetches, sainfoin, then grown extensively on the Cotswolds, lupins, melilot, lucern, meadow vetchling and furze as fodder crops. About this time Voelcker was experimenting on clover seeds.[36]

These experiments and the volume of advice that was constantly being repeated had little general effect. H. S. Thompson, who had travelled all over the country to see grass, and thought money spent on grass better invested than expenditure on arable land, found efforts to improve grassland in 1872 'very desultory and entirely without system'. Weedy poor grass on a farm 'excited no criticism'. The best management was to cut thistles while young, and to scythe out coarse grass, or tether an old horse to eat it off. Deterioration could be arrested by feeding concentrates to grazing animals, a practice that was increasing. Artificial fertilisers were good, but an occasional dressing of compost or farmyard manure must be given. He had used 1 cwt. nitrate of soda, 2 cwt. mixed super and 3 cwt. kainit for pasture. On mowing land $\frac{1}{2}$ cwt. nitrate of soda was good. Judicious manuring was now generally regarded as necessary. Bones and dung were perhaps best; guano was very stimulating, and should be used sparingly mixed with bone dust. Gypsum, lime, salt, soot and compost were all well spoken of. Macdonald complained that the farmers had an idea that grassland possessed a mysterious quality of perpetual fertility, and advised moving the grazing animals from one spot to another so that their dung should not kill the better grass and introduce coarse and unpalatable plants, a note continuously struck throughout the literature.[37]

There was still no trustworthy evidence whether old pasture was better than new in 1888. It was no less than sacrilege to think of ploughing it up, cropping and laying down with new grasses. Proper management was rarely thought of. Old pasture had some merits. It often contained condimental or medicinal herbs not to be found in new, and these herbs had some influence on the health of animals but just what was not known. The whole subject required careful investigation. The Wensleydale meadows were of this kind being full of herbs, so that the hay was very rich and the dairy cows there lived on nothing else. Fream however who examined many turves taken from old pastures came to the conclusion, as William Marshall had so long before, that rye grass (*Lolium perenne*) and clover (*Trefolium repens*) were found in old pastures all over the country. Lawes' visit to Leicester proved that it was these plants that gave Leicester its great reputation. Besides these Agrostis, Yorkshire fog (*Holcus lanatus*), Meadow foxtail (*Alopecurus pratensis*), and Cocksfoot (*Dactylis glomerata*) were found as minor contributors in that order. This confirms the guess made above at the botanical composition of the old common grazing of Tudor days, and more, suggests that the old pastures had much the same composition as the sown ley, but possessed some herbs in addition to the ordinary grasses and legumes. William Carruthers brought up another point, that it was the soil on which the grass grew rather than the mixture of plants that provided better or poorer nutrition. Robert Bruce suggested that cattle grew larger feeding on limestone pastures than on gravel soils. Carruthers added that the inferior grasses predominated in several famous pastures where the useless plants flourished because the cattle did not like them.[39]

After 1880 the making of grassland, or its casual occurrence because the land was no longer tilled, increased very rapidly for reasons that are all too well known. The disasters of 1879 and the years before really disorganised English farming. Farmers, faced with ruin from the loss of crops and stock, did not know which way to turn. It is easy to condemn them for making false economies, neglecting drainage, hedging and gates, and leaving land unploughed because the return was less than the cost. But men who have no money in their pockets, and nothing but overdrafts in their banks, are in no position to make capital outlay when they cannot meet current expenses. The beginning of the flood of overseas corn made conditions no better. Prices remained consistently low, especially corn. Meat and dairy produce prices were slightly better, and the growth of the dairy industry, for the produce of which there was an increasing demand, was stimulated.

Then conditions not only encouraged a turnover to grass, but required that change. In the decade ending 1887 about 1·5 million acres were allowed to fall or were laid down. Answers to a questionnaire sent out by James Caird showed that a very great variety of seeds mixtures were used, and this is not surprising because the writers of the numerous articles on the subject, and the seedsmen who supplied ready made mixtures, all had their own ideas of what it was proper to sow.

The management of grassland as practised by our earlier dairy farmers, when they managed it at all, could not be injected with much novelty by the nineteenth century man. The extirpation of weeds like thistles and docks, drainage to lay the land dry, the suppression of acquatic plants and encouragement of more nutritive ones, had all been done sporadically for centuries. Sometimes the meadows had been dunged or composted, and bush harrowed to spread the manure properly. Now it was suggested that the heavy harrow or scarifier should be used in the spring to tear out the foggage (tufts of old grass) which should be burnt and the ash spread. Bones were the most valuable manure, but grass always benefited by superphosphate of lime. Lawes and Gilbert advised a mixture of the new fertilisers: 3 parts guano, 1 of nitrate of soda, 1 of sulphate of ammonia, applied at $2$-$2\frac{1}{2}$ cwt. per acre per annum. Ten to twelve tons of good rotten dung should be spread every four or five years in addition to the artificials. Some advised not to graze the hay meadow after Christmas, and to graze the aftermath down close; but others considered April early enough to stop grazing. Great judgment must be exercised in stocking the pastures as harm could be done by putting in too many beasts, and too few would let the grass run away to fibre and seed. Stones ought to be picked up to spare the scythe, or the cutter of the new mowing machines that were being sparingly used in the 1890's.[40]

Maize, which had been tried unsuccessfully by Blundell about 1700, was one of the new fodder crops that enthusiasts advised dairy farmers to grow. James Long said that South of Trent it would grow almost as readily as cereals. It can be grown, but it has not become popular any more than lucern, and some of the so-called artificial grasses. Long's suggestion of sorghum, a giant forage plant, was not adopted, but other plants had been, and the dairy farmer of 1900 was in a very favourable position to support his cows compared with his Tudor ancestors. The alternate husbandry had provided him with the short ley, and the root crops, turnips, mangold and swede. The cabbage, kohl-rabi and rape formed other supplies of home-grown feed. The new fertilisers had enabled him to grow better crops on his arable, and to improve his grass if he wished to do so. The ample supplies of clean seed of indigenous and imported grasses enabled him to cultivate short ley, long ley and permanent pasture alike. Supplies of oil cake, blood meal and other prepared feeds supplemented home grown feeds. Progress had been remarkable, most

I

marked, of course, in the nineteenth century, though there was still much to be learned about the management of grassland and herbage crops and still more to be practised.

### (iii). Haymaking and forage conservation

Some villages in Tudor England must have taken a little care of their common meadows as the order-makers of Cottenham did, but there was little encouragement for the individual farmer to do so. In many places the strips of meadow, their boundaries possibly indicated by mear stones, were annually balloted for, and likely to be in different ownership each hay season. It was only when closed from grazing, so that the grass could grow enough to be harvested as hay, that the individual knew what part of the meadow he would be entitled to mow. Examples are numerous. The method of allotting the pieces varied, and were often complex as at Brotherton Ings, Yorkshire, though in other places the system was simpler. Lot meadows as they were called, were frequent in Gloucestershire at the end of the eighteenth century. The system continued in Somerset until the nineteenth century, and was even practised at Yarnton, Oxfordshire quite recently.[1]

These meadows were open to grazing until rather late in the season. Some were closed as early as February, but more often the early bite was so valuable that the village cattle were allowed to roam over them until April or May. Undoubtedly the hay crop suffered where this was done. In these circumstances there was small encouragement for the farmer to spend time following the good advice to treat the meadows by spreading ant and molehills, weeding and draining and picking up stones and rubbish, and it is rather unlikely that anything of the sort was done by communal effort or under the compulsion of the manor court. Whether they were cultivated by any of these methods or not, the meadows were duly closed to grazing at the traditional date, either early or late in the season, according to local practice. The fortunate owners of several closes, the lord of a manor or the more successful tenant, could close up their meadow land according to their own judgment.

The meadow grass was ready for cutting in June, or, if delayed by late grazing or any other cause, must be cut early in July, because it would be a great nuisance to have both hay and corn harvest in hand at the same time. Tudor ideas about winning the hay in proper condition were much like our own, though some differed. Few modern farmers would bother about the phase of the moon, but Surflet was emphatic that grass should only be cut in the new of the moon, never in its decrease. Both he, and Fitzherbert a century before him, agreed that mowing should begin while the grass was somewhat green and not thoroughly ripe. It would then be all the softer and sweeter as feed, would fatten better and would increase, or keep up, the milk yield. Naturally hay cut rather under-ripe would need more careful making, but the later grass was dry and hard, 'and the worse for all manner of catel'. In dry weather it would 'dry and burn' on the ground, and the seeds most likely shed or lost. If the first cut was made fairly early, the second crop or aftermath had a better chance, but great judgment was necessary because grass carted too green would putrify in the mow or barn. The hay must be dried on the ground for two or three days and a heavy crop ought to be shaken out by hand, or with a short 'pyk forke'. Good tedding was the secret of making good hay. At night it was cocked and each morning spread again till 'widdred all a like', when it was ready for carting.

The yield of hay from what were almost natural or wild grass meadows should have been less than the modern harvest. 'Land meadows produced not more than one good wain load, but low meadows usually two, or more occasionally'. Assuming that the load was the same as the modern one, and that is quite an assumption, the hay harvest was not so much lower than ours, ranging from a ton an acre upwards. This is all

the more surprising when placed in opposition to the generally accepted belief in the shortage of winter fodder before
the artificial grasses and root crops were cultivated, but the
explanation must be that each man only occupied a trivial
area of meadow.

The Tudor farmer had to plan the work. Labour was
limited and all hands were recruited, men, women and
children, the village tradesmen, and those from the neighbouring market towns, but it was the part of wisdom only to
cut as much each day as the number of hands could deal with.
In Tusser's words:

> If weather be forward, be mowing of some
> But mow as the makers may well overcome.

The mowers needed watching too. The farmer must see
that the hinder end of the scythe was well down so that it did
not indent the grass. The mower must cut clean through to
the previous cut, and not leave a mane between. The aftermath must be cut without fail by the end of September,
though this did not make such wholesome feed as the first cut.
The value of a good crop of hay to the farmer can hardly be
overestimated. Every bale of hay, and indeed of straw, was of
vital importance. In bad years it sold for very high prices. For
example in the spring of 1643 it fetched £8 14s. a ton in the
south west 'nearly the value of three fat bullocks'. This sale
of hay was a comparatively new thing and had been almost
unknown in earlier times.[2]

According to an old couplet from Oxfordshire:

> Hay is for horses, straw is for cows,
> Milk is for little pigs, and wash is for sows.

This may have been true in the county of origin, but hay was
certainly used to feed in-calf cows elsewhere, and some of it
was most probably used for the same purpose there. (see
supra pp. 57, 63).

Hay making was fun as well as work, and it was a time for
rejoicing almost as great as the corn harvest. It took second
place to harvest, but came before it in time, and must be
cleared up before the cereal crops were ripe. Matthew Stevenson became almost lyrical about it in 1661. In May the scythe

and the sickle, the mower's furniture, must be made ready. The following month the haymakers were mustered to make an army for the field where, not always in order, they marched under the bag and bottle. Great force of arms was then seen betwixt the fork and rake. The work often ran on into July when the courteous countryman made hay while the sun shone.[3]

Blagrave in 1675 repeated Fitzherbert's advice of 1525 demonstrating that the system had not changed in two centuries. It was probably very much older. If the crop was heavy it should be tedded with the hands so that it all withered alike, and when one side was cured it must be turned before noon as soon as the dew was gone. This was done again the following day, and at night the hay was windrowed. When evening approached the next day, after the windrows had laid open all day, the crop was put into small cocks to stand one night or more to sweat, after which it was loaded, carried and stacked as soon as the farmer judged it dry.[4]

More detailed descriptions of methods of making hay in different parts of the country appeared in the eighteenth century, but the general principles remained the same. The time occupied varied with the weather and the practice of the locality, or with the condition and composition of the crop. Careful judgment was necessary to decide when to cut. Some cut it when in full bloom, others, especially on light land, before it began to wither, but it must not be housed or ricked too green or it would be liable to mow burn, or even to fire, as every modern farmer knows. If made up wet with rain it turned to filthy, stinking mould. Some degree of mow burn might however be useful, particularly in coarse hay; it made it tender and succulent or sweetened it. Good hay was made of mere sedge near North Bank, between Wisbech and Peterborough. Hay made of sedge and rush would cause cattle to eat and drink plentifully. The Vale of Aylesbury farmers even tried to make their hay a little dampish so that it would mow burn slightly. The Norfolk method was slightly different from the general. The mown grass was left in the swath for three days or more and then turned. Afterwards it was thrown up into windrows, and thence cocked while hot in the sun, and loaded off as soon as possible. Norfolk men, like those of Aylesbury, thought it none the worse for a trifle of mow burn. Everybody agreed that it was a sensible way of increasing the crop to cut the grass on the headlands and all grass patches in the arable fields.[5]

Early in the seventeenth century Sir Hugh Plat had suggested a type of open sided Dutch barn with an adjustable roof that could be raised or lowered on its supports to house crops. This would permit varying quantities to be stored. Whether his advice was followed by anyone at that time is not known, but Ellis reported that one man had put up a Dutch barn in 1738. He does not say where, nor does he describe this building.

The yield of hay had not materially increased since Tudor times. The Vale of Gloucester meadows were held in common, and individual plots marked by boundary stones. The hay was private property, but the after grass was common, either stinted or not. Here the natural grasses were ray grass, clover and some crested dogstail, and the yield was about one and a half tons an acre, occasionally two tons. This was not very different from Suffolk, where the yield ranged from one to two tons an acre. The method of making in Gloucester was much like that of Yorkshire. The grass lay in swathe the day it was cut, being 'broken' tedded and cocked the next day, a process that was continued for some days, after which it was first made into small stacks, and finally into one large stack. Suffolk men were inclined to let the grass lay too long after the scythe. They paid too little attention to the grass cocks, and made their stacks too loose. They mowed too much for sale to towns.[6]

There were slight variants in every district, but the main principles were the same, as indeed they must be unless the grass is cut green for drying or ensilage in the modern manner. The artificial grasses, mainly clover and rye grass, had necessarily to be treated differently. The usual yield was from one and a half to two tons an acre, but if properly made, the feeding value was greater than ordinary meadow hay. This crop was generally withered gradually in the swath. If it was tedded or spread like meadow grass the leaves and blossom would all be left in the field, and the stalks dried to a stick. The usual way was to let it lie for a day or two, turn it and leave it for another day or more as necessary, pitch it into cocks for another couple of days, and carry it home. Mr. Eccleston, a farmer in Lancashire, took measures to prevent his stacks firing. He made a chimney in the stack by placing a basket in the middle. As the stack was built the basket was drawn upwards by a rope thus making a ventilating shaft in the centre. This practice was also common in Middlesex, but Thomas Davis of Wiltshire did not think this was necessary if the hay was properly prepared before carrying. 'Rather let an ox-feeder in Wiltshire be consulted in the art of haymaking than a farmer in Lancashire', he said. John Lawrence thought an improved system of haymaking had long been a desideratum.[7]

There was certainly a good deal of disagreement about the best stage at which to cut the grass, whether natural or cultivated. James Anderson did not like the usual methods of making hay from the artificial grasses. He thought that letting it lie for some days in the swathe, and spreading and tedding in the sun tended to bleach it. He never cut his until it was quite dry, and then made the gatherers follow close upon the cutters, making it into as small cocks, about three feet high, as would stand. A few handfuls of hay were laid on the top of the cock as a slight kind of thatching. When once in that state he felt that the hay was in a great measure out of danger, but it is possible that leaving it so late before cutting may have caused some leaf to fall off and be lost. These cocks could be left for two or three weeks until ready to be put up into larger cocks. It was not uncommon for the grass to be cut too early, not only before it was in blossom, but even before it was in ear as in North Wiltshire where the dairymen kept up the milk of the cows that calved early by feeding this young hay, and also fattened their calves on it. Wiltshire graziers and dairymen obtained an early aftermath and this compensated for any loss in quantity of the hay crop.[8]

The Midland farmers spread the swathe immediately after cutting, and left it until dry no matter how long. The Somerset men processed it for three days if the crop was not more than 30 cwt. an acre. The method of the North Riding farmers, where hay was the grand object, had two very general faults. The grass was left too long unturned after the scythe, and the pikes (cocks) left too long in the field. Ordinary methods were usual in Cheshire. The Lincolnshire farmers let their meadow hay lie for some days in the swathe as others did cultivated grasses. Like the Middlesex men they tried to make it green. Parkinson had found that fine green hay made a difference of about 3 pints of milk a day as compared to feeding brown hay. In the Tees valley, where they got the normal yield ranging between one and two tons an acre, they stacked the hay in the middle of the field, and foddered the cattle all over the field all through the winter. Dorset hay was not made in any regular way, and a great deal of the work was done by women. One farmer, Groves of Battiscombe, built his stacks over a triangle of timber in order to make a flue for ventilation, and to prevent firing—like Ecclestons' basket, but the triangle was left in the bottom of the stack.[9] All these and other local methods would no doubt have been strongly confirmed by the farmers who used them, not only because they were more or less traditional in the neighbourhood, but because long experience had shown the best way to do the job. Some would have been justified in their particular system by considerations of elevation and climate.

The desire to improve haymaking aroused some criticism of the tools used, and inspired some inventiveness. Marshall considered haymaking ill done in the West of England, partly through the fault of the tools in use there. The scythe was too short, and 'laid in too near the handle', so that work went on slowly. If done quickly the heel could not be kept down, and a line of uncut herbage was left between each stroke, something Fitzherbert had complained of three centuries before. The 'prong' was ridiculously small, 'fitter in the hands of a cook than a haymaker', and the loading forks were no longer than a man-of-war's beef fork.[10] With such tools the work must have been more laborious than necessary, but no doubt the workers were skilled in the use of tools they had been familiar with since childhood.

In the more hilly parts of the west the hay crop was carried home in crooks on a pack saddle, just as it had been in the late seventeenth century when Celia Fiennes passed that way, but elsewhere upland hay was dragged down on sleds as in Wales and Yorkshire. The hay sled was used somewhat like the modern hay sweep. It was dragged along a swathe by two horses, one at each side, until filled and then hauled to the stack. The horses were then turned round, and the sled drawn out back from under the load. It took much less time than a cart. Such sleds were used until quite recently in Westmorland, and it has just come to light that something of the sort has only recently gone out of use in East Anglia. A horse-drawn hay-sweep was designed by Mr. Middleton, presumably the writer of the report on Middlesex, for use on flatter lands. It was drawn like the sled by two or four horses from the outside edges of the device, and the hay swathe swept upon the prongs and held in place by the fencing at the sides and back. A few horse-drawn rakes for windrowing were in use at the turn of the eighteenth century, but this implement was not extensively used until much later, and Robert Salmon of Woburn designed a haymaking machine or tedder at about the same date, which was speedily adopted by the Middlesex hay farmers, being in general use near London by 1831.[12]

It was in the direction of mechanisation that development was possible in the nineteenth century. Methods of handling and curing necessarily remained much as they had always been, but the work gradually became less laborious as new machines were designed and came into use.

The textbooks advised that hay should be cut in bloom, and before the seed had formed. No doubt the generality of farmers agreed, and did as their experience and this advice directed. Water meadow hay, which was often large and coarse, had to be cut while still young, or its value decreased. Cultivated grasses required more careful handling than natural meadows, though some of the latter must have had a somewhat similar botanical composition, but with more varieties.

The length of time occupied in curing varied in different places, and according to the weather, as it had always done. Some thought the swathe should not be touched on the day it was cut, but should be left to soak in its own sap, and that it should be left in the cock for the same purpose. Others thought that cutting should be done before 9 a.m., and the hay tedded the same day, windrowed and cocked the second, and the same the third. The mechanical haymaker, or tedding machine, originally invented by Salmon, was widely used towards 1850 as was the horse drag rake. The first of these did work formerly done by women, and one machine was estimated to be equal to 20 manual workers. Mowing machines were included in the Royal Agricultural Society's trials in 1857, and one machine was used in 1859 near Kenilworth. This machine must have been making parallel progress with the reaper,[13] and, of course, did much more work than the acre or so a man could mow in a day with a scythe. But only on level ground, i.e., not ridged up, could it be used conveniently and it was not generally used until much later. Cutting with the scythe lasted until the end of the nineteenth century in some places. Straw elevators had been designed for use with the threshing drum in the 1860's, and were adapted to the hay harvest, but these were another development that had to wait until after the first world war for acceptance. A straw trusser was presented to the public in 1881, and could have been used for hay, but was not until comparatively recent times, although it was included by John Walker in a list of mechanical necessities required for haymaking in 1888. The other machines Walker recommended were a 2-horse mower, tedding machine, and horse rake. Upton specified the following implements for a 50 acre dairy farm: mowing machine with reaping gear for two horses, a 1-horse haymaker, horse rake, horse drill, 2-horse roller, two sets harrows, plough, liquid manure cart, turnip cutter, chaff cutter, and other barn machinery.[14]

Another nineteenth century development was an attempt

to introduce making silage in place of hay. The use of silos for storing cereals is very ancient. It was known in classical times, and probably earlier, and the primitive North American Indians were using the system for storing maize when the Pilgrims landed. It seems to have been only in the nineteenth century that it was adapted to the preservation of forage crops. It was first practised on the Continent, and Professor J. F. W. Johnston described the process in the Transactions of the Highland and Agricultural Society for 1843. This was making pit silage in a pit lined with boards or brick. As always the grass, clover or vetches were put in as cut. It was sprinkled with salt at 1 lb. to 5 cwt. Sometimes it was watered. The whole was then trodden down by a gang of men, and rammed tight with wooden rammers. When the pit was full it was covered with boards or a well fitting lid on which about eighteen inches of earth was laid to exclude the air. In a while the contents sank lower, and more was added till a compact mass was secured. The process was also described in Stephen's *Book of the Farm,* 1844, and in later editions, but nobody here was sufficiently impressed to try it until 1875. In that year Earl Cathcart made some silage on his estate at Thirsk. Others then took it up, and by 1884 there were known to be forty farmers practising it. Silos of various kinds were used, wholly below ground level, partly below and partly above, and so on. The silage made was usually successful, and the cattle ate it with appetite. The wet seasons too encouraged its spread, and in 1888 many farmers made silage instead of hay, because they could not have cured hay. Some of these made stack silage.

A number of patents was taken out in connection with the process, mainly concerned with methods of compressing the material in the pit and the stack, but it did not at that time become a usual process.[15] It was indeed not unusual at the turn of the century and later to see substantial silos, erected at some expense during the period of enthusiasm, standing disused. The process was greatly stimulated in World War II, and it is only since that it has become popular.

NOTES TO CHAPTER II (i)

1 H. Ian Moore. *Gold in our grass*. Agriculture. LXII (Jan. 1956). p. 457. A. G. Thomason. *The Small dairy farm*. 1955. p. 86.
2 H. I. Moore. *The science and practice of grassland farming*. 1949. p. 2. Gordon Manley. *Climate and the British scene*. 1953. pp. 278, 280.
3 S. F. Armstrong. *British grasses and their employment in agriculture*. 1937. pp. 162–164.
4 Myrddin Williams. *Milk and money from grass*. 1952. pp. 40–44. A. G. Thomason. *op. cit.* p. 88.
5 R. G. Stapledon. *The land, today and tomorrow*. 1942. p. 78. *idem.* & W. Davies. *A grassland survey of Kent*. Kent Farmers' Jour. vol. 54. no. 4. cited in G. H. Garrad. *A survey of the agriculture of Kent*. 1954. p. 85.
6 Moore. *op. cit.* note 1. p. 459. T. Bedford Franklin. *British grasslands*. 1953. p. 33.
7 E. J. Lowe. *A natural history of British grasses*. 1862.
8 Fitzherbert *Husbandry*. ed. of 1767. p. 70. *Surveyinge*. pp. 80, 81. H. J. Hewitt. *Medieval Cheshire* 1929. pp. 21–24. A. L. Rowse. *England of Elizabeth*. 1950. p. 81.
9 Surflet, *Countrey Ferme*. 1600. p. 634. Fitzherbert. *Surveying*. 1523. pp. 7, 8, 81. Tusser. *Five hundred points*. 1577. (ed. Mayor, 1812) p. 44.
10 J. Llefelys Davies. *Grass farming in the Welland Valley*. 1926; but see P. F. Astell. *Grazing in the Midlands*. Imperial Bureau of Plant Genetics. *Herbage Plants*. 1933. Bull. No. 10. Gervase Markham. *The English husbandman*. 1613. p. 83. W. Folkingham. *Feudigraphia*. 1610. p. 25.
11 T. S. Willan. *River navigation in England, 1600–1750*. 1936. pp. 9, 19, 45. Lord Leconfield. *Petworth manor in the 17th century*. 1953. L. Dudley Stamp. *Men and the land*. 1955. Fitzherbert. *Surveying*. p. 75. Surflet. *op. cit.* p. 637. See E. Kerridge. *The sheepfold in Wiltshire and the floating of water meadows*. Econ. Hist. Rev. 2nd ser. VI. 1954.
12 Barnaby Googe. *Foure Bookes of Husbandry, 1577*.
13 Surflet. *op. cit.* p. 634 ff. John Norden. *Surveyor's dialogue*. 3rd ed. 1618. p. 208. Googe. *Whole art of husbandry*. 1614. p. 42. Ernle. *English farming*. 1961. p. 99. E. S. Rohde. *Story of the garden*. 1933. pp. 86, 93, 94, 133. Idem. *Shakespeare's wild flowers*. 1935. p. 11.
14 C. E. Raven. *English naturalists from Neckham to Ray*. 1947. pp. 58, 133. Paul Lindemans. *Geschiedenis van de landbouw in België*. 1952. ii. p. 155. Russell M. Garnier. *Introduction of fodder crops into Great Britain*. Jour. R.A.S.E. 1896. Franklin. *op. cit.* p. 86.
15 *Inrichment of the Weald of Kent*. p. 5. Giles Jacob. *Country gentlemen's vade mecum*. 1717. p. 4.
16 *Legacy*. 1655. p. 39. Mildred Campbell. *English Yeoman*. 1942. p. 204.
17 A. B. Beddowes. *The rye grasses in British agriculture*. Welsh Plant Breeding Station. Bull. H.17. 1953. p. 10, and the authorities therein cited. Nigel Harvey. *Farming kingdom*. 1955. p. 28. William Davies. *The grass crop*. 1952. p. 76.
18 J. Worlidge. *Systema agriculturae*. 2nd ed. 1675. pp. 15–24. John Smith, Gent., *England's improvement reviv'd*. 1670. pp. 12–14. Joseph Blagrave. *New additions to the art of husbandry*. 1675. pp. 3–6. Richard Blome. *Gentleman's recreation*. 1686. pp. 209, 210. Giles Jacob. *op. cit.* pp. 3, 4, 8.

Tim Nourse. *Campania felix.* 1700. p. 47 ff. Anon. *Dictionarium rusticum.* 1717.

[19] William Ellis. *Modern husbandman.* 1750. I Jan. pp. 82–84. Feb. pp. 113, 114. June. p. 86.

[20] Richard North. *Account of the different kinds of grasses propagated in England.* 1759. Country gentleman. *Complete grazier.* 1767. p. 120. See my Benjamin Stillingfleet. Notes & Queries. 29 May, 1948. William Curtis. *Practical observations on British grasses.* 1790. Rev. G. Swayne. *Gramina pascua.* 1790. Gustavus Harrison. *Agriculture delineated.* 1775. p. 377. Kent. *Hints to gentlemen of landed property.* 1776. p. 35. Nigel Harvey. *William Curtis & the British grasses.* Agriculture. Jan. 1951. also my *Pure strains of grass seed.* ibid. Feb. 1951. cf. J. L. Knapp. *Gramina Britannica, or representations of British grasses.* 1804. *passim.*

[21] Young. Northern tour. 1771. I. pp. 32–36.

[22] Marshall. *Gloucester.* 1796. I. pp. 154–160. *West of England.* 1796. I. pp. 207, 211. II. p. 146. *Midlands.* 1790. I. pp. 268, 269.

[23] James Anderson. *Essays relating to agriculture.* 1773. (4th ed. 1797.) p. 172 ff. idem. *Recreations in agriculture.* 1800. III. p. 175. John Lawrence *New farmer's calendar.* 4th ed. 1802. pp. 432, 435–439. T. Bedford Franklin. *op. cit.* p. 94. Thomas Rudge. *General view of . . . Gloucester.* 1807. p. 179. J. Billingsley. *Gen. view Somerset.* 179. p. 119. for a full discussion see A. R. Beddows. *op. cit.* pp. 18, 19, 32 fn. 28.

[24] Society of gentlemen. *Complete farmer.* 1766. art. *Timothy grass.* James Adam. *Practical essays on agriculture.* 1787. II. p. 451.

[25] Lawrence. *op. cit.* p. 3 Jan. & p. 15 March. Robert Forsyth. *Principles and practice of agriculture.* 1804. II. p. 58. Young. *New farmers calendar.* new ed. 1804. April. p. 221. Sept. p. 464. R. W. Dickson. *Practical agriculture.* 1804. II. p. 817 ff.; he discusses the grasses at length. References could be multiplied, but this is a sufficient specimen.

[26] F. L. Olmstead. *Walks and talks of an American farmer in England.* 1852. p. 173. John Coleman. *Farm prize competition, 1884.* J.R.A.S.E. 1884. p. 519. A. D. Hall. *Pilgrimage of English farming.* 1913. p. 223.

[27] Francis Blaikie. *The conversion of arable land into pasture.* 1833. George Sinclair. *Hortus gramineus Woburniensis.* 1816. Franklin. *op. cit.* p. 96. Beddows. *op. cit.* pp. 22, 23.

[28] David Low. *Elements of practical agriculture.* 4th ed. 1843. p. 522 ff.

## NOTES TO CHAPTER II (ii)

[1] Worlidge. *Systema agriculturae.* 1669. p. 28. *Dictionarium rusticum.* art. Sainfoin. John Aubrey. *Memoires of naturall remarques in the county of Wilts.* ed. by John Britton 1847. A. Speed *Adam out of Eden.* 1659. p. 108. cf. J. R. Thompson. *History of sainfoin.* Jour. Min. Agric. XLV (1938). pp. 331–337.

[2] Martin J. Sutton. *Permanent and temporary pastures.* 5th ed. 1895. p. 86.

[3] John Norden. *Surveyor's dialogue.* 3rd ed. 1618. p. 208.

[4] Ernle. *English farming.* 1961. pp. 99, 100. Barnaby Googe. *Foure bookes of husbandry.* (translation of Conradus Heresbachius). 1577.

[5] Paul Lindemans. *Geschiedenis van de landbouw in België.* 1952. I. p. 430.

See also his edition of Sir Richard Weston. *Verhandeling over de landbouw in Vlanderen en Brabant, 1644–1645.* 1950.

6 Robert Brown. *Treatise on rural affairs.* 1811. II. p. 155.

7 J. F. Benese. *Anglo-Dutch relations from the earliest times to the death of William III.* 1925. pp. 125, 126.

8 Naomi Riches. *Agricultural revolution in Norfolk.* 1937. pp. 88, 89. Samuel Copland. *Agric. ancient & modern.* 1866. I. p. 502. The import figures were obtained from the Port Books with the help of the Milk Marketing Board.

9 Blith. pp. 178–186. Speed. *op. cit.* Chap. V.

10 Westons' book was not only plagiarised by Hartlib, but was several times reprinted without acknowledgment, e.g., by Gabriel Reeve. *Directions left by a gentleman to his sons for the improvement of heathy and barren land . . .* 1670. (Roger North) Person of honour in the county of Norfolk. *The gentleman farmer . . .* 1726.

11 Samuel Hartlib *his legacy.* 1655. pp. 239, 240, 247. Andrew Yarranton. *The improvement improved by a second edition of the great improvement of lands by clover.* 1663. Francis Forbes. *Modern improvements in agriculture.* 1784. William Davies. *The grass crop.* 1952. p. 76. *Account book of a Kentish estate.* ed. by Eleanor C. Lodge. 1927. Stevenson. *Gen. view of Surrey.* 1809. p. 242. Marshall. *Southern counties.* 1798. I. p. 145. R. Lennard. *English agriculture under Charles II.* Econ. Hist. Rev. IV. (1932). p. 23 ff. E. Kerridge. *Turnip husbandry in High Suffolk.* Econ. Hist. Rev. 2nd ser. VIII (1956). p. 392.

12 J. H. Plumb. *Studies in social history.* 1955. pp. 184, 185.

13 Mary Sharp. *Beenham, Berks.* Berks., Bucks., & Oxon. Arch. Jour. XXII. 1916. W. G. Hoskins. *Leicestershire farmer in the 16th century.* Trans. Leics. Arch. Soc. 1941–42. Julian Cornwall *Farming in Sussex 1560–1640.* Sussex Arch. Collec. 92. (1954) pp. 57, 72.

14 Franklin. *op. cit.* p. 90. Edward Lisle. *Observations in husbandry.* 1757. (these relate to dates from 1690 to 1715) pp. 240–262. John Mortimer. *Whole art of husbandry.* 4th ed. 1716 (1707). I. pp. 32–36. Gervase Markham. *Inrichment of the Weald of Kent.* 1625. George Atwel. *Faithful surveyor.* 1662. p. 101.

15 Robert Plot. *Natural history of Oxfordshire.* 1676. cf. Nigel Harvey *Farming kingdom.* 1955. p. 28.

16 H. C. Darby. *Drainage of the Fens.* 1940. pp. 54, 62, 77, 84.

17 See my *History of cole (Brassica sp.)* Nature. 9, July, 1955.

18 Tim Nourse. *Campania felix.* 1700.

19 Ernle. *op. cit.* but see E. H. Carrier. *Pastoral heritage of Britain.* 1936. p. 84. L. Dudley Stamp. *Man and the land.* 1955. p. 79 both of whom subscribe to the infrequency of these crops at this time. L. W. Moffitt. *England on the eve of the industrial revolution.* 1925. p. 6. inclines to my view. C. E. Raven. *English naturalists.* 1952.

20 Margaret Blundell (ed.) *Blundell's diary and letter book, 1702–1728.* 1952. p. 32. Edward Hughes. *North country life in the 18th century.* 1952. p. 143.

21 *Tusser redivivus.* 1710. April. p. 8. Dec. p. 14. Giles Jacob. *op. cit.* pp. 3, 4, 8. *Dictionarium rusticum.* 1717. art. Pasture. Stephen Switzer. *Ichnographia rustica.* 1718. III. p. 236.

22 William Ellis. *Practical farmer.* 1732. pp. 49–82. *idem. Mod. Husb.* 1750. *passim.* cf. Thomas Hale. *Compleat body of husbandry.* 1756. T. H. Marshall. *Jethro Tull and the new husbandry.* Econ. Hist. Rev. Jan. 1929.

[23] B. Cozens Hardy (ed.) *Diary of Sylas Neville, 1767–1788*. 1950. pp. 100, 101.
[24] See my *John Wynn Baker: an "improver" in 18th century Ireland*. Agric. Hist. (U.S.A.) V. Oct. 1931. pp. 151–161, and the references therein cited. James Adam. *Practical essays*. 1787. I. p. 473 ff. Anderson. *Recreations*. 1800. III. p. 175.
[25] Rev. W. Thorp. *On the failure of the red clover*. J.R.A.S.E. 1842.
[26] Holland. *Cheshire*. 1808. pp. 156–183. Bailey. *Durham*. 1810. pp. 175–177. Young. *Norfolk*. 1804. p. 370. Batchelor. *Bedford*. 1808. p. 431. Priest. *Bucks*. 1813. p. 234. Mayor. *Berks*. 1813. pp. 238–239, 284–296. Stevenson. *Surrey*. p. 250. Young. *Sussex*. 1808. pp. 146–153. Gooch. *Cambridge*. 1813. pp. 184–190. Plymley. *Salop*. 1803. pp. 180–208. Pitt. *Northampton*. 1809. pp. 113–118. Murray. *Warwick*. 1815. pp. 128–134.
[27] A Farmer. *Rural recreations*. 1802. May. pp. 10–12. 16. R. W. Dickson. *Pract. agric.* 1804. II. pp. 839 ff. Robert Forsyth. *Principles and practice of agriculture*. 1804. II. pp. 77, 90, 95. Bailey & Culley. *Northumberland*. 1813. pp. 113, 116. *Cumberland*. p. 228. Brown. *W. R. Yorks*. 1799. pp. 113, 116, 118.
[28] Sir George Head. *A home tour . . . 1835*. 1836. pp. 258, 259. For a general discussion of the depression see G. E. Fussell & Maurice Compton. *Agricultural adjustments after the Napoleonic Wars*. Econ. Hist. Suppt. of Econ. Jour. Feb. 1939. pp. 184–204.
[29] Baxters' *Library of agricultural and horticultural knowledge*. 3rd ed. 1836. art. by George Sinclair p. 276 ff. & p. 142 ff. John Donaldson. *Treatise on manures*. 1842. pp. 278–300. David Low. *Pract. Agric.* 4th ed. 1843. pp. 509–538. C. Hillyard. *Practical farming*. 3rd ed. 1840. MSS. *Account book of Riplingham Grange 1839–1874*. fol. 50v. George Nicholls. *The Farmer*. 1844. p. 19. Alexander Taylor. *Farmer's guide*. 1829. pp. 11, 212. G. H. Andrews. *Modern husbandry*. 1853. pp. 264–286. Henry Evershed. *Farming of Warwickshire*. J.R.A.S.E. XVII (1856) p. 485.
[30] William Davies. *op. cit.* pp. 77, 78. Donaldson. *op. cit.* pp. 276, 314. Twamley. *op. cit.* pp. 91, 113 ff. Benjamin Axford. *Extirpation of plants noxious to cattle*. Letters and papers . . . Bath . . . Soc. I. (1788). p. 208. Robert Smith. *Management of grassland*. J.R.A.S.E. 1848. pp. 2, 23. C. W. Johnson. *Gypsum as manure*. id. 1842. pp. 107–110. J. Dixon. *On manuring grass*. id. 1858. p. 204. ff. Rev. W. Bowditch. id. p. 217 ff. H. S. Thompson. *On laying land down*. id. p. 260 ff. Lawes and Gilbert. *Reports on experiments . . .* id. 1858. pt. I. 1859. pp. 2, 3, 4.
[31] T. Horsfall. *Management of dairy cattle*. J.R.A.S.E. 1856. p. 281.
[32] See my Sewage farming. Agriculture. June. 1957.
[33] L. Rawstone. *Some remarks on Lancashire farming*. 1843. pp. 19, 26. H. Badcock. *Practical observations on husbandry of . . . East Cornwall*. 1845. p. 16.
[34] C. S. Read. *Farming of Bucks*. J.R.A.S.E. 1855. p. 298. H. Evershed. *Agriculture of Stafford*. id. 1869. p. 270. Maude Robinson. *Southdown farm in the sixties*. 1947. p. 60.
[35] M. H. Sutton. *Laying down land to permanent pasture*. J.R.A.S.E. 1861. pp. 416–420. Morgan Evans & T. Bowstead. *Report on laying land down*. idem. 1875. pp. 443–503.
[36] Lawes and Gilbert. *Effects of different manures on mixed herbage of grassland*. idem. 1863. pp. 131, 132, 528. James Buckman. *On clovers*. idem. 1866. pp. 449–466. On clover allies as fodder crops. idem. 1866 & 1868.

Clement Cadle. *Improvement of grassland. idem.* 1869. pp. 318–334. He states that Wheeler and Sons of Gloucester had issued a book on grasses giving grasses suitable for each geoglogical formation. It was on such firms of seedmen that farmers usually relied.

37 H. S. Thompson. *Management of grassland. idem.* 1872. pp. 164–179. R. O. Pringle & Prof. Murray. *Practical farming; stock.* c. 1865. pt. II. pp. 2–18. D. F. G. Macdonald. *Cattle, sheep and deer.* 2nd ed. 1872. pp. 14–40. cf. Ward and Lock's *Book of farm management.* c. 1880. p. 300.

28 R. Scott Burn. *Outlines of modern farming.* 6th ed. 1888. Pt. IV *The dairy.* p. 25. W. Livesey. *Wensleydale and its dairy farming.* Jour. Brit. Dairy Farmers' Association. 1879. I. pt. 2 p. 45.

39 William Fream. *Herbage of old grassland.* J.R.A.S.E. 1888 pp. 422–443. *idem. Herbage of pastures. idem.* 1890. pp. 390–391. William Carruthers. *Composition of some famous ancient pastures. idem.* p. 756. *idem. How to estimate seeds mixtures for grass and hay. idem.* 1894. p. 797. Robert Bruce. *Influence of locality on breeds of cattle.* Jour. Farmers Club Dec. 1895. p. 24. L. Dudley Stamp. *Man and the land.* 1955. pp. 99–104.

40 James Caird. *Recent experiences in laying down land to grass.* J.R.A.S.E. 1888. pp. 125–149. Henry Evershed. *Laying down arable land to pasture.* Jour. Farmers Club. Nov. 1880. Martin Sutton. *Conversion of arable to grass. idem.* Feb. 1895. James Howard. *Laying land down to grass.* J.R.A.S.E. 1880. pp. 435–440. Faunce de Laune. *On laying down. idem.* 1882. pp. 229–257. R. Scott Burn. *Directory for the improvement of landed property.* 1881. pp. 418–426. *idem. op. cit.* (note 38) p. 26. John J. Pilley. *Scientific agric.* 1881. pp. 164–172. H. M. Upton. *Profitable dairy farming.* 1888. pp. 23–43.

## NOTES TO CHAPTER II (iii)

1 J. A. Venn. *Foundations of agricultural economics.* 1923. pp. 17 ff. Ernle. *English farming.* 1961. pp. 26, 230. cf. E. C. K. Gonner. *Common land and enclosure.* 1912. p. 30 fn.

2 Fitzherbert. *Husbandry.* pp. 24–26. Tusser. *Five hundred points.* 1577. (ed. Mavor 1812) p. 162. Surflet. pp. 637, 638. Harrison. ii. p. 133 cited in and discussed by M. E. Seebohm. *Evolution of the English farm.* 1952. pp. 214, 296. Nigel Harvey. *Farm and estate under Elizabeth I.* Agriculture. June, 1953. p. 106. Mildred Campbell. *English yeoman . . .* 1942. p. 204. Barbara Winchester. *Tudor family portrait.* 1955. p. 182. George Roberts. *Social history of the southern counties of England.* 1856. p. 196. Thorold Rogers. *Six centuries of work and wages.* 1906. p. 73.

3 Matthew Stevenson. *The twelve moneths.* 1661.

4 Blagrave. *Epitome.* 1675. pp. 36, 37.

5 *Tusser redivivus.* 1710. June. pp. 3–9. July. pp. 3, 4. Ellis. *Mod. Husb.* 1750. II. June. pp. 97–101. Matthew Peters. *Winter riches.* 1771. pp. 125, 127.

6 Marshall. *Gloucester.* 1796. I. pp. 170, 201, 202. Rudge. *Gloucester.* 1807. pp. 183, 184, 186. Young. *Suffolk.* 1797. p. 140.

7 John Lawrence. *New farmers calendar.* 1802. June. pp. 75–77. John Holt. *Lancashire.* 1795. p. 76. Francis Forbes. *Modern improvements in agric.* 1784. p. 387.

[8] James Anderson. *Essays.* 1797 (1773). I. pp. 379, 380. III. p. 560. Thomas Davis. *Wiltshire.* 1811. p. 186.

[9] Marshall. *Midlands.* 1790. I. p. 289. Billingsley. *Somerset.* 1797. p. 121. Tuke. *N. R. Yorks.* 1800. pp. 173–176. Holland. Cheshire. 1808. pp. 184–186. Parkinson. *Experienced farmer.* 1807. II. pp. 107, 111. Bailey. *Durham.* 1810. p. 176. Stevenson. *Dorset.* 1815. p. 306.

[10] Marshall. West of England. 1796. I. pp. 209, 210.

[11] Dickson. *Pract. agric.* 1804. II. p. 947. Frank W. Garnett. *Westmorland agric. 1800–1900.* 1912. Illustration opp. p. 22.

[12] See my *Farmers' Tools, 1500–1900.* 1952. pp. 140, 141. This work relates the further history of hay making machinery, a subject that can only be touched upon here.

[13] Robert Smith. *Management of grassland.* J.R.A.S.E. 1848. p. 20. G. H. Andrews. *Modern husbandry.* 1853. pp. 359, 361. Thomas Horsfall *Dairy Management.* J.R.A.S.E. 1857. p. 182. T. Bowick. *Recent improvements in haymaking. idem.* 1862. p. 50. John Donaldson. *British agric.* 1860. III. pp. 684, 685. Copland. *Agriculture . . .* 1866. II. pp. 178–180.

[14] John Walker. *Farming to profit.* 1888. p. 38. H. M. Upton. *Profitable dairy farming.* 1888.

[15] H. M. Jenkins. *Report on the practice of ensilage . . .* J.R.A.S.E. 1884. H. Kains Jackson. *Experiments in making ensilage. idem.* 1888. James Long. *Dairy farm.* 1889. pp. 35–37.

# CHAPTER III

## *Buildings*

### (i). Cowsheds or houses

The Tudor textbooks pay little attention to the housing of cows. Many of the animals were out-wintered, and took their chances in the trying vagaries of our climate, which may have been somewhat more severe than it is today. Garnier believed that there was no country in Western Europe where so few cows were housed as in eighteenth century England, but this is a comparison that it is impossible to test. In France then only the oxen belonging to the peasant small holders lay abroad in winter; in Holland the cows were housed in winter, and were clothed when feeding in the fields in autumn; the cowstalls were washed daily. There was a good deal of summer stall feeding as well, both in the Low Countries and in Germany.[1]

In the larger Tudor establishments the auxiliary buildings were generally separate from the dwelling house, but not so distant that the farmer could not oversee them from his bedroom, a point of vantage that was long taken into account in designing the layout. Leonard Mascall in the early seventeenth century was slightly more explicit. He recommended that cowstalls should be built on an east to west line, with a blank wall on the north, and windows and doors in the south elevation. Surflet described the ideal ox-house, and this may perhaps be applied to the cow house as well, but his was an ideal, or, at the lowest estimate, a building that could be only considered by a rich man. His idea was a stone house, sited on sandy or gravelly soil, with a slope to the floor for drainage. He agreed that a south elevation was best. It made for dryness, and was less subject to cold and frosty winds. The house was to be nine feet wide, and only high enough for the animal to stand upright. These dimensions would allow the herdsman to go round to feed, and would prevent the animals goring each other.[2] Few modern designers would approve so low a building.

Some confirmation of Garnier's contention may be found in the lack of any more information about cowhouses until the end of the seventeenth century. Even then all that A. S., Gent, has to say in 1697 is that the stalls or houses should be 'adjoyning to some warm, inclosed Pasture', and that the stalls should be 'Yoak wide, about seven foot from the ground'. At Halsall, Lancashire, in-calf heifers were housed at night a little before Christmas, or according to the weather. Nothing is said about the house itself, but the cow's neck was tied with a sow (of bent wood) made fast to a stake by the side of the stalls with another ring, called the Frampas, 'which is put to the stake that the heifer may lift her head up and down'. In front of her was a 'cratch' with fodder, about eighteen inches high from the ground. This method of tying, which, with different apparatus, lasted until recent years, was intended to make her tame and easy to milk.[3]

Some thirty years later Richard Bradley partly endorsed and partly contradicted Surflet's advice as well as expanding it with more detail. The site should be chosen so that it was dry, and not too much exposed to the sun. He did not like the floor to be stone-pitched as some advised, but rather to be of the small Dutch bricks known as clinkers, set edgeways, as used in stables, and the floor should, as Surflet said, be laid slopeways to carry off the moisture. Bradley did not like the windows to face south, because that would make the house too hot for health. Preferably they should face north or east to get the morning sun, and the cooler air in summer. The doors should be large, and in winter opened occasionally to let in the sun or warmer air. The stalls should be eight feet wide to provide room enough to lie in, and so that the pregnant cows should not hurt each other, nor the stronger ox hurt the weaker. This advice, much of which could be respected to-day, was repeated by a Country Gentleman in 1767.[4]

A Practical Farmer (David Henry?) laid down the buildings necessary to equip different sizes of farms in 1772. For a small farm of £50 a year a cowhouse large enough for four cows with a part partitioned off for two calves was all that was required. A mixed farm four times as large ought to have accommodation for ten cows and four calves, the proper number that one dairymaid could cope with. Generally the cowhouse ought to be sited at one side of the dwelling, and in line with it. Proximity was an advantage for the obvious reason that the daily work of milking and so on was at hand. A farm of 500 acres (£200 rent) ought to have a cowshed sixty feet long by thirteen wide. A wall of moderate height 'should connect the whole'. It should be built of brick, as timber buildings always proved much the dearer in the end. The walls should be plain 9" wall, 5½' high in front, and 10' behind, strengthened with 14" piers. It should be bonded about the middle, and the roof tied in three or four places with tie beams, 3" x 6". The rafters, 3" x 4", should be notched and spiked to the wall plates, and should fall over the front about 8". The roof should be pan tiles, and the gables fitted with oak lathes, latticed for free admission of air, because horned cattle should never be kept hot.[5] A stream of water should be let through the buildings, if possible; if not, a reservoir should be made round the pump. Such buildings as Henry planned were not impossible. They may have been infrequent, but as the new layout of the land took place following enclosure, and farmhouses and buildings set up in the fields instead of in the villages some cowsheds like these were built.

William Ellis had a much more elaborate scheme, reminiscent of a modern milking bail on a permanent site, but rather fantastic in the conditions of 1750. Its essence was that eight sets of buildings should be put up on convenient sites in a hundred acre field of sainfoin. These were thatched sheds ten feet high and thirty feet wide, each one hundred and twenty five feet long. Under the highest part, directly in the middle, a slight partition of lathe and plaster supported the roof. The sides were supported by square wooden posts about eight feet

high at suitable distances apart. On either side of the partition a feed rack was to run the whole length of the shed, high
enough to suit the cow's feeding. The cows were to stand in
stalls about five feet wide, and just long enough for the cow
to be prevented from walking backwards by a crossbar behind
it. Every shed would hold 50 cows, 25 on each side of the
partition.

One man would be able to clean such a cowhouse and carry
off the dung. He could also mow the sainfoin every day, and
give it to the cows by placing it in the rack. The cowman was
to be allowed a proper proportion of the growing crop, and
if he began to mow at one end of it that part would be fit to
mow again by the time he reached the other. Provision was
made for the dairymaids to live on the premises. At each end
of each shed a slight brick room of thirty foot square was to
be built and divided, crossways, into two, each fifteen by
thirty feet. The section nearest the cowshed was floored with
tiles to serve as a dairy, the other floored and windowed to
be a lodging room for the dairymaids. Each shed needed five
maids, one to every ten cows. They were to deal with cows
on both sides of the partition nearest to their dairy.

The modern touch was that all along both sides of the
partition about a foot about the ground, a strong lead pipe, a
little less than 1 inch in diameter, was to be fixed so that there
was a slight gradient from the highest point in the middle of
the shed down to where it was run through the dividing wall
into the dairy. There the two ends were joined so that whatever descended through them was discharged at only one
mouth; this must be made quite small.

The combined discharge mouth of the lead pipes was neatly
fitted into the end of a strong wooden axle tree. This job must
be skilfully done because the axle had to revolve rapidly, and
in doing so must not damage the pipes. This axle carried a
barrel churn capable of containing at least three times the
milk it is intended to use. The axle was fitted with the six
dashes or wings then usual in such a churn. An inspection
port, tight fitting when closed, was put in some convenient
place in the exterior of the barrel. Tightness could be secured

by lining the inside and edges of the port with cheese cloth. The solid end of the axle tree was designed to project about five feet beyond the barrel and to rest on square wooden posts having the tops hollowed out and filled with grease to serve as bearings. The end was fastened into a wheel to be turned by dogs running round inside it on the principle then employed in turning spits on which joints were roasted.

The purpose of the lead pipes was, of course, to deliver the milk to the dairy. Near the side of each stall a small hole was made in the top of the lead pipe. When not in use this hole was closed by a small screw attached to the pipe by a litte chain so that it could not be laid down and lost. A special milking pail was necessary to enable the milk to flow into the pipe without spilling. It was very shallow and broad and stood on three legs, tripod fashion, about a foot high. To a point on the bottom of the rim a long tin pipe, rather like the neck of a still (everyone made distilled waters in those days) was attached. Its nozzle was put in the hole in the main pipe to empty the milk into it. This adjustment was made before milking began, and the milk drawn from the cow flowed straight from the pail into the pipe. To keep the milk free from hairs and other dirt, a straining cloth was put in the pail over the vent that led into the nozzle.

By gravity the milk flowed down the pipe into the hollow axle, and from it through holes provided in its outer structure into the barrel it worked in. In the morning and evening before they began to milk, the maids put the dogs into the large driving wheel, and so the churn began to turn immediately before the milk commenced to flow into it.

The optimistic designer of this elaborate apparatus believed that a much larger quantity of butter would be produced in this way than in the ordinary way of setting milk for cream. Again the cheese made from the buttermilk could be reckoned amongst the richest and best kind in England. Nowhere is it suggested that any experiments had been made to prove these contentions, nor is it suggested that anyone anywhere had erected such an installation for practical use.[6]

The ordinary farmer was much less exacting, and would

have been much more likely to take the advice of Thomas Comber, jun., of East Newton, Yorkshire, who believed in housing cows for convenience in milking and feeding. He suggested that a 'helm' (hovel or shed) of any coarse wood could easily be put up against a convenient south wall. The eastern and western ends could be protected by a wattle of thorn or furze if stones were wanting. It could be covered with a few waggon loads of furze, broom or heath, and thatched 'slightly'. Such a shed would last many years, and was of a cheapness to appeal to the small farmer with little capital. The stalls, so long as they were kept dry, could be formed of any kind of 'offal' wood. A channel of coarse stones was easily made to carry off the urine.[7] Though not ideal, this must have been quite a popular way of housing the cows, and would serve the purpose quite well. It was similar to the linhays Marshall saw in the west of England, where the cattle yards were furnished mostly with open sheds with troughs or mangers in the back parts to hold fodder. Some were double, the same roof space covering two ranges of sheds which served two yards, and divided only by a fence partition running along the middle. These open sheds were used for cows and young cattle, and Marshall thought them efficient.

Modern cowsheds were more in line with David Henry's ideas, as Marshall described them in 1790. They were provided with a gang way before the heads of the cattle, mangers for dry food, and water troughs. The cows stood in pairs with only a simple division (boosing) between each pair, consisting of an upright post in front of the manger or between the troughs, with a natural or artificial arm springing near the ground, and rising to the same height as the post the upper part forming the letter K. This was stiffened by slots or bars running through the two pieces. The cows were fastened by chains round their necks and playing by means of rings fitted on stakes fixed to the sides of the partition posts. This prevented the cows goring each other, and they were as free to rest as if there were no guards between them. Marshall admitted that cowsheds of this kind were expensive.[8]

Ventilation, drainage and cleanliness were all important.

141

When the cowhouses were in the form of sheds ventilation was often defective. Sometimes the cows were seen to be smoking and the rafters wet with the exhalations of their breath. These were symptoms that more air holes were required. If there were gabled windows they ought to be latticed, as Henry had advised, or provided with board closures that could be removed to admit air. The stalls ought to be designed to keep the cows perfectly dry, airy and cool, and should have suitable drains to carry off the urine. A space behind the cows to allow the dung to be removed was a further aid to cleanliness. A pond of clean water in the adjoining yard was a desideratum. The floor should be regularly washed.

There was some difference of opinion about the placing of the cows, especially if kept in two rows. Some thought they should face each other, but others that their heads should be against the wall where the manger and water troughs were fixed. Again placing the calf pen caused some argument. It was a convenience to have it under the same roof as the cowshed so that the maids would not have to carry the milk any further than was necessary, but if the cows could hear the calves bawling they were disturbed with bad effects. For this reason it was better to have the calf pens some distance away from the cowhouse. Each farmer had to decide this question in the way that suited him best.[9]

A curious patent was taken out by George Adams in 1810 (No. 3350). It was, amongst other things, for a cowhouse fitted with troughs for food and water, and mounted on wheels so that it could be moved from one place to another on rails or otherwise. Here again is a forerunner of the moveable bail!

Clearly by 1800 the general outline of a modern cowshed had been designed, and the main principles of management laid down: but to what extent the best type of cowshed was present on the farms is impossible to determine. The materials used were not, of course, so readily kept clean as the present day tubular steel fittings. Wooden posts and partitions must have accumulated dirt in their pores however careful the cowman was, and brick or paved floors could never have been kept free from dirt, but the arrangement of the tyings, the feed mangers and water troughs was much the same as it is today. Many farms must have lacked these conveniences, and when a man had only one or two cows they were usually kept in a building that was little more than a stable of a quite primitive kind. Loose pens were still considered best in north-east Gloucestershire in 1850 because the cows were cleaner, less litter was necessary, and less hay was wasted. A shed nine feet deep divided into pens eight feet wide with an outlet of nine to ten feet, besides space for crib and water was usual there.[10]

The design of the nineteenth century cowshed was influenced by the large town dairies. The Harliean dairy in Glasgow housed some 300 cows and has been widely discussed. A large number of cows were fed on grains in Whitbread's dairy in Battersea. A metropolitan dairy in Edgware Road housed 360 cows about 1830. An 1846 plan of a cowhouse, suggested by the byre of Mr. Race, the extensive dairyman of Newcastle-on-Tyne, was one of these.

It was designed to provide accommodation for 20 cows, and was forty two feet by thirty six feet, having two rows opposite each other, five stalls on each side, each stall being for two cows, eight feed wide and eight feet from back to front, with a space eight feet between them along the centre of the building at the tails of the cows. A passage four feet wide was left on each side at the heads of the cows, running the whole length of the building, for supplying food. At one end there was a shed for a boiler and apparatus for steaming roots, and preparing food for the cows, calves and pigs. Further details are supplied by G. H. Andrews. The partition between each pair of animals was of stone or a slate slab if easily obtained, but wood was preferable. The mangers should not be less than 20 inches above the floor. They were often put on the floor, but this was objectionable because the animals had to bend their heads so much when biting turnips and other food. The cows were secured by a chain on a ring that slid up and down a post, the other end being fastened to a strap round the throat. Instead of chains a 'bakie' could be used as a tie, i.e., a piece of hardwood with cords at each end, one with an eye to slide up and down the post, and the other tied round the cow's neck. An open drain formed of bricks was made at the back of the cows. The floor was paved with hard material, rammed chalk, clay, or smith's ashes and pitched flints with a fall for run-off of liquid manure. Ventilation was provided by flaps to open at the side of the shed close under the wall plate, and above the animals' heads, and hoppers in the roof to let the hot air out. The building itself could be of brick to four feet high, and above that of close boarding. Water ought to be laid on to a drinking trough at the head of each cow.[11] This was the more common type of cowhouse in 1860, but many were mere sheds with a trough along the inner side and an upright post every 4 feet carrying the sliding ring and neck strap. Such sheds were open to the south, and partly closed to the weather in winter by wattled gates or some similar device. Others were a series of loose boxes only used in winter. It had long been thought the byres ought to be high in the side walls with no lofts over them.[12]

It was much on these lines that the Prince Consort built the new cowhouse for the royal dairy at Windsor. George III had adapted some old buildings as a dairy homestead making a cowhouse of the orangery put up by Sarah, Duchess of Marlborough, when she was Ranger of Windsor Great Park, but it was not satisfactory. When the Prince Consort examined the buildings in 1851 he discovered that they flooded if the Thames overflowed, and the cattle, many of them valuable pedigree animals, suffered in health. Several died of pleuropneumonia in 1845-1846, so there was good reason for the rebuilding. The new cowhouse had a wide central gangway and a lofty roof provided with carefully thought out arrangements for watering and draining. The stalls were nine feet wide, for two cows each, separated by slate partitions. An iron trough, divided into three parts was set up in each stall, the middle one for water, brought in by pipes below the floor. The stall and passage floors were asphalt with a gutter to allow water to run away. They were laid upon a bed of concrete to the consternation of any rats that tried to penetrate it. The feed and litter stores were so arranged as to be of easy access.[13] Similar buildings were created by some of the great landlords, for example, the Duke of Norfolk at Arundel. Asphalt for flooring began to be recommended to the ordinary farmer at this time, but was apt to be too smooth. The ideal floor was one hard enough to wear, and rough enough to give good foothold while being non-absorbent of manure and easily cleaned. Musgrave stable flooring bricks were excellent. It was good practice to sweep the floor twice a day at least, all dirt and litter being sedulously removed. No more feed must be given than the cows could clear up at a meal, or the leavings of stale food might contaminate the milk.[14]

The two cow partition was usual, but came in for some criticism in the 1860's. Henry Stephens thought each cow should have its own stall. She could then go in and come out without interfering with the other cows, and learn to stand quietly waiting for the man who fed, and the maid who milked her. R. Scott Burn described the double stall system in detail, but preferred each cow to have a single stall. She might quarrel or refuse to give milk if beside another cow.[15]

The pattern of the cowhouse was stabilised by the 1880's. By then corrugated iron had begun to be used for roofing. It was sometimes lined with boards, a very sensible precaution. Emphasis continued to be laid upon the necessity for proper ventilation, which was often inadequate. The cows should be kept warm, for they required 33% more food if they were cold; a reasonable assumption. The size of the byres varied a foot or so according to choice, and the materials used were a mixture of brick and timber. Upton in 1888 suggested that each cow should have 600 cubic feet of air space, and this was approved by the authorities. Later the Local Government specified 800 cubic feet for each cow unless habitually grazed on grass. The optimum temperature of a cowhouse was a few degrees below 60°F. Otherwise the principles that had been discussed for so long were accepted.[16]

145

Nevertheless right down to 1900 there were many rough and ready sheds or barns in which cows were housed either for a few hours daily, for milking or at night as necessary.


## (ii). The dairy


A great many farmers who lived in Tudor and Stuart times owned a cow or two; some owned large herds. Those who did not aspired to. The ownership of a milch cow meant a better standard of living, and a possible source of money income, but even those who owned substantial herds cannot have been very particular about the construction of the dairy in which they worked up the products; or it may be that there was a common standard which the textbook writers thought so customary that they need not describe it. For whatever reason there is very little to be gleaned about the arrangement of the dairy before the eighteenth century.

Miss Seebohm states that the Tudor dairy, bakehouse, brewhouse, and stable were generally separate from the main building, but near enough for the farmer (goodman) to see what was being done when lying in bed. Andrew Boorde wanted the slaughter-house and dairy to be on a site a quarter of a mile away from the house. These arrangements could only have been on large estates or farms, and could not have been possible for the ordinary farmer.

Surflet, who described the lay-out of a large farmhouse and the necessary outbuildings in detail, placed the dairy at the entrance of the kitchen in a cool situation and not exposed to the sun. It should be a small vaulted, paved room

> 'lying slope-wise and with a gutter . . . for the auoiding and conueying of all such washings as she is to make about the milke vessels'.

In this room the housewife did all her business concerning the making of butter and cheese.[1]

In many of the Tudor farmhouses of East Anglia, which

are lived in and worked in today, there is a dairy room as an integral part of the building. It is usually placed adjacent to the kitchen with which a door communicates. Stone flags form the floor, and there are substantial wooden shelves. The window is usually unglazed, and only partly closed by vertical parallel bars an inch or so apart. These dairies are not now used for butter and cheese making as they must have been in the past. Doubtless there are similar dairy rooms in old farmhouses in other parts of the country. Accommodation of this kind must have been sufficient and acceptable to the busy housewife's dairy work until the late eighteenth century, when a more elaborate arrangement was considered necessary, an arrangement that was more or less uniform throughout the nineteenth century with only minor local variations.

Blundell, the improving and experimental Lancashire landowner, wanted to make his buttery into a dairy in 1711, but his wife had social ambitions. She wanted a second parlour instead. On August 19th of that year a mason and his partner actually came to the place to begin making the buttery over into a dairy, but Mrs. Blundell enlisted the aid of friends to overrule her husband, and two gentlemen visitors persuaded him to do what his wife wished. She got her second parlour, and the dairy work had to be done in the unimproved premises where it had formerly been done. This was an unusual obstacle to progressive farming.[2]

The necessity for ample water and a cool temperature in the dairy had been realised at an early date. Richard Bradley in 1728 had known dairies that had a stream of water running through them. The lattice window too had long been preferred to glass. Wire and shutters to open and close as the sun changed its course were fitted instead. Bradley, too, preferred thatch for roofing. It was much cooler than tiles, a subject that was discussed at length in later textbooks. He thought that whatever would keep off the sun should be practised.[3]

Theory had advanced no further sixty years later. North windows were best, and ought to be fitted with a sliding frame to close when necessary, made of oiled paper fixed with adhesive to a network of packthread. This would admit light but keep out sun and wind. The dairy floor should be neatly paved with red brick or smooth hard stone with a slope so that no water should lodge. The floor must be well washed every day in summer. Churns and other utensils ought not to be washed in the dairy. The steam would injure the milk. Nor should cheese or rennet be kept there for the same reason.[4]

Practice was perhaps much the same as it had long been. Marshall, who was impressed by the dairy farming of Gloucestershire and North Wilts., has left a rough description of the dairy rooms in that area, and the Board of Agriculture published ideal specifications before the end of the century.

The Gloucestershire dairy room had generally an outer door opening into a small garden or yard. This gave freer and more general air, and better and more commodious light. In the garden or yard there was or ought to be a well with proper benches for washing and drying the utensils. A medium sized dairy room was usually about fifteen feet by eighteen, and the churning and cheese-making was done there. The floor was paved with stones, and the shelves constructed of elm or ash. When well placed the outer door opened near the north-west or north-east corner, and the window was on the north side. An inner door opened into the kitchen.

North Wiltshire dairies were more spacious and commodious. For a farm with 40 cows the dairy was twenty feet by sixteen; for 100 cows thirty feet by forty, besides a lean-to for leads and other implements. The building was provided with outer doors frequently opening under a lent house, or open lean-to shed. This Marshall approved of; it afforded shade and shelter, and kept the dairy room cool. One he saw had two doors, an ordinary door on the inside, and an open paled door outside it. An even more elaborate building was owned by Mrs. Badow, comprising a shelf room immediately over the dairy and lofts over this room with trapdoors in each floor to hand the cheeses through, a plan that saved much awkward carriage.[5]

By an Act of 1796 windows in dairy and cheese rooms were

exempted from the window tax, but only if they were not glazed. Untaxed lights in these rooms must be made with splines, wooden laths or iron bars. The doors had to be painted in Roman letters two inches high with the words 'Dairy and Cheese Room'. This provision perhaps indicates a realisation of the increasing importance of the dairy industry. No dairy farmer would have been likely to take exception to the specification of the kind of light required to secure exemption from tax. It was in line with approved practice, and relief from the tax was an early example of direct government aid to farmers. It may have been partly in consequence of the habit of great ladies and their friends to visit the dairy of their country mansions, which were sometimes elegant and decorated with a collection of old china, to drink syllabubs and milk warm from the cow.[6]

The design of farmhouses, cottages and buildings was a subject that engaged the attention of the Board of Agriculture, and there was a number of architectural treatises published dealing with the ferme orné at about the turn of the century. Ideal designs were described in the first volume of the *Communications to the Board of Agriculture* issued in 1797, and widely subscribed to by subsequent writers.

Whether the dairy was primarily devoted to the production of butter or cheese it required three rooms. A butter dairy must have a milk room, a churning room provided with a boiler for scalding utensils, and a room for keeping and drying them when this could not be done in the open air. A cheese dairy similarly must have a milk room, a scalding and pressing room, and a salting room. Where liquid milk was sold, usually only near large towns, it was only necessary to have a room where the milk could be put before disposal. A north exposure was to be preferred. It was cool in summer and warm in winter. The buildings should be as much under the shade of trees as possible. An apartment over the dairy was thought by some to be an advantage, others did not approve, as noticed above. If there was no such room, the roof should be thatched over tiles. Stone walls were better than brick as not so pervious to heat and cold if of proper thickness. The temperature should be between 40° and 50°F. if possible. The ceiling of the milk house ought not to be more than seven feet high, but this was not always agreed. Some thought it could not be too high. Both walls and ceilings ought to be plastered very smooth with no cracks. Such a ceiling prevented dust from the thatch falling into the milk. Some dairy walls were covered with Dutch tiles a foot or so above the shelves. The latticed windows should be fitted with slight frames of gauze to let in air and keep out insects, an improvement upon Hazard's oiled paper. Freestone paving flags or square paving bricks, properly jointed, could be used for flooring, but marble or black slate from Penrhyn, North Wales, was better. It should have a gentle declivity to the centre to carry off the water. The churning room, adjoining the cheese room, should have shelves round the walls to hold milk vessels. It should be fitted with a furnace, fireplace and proper boiler as well as a pump with spouts for filling the copper. A spout below the copper to empty it was a convenience. The utensil store ought also to have a small fireplace for airing and drying properly when it was not possible to set the things out in the sun, the best method. Stone shelves to store these things on were another requisite. The three rooms in the cheese dairy were much the same, but should have a loft above.

Anderson made his specification rather more elaborate with double walls, either of lath plastered on both sides or of brick. A cheap building was quite as good as the expensive ones often put up by noblemen and gentlemen. A rill of water should be made to run through the house, if possible, and an interior passage four feet wide round the milkhouse was desirable. It could be used for storing butter. Near towns where ice could be sold in summer it was useful to make an ice house near the dairy. He thought the correct temperature 50°-55°F. This disparity shows that the proper temperature had not yet been determined with sufficient accuracy. Some farmers used the churning room and utensil store as a brewhouse and laundry, and had bedrooms for dairymaids and

MODERN MILK TRANSPORT IN 1800

A MILK CARRIAGE ABOUT 1800

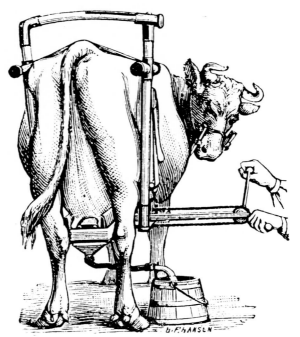

THE DANISH COW MILKER

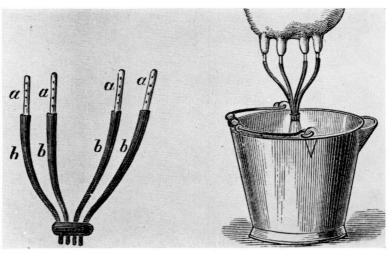

THE EARLIEST ARTIFICIAL MILKMAID. A SIPHON MILKING MACHINE

other servants over them, but this was not desirable. This was the plan of Wakefield's well known dairy at Liverpool.

Young, too, set out his ideal. It seemed to him necessary that the entrance to the milkroom should be through the scalding room so that the heat might be as far as possible from the milk. The boiling water should pass by a cock in the bottom of the copper through a pipe across the scalding house, with a cock there for washing the smaller implements, and so through the wall into the milk leads to purify them. The dairy could be circular, and, if expense was no object, a fountain of water might be arranged to play in the centre of it in summer, a forecast of the arrangement in the Prince Consort's model dairy of half a century later. Parkinson suggested that the dairy should, if possible, be sunk three or four feet below the level of the ground with proper drains, and an area made round it to prevent damps, a suggestion that was frequently repeated in the following century, e.g., by Alexander Taylor in 1829. Some dairies were provided with plaster floors rendered as hard and smooth as marble, and in Staffordshire shelves of this material took the place of the wood or stone usual in other places.[7]

The importance of keeping an even temperature in the dairy house was constantly stated, and plans to secure it were numerous. Anderson proposed that a barrel filled with boiling water and close stopped would diffuse a gentle heat in winter. Young's advice that a fountain or jet d'eau, if it could be made, was a great convenience for reducing the temperature in summer was often repeated. Loudon said that if a cistern was placed over the steaming room water could be raised to it by a forcing pump worked by the general wheel, and would supply water for the jet and all other purposes. A small quantity of ice placed in the milk room would counteract the rise in temperature caused by bringing in warm milk in summer, and this could easily be supplied if a simple ice house were constructed near the dairy. From 50° to 55°F. was pretty well agreed to be the optimum.[8] As time passed only in the use of new materials was there any change in ideas about the design of farm dairies. Slate, for instance, was not only used in the internal construction, but James Jackson (1840) thought it preferable to tiles for the roof. He introduced a novelty when he proposed that the flagstone floor should be raised a little above the level of the ground outside. If it was so placed the open drains inside would readily carry away water used for washing down and for cleaning utensils. Most people preferred the dairy floor to be sunk a foot or so below ground level. Everybody knew that smelly things, rennet, for example, would give a taint to milk if kept in the milk house. David Low added to care inside the house the need to see that nothing immediately adjacent to it should give off a nauseous odour. Manure heap or midden must be well removed from the site.[9]

Some rich dairy farmers made the dairy an exhibition of their wealth. Their extravagance was not without good reasons in the handling of milk, but it is unlikely that such large capital outlay was economic. Mr. Littledale's dairy farm at Liscard, Cheshire, was one of these. It adjoined the farmhouse, and was an oblong room with a floor of Kean's patent cement laid in one piece, but with white lines of composition let into grooves. This device made it look like a fine pavement in large squares. Two large tables, one on each side, of sycamore wood, with turned legs, were snowy white with continual scrubbing. A massive marble table was at the far end. Three large octagonel lead milk coolers stood in the centre each on an ornamental pedestal. The walls above the tables were faced with glazed Staffordshire tiles twenty inches high, resembling small squares of veined marble. Tiles of this kind had been used in some dairies from the mid-eighteenth century, but only in a very few. They were easy to wash down and keep clean, but could not compete with the eighteenth century eccentric who lined his Wiltshire dairy throughout with lead, a very costly method, but one that would last from generation to generation without repairs, and always had a large intrinsic value.

Littledale's dairy roof was covered and groined with a handsome foliated centre piece in open work which led the air to a large ventilator at the top of the building. The walls most exposed to the sun had a hollow space of three inches in them through which a current of air passed, and there was a double ceiling for keeping an even temperature summer and winter. Copland thought this a first class establishment of the kind.[10] It was certainly not much below the exalted standard of the Royal Dairy at Frogmore.

When the Prince Consort decided to reconstruct it the old Frogmore dairy comprised two rooms, one octagonal, the other oblong, connected by an opening in the wall between them. There was a small fountain in the eight-sided room. A temporary lean-to shed had been added to house surplus milk, and the churning and butter rooms were detached. The drainage was completely insanitary. Quite close to the wall and directly under the windows of the milk room there was a large cess-pit. Ventilation, too, was deficient. The milk would not keep in hot weather, and had to be stored in the cellar of the neighbouring bailiff's house.

The Prince Consort drew up new designs, and had the whole thing rebuilt. The new dairy was sheltered from the south and west, and was in an open situation with no tree closer than thirty feet from the walls. It was provided with proper ventilation on 'Watson's Principle', the most modern system available, and with means of regulating it. Double windows excluded heat in summer, and cold in winter. A plentiful water supply was arranged and no cesspool allowed anywhere near the dairy. Both floors and walls were covered with ornamental glazed tiles, some to the Prince's own designs. Tables and shelves were of marble and slate. Cavity walls were built, and the roof constructed so that changes in the weather should not affect the milk. At either end of the dairy there was a majolica fountain of ornate design, and on the south side another even more elaborate. Externally the building was of Victorian gothic and the bailiff's house was ornamented to match it. The size of the milk room was thirty six by twenty feet, and about twenty feet high. About 240 gallons of milk could be stored in the white ware dishes it contained. It was easy to keep clean and there was a plentiful supply of fresh water and good ventilation. Any possible source of contamination had been removed to a reasonable distance.[11] No doubt the milk supply of the royal household was by so much improved and protected, but it would have been quite impossible for the ordinary farmer to emulate such a milk palace. He could have provided the essentials, but only in a much more simple fashion.

Most small dairy farms used a small apartment in the house, but larger ones had a separate building. Thatch was favoured for roofing both in Cheshire and Buckingham. A substitute for a hollow wall could be supplied by a wall of peat raised round the exterior of the building. A verandah was expensive but perhaps best. From the boiler it was desirable to have a pipe running through the rooms, the flow regulated by a stopcock, and the pipe perforated along its length to act as a sprinkler. If the inside walls were covered with white pottery it was not only elegant but useful. Dutch tiles, Kean's cement or glass might be used in its place. Besides fly gauze the windows could be fitted with Venetian blinds then a household novelty, or shutters to open outwards.[12]

The example of the Prince Consort was often quoted in textbooks printed after he had rebuilt his dairy, but his building was impossibly costly. In most dairy districts the farmhouse had an old-fashioned dairy room attached or under its roof e.g. in Gloucester and Somerset. It was often damp and filled with impure air. Frequently it was much too close to the stables and piggeries, the smell of which could so easily taint the milk. 'Our forefathers,' complained Joseph Harding of Marksbury, near Bristol in 1868, 'had one object in view, viz., shelter from the sun's rays, but however desirable a cool dairy may be unless it be thoroughly dry and sweet milk will keep longer in a higher temperature'. In the main his ideas were those promulgated for so long, but he wanted the escape drain covered with a patent sink trap, and the ceiling to be at least ten feet above the floor. Skirting should be stone or tile, ten inches deep rather than wood, and the milk ought to be brought in by a pipe through the wall so as to avoid the necessity for the milkers to bring it in. They often had dirty boots and so on, and introduced filth if they entered the dairy. Dirt was difficult to remove completely from corners and so Pringle and Murray (c.1865) advised that all corners should be rounded. Macdonald (1872) would have calico blinds over the windows in addition to shutters and wire gauze. Calico could be wetted in hot weather to assist in keeping the temperature at the optimum level. If a thermometer was hung up so that the temperature was precicsely known it was an obvious advantage.[13]

For the small farmer whose ambitions did not soar so high, but who wanted to build a dairy in the 1880's, a cheap building framed of quartering, with the outside cased in half inch slates was all that was necessary. The cavities between the quartering could be filled with solid concrete, or brick or stone rubble plastered smooth inside with a trowel and lime washed. The floor could also be of slate, laid on four inch thick concrete, made of seven parts of gravel and one of fine stone quick lime on a bed of mortar, which sounds rather elaborate. Another idea was an extension of the peat wall of some years before. Where peat was not to be had an outer wall of sods 4 inches thick, rammed firm would serve. If this was used the inner wall need only be one brick thick, or even lath and plaster, insulation being obtained by the cavity between. A large tin funnel with a trap to open and close provided cheap and effective ventilation. Farmers on this scale would not be likely to have an ice-house in which they could store their butter as Scott Burn proposed, nor supplies of ice to place on the tables in the dairy, nor an ice safe. Such things were confined to the great houses.[14]

The standard of three rooms that had been the minimum accommodation for so long continued to be discussed until the end of the century with emphasis on the optimum temperatures. It was slightly higher than formerly, ranging from 60° to 65°F. There were few opportunities for rebuilding from the 1880's onwards. Farming was not prosperous enough, and the landowners were restricted in their expenditure by the low state of farming. There must have been many dairies where the minimum rooms were to be found, but there were many more where the dairy was a room in the house, probably looking out over the yard as in Shropshire and many other counties where the disused dairy is still to be seen. In Cumberland and Westmorland the dairy remained in its original position, often badly placed under the staircase, or adjoining the living room, close to a fireplace, with a window looking out over the main midden or other insanitary spot. It was frequently used as a larder as well. How could it be otherwise in farmhouses that had stood for centuries? In modern farmhouses the arrangements conformed to modern ideas, and there were light, airy and well ventilated dairies. The same could no doubt be said with some truth of other parts of the country where some of the farmhouses and buildings are ancient.

Very few of the advisers who were writing during the eighteenth and nineteenth centuries supplied any dimensions of the dairy rooms. The most they did was to lay down that the ceiling should be not less than eight feet high, some said not less than ten feet. Of other measurements there are none or very few, and these are usually of fine dairies like that of the Prince Consort.

A dairy six feet wide by fifteen feet long and twelve feet high with one door to the kitchen and another to the churning room was Horsfall's ideal in 1856. A trellis window on the north side provided light and air. The room should be provided with two shelves one above the other, the top shelf being covered with charcoal to act as a deodoriser. In winter the door to the kitchen should be kept open so that the warmth could seep in, and the window closed with a shutter. The window should be covered with a cloth dipped in salt water and kept wet all day in summer. By these means an even temperature was secured.

George Gibbons estimated in 1890 that a dairy house on a Somerset farm where there was a herd of 50-60 cows should be at least twenty four feet by fifteen and ten feet high. Glazed windows four feet by three ought to be provided in the north-east and south walls, and fitted with sliding casements. The adjoining boiler house on the west of the main building should be twenty one by fifteen feet with a concrete floor and windows similar to the dairy. The whey room was set to the north of the boiler house and was fifteen by seven and a half feet with windows east and west. It was two feet lower than the dairy so that the whey could pass by open 'shoots' from the cheese tub to a cistern on stands, from which two inch glazed pipes led to a whey vault capable of holding at least 100 hogsheads. Over the dairy and boiler house should be cheese rooms reached by an easy staircase. These rooms should be nine feet high to the wall plates, and sealed with roof joists, boarded and covered with felt. The floor joists should be eleven inches by three, and the boards tongued and grooved.[16]

Little more can be said. Nothing of import was added to the old ideal in the last days of the nineteenth century; the same requirements are demanded in a recent textbook. W. J. Malden did warn people against the prevailing tendency to over elaboration in the 1890's. He said that a classical hero fed his horses on gilt oats out of ivory mangers. Some model dairies of his own time were planned and carried out on much the same lines. He might have taken comfort in the thought that on many farms the dairy was, to put a low figure on it, nothing like this.[17]

## NOTES TO CHAPTER III (i)

[1] Russell M. Garnier. *History of the English landed interest.* 1893. II. p. 264.

[2] M. E. Seebohm. *Evolution of the English farm.* 1952. p. 198 citing Mascall. Surflet. *Countrey Ferme.* 1600. p. 126.

[3] John Houghton. *Collection of letters.* 1681–83. II. pp. 155, 156.

[4] Richard Bradley. *Gentleman and farmers guide.* 3rd ed. 1739. (1729) pp. 172, 173. Country Gentleman. *Complete grazier.* 1767. p. 23.

[5] Practical Farmer (David Henry). *The complete English farmer.* 1772. pp. 22, 23, 26, 29–30, 35.

[6] William Ellis. *Mod. Husb.* 1750.

[7] *Museum rusticum . . .* V. (1765) p. 128.

[8] Marshall. *West of England.* 1796 I. p. 61. idem. *Midlands.* 1790. I. p. 32 c.f. *Communications to the Board of Agriculture.* 1797. I. pt. i. pp. 21-29.

[9] A Farmer. *Rural recreations.* 1802. July p. 34. Aug. p. 50. Sir John Sinclair. *Code of agriculture.* 1817. p. 194. R. W. Dickson. *Practical agric.* 1804. I. pp. 52–55.

[10] John Bravender. *Farming of Gloucester.* J.R.A.S.E. 1850. p. 152.

[11] J. E. *On the arrangement of farm buildings.* The Plough. vol. I (Jan.–June, 1846) pp. 575, 576. G. H. Andrews. *Modern Husbandry.* 1853. pp. 78, 79.

[12] J. C. Morton. *Handbook of dairy husbandry*. 1860. pp. 36, 37. Alex. Taylor. *Farmers guide*. 1829. p. 229.

[13] J. C. Morton. *The Prince Consort's farms*. 1863.

[14] Pringle and Murray. *Practical farming*. c. 1865. pt. ii. p. 19 ff. Copland. *Agric. ancient and modern*. 1866. I. pp. 751, 752.

[15] Stephens' *Book of the farm*. 3rd ed. 1877. I. pp. 177, 189. Burn. *Directory . . .* 1881. pp. 50–53.

[16] Pilley. *Scientific agric.* 1881. p. 218. F. Impey of Birmingham. *My small dairy farm.* appendix to C. W. Stubbs. *The land and the labourer.* 1885. p. 195. Upton. *Profitable dairy farming.* 1888. pp. 7, 9, 13. Robert Wallace. *The farm livestock of Great Britain.* 1889. p. 139. James Long. *The dairy farm.* 1889. pp. 46–48. Prof. Muir. *Maintenance of dairy cows.* Jour. Bath and West Soc. 4th ser. (1895) p. 57, 60, 61. Hugh A. Macewen. *Public milk supply.* 1900. pp. 95–116.

## NOTES ON CHAPTER III (ii)

[1] Seebohm. *Evolution of the English farm.* 1952. p. 198. Surflet. p. 22.

[2] *Blundell's diary.* 1952. pp. 53, 54.

[3] *Country housewife.* 6th ed. 1736 (1728). p. 88.

[4] Hazard. *On making butter and cheese.* Letters and papers of the Bath and West Soc. III (1788) pp. 137, 138. Willich. *Domestic Encyclo.* 1802.

[5] Marshall. *Gloucester.* 2nd ed. 1796. I. pp. 265, 266 II. pp. 157, 158, 179.

[6] Rosamund Bayne-Powell. *Housekeeping in the 18th century.* 1956. pp. 61, 62.

[7] Anderson. *Recreations in agric.* 1800. III. pp. 402–419. A Farmer. *Rural recreations.* 1802. Sept. pp. 66, 67. Robert Forsyth. *Principles and practice of agric.* 1804. II. p. 449. R. W. Dickson. *Practical agric.* 1804. I. pp. 56, 57. Loudon. *Encyclo. of agric.* 1831. p. 1037. Young. *Farmers calendar.* new ed. 1804. April, pp. 234, 235. Parkinson. *Treatise on livestock.* 1810. I. pp. 36–39. J. Twamley and ors. *Essays on management of dairy.* 1816. pp. 3, 104 fn.

[8] A. Lawson. *Modern farrier.* 8th ed. 1925. pp. 381, 382. Taylor, *Farmers guide.* 1929. p. 231. Loudon. *Encyclo.* 1831. pp. 1037–38. Baxters *Library.* 1836. p. 141.

[9] James Jackson. *Treatise on agric. and dairy husb.* 1840. p. 108. Low. *Pract. agric* 1843. p. 641. George Nicholls. *The farmer.* 1844. p. 179. J.E. *On the arrangement of farm buildings.* Plough. I (1846) p. 575.

[10] *Farmers Magazine.* 1848. Copland. *Agric.* 1866. p. 744.

[11] Morton. *Prince Consort's farms.* 1863. c.f. Burrett. *Walk to Land's End.* 1868. p. 341.

[12] Olmstead. *Walks and talks.* 1852. p. 101. Milburn. *The cow.* c. 1851. pp. 79, 80. Andrews. *Rudimentary treatise on agricultural engineering.* 1852–3. idem. *Mod. husb.* 1853. pp. 88, 89. C. S. Read. *Farming of Bucks.* J.R.A.S.E. 1855. p. 299.

[13] Joseph Harding. *On the construction and heating of dairy and cheese rooms.* J.R.A.S.E. 1868; also in Jour. Bath and West Soc. 1868. Morton. *Handbook.* 1860. pp. 48, 68. Voelcker. *Milk.* J.R.A.S.E. 1863. pp. 291–293. Pringle and Murray. *op. cit.* pp. 35, 45. Macdonald. *Cattle, sheep and deer.* 1872. pp. 118, 119. J. Bowen Jones. *Somerset prize farms.* J.R.A.S.E. 1875. pp. 529, 547. Coleman. *Cattle, sheep and pigs.* 1887 (1875) pp. 92, 93. Stephens *Book of the farm.* 1877. II. pp. 239, 242. Roland. *Farming.* 1879. pp. 52–59.

[14] Ward and Locks' *Book of farm management.* c. 1880. p. 328. Scott Burn. *Directory.* 1881. pp. 50–62. Pilley. *Scientific agric.* 1881. pp. 229, 230.

[15] Coleman. *Farm prize competition*, 1884. J.R.A.S.E. 1884. F. Punchard *Dairy farming of Westmorland and Cumberland*. Jour. B.D.F.A. VII (1892) p. 112. See also James Long. *British dairy farming*. 1885. *idem. Dairy farm*. 1889. p. 20. John Walker. *Cow and calf*. 1886. pp. 75–77. Scott Burn. *Outlines*. 1888. pt. iv. pp. 36–39. Sheldon. *The farm and the dairy*. 1889. p. 62.

[16] T. Horsfall. *Management of dairy cattle*. J.R.A.S.E. 1856. p. 275. George Gibbons. *The practice of Cheddar cheese making*. *ibid*. 1890. pp. 101, 102.

[17] James Muir. *Manual of dairy work*. 1893. pp. 85–87. Henry J. Webb. *Advanced agric*. 1894. pp. 608, 609. W. J. Malden. *Farm buildings*. 1896. pp. 32–34, 40, 56, 147. C. W. Walker-Tisdale & Theodore R. Robinson. *Butter making on the farm*. 1913 (1903). pp. 10–16. c.f. Ronald T. Needham. *Modern farm dairy equipment*. 1952. pp. 1–4.

# CHAPTER IV

## *Equipment*

### (i). The age of simplicity

The Tudor dairy farmer had no very great range of equipment. All the work from milking to the processes of butter and cheese making was done manually. The most valuable piece was therefore the human hand, that of the much praised and criticised dairymaid. A skilful, cleanly wench was beyond price in the dairy and it was not until the end of the nineteenth century that her experience and ability began to be superseded by machines.

The Tudor preference was for twice milking. There were advocates for three times, but Markham, writing in the early seventeenth century, thought two good milkings better than three poor ones, an irrefutable argument. It was the housewife's business to set the time for milking in the morning and evening at a convenient hour, and when the cows were at rest. The best times were between five and six in the morning, and six and seven at night. The best milkers sat on the near side of the cow, and handled her gently at first, stretching her dugs and moistening them with a little milk. They were very careful to fix the pail firmly on the ground until the cow was settled, but had to be on the watch all the time, and the milkmaid who moved jerkily or suddenly only startled the cow; she must have a care to be gentle. If after some trial a cow was not 'gentle and affable to the Maid and patient to have her dugs drawn without skittishness, striking or wildness she is utterly unfit for the dairy', and ought to be culled.

Great emphasis was laid upon the necessity for hygiene in the milkhouse and dairy, a subject that many later advisers insisted upon when the sources of contamination were better understood, and methods of control worked out. The best that the Tudors could do was to keep their premises very clean, and, if their practice had been as good as their precept, it would have been a very good best. The maids must see to it that the buildings harboured 'no least moat of any filth', and to keep it so 'void of sowerness or sluttishness that a Prince's bedchamber must not exceed it'. She must keep her milk vessels sweet and clean. The housewife, too, must be exacting in her supervision. As Tusser put it:

> The housewife, to make her own cheese,
> Through trusting of others, hath this for her fees;
> Her milk pan and cream pot, so slabbered and sost;
> That butter is wanting, and cheese is half lost.

Surflet added the odd precept that 'none of her maides have anything to do with either the butter or cheese when they have their termes'.

Opinion had not yet decided whether wood, earthenware, or lead was the best material out of which the milk pans should be made, but each had its virtues. Dr. W. E. Minchinton has recently suggested that tinplate was sometimes used, but, if so, it was not mentioned in the textbooks. It is therefore rather doubtful, and, if ever used, must have been so rare as not to excite comment. Earthenware pans were principally used when it was necessary to keep the milk for a day or two; leaden vessels raised the most cream and shallow circular wooden pans were best if kept in a cold vault. Whatever material they were made of the milk pans and other things ought to be carefully scalded once a day, and set in the open air to sweeten, 'lest getting any taint of sowreness into them, they corrupt the milk that is put in'.

The complete range of dairy equipment was limited to buckets, milk pans, cream pots, churns, cheese vats, a syle dish and straining cloths. The steward's accounts of Sir William Darrell's estates at Littlecote and Axford, Wilts., show purchases of all these things except a syle dish, and that was a necessity. Shakespeare, whose work describes so many phases of country life, only mentions churns when Puck mischievously interferes, and 'Bootless makes the housewife's churn'. The churn was 'a vessel rather deep than big, round and

Gilander fashion; although in some places they have other kind of Charmes low and flat wherein . . . they so stroke the milke'. Cheese presses were another essential, and are included in many Bedfordshire inventories dated 1619 and 1620.[1]

As soon as the milk was brought home—the cows were often milked in the pastures—the dairymaids strained it from all unclean things 'through a neat and sweet kept Syledish, the forme whereof every housewife knows'. Markham consequently did not describe it for posterity. Hale was more detailed a century and a half later. The syle or soiling dish was a wooden bowl with the bottom cut out, and, when in use, the bottom was covered with a very clean washed linen cloth of very fine mesh that would not allow the least mote or hair to pass through it.[2]

Milking in the pasture was not confined to the good weather if Shakespeare's casual reference to the season when 'milk comes frozen home in the pail' is any guide. Evelyn, when laying out Sayes Court in 1652, set out a pleasant plot beyond the east wall of the bowling green to be called the Milking Close. It was planted with eight walnut trees under which the cows were milked. The milkmaid was a favourite with the seventeenth century 'character' writers, and Isaac Walton saw a mother and daughter engaged in this idyllic occupation in Hampshire in 1653. They sang one of Kit Marlowe's ditties and another of Raleigh's, 'like nightingales', and were so happy that Isaac was enchanted and as he listened he was surprised to see them set to work again. This pleased him so much that he then and there decided to make them a present of a chubb he had just caught.[3] These maids were none too highly paid, and were expected to do other household work besides milking, and butter and cheese making. About £2 a year plus board and lodging was usual. At Broadway, Worcestershire a dairy maid or chief maid was paid £2 in 1663. The Purefoy family, who lived in Buckinghamshire, wanted a maid in 1737 who could cook, and, if she turned out well, offered to provide a young maid

'to stand at the Buck tub (wash tub), milk the cows, serve

the hogs, and help scald the milk vessels. The first, who would milk the cows at the gate by the house, was to be paid £3 to £3 10s. and the second £2 a year'.[4]

Farmer Clerk of Holt, Wiltshire thought a good maid could milk six cows even though his wife had done eight, as this was an exceptional number. Both Chivers and Stephens of that county agreed and if they meant in an hour this was about the rate of working that was normal until the coming of the milking machine. James Adam, nearly a century later, was more ambitious. A good Norfolk dairymaid could take care of twenty cows, and John Billingsley then thought a Somerset maid could do the same 'so far as indoor work is concerned', which may mean making butter and cheese. Though it varied from district to district the average may have been ten.

The *Dictionarium Rusticum* of 1717 repeated Markham's advice about hygiene, the use of milk pans made of different materials, methods and times of milking, so it may be assumed that there had been little or no change in practice or equipment in the seventeenth century. Lisle advised that the milk should be allowed to stand to cool before it was strained, and put in the milk pans, otherwise the cream would not rise so well. Moreover the milk coming hot into the dairy steam heated the air in the room to the loss of cream. Susanna Whatman emphasised this point adding that in hot weather it was sometimes necessary to put some cold pump water into the pans to make the milk throw up well and everyone agreed upon the necessity for completely stripping the cows and milking them gently at regular hours.[5] The controversy about twice or three times milking continued—with a definite preference for morning and evening only.

For a dairy of twelve cows William Ellis said, in 1750 that four large milking pails were required, made with oak bottoms and ash sides, which ought to be rinsed with cold water every night. After the following morning milking they must be scrubbed with ashes or sand, and boiled about two minutes in the copper. A cooling tub to hold 30 gallons was used before the milk was poured into 'kivers' to set the cream.

These were round and shallow wooden tubs on leaden stands. It was a good idea to have some of each. The wooden ones were made of oak with broad ashen hoops. Leaden stands made of milled lead fastened in deal frames were provided with a cork hole in the middle of each for letting out the milk, and leaving the cream behind, a principle that came more into fashion later. Apparently these leaden stands were invented at Leighton Buzzard where there was one five feet long by three feet wide, costing 20s. The wooden vessels were brushed with a hard brush and boiling water, then rinsed and set to dry. Small ones could be conveniently boiled in the copper. The leads were cleansed with a wisp of straw or hay, wood or bean straw ashes and boiling water. Besides these, twelve earthen cream pots were necessary which after use must be boiled in the copper. An oaken barrel churn, two feet diameter and three feet long on a wooden stand and fitted with two handles to turn it was all else a butter farm required. It too must be carefully cleaned, first rinsed with a pail of warm water, and then two pails of boiling water put in to stand for fifteen minutes. Bradley (1735) knew of some places where the farmers did not know the use of the churn. Their cream was agitated by hand to make butter as the scalded cream of the southwest was for so much longer. He did not approve, saying there was no better way of making butter than in a churn, or something equivalent to it.

Ellis preferred the barrel churn to the old plunger type that had been in general use for so long as it made for 'dispatch, ease and profit'. He had one of firkin size which the Cambridge dairy farmers all used. He also preferred the square wooden cooler lined with sheet lead used in that county for setting cream 'in place of the old-fashioned brass pan', nowhere else mentioned, that gave a slight tang to the cream. Earthen glazed pans were a good substitute for those who could not afford leads. A great oval or round tub was constantly used in summer to cool the milk before it was put into the leaden 'kivers', while warm water was sometimes used in winter to adjust the temperature. The other requisites were, he said, well known to every dairymaid and to some sorts of shopkeepers. Straining sieves, pails, trenchers, weights and scales, baskets, trays, and other things formed his incomplete list.[6]

Some gentlemen, who were encouraged by the current enthusiasm for agriculture, rather over-elaborated their dairies by introducing imported China utensils. These had a highly glazed surface and were easy to clean, but in Hales' opinion were no whit better than glazed earthenware of which the surface was obtained in the same way. Hale preferred glazed earthenware to lead or wood, but others thought wood the best material and it became a question that was never definitely answered. Lead setting pans were used for setting cream long after the cream separator was invented.

William Marshall towards the end of the 18th century studied the dairying of Gloucester and North Wilts with great care. In that area the cows were brought home to be milked if the pastures were near the house, but if more distant the pails were carried to the cows. The milking pail was made of oaken staves with ash hoops, and a handle formed of one stave rising three or four inches above the rim rather like the similar Yorkshire 'skeel' with one handle. It was about ten inches deep and fifteen in diameter. Near Swindon the milk pails were hooped with iron, and fitted with an iron bow so that it could be carried on yokes in the London manner. Some Gloucestershire dairymen used a horse and barrel cart to bring the milk home from distant pastures. The other utensils used were:

Milk cooler, provincially termed a 'cheese cowl', a wooden vessel 18" to 2' deep, provided with two opposite staves rising above the rim, each having a hole in it large enough to take a pole for carrying on the shoulders.

Strainer or milk sieve 12" to 14" diameter and 5" to 6" deep, some having hair and some cloth bottoms, which were taken out every day to wash. This was the syle dish. A frond or leaf of fern was frequently put at the bottom of the sieve to prevent milk flying over.

Sieve holder or ladder laid across the holder to place the milk sieve on, and fixed by two crossbars that fitted one handle of the cooler.

Lading dish 1′ diameter.

Pail brushes, i.e., common hard brushes with hard bristles at the end to clean out angles of utensils more effectively.

Pail stroke—a bough with many branches firmly fixed in the ground, each branch a peg to hang a pail upon.

Skeels—broad shallow vessels of oak and ash for setting cream.

Skimming dishes. By this date chiefly made of tin, 8″ diameter, $\frac{5}{8}$″ deep. If of wood these must be very thin.

Cream jars—earthenware of middle size.

Cream slice—a wooden knife shaped like a table knife, 10″-12″ long.

Churns—upright or barrel churns (John Raistrick had taken out the first patent for one of the latter in 1777, but some were in use before then). In Gloucestershire barrel churns were fitted with one loose and one fixed handle.

Butter board and trowell, prints and scales.

Cheese knife, a wooden handle 4″ or 5″ long furnished with 2 or 3 blades 12″ long by 1″ broad at handle: $\frac{3}{4}$″ at point with a space of about 1″ between each blade: flat sides towards each other: later known as curd knife or curd breaker.

Cheese vats made of elm, 15″ diameter: $1\frac{1}{2}$-2″ deep, some with but some without holes.

Cheese cloths.

Cheese press—of various construction: some single, some double: pressure mostly a dead weight: raised by a roller and falling perpendicularly on the cheese. In Wilts. a box filled with sand or gravel weighing 4 cwt. was used.[7]

Both in Gloucester and in Wiltshire the whole strength of the family and servants was enlisted at milking time with the one exception of the teamsman, and the cows were milked 'unfettered', the milkers sitting on four-legged, square topped stools, resting one side of the bottom of the large pail against two legs of the stool. At least one man was employed about the dairy to help the maids with the heavier work, which was a surprise to Marshall who thought it highly desirable;

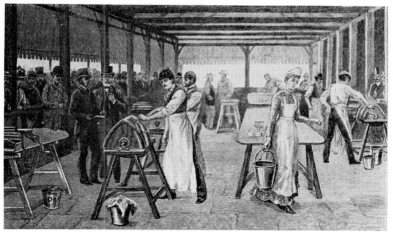

THE BUTTER MAKING COMPETITION AT THE ROYAL AGRICULTURAL SOCIETY'S
SHOW AT WINDSOR, 1889

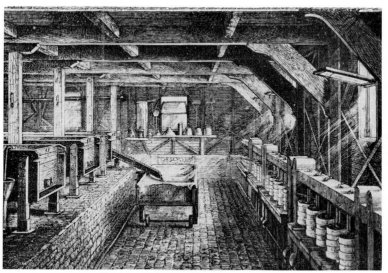

LONGFORD CHEESE FACTORY—INTERIOR

MILK AND BUTTER MAKING IN THE OPEN AIR, 1835

WORKING A PLUNGE CHURN

the women were still moving heavy cheeses and doing other unsuitable labour in the middle of the nineteenth century. In Essex men did the milking if not the butter making.

Marshall could find little to say about the Norfolk dairy-women that would redound to their credit and his exhortations to cleanliness as the basis of the whole art, emphasise his criticism.

'A dairymaid should not be allowed to sit down under a cow with a pail a fine lady would scruple to cool her tea in; nor until she has washed the teats of the cow and her own hands: and for the purpose clean water and a cloth should always be at hand'.[8]

The cheese vats used in the Midland counties were merely hoops of ash with a broad bottom, fifteen inches diameter and two inches deep. A fillet, formerly of ash about one inch wide, was fixed to the top when necessary. Tin fillets were used in place of wood at the end of the eighteenth century. These were admirable but care must be taken to prevent them rusting.[9]

By that time inventors had become interested in producing new designs of churns and other well established dairy implements and utensils. Most of their ingenuity was devoted to churns and cheese presses, the only two articles then in use that could be adapted for easier working by the application of simple mechanical principles. In the North there were at this date butter churns worked by horse gear, and possibly horse gears had been put to this use elsewhere, but it must have been the exception rather than the rule as it remained throughout the nineteenth century. Willich applauded the new inventions as the churns in general use were inferior. C. Harland of Fenchurch Street had produced a plunger churn fitted with a wheel and crank to make the motion smooth. Similar appliances were attached to barrel churns for the same purpose. W. Bowler was awarded a prize of 30 guineas by the Society of Arts in 1795 for a barrel churn agitated by levers, and given a semi-rotary motion. It was fitted with internal blades. This was also known as Bowles' pendulum churn. Both Anderson and Twamley however preferred the old

M

fashioned upright churn to all others because it could be easily cleaned, and it continued to be used, though in what relative numbers cannot be determined. It was used in Westmorland until the 1840's. The butter churn must have held a peculiar fascination for inventors. Innumerable patents were taken out during the nineteenth century, and the designs were as ingenious as they were various: but the general principle in all of them was dictated by the fundamental necessity of agitating the cream until the butter came.[10]

The advances in chemistry that were being made caused some advisers to be chary of the metal pans that had for so long been used for setting cream. A strong preference for wooden vessels was expressed as lead, copper and cast iron were all easily soluble in acids, and the solutions of the first two poisonous. The third was innocuous, but the taste of it might render the products disagreeable. Twamley (1787) thought wood very much better than the lead or earthenware then recently in request for pails, sieves, bowls, creaming dishes and churns. The cast iron setting bowls, which had just been produced by Baird of Shott's Ironworks, Whitburn, were more durable than wood. They were softened by annealing in charcoal, turned smooth inside and given a thin coat of tin to prevent the iron coming into contact with the milk, or forming rust. The outside of the pan was painted to prevent rusting. It was the least objectionable of all the metal pans in Lawson's view, cooler than wood, and throwing up one-third more cream. It was first made in 1806. Lead, brass and copper were 'altogether inadmissable'. The lead glaze used on earthenware vessels dissolved in the milk acids as did the lead lined vessels to form a poisonous compound. This was a strong argument against their use, but the farmers may have paid little attention to all this discussion. They went on using utensils made of all these materials.[11]

The process of milking remained manual throughout the century, but a very modern note was struck by John Lawrence a hundred and fifty years ago. He liked the cows to be hobbled when they were being milked, but in addition he advocated the Continental practice of currying and brushing the cows. The bag should be kept well trimmed, and the teats perfectly clean, especially during the winter when liable to be chapped. Milk should not be used for washing, but warm soap and water, and the parts carefully dried with a cloth. The tails also ought to be kept clean. The necessity for scrupulous cleanliness in all parts of the dairy was a corollary, and was strongly advised by all the writers. The largest number of cows that could be handled effectively by one maid was agreed to be no more than twelve or fourteen, and the time occupied in milking remained constant. Detailed supervision was the most important thing in dairy management. This could not be entrusted to a hireling, but was the important office of the farmer's wife and daughters. The hours worked were very long; Young thought a dairymaid should be up at 4 o'clock in the morning and often they worked from that time until 10 o'clock at night—even longer at busy seasons in butter and especially in cheese dairies. These long hours were worked until at least 1868-1869. As prosperity increased during the wartime inflation some wives and daughters tried to avoid all this work, and some of it was given up in favour of suckling calves, but the extent of this change may have been exaggerated.[12]

In Cheshire all the man had to do was to provide a proper stock of cows, and look after his white and green crops. The fair dairywomen of the county, of whom it was impossible to speak but in terms of approbation, did the work that made up his rent. They used the plunger churn if the dairy was small, but a barrel churn was installed in the larger dairies as it was in Gloucester and Essex. The Cheshire milk cooler stood on feet like a table, and was a lead cistern nine inches deep, five feet long, two and a half feet wide, with a cock or spigott at the bottom for drawing off the milk. In some places extensive dairies used very large coolers 'several feet or even yards long'. One or two writers mention the patent box churn in the late 1820's, but the number of types was then increasing very rapidly. Loudon mentions the new lactometer, a glass tube with a funnel at the top graduated for measuring cream. He also subscribed to the idea of washing the udder and teats with warm water before milking, as did James Jackson. By 1840 it was common to employ male milkers in the south and midland counties, but Jackson thought females better. They were likely to do the work in a more gentle and cleanly manner, something of essential importance.[13] The heavy work and protracted hours of women on the dairy farms was unfavourably commented upon in 1843 and in 1867-8, especially that involved in turning cheeses. On farms where butter was the main object the work was less arduous.[14]

Jackson, in 1840, was able to say that dairy utensils were very numerous, but that in form, with few exceptions, they were very much alike throughout Great Britain and indeed in other countries as well. The majority were made of wood and that was generally approved. Some of the best dairies then had coolers of cast iron, wood lined with tin, or glazed earthenware. In Westmorland lead pans began to be used in the 1830's, but tin had supplanted them by 1912. Zinc was beginning to be used in the 1840's, and was thought, like lead, to throw up more cream. Marble or slate was recommended. Excellent slate ones were made by Mr. Hind, Slate Pits, Swithland, near Leicester, and it was thought that the black slate found on Lord Penrhyn's estate might be good as the material would take as high a polish as marble.

Churning, too, had begun to be done by machinery, either horse or water power, or 'attached to the threshing machine'. The plunge churn was most commonly used, the plunge worked by a lever with a shaft and crank moved by a wheel outside the dairy. In the 'syle' dish a hair or wire gauze sieve, sometimes of silver had been introduced to take the place of the linen cloth of earlier days.[15]

By 1850 invention had come to the aid of the dairy farmer as it had to most other trades, but only to a limited extent. On many farms power was beginning to be used to do the more arduous work, and new utensils were offered. The age of simplicity was drawing to its end, but it had not passed away entirely by the end of the century. The old ways were still followed, especially in the smaller and more remote farms, but everywhere new apparatus was then being installed. The developments in the last fifty years of the nineteenth century laid the foundations of the modern dairy industry.

## (ii). A half century of inventions

Horse power was first applied to driving churns in the eighteenth century. The apparatus was very large because the gearing was made of wood by a local millwright. Mechanism of this kind was used in such widely separated places as Buckingham and South Wales. The horse walked round in a circle of thirteen to fifteen feet diameter, and the harness was attached to a large overhead wooden gear wheel having about 240 teeth by means of a fork suspended from the wheel. The movement was transmitted through two gear wheels on a vertical spindle to a barrel churn. The method is clearly shown in the illustration—much better than it can be described verbally.

The Science Museum had in 1930 three models of plunger churns originally submitted to the Highland and Agricultural Society early in the nineteenth century. In each of these the churning was carried out by paired plungers reciprocating vertically in a pair of churns.[1]

By 1853 there were a good many different types of churn on the market. Of these the barrel churn and the dash churn were the oldest types, the former being at least a century, and the latter several centuries old. Internally the barrel was studded with perforated beaters, revolving on two axles or gudgeons, and thus agitating the cream. The dash churn was worked with a piston perforated with holes attached to the bottom end of a piston rod pushed up and down. Both types were sometimes on a large scale, and worked by mechanical power.

Dray's double action churn was one of the last. It had a 'double perpendicular action by which the plunger of the downward strokes forced the cream through the middle partition of the vessel, following the upward plunger; so that at the reversion of the cranks, the cream was met by the plungers and forced backwards and forwards in rapid succession, "crasing" and agitating it in a few minutes into small particles of butter; after which, by slowly turning the crank, the small particles adhering to each other, quickly become into a condition to be taken out'.

Two American churns then being imported were modifications of the box churn. Dolphin's was made on a self-adjusting rotary principle. Internally it was fitted with slats set at such angles as to force the cream to the centre where it was met by moveable floats which stood open when revolving, and caused the cream to move outwards. These various and contrary motions so agitated the cream that butter was soon produced. Anthony's churn was a simpler version of this type being fitted with fixed instead of moveable slats. Motion was given manually by turning a handle.

The box churn was simply a box in which four dashers worked on a spindle that passed through its centre. The dasher was composed of slats of wood fixed at intervals on two pieces which radiated from the spindle. As these were made to revolve they agitated the cream. The American churns had 'cellular' slats, which presumably means perforated, and this caused a larger quantity of air to be carried down to the cream as churning proceeded, and therefore expedited the separation of the butter.

Glass and metal had then recently been introduced for making the boxes and barrels of churns, but the dairymen preferred wood, although it was more difficult to keep clean.[2]

The principle of forcing air into the cream was not limited to the American type of box churn, but was introduced in the so-called 'atmospheric' churns that appeared at about the same date or a little later. Examples of these were included in the Science Museum collection in 1930. One was a rectangular box fitted with a horizontal axle carrying four radial paddles, these being alternately perforated and solid. The cover of this churn had two handles which were hollow and served as air passages. Another was a portable tin cylinder within which a disc or piston slid freely. This piston was fitted with a tubular rod, terminating in a cross handle so that it could be reciprocated. The disc and rod were heavily perforated, and jets of milk or air were forced through the holes as the churn was worked. A removable cover closed the vessel and prevented splashing. If worked fairly quickly it caused the butter to come in 10 or 15 minutes. Large churns of this pattern were made with a crank motion for driving, and they seem to have been very similar to what was known as the common Sussex churn in 1860, a fixed horizontal tin cylinder with a horizontal axis, and beaters of flattened tin tubes. Rowan's churn of this date was an oval tub open at the top, and divided vertically into two parts, one containing the beaters and the other with a wire screen to catch the butter globules as they were formed. Clyburn had produced a churn driven by steam at this date, and Standing of Preston had patented a sun and planet churn.[3]

A trial of churns was made in 1851, but it is difficult to decide whether this was undertaken in connection with the Great Exhibition, or at the annual Royal Show. Two trials were run. Thirteen churns competed at the first, and medals were awarded to the Lavoisie a French design, the Wilkinson, an English and that of Burgess and Key, an American. The Duchene, a French churn, was also considered entitled to a medal and this may mean that it received one. These, and the Clare, another French churn not included in the first trial, were given a shorter test in the second trial. No more detail of this equipment is provided beyond the fact that the Lavoisie and the Clare were made of tin, the Wilkinson and the Burgess and Key were wooden box apparatus, and the Duchene a wooden barrel churn.[3a]

In spite of all these inventions Pringle and Murray did not think it necessary to include a description of mechanical churns in their *Practical Farming*, 1865. The plunger churn, though laborious in use, was then used on most farms, but where there was a large quantity of milk it was worked by a machine crank. The barrel churn was even then competing strongly with it, and had, according to Roland taken its place by 1879. This is too definite for some plunger churns were in use much later. Burgess and Key's American dasher churn is mentioned by Pringle and Murray. Common box churns were more used by 1879 and so were power churns. The dimensions of a common box churn about 1880 were 17″ x 12″ x 16″ deep, rectangular in form, but bevelled below so as to present an octagonal section in the vertical plane. It was fitted with beaters that revolved inside it. The barrel churn was 18″ long by 18″ at its largest diameter, and was fitted with two internal beaters. This size was effective for a dairy of 6 cows. For a smaller number a plunge churn was still extensively used. Allways then produced a tin barrel churn and an oscillating rectangular churn was on the market, amongst numerous other designs.[4]

Trials of churns were again made with the other dairy implements and machinery tested at the Bristol 'Royal' Show in 1879. Two classes were examined, the first being of churns capable of dealing with enough milk to produce not more than 20 lb. of butter and the second of those capable of dealing with enough cream to produce the same quantity. There were nineteen entries made by fourteen manufacturers in the first class. Of these all came to trial. In the second class there were thirty nine entries but only sixteen came to the test. A line of shafting driven by a steam engine was fixed in the trial shed to provide power. Most of the churns were barrel churns, which either revolved or were fitted with internal beaters or dashers that were turned inside them. The most outstanding in the milk class was Ahlborn's prize Holstein churn, which differed materially from anything used in this country. It was a vertical barrel, slightly conical in shape, hung from central pivots so as to be easily turned upside down for cleaning or emptying. It was supported on a wood frame. A wooden spindle, with two thin wings or strips of wood 3″

wide, ran on a central boss in the middle of the churn, a plunge motion being communicated by bevel gear wheels actuated by a pulley driven by a strap. It was in effect a mechanical plunge churn. The cream churns were either barrels with revolving beaters or barrels with fixed beaters, but Thomas and Taylor entered a six-sided eccentric churn operated manually by a handle. This won the first prize. Another point of variation was the system of ventilation, which was by an air valve that in some designs could readily be made self-acting. These trials led to no very firm conclusion.[5]

The innumerable variety of churns was remarked both by James Long and J. P. Sheldon in the 1880's. Both described the same types, and presumably chose them for efficiency. The former in 1889 considered a steam or gas engine or strong horse was necessary on a dairy farm to provide power for working the dairy implements. The Holstein churns were prominent in Sheldon's mind, but both he and Long praised the Victoria churn made by Waide of Leeds. This was a cylindrical container with no inside beaters, swinging on two vertical supports and turned end over end by the handle in work. This motion was thought to provide sufficient agitation without beaters. Other end over end churns were roughly rectangular in shape with rounded corners. Waide also made a barrel churn which stood on one end, and was worked manually with a plunger like the old plunge churn, as well as a barrel churn placed horizontally on supports and turned with a handle. The absence of internal fittings made these easy to clean. Bradford's Diaphragm churn was fitted with internal beaters. Another design was the Steamlet churn. This was a flat circular container fixed on a stand, in which beaters were turned by a wheel. Steam, horse and even dog power were used to give motion to the action.[6]

A new principle was introduced by J. H. Duncan of 39 Coleman Street, London in 1893, when he showed his Disc churn at the 'Royal' Show. The judges considered it one of the chief features of the implement yard. It was an oblong box with a circular bottom in the centre of which a plain wooden disc was mounted on a shaft and revolved vertically.

The motion given by the handle was multiplied by gearing so that 40 r.p.m. of the handle gave about 600 r.p.m. to the disc, which, for 8 quarts, was about 15" diameter, $1\frac{1}{8}$" thick at the shaft and bevelled to a knife edge at the circumference. The top of the box was open, but the disc was covered by a hood or dasher, a sort of inverted trough about 3" wide. Worked half full of cream the effect was to pick it up on the disc, and throw it with some force against the hood, thus causing the butter granules to form. It worked effectively and quickly when tried, and could be used to wash the butter if water was added.[7]

It was partly the exhibition of this quickly working churn and the award made to it that determined the Royal Agricultural Society to hold a third series of comprehensive trials at Cambridge the following year, but their decision may have been partly the result of the Show being held in a district where there was some dairy farming. The churns tried were again divided into two classes, those capable of dealing with 10 quarts of cream and more, and those using 5 to 10 quarts. Neither class was to require more than one man-power to work it.

Two other disc churns competed in the first class. They were on the same principle as the Duncan Disc Churn, but both had twin discs. In one the discs were concave at the periphery; in the other divided into points and therefore called star discs. Vincent's churn, another entry in the first class, was a box churn in which a dasher was placed upon an oblique spindle, and made to revolve quickly by cog-wheel gearing at the upper end of the spindle. Bradford's Fishback was a box churn in which a cylinder of wood studded with pegs, placed horizontally, was made to revolve quickly by chain gearing. The same firm's Horseshoe had no novel features except an arrangement of a fan and temperature cans for regulating 'temperature and ventilation'. 'This arrangement', reported the judges succinctly, 'is not a success'. Indeed the temperature chambers fitted to the entries were seldom used in practice, and were probably of no advantage. The other entries were so well-known that the judges thought they required no description. They were some of the end over end diaphragm churns mentioned above, and these were successful in securing the three prizes awarded in the first class.

The first prize was won by Bradford's end over end diaphragm churn, and the second by Llewellin's very similar apparatus. Llewellin's also received the third prize for a churn which worked in the same way but had a different shaped container. It was called the Royal Triangular, and apparently made of metal. The Dairy Supply Co's Victoria churn was another end over end barrel churn. The Star Disc churn was the last on the list. The power required to do the work was measured by using an electric motor, and the disc churn used an 'excessive amount' beyond the one man-power specified. It was difficult to clean because the fitting on which the disc revolved was inaccessible, and a brass top for drawing off the buttermilk was liable to verdigris.[8]

The 1894 churn trials were made at the time when farmers were turning to dairy farming as one way out of the economic difficulties that they were faced with as the world market in agricultural produce developed. Their object was largely the sale of liquid milk rather than the manufacture of butter and cheese. It is therefore probable that their demand for butter churns did not increase, but was already declining by 1914, and thereafter became negligible.

Both whole milk and cream were used for churning into butter. If cream alone was used it had to be separated from the milk, and there had been an ancient and prolonged controversy about the best materials out of which the cream raising pans should be made. Before putting in the setting pans the milk was cooled and strained, and the use of ice had been suggested as early as about 1830 for reducing the temperature of the milk as well as for keeping the temperature of the butter store low. G. A. Dean enlarged the idea in 1849.

That the best possible situation for the butter store and cooling room was inside the ice house was not thought of until about 1880. Very optimistically R. Scott Burn said that a simple arrangement of shelves in the ice house was all that was necessary. If this method was not adopted the temperature could be kept at the correct level in a separate store room by putting masses of ice on tables or having ice safes in it. A building with hollow walls and roof filled with insulating material, and a grating under the floor in which ice could be placed was another suggestion. Again ice boxes could be put in the ventilating shafts which supplied the building with air.

By the date of Sheldon's exhaustive treatise on dairy farming large quantities of milk were being carried long distances by rail so that it was essential for it to be cooled before it was sent to the station just as it was before it was set for cream. Sheldon was acquainted with the Swedish method of using ice and snow for raising cream, and considered it more efficacious than the old system of setting the milk in open pans without any cooling agency. He made elaborate calculations of the quantity of ice required by a dairy using these methods. For 50 gallons a day in a district where the mean annual temperature was 50°F. about 36 tons would be required per annum, so that about 50 tons would have to be stored to allow for waste by melting. For this quantity a space about 2,600 cubic feet was necessary.

An ice house to hold this amount could, he said, be built on any farm at a moderate cost and in a simple manner. The cheapest was that partly underground, and where good drainage was easy to arrange. He thought that in England it was perhaps better to store snow because it could be trodden into a solid mass easily, and was generally to be had even in winters when there was no ice.

The use of natural ice in the dairy had a short life. The coming of large scale refrigeration and cold storage did away with the need for collecting ice to preserve butter and other perishables. It was superseded almost as soon as it was thought of for pre-cooling milk. Lawrence's so-called refrigerator was cheap and efficient and used only water. This cooler was shown at the Royal Show at Cardiff in 1872, but before this it had been used by brewers for cooling beer. The judges thought it equally useful for cooling milk before sending it away by rail, and before setting it for cream.

The principle is the same as most modern coolers. A small quantity of cold water, passing upwards in a very thin stream between two corrugated sheets of metal rapidly abstracted the heat from two very shallow streams of milk descending outside the metal sheets. The water inlet was at the lowest part, but the supply came from a higher level, and so flowed upwards though the cooler by gravity being let out by a pipe at the top. A tank was placed above this into which the milk was poured. A tap in the bottom of the tank regulated the flow of milk into a small perforated trough at the top of the refrigerator. The milk flowed through the holes and was spread in a fine sheet that followed the corrugations in the surface of the metal. It gradually cooled as it descended, the water warming at the same rate as it ascended until exhausted at the top. The descending milk fell into a container below the apparatus. By this process 'the odour of the cow', too, was removed from the milk. The dairy farmers were not slow in adopting so useful an adjunct, and by 1879 it was already well known to the farming community. In that year it was the only cooler actually tried at the Royal Show though there were four other exhibitors. Two years later H. M. Jenkins thought it so well known that he need do no more than allude to it.[9]

Milk that had been cooled in the Lawrence refrigerator was ready to go to the station or to be set for cream. The common method of setting in pans continued to be used, and the material best for this purpose to be argued until the end of the century when the old leads were still to be seen in some farm dairies. Jenkins, when he went to Sweden for the Royal Agricultural Society found that an ingenious farmer there had perfected a method of raising cream that allowed the Swedish farmers to abandon their ancient way of making butter from sour cream. He was Swartz of Hofgarden near Wadstena.

His system was simple and effective, and its general adoption by Swedish farmers had lent a very high reputation to Swedish butter. Deep cans, oval in shape, about two feet long, twenty inches deep and six inches wide were nearly filled with milk. They were placed upright at intervals in a trough or tank containing a mixture of water and ice, and kept at a temperature of about 39°F. The cans each held 10 gallons, and a moderately sized cistern would hold eight to twelve cans.

When used in England the tank was supplied with a constant flow of cold water from a faucet at one end, and the milk very rapidly cooled from its natural temperature to 50° or 60°F. In hot weather lumps of ice were added to the water. Herbert J. Little who reported on the working dairy at the Royal Show in 1881 thought that this method controlled the germs or organisms which in warm weather 'turned the milk so frequently in old-fashioned dairies with shallow settings'. Sometimes the Swartz cans were fitted with lids, but in the main the narrow surface of the cream exposed to the atmosphere was considered sufficient to protect it from absorbing smells and off-flavours from other things placed in the dairy for coolness sake, or that were adjacent to it.

In America a similar system was worked out. The Cooley creamer, made by the Vermont Farm Machinery Co., and sold by a London firm, was first exhibited in the Kilburn Royal in 1879. It was considered a great novelty, but was recognised to be of the same character as the Swartz. The milk containers used in this system were cylindrical, about twenty inches deep, and eight and a half inches in diameter. They had watertight covers, and were carefully immersed in a watertight container rather like a domestic refrigerator of the time, but having inlet and outlet pipes and a thermometer in the front so that the temperature of the water could be kept even. By using it sweet milk and sweet cream could be obtained even in hot weather. For large concerns, who would preferably use the Swartz system, the water could be kept at a cool, even temperature by a refrigerator similar to that used in brewing.

There was general agreement that these systems were better than the shallow pan method, but in America the shallow pan method was adapted to the water cooling system in the Centennial Milk Pan and Cooler, the essence of which was that the shallow rectangular pans in two sections longitudinally were set in series in a stand about as high as a table. The stand was made to contain water, which flowed in from a faucet at one end and out of a pipe at the other. The flow of water was directed along and across the stand by the transverse bars of wood that supported the milk pans. A tube from the bottom of each pan led through an opening in the stand so that the milk could be drawn off at the proper time, leaving the cream in the pan, whence it could readily be collected.

There was also a cheaper form of the Cooley known as Weldon's Cream Raising Apparatus. The chief difference between it and the Cooley was that the milk cans had perforated foot rings that allowed a free circulation of the water under the cans. The cream was removed from the surface with a long handled conical dipper. This was not so easy nor so efficient as the Cooley system which allowed the milk to run out through a tap so that no skimming was needed, a great saving of time and trouble.

In two other American systems ice only was used. The Harden was a chest having a shelf above the space for the milk cans upon which blocks of ice were placed. The cans stood in about four inches of water, and the cooling was effected by the circulation of cold air, not cold water. Mr. L. S. Hardin, the inventor of this system, condemned the open pan method, even when it was aided by cold water as in the Centennial.

'If the milk is set in water (in open pans), and thus kept cooler than the air, it, of course, condenses the moisture of the air into the surface of the cream, thus drawing down into the surface of the cream all the impurities of the air'.

A much more elaborate creamer was the Bureau Creamer and Refrigerator. This, like the Hardin, used ice placed on shelves above the milk receptacles, but differed chiefly from that in its size and the number of its compartments. It depended on shallow and not deep setting of the milk. The inventor argued that the best keeping butter was made from cream more perfectly separated from the milk than it was in the deep setting systems. The cream ought also to ripen by remaining a longer time on the milk. Contamination by atmospheric impurities was prevented by having the shallow pans accessible to only a little air(!), and that cooled by ice stored above the milk.

This is not a complete list of this type of creamer in all its varieties. Many makers of dairy utensils contrived them. Two well known types were the Jersey and the Dorset, both made by English manufacturers. A great deal of ingenuity was exercised all over the world in designing these creamers, but inventors were most active in this direction during approximately the two decades, 1860-1880. As soon as the centrifugal cream separator was invented all of them were rapidly superseded though authority still recommended the Swartz and Cooley cans in 1894, and put the mechanical separator last in the list of equipment for the small dairy.[10]

The cream separator had been known for some time in Germany, Denmark and Sweden before the de Laval was exhibited at the Royal Show at Kilburn in 1879. It won a silver medal, and was regarded as the most novel exhibit of the year, but farmers felt a little doubtful of its practical value to them. It was likely to be more useful in a butter factory, where its merits in producing perfectly fresh cream, dispensing with ice and saving space and apparatus were mainfest.

The Laval was the first to be shown in this country, but there were several others in use on the Continent. J. P. Sheldon saw an odd one at the International Dairy Show at Hamburg in 1877. It consisted of two wheels on a stand, one of which moved the other by means of a belt. In the upper wheel four glasses holding the milk were fastened securely to a flat bar across the diameter. The lower wheel was then turned by hand giving the upper motion at over 1,000 r.p.m. This whirling motion brought centrifugal force to bear on the tubes, and caused the lighter cream to collect at one end. The separation was said to be complete and well defined, but it was not introduced into this country in competition with the bowl type separator.

Two years after the Laval had been first shown three machines were exhibited at the Royal Show, and by 1882 the importance of the apparatus had been so far established that the Society offered two gold medals for competition. One was given to the Laval shown by Hald and Co. This early machine was practically the same as that used on so many farms today. The milk was put into a metal bowl which was made to revolve at from 6,000 to 7,000 r.p.m. This made the heavier portion, the skim milk, fly to the sides whence it was forced upwards and discharged through a convenient pipe. The cream was left behind, and expelled through a separate pipe. The high speed of working of this machine was rather a disadvantage to the small dairy farmer, whose barn was not equipped with steam power, but the British makers pointed out that it worked perfectly in Sweden when worked by horse gear. The only necessity was that there should be 'intermediate motion'. In other words it should be geared up. Once the farmers were convinced that it could be worked in that way, it would quickly come into general use, as, in fact, it did.

A German machine, the Lefeldt, one of those entered in 1881 and 1882, was similar in principle to the Laval, and had some advantage in its slower rate of work, but was heavy and cumbersome in design. This coupled with its high price of £90, hardly compensated for its slower rate of working, 2,400 r.p.m. A Danish machine, the Neilsen-Peterson, was shown in 1881, and competed for the gold medal in 1882. It was large and rather complicated, and cost £80 as against the Laval price of £37. Its rate of work was only 1,500 r.p.m. and thus was better adapted for horse-gear than any of the others, but the high price was a formidable obstacle. Some other machines were entered, but were prevented from competing because of patent right litigation. The British Dairy Farmer's Association, formed in 1876, recognised the importance of the Laval separator by the award of a gold medal in 1884. It was the foremost of the two makes that shared the market for some years. The other was the Hamburg or Petersen, which did not share the simplicity of the Laval design.

The appliance was of such obvious utility that in a few years other firms were encouraged to produce competitive types. The Laval had been improved by 1887. The following year Freeth and Pocock exhibited the Victoria separator made by Watson, Laidlaw and Co., both at the Royal and the Bath and West Society's shows. This appliance possessed some desirable features. It was constructed so as to be self-skimming, and the Royal judges thought the parts easily accessible for cleaning, an opinion not shared by those of the Bath and West. The Victoria, manually operated, was however used at the Royal Working Dairy in 1889. Listers produced a power driven machine, the Alexandra, in the same year, and several other manual and power separators were to be seen at the Bath and West Society's show.

The use of a separator in the working dairy at the Royal Show was one indication of the growing importance of this implement. The Society recognised this in another way. Both in 1891 and in 1899 it held trials of separators in conjunction with the Show. No new makers entered machines in 1891, but internal discs had then been added to the bowl of the Laval. This was a series of thin steel plates one above the other kept separate by projections on each. They were loosely arranged round the spindle. Later on other firms added something of the same kind to the bowls of their appliances, and the judges in 1899 were so convinced of their utility that they declared that the day of the plain bowl was done. The Dairy Supply Co., won the first prize in 1891 for their Alpha-Windsor machine. Ingenuity was not idle in the 1890's. Freeth and Pocock showed their 'Express' in 1894, and Listers their 'Farmer's Cream Separating Plant' in 1895, the latter being rather elaborate. Wallins' 'Butter Accumulator' an American apparatus, separated the cream and made butter in one operation. It was shown in 1896. The Melotte cream separator was added to the list in 1898, and was tried with other power driven machines, made by Watson, Laidlaw of Glasgow, Fram Dairy Machinery Co. of Holborn Circus, and the Dairy Supply Co., in 1899. Manually operated machines were produced by these firms, by Pond and Son, Blandford,

Dorset and Vipan and Headley of Leicester. Most of these continued to exhibit machines until 1910 when Fullwood and Bland were added to their number.

One early enthusiast, Waldren of Chilcombe Farm, near Bridport, not only used a separator for the milk from his own cows, but also borrowed milk set in pans and skimmed by hand from his neighbours. When he put it through his separator he got an extra quart of cream from five gallons. This proved to his own satisfaction an irrefragible economic argument in favour of the separator.[11]

Butter had been worked manually for centuries, but in the nineteenth century a variety of manually operated butter workers was designed. One of the great advantages of these appliances was that the butter was not touched by hand. The dairymaid with a warm hand was therefore under no handicap. She need not be jealous of her sister who possessed the much valued cold hand.

The design of the appliance was varied as much as possible by the different makers in order to give their special product an individual character, but the main principles of all of them were the same. Some examples were entered for the prizes offered by the Royal Agricultural Society at Bristol in 1879. The entries were divided into two classes, one for large, the other for small dairies. Ahlborn's larger worker won the first prize in its class. It was a circular table, slightly sloping from the centre to the circumference, with a rim at its edge about two inches high. Round the outer edge of the table was a shallow groove to receive the expressed fluid which then flowed through a pipe into a container below. The butter placed on the table was carried by the rotary motion of the top under a fixed fluted roller actuated by a manually operated wheel. The roller was held in position by a thumb screw, and the pressure was easily regulated.

An American appliance made by H. E. Mines consisted of a fluted roller made to work backwards and forwards along an inclined rectangular table. This was the design adopted by several makers. Some, like that made by Ahlborn, were very simple. It was a board three feet long by ten inches wide, with a lip above the edges at either side about one inch high. A fluted roller with grooves to run along these lips was pushed up and down the board by handles on each side. The end near the operator was supported on two legs, the other end resting on a tub or other container. A similar one was made by Waide of Leeds. Bradford's Albany butter worker was a more elaborate design of this kind. It was awarded a silver medal at the Royal show in 1883. A fluted roller made of sycamore worked in a rectangular tray or table on a strong frame, both made of American maple, a close-grained, non-absorbent wood. The carriage carrying the roller worked in grooves on the outside of the table. Both hands were used. The left hand worked the roller backwards and forwards from end to end of the table by means of a knob handle on the top of the carriage, while the right hand revolved the roller by a crank handle. The pressure adjusted itself automatically to the quantity and consistency of the butter on the tray through an ingenious wood screw. The roller and carriage were removable, and could be placed in a frame below so that the top could be used as an ordinary table.

Other types had conical fluted rollers turned by hand on a suitably shaped table with rather higher sides, or a long, squared wooden lever with a hand grip to enable it to be pressed or rolled over. Both these must have been rather laborious, but the squared lever was also used on a round table being loosely fixed at one edge so that it could be moved all over the surface. Another lever design was an inclined plane on legs having bevelled sides about three inches high, the slab being four feet by two tapering down four inches at the lower end where a crosspiece with a slot to take the end of the lever was fixed. Here, too, there was an opening for the escape of the buttermilk. In this the lever had either four or eight sides, its end fitting loosely into the slot so that it could be moved in any direction. Workers of these kinds made by several manufacturers were used until the end of the century.[12]

One more elaborate machine was awarded a silver medal in 1886, and came in for a good deal of recommendation by such authorities as James Long and J. P. Sheldon. It was a French invention, known as the Délaiteuse, or Centrifugal Butter Worker. Both power and manual types were produced. The machine, externally rather like a separator consisted of a perforated cylinder mounted on a vertical spindle, and driven through cones at about 800 r.p.m. This cylinder fitted inside a fixed container. The butter, after churning, and while in a granular state, was put in a thin canvas bag, fitting inside the perforated cylinder. At the appropriate rate the centrifugal force became sufficient to drive the buttermilk outwards through the granular particles of the butter into the space between the perforated cylinder and the outer case from which a waste pipe carried it off. The machine, despite the high praise the authorities gave it, had one limitation. Its efficient working depended largely upon the condition of the butter when put into it; besides that it must have been costly.[13]

The composition of milk, even from cows in the same herd, is liable to wide variation from causes not very well understood by our ancestors. This led to differences in the quality of butter and cheese that seemed to them to be the result of unexplained chance and unavoidable. Naturally it would be an advantage if there was some means of testing the quality of milk before it was manufactured. Several devices for this purpose were prepared in the early nineteenth century. One of them, the so-called 'lactometer' is mentioned above.

Another, invented by Dicas of Liverpool about 1795, was 'for ascertaining the richness of milk from its specific gravity, by its degree of warmth taken by a thermometer, on comparing its specific gravity with its warmth' had no success. Mrs. Love of Edinburgh made another about 1825. It consisted of aereometric beads, by which the specific gravity of the milk was tried first as it was drawn fresh from the cow, and again after the cream had been removed.

'Where milk is tried as soon as it cools', said Loudon, 'and again after it has been thoroughly skimmed, it will be found that the skimmed milk is of considerably greater gravity; and as this increase depends upon the separation of the lighter cream, the amount of the increase, or the difference between the specific gravity of the fresh and skimmed milk will bear proportion to, and may be employed as a measure of, the relative quantities of the oily matter or butter contained in different milks'. To determine its value for cheese making it was only necessary to curdle the skim milk, and ascertain the specific gravity of the whey. The method was well regarded by the Highland and Agricultural Society, but there could not then have been many dairy farmers who would be prepared to take this trouble, or indeed were of sufficient education to enable them to use it.[14]

None of these was very satisfactory, and Voelcker in 1863 still thought an instrument to determine the percentage of cream in milk, accurately and readily, would be most valuable. Creamometers had then been recommended. These were a cylindrical measuring glass with a glass foot, and divided into 100 equal degrees, or wide graduated glass tubes. The graduations read downwards from a point near the top marked zero, each indicating one per cent. of cream. Several tubes were set upright in a frame in a cylindrical tin box, which could be filled with water at 62°F., and covered with a lid provided with an aperture for a thermometer so that the temperature could be controlled. The tubes, filled with milk to zero, were left for twenty-four hours, and the percentage of cream then read off. It had two disadvantages, one the fact that the cream often varied in composition, the other that after agitation, as when sent by rail, the milk threw up less cream than when it had not been disturbed.

Donne's lactoscope was designed for the same purpose. It was a telescopic tube. The observer looked through this when it was filled with milk at a candle placed three feet distant. The more opaque the milk was, i.e., the richer in cream, the shorter the tube through which the candle could be seen. This seems difficult to use, and, as can be easily understood, did not give accurate results.

Marchand's lacto-butryometer was another graduated tube, divided into three parts, marked milk, ether and alcohol respectively. A marked indicator slid up and down the tube. It worked in a wider tin tube or casing, which served as a water bath when the milk was being tried. The tube was filled with milk up to the second division marked ether. Two or three drops of a solution of caustic soda were added, and then ordinary ether up to the division marked alcohol. The milk and ether were next shaken up, and afterwards the third division filled up with spirits of wine containing 86% to 90% of absolute alcohol. When the milk was shaken up with the ether, its fatty matter was completely dissolved. On adding alcohol, it was again almost entirely precipitated. The maker claimed that the quantity of fatty matter dissolved in the ether remained constant. Finally the tube was plunged into warm water at 104°F. and kept there until the butter was quite melted and formed a layer readily measured by the sliding indicator. Such a complex series of chemical manipulations were hardly suited to the capacity of an ordinary dairy farmer, and Voelcker admitted that chemical experience was necessary, but the use of this apparatus was recommended by some. Other systems dependent upon specific gravity were developed in France, and Voelcker's experiments led him to the conclusion that, within certain limits, specific gravity was a trustworthy indication of the quality of milk.[15]

Seventeen years later Voelcker confirmed his opinion of the unreliability of the creamometer. He preferred instruments on the optical principle, and failed to understand why Donne's lactoscope had not been generally adopted. A simpler version of this apparatus was invented by Fesser of Munich, and Voelcker carried out exhaustive tests of it. It was simply a wide glass tube, closed at the 'alternated' end, with an opening at the opposite end that could be closed by the thumb. In the narrow end a smaller cylindrical closed tube was fused in, made of white, so-called milk, glass. This was marked with black lines that became invisible when milk was poured in and only a little water added, but were clearly seen as more water was gradually added. The richer the milk was in butter fat, the more water must be added before the black lines became visible. In use water was slowly added, and the mixture shaken up. The process ceased as soon as the black lines could be plainly seen. Figures on the right side then showed at once the percentage of pure butter fat. Other figures showed the amount of water that had been added, but this information was unnecessary and only confused the issue. The operation was simple and speedy, and shown by Voelcker's experiments to be reasonably accurate. The apparatus was extensively used by dairymen and others on the Continent, but there is no evidence to show that it ever became popular in this country.[16]

The Lactocrit apparatus involved a more complex chemical process.

> 'The coagulated portion of the nitrogenous matter in a measured quantity of milk, precipitated by continuous boiling of the milk with a mixture of glacial acetic acid and sulphuric acid is first completely dissolved, and the fatty milk globules, which have been melted at the necessary temperature, thoroughly incorporated with each other, are enclosed in test tubes, and subjected to centrifugal force in the Lactocrit. The percentage of fat is estimated by the observed volume of melted fat'.

At first this method was only used for testing whole milk, but by 1890 chemical modifications enabled it to be used for determining the fat in skim milk and butter milk. The machine used was bolted to a table, and the container at the top revolved by a handle turning gearing enclosed in the vertical pillar supporting it. The process was complex and more suited to a laboratory than to the dairy room of a farm.[17]

Fjord's centrifugal milk tester was used in the working dairy at the Royal Show in 1888, and was assumed to be so well known that a description of it was superfluous. Four years later R. A. Lister and Co., exhibited Babcock's 'Positive' tester, invented by Dr. Babcock of Wisconsin, U.S.A. This method, which was widely accepted, was simple in construction and worked by hand. A circular pan about four inches deep, revolved on a spindle. There were four or more pockets in the pan to receive the test tubes; an even number must be used, and placed opposite to one another to maintain equilibrium. A measured quantity of milk was put in a test tube having a graduated neck or stem to which a measured amount of sulphuric acid was added, and the whole shaken up and mixed. The mixture turned quite black, and the glass became very hot. It was immediately put in a pocket and the pan rotated for seven or eight minutes at 400-500 r.p.m. The test tube was next filled up to a mark on the stem with hot water, and hot water put into the pan to about two inches deep. The pan was again rotated for about one or two minutes, the glasses taken out and filled with more hot water to a mark on the stem. More hot water was put in the pan if necessary, and it was turned once more for a short time. When the test glasses were taken out, a portion of the contents had separated and risen above the hot water. This quantity could be read off on the stem, and showed approximately the amount of butter-fat in the milk. The judges after tests, con-cluded that it would only be satisfactory if used by a skilful operator. Though they held the same opinion the following year, they were impressed by the improvement of hinged holders for the test tubes, which allowed them to swing from the centre outwards by centrifugal force. The results were clear and easy to read, and a printed table supplied the per-centage of butter-fat obtainable by the churn, and by analysis also the solids-not-fat and total solids. It was quite suitable for use on the farm, 'not only in simplicity but also in price'. Three other patents were applied for in 1892 and 1893 to protect other kinds of milk-testing apparatus, but the Bab-cock method became standard practice. The Gerber milk tester was a device that worked on much the same principles.[18] Another measuring machine that came before the dairy far-mer at about this time was the Acidmeter, which as its name implies, was used to measure the degree of acidity that ob-tained in milk.

In cheese making one of the most laborious processes is breaking the curd. Much of it was done by hand supple-mented by the curd knife with several blades or one shaped like a barley hummeler. A semi-mechanical curd breaker was invented by Robert Barlas of Edinburgh, and had been used on some farms for several years when it was described in the

*Quarterly Journal of Agriculture.* This consisted of a wooden hopper, 17½ by 14 inches at the top, with sloping sides to a smaller perforated bottom, through which the broken curd fell into a container beneath it. At the bottom of the hopper a wooden cylinder, 3½ inches diameter and 6¾ inches long, was fixed. It was studded with hardwood pegs projecting ⅜ inch. This was turned on an iron axle by a handle outside the hopper, and the curd pressed down upon it by the disengaged hand. Two wedges, also studded, rested between the ends of the cylinder and the sides of the hopper. All parts could be easily dismantled for cleaning.[19] It was cheap and efficient and saved a good deal of labour.

It was one, perhaps the first, of many such appliances made and patented during the next seventy years. It would be tedious to give details of them all, but perhaps three examples may be described. Pugh's patent cheese making machine was exhibited at the Royal Show in 1856, and gained some praise from the judges because it was simple and easily managed by a dairymaid. It was sold at prices well within the reach of any dairy farmer. The maker was Francis Mellard of Uttoxeter. It consisted of a circular metal pan provided with taps for drawing off the whey. Above it a vertical rod or rack carrying a perforated pressing plate or sinker was supported by two iron uprights, and a cross beam, giving an effective system of leverage. The sinker was raised or lowered by means of a counterweight, which acted like the weights in a sash window. When the plate was raised it could be set in an upright, inclined or horizontal position to give access to the curd, and could revolve for easy cleaning. The whole thing was mounted on rollers so that it was easily moved from one place to another. A novel set of curd knives, rather like a steamship screw, revolved upon a centre in the pan, and were so made that one half cut the curd downwards, and the other cut it upwards simultaneously. This movement could be reversed. The whey was forced up through the perforated presser, and when this was completed, the presser was used to force the curd down into the vat. The pressure on the curd in the vat was self-acting, and could be regulated from 1 cwt. upwards so that the operator need not be in attendance all the time. It was the first apparatus that enabled the whole process of cheese-making to be done in one vessel.[20]

I have been able to find no evidence that this apparatus was extensively used. Two others, invented at a rather earlier date, did take the fancy of the cheese makers, and were used for a good many years. Cockey's patent was not very spectacular, but it was used in the larger Somersetshire dairies for at least twenty years and probably longer. It was a water jacketted cheese vat, heated and cooled by a flow of water carried through pipes from an adjoining room. The tub had a double bottom into which hot or cold water was introduced as required. Its advantage was that it saved the labour of carrying the milk to a furnace in another room.[21]

Keevil's patent was a cylindrical tub fitted with a set of knives, which revolved round a central vertical spindle. These knives were fixed on two radial arms, one upright and the other horizontal. They were turned by a handle at the top. The whey was run off without any labour through a filter in one side, and a plug was drawn to allow it to drain away completely. The curd was finally dried by a pressing plate and screw thus saving loss and damage by hand drying. This apparatus, made by T. F. Griffiths and Co., of Birmingham, won a number of prizes and was made in various sizes.[22]

In 1879 several mechanical curd mills, having internal rollers with spiked teeth, were entered at Bristol, in addition to the older manual types. One was a galvanised metal slotted concave in which was geared either one or two rollers fitted with hooked teeth. These worked in the slots in the concave, carrying portions of the curd with them as they revolved. Wooden rollers were used, but more commonly these were made of galvanised iron. They were driven by hand at high speed. One of this kind, shown by William Gilman, was praised. It was fitted with two wooden rollers carrying iron spikes in rows, which revolved at different speeds, 'thus insuring greater regularity of feed and better work'. It did not win the prize which was awarded to Bamford's mill, an apparatus wholly of galvanised iron. This was fitted with two spiked rollers working up to a spiked breast. The hopper when turned back released the rollers, and the whole appliance could be easily dismantled and cleaned.[23]

Some of the heaviest work in the cheese-making dairy was the turning of the cheeses to ensure uniform ripening. Before 1860 sets of ingeniously contrived shelves that could be turned more or less automatically had been produced to facilitate this work. One of the earliest was invented by William Blurton of Fieldhall, Uttoxeter. It had so-called tumbling shelves. Three makers competed for the prize offered at Bristol in 1879. H. E. Mines, 79, Redcliff Street, Bristol; Bamford and Sons, Uttoxeter; and Carson and Toone, Warminster, Wilts. All worked on the same principle, though differing in detail, and none possessed any novelty.

The prize was awarded to Carson and Toone. Two cast iron standards, springing from a base which rested on the floor, and secured in position by a top and bottom brace, brought the frame into the form of a square. Attached to the standards was an inner frame, hung on a central pivot on which it revolved. This inner frame was a series of wooden shelves, braced and supported by wrought iron. The turners were in lengths of about six feet, and held a total of thirty to forty cheeses; even when evenly loaded they were easily turned by a crank handle fitted on the end of the centre pin. On one side of each board a quadrant shaped piece of lattice prevented the cheeses slipping off when being turned.[24]

But the old methods persisted alongside the new, and were probably much more usual as long as farmhouse butter and cheese making continued. Cheese vats of elm wood 'turned out solid of the size of the cheese' were used in Gloucestershire, $2\frac{1}{2}$ inches deep for single, $4\frac{1}{2}$ inches for double Gloucester and $15\frac{1}{2}$ inches in diameter. The best material for setting dishes was discussed as it had been for so long. It was a controversy that was unlikely to reach an end. Within my memory Dorset farmer's wives set milk for cream in the ancient lead lined pans, and churned the cream in the upright churn. No doubt the same sort of thing was happening at the same date in other dairy districts.

The milking machine, now so general, was not brought to perfection enough for practical use until the last decade of the nineteenth century. Many ingenious people had tried to find a mechanical means of overcoming the process that occupied so much time morning and evening and demanded so much skill on the part of the milker. The first patent for an apparatus of this kind was taken out by William Blurton of Field Hall, Staffordshire in 1836 (No. 7045). It was of the utmost simplicity. A small tube was inserted in each teat so as to keep the muscle distended and cause the milk to flow. The four tubes were fixed to curved pipes that were connected just above the pail. The inventor stated that it should have a small vessel attached to the end to act as a trap to prevent air entering the udder. It must have been fairly widely discussed if not used. Charles Hillyard heard it did not answer. Blurton himself found it not altogether satisfactory, and later used only two tubes while milking the other two quarters by hand, a procedure that must have been very awkward. The tubes were made of ivory, bone or metal, and must be carefully cleaned after use.

This principle, called siphoning, which was a misnomer, continued to be advocated, and modifications of greater or less significance to be patented. Milking tubes were marketed by Cooper and Co., of Sheffield, consisting of four smooth rubber tubes about the thickness of a goose quill, six inches long. A two inch electroplated perforated tube closed at the top, was attached to one end and the other to a three quarter inch metal tube, the four of these being held together by a rubber band, and the ends below dropped into the pail. William Edward Newton had taken a like precaution in 1851 (No. 13498) by having a guttapercha bag to fit over the udder and be held tight by an elastic band the tubes being attached to the bag so that they could enter the teat. Margaret Barland patented something like this in 1863 (No. 1044). It was known as the 'pocket self-milking apparatus'. She added the refinement that the milk vessel should be shaped like a cow's udder and placed in a raised position. Straps were advised to keep the cow quietly standing over a trough to avoid waste by spilling. Patent no. 1082 of this year was for a similar system. Stanley and James (No. 1452 of 1874), Jordan (No. 3628 of 1878), McIntyre (No. 1423 of 1889) used the same principles.[25]

Newton made an advance on his previous patent in 1860 with patent no. 2634 which introduced a pumping action. The specification was for a pail with a fixed half cover to it, in the middle of which a tube was fixed connected with a chamber having on each side another chamber. Each of these second chambers had two pipes ending in a cap which fitted one of the cow's teats. One side of each chamber was made of flexible material with a metal disc in the centre. The openings leading to the teats and the central chamber were fitted with valves, so that by pressing the metal discs in and out a pumping action was set up which drew the milk from the udder into the centre chamber whence it ran into the pail. The discs were worked upon by a pair of lever handles. The teat cups were conical, and fitted internally with a series of rings which held the teat firm, and made an airtight joint.

Newton's appliance did not make the furore nor capture the public imagination like the American machine shown in 1862. It was protected in this country by Francis Watkins (No. 2686 of 1862). He was a member of the firm of Watkins and Keene of Birmingham, who paid £5,000 for the patent plus a royalty on sales, if any. The appliance seems to have been very similar to that protected by Newton. The teat cups were of rubber and flexible wire, and attached to four tubes leading to a vessel having a diaphragm at the top in the centre of a metal disc, and worked by a lever handle. A vacuum was caused by working the lever, and the milk thus drawn—it was said—at the rate of a gallon a minute. A prize medal was awarded to this machine at the International Exhibition of 1862.

John Fairless protected another somewhat similar device in the same year (No. 3441), which had an elastic pipe with four branches to fit the teats, and at the other end an air pump in the lid of an ordinary milk pail. This lid was hollowed to hold the valves. As the pump exhausted the air from the pipe or tube the milk was drawn and ran down into the pail. W. E. Gedge added to the list in 1863 (No. 1688) with his suction milker fitted with a pump. A vacuum was formed in a flat cylinder, taps opened in the connecting tube and teat cups, and the milk was then drawn. No. 1082 of that year by E. H. Cradock was not very different. Bowick added another teat cup and pump machine in 1878 when he took out two patents, nos. 3076 and 5191. Keevil's 'siphon' machine of 1871 (No. 1126) had an air pump but the reason for this, unless it was to pass the milk along the tubes, is difficult to determine.

These machines must have been talked about, and there were a good many others produced in America, Germany, Denmark and Sweden. The Royal Agricultural Society therefore offered a prize for an efficient machine in 1879, but no inventor was bold enough to enter an apparatus for it. Farmers had not apparently been convinced of its utility, and they were right to be cautious. The apparatus was as yet very imperfect.

The next development was the Crees milker provided with travelling rollers for squeezing the teats. (No. 3831 of 1881), a principle that was repeated in the Nyrop apparatus (No. 7654 of 1885). The last squeezed by pressing handles, but the Frazey of the same year (No. 2705 of 1885) was a bulb put on a teat and squeezed manually by a hand put through a hole covered by a flap so made as to fit the milker's wrist. The Horlyck was another pressure milker (No. 17959 of 1890) and the Vaughan (No. 5395 of 1890) was an elaborate machine worked by an endless chain to press the milk out, the pressure being applied manually. So far as I know at present none of these was ever installed on a farm for practical use. My information on this point is not likely to be exhaustive.

Marchand's (No. 15210 of 1889) had a better destiny. It's principle was continuous suction like so many of its predecessors and the vacuum was formed by water worked by gravitation. Its first erection on David Shaw's farm at Haining Mains was intended to offset a shortage of milkers in this district, and other farmers there took it up. Those who did so were not numbered, but were doubtless only a few.

Nicholson and Gray (No. 2709 of 1891) showed their apparatus at the Royal Show in the year it was patented, and W. N. Nicholson and Sons the Neilsen, a Danish design (No. 6520 of 1891). Both these worked by a vacuum giving continuous suction and the first was awarded a silver medal. All of this type of milker had the disadvantage that they were too drastic, and had a bad effect on the teats, often leaving them in a congested state, in spite of the inventor's attempts to imitate the action of a calf suckling or of hand milking. This was finally achieved when Dr. Alexander Sheilds adopted the pulsator principle (Nos. 9547, 10259 and 20889 of 1891) on the Thistle Mechanical Milker which he exhibited in 1895. It had some success both in this country and abroad, but was very noisy and difficult to keep clean. Many other patents were registered between this date and 1914. J. & R. Wallace of Castle Douglas began making milking machines in 1895, and won a silver medal in that year. Its improved design and utility were commended by the Royal Judges in 1908. Two years later Vaccar Ltd., produced a machine that milked cows in the field.

The utility of the milking machine, both siphon and suction, was questioned by many writers from 1850 onwards, and Scott Burn, who thought in 1888 that it might be generally and successfully introduced into English dairies was a voice crying in the wilderness. Sherer and Milburn about 1850 were tentative. The former was rightly dubious about the siphon system, which caused flaccid teats and self-milking. Both writers considered the American machine more satisfactory, and Milburn that it was not altogether void of feasibility. Thirty years later Ward and Lock's *Book* insisted that nothing was so good as hand milking, and James Long was non-committal in 1885, though he provided descriptions of the Barland and Durant machines. Robert Wallace declared all machines to be unsatisfactory in 1889, the siphons being apt to injure the teat and troublesome to fit, and the suction type likely to draw blood at the finish. The

Principal of the Royal Veterinary College was equally doubtful in 1896. Inflammation of the udder was caused by the
siphon type, and the self-acting milking machine with its
rubber tubes was a good way of introducing germs unless
sterile when used. On no account ought it to be used on a
healthy cow. The siphon had been abandoned as it well
deserved to be, but the disadvantages of the suction system
were overcome before 1914. Nevertheless many years passed
before it came into general use.

No such doubts existed about the cream separator, the invention of which had marked 'an era in dairying', but the
benefit of the scientific discoveries of the fifteen years before
1896 had passed the small farmer by, though even he had
realised the value of the thermometer and greater mechanical
accuracy. The new methods appeared to him difficult and
costly, especially those employed in butter making. The working dairies put on by the great agricultural societies had done
nothing to increase his confidence. The farmers were
appalled, wrote Malden in 1896, by these and by model
dairies, which used so great a variety of articles. Their
response was that they could not afford all these things.

As late as 1911 labour saving machinery on the dairy farm
did not play so important a role, especially in butter and
cheese making, as did good and cheap hand labour. Hermann
Levy's considered opinion then was that the dairy farmer producing on a large scale, selling wholesale and using machinery, had few advantages and very important disadvantages
compared with the small farmer who did the work himself
with the help of his family, sold his products in person, or
through his wife, and employed little or no outside labour.
The separator was, as Bear had said, the most important accession, but even that was relatively cheaper for large quantities
than for small. The price of the Pasteurising machine was
prohibitive to the small farmer. The cooling apparatus was
relatively cheaper and was widely used. Churning machines
were cheap enough for the small man, but again relatively
dearer than in relation to large production. But machinery

was not necessarily a pure advantage so long as no satisfactory milking machine was to be had.[26]

The new machines that had been put at the disposal of the dairy farmer by ingenious inventors of the nineteenth century had affected the industry in a comparatively minor degree. Many gentlemen and large dairy farmers had adopted them, but the main body of the industry was composed of small enterprises most of which were worked by family labour, and on these the mechanical genius of the century had less effect. Milking was still usually done by hand; it is perhaps not too much to say that most cream was set in open pans, and that only on a small proportion of farms had the new mechanical churns and cheese making machines been adopted; but this conclusion must not be accepted without taking into account the numerous farmers who had been far-seeing enough and financially able to utilise the new things that the mechanical age was placing at their disposal for facilitating their work. The propaganda of the British Dairy Farmer's Association, formed in 1876, too, must not be underestimated.

## NOTES TO CHAPTER IV (i)

[1] Hubert Hall. *Society in the Elizabethan age.* 1887. pp. 23, 201. W. E. Minchinton. *British tinplate industry.* 1957. p. 3. Shakespeare. *Midsummer night's dream.* I. ii. Heresbach. *Foure bookes of husbandry.* 1586. Book III, p. 146 v. Surflet. *Countrey ferme.* 1600. p. 88. F. G. Emmison. *Jacobean household inventories.* Publns. of Beds. Histl. Rec. Soc. XX 1938 passim. Markham. *English housewife.* 1653 (1615) p. 144.

[2] Markham. *ibid.* Hale. *Compleat body.* 1756. p. 561.

[3] *Love's labour lost.* VII. ii. W. G. Hiscock. *John Evelyn and his family circle.* 1955. p. 28. Walton. *Compleat Angler.* 1653.

[4] G. Eland. *Purefoy letters, 1735—1753.* 1931. I. pp. 144, 145. R. C. Gaut. *History of Worcestershire agriculture.* 1939. p. 101. Thomas Balston. *Housekeeping book of Susanna Whatman, 1776–1800.* 1956. p. 26. J. Jean Hecht. *Domestic servant class in 18th century England.* 1956. pp. 9, 68.

[5] Lisle. *Observations.* 1757. p. 298, 301. Adam. *Practical Essays.* 1787. Billingsley. *Somerset.* 1797. p. 250. Balston. *op. cit.* p. 36. Anderson. *Recreations.* 1800. III. pp. 253, 255.

[6] *Mod. husb.* 1750. II. June. pp. 164, 165. May. pp. 127, 135. Ellis' *Husb. abridg'd.* 1772. II. pp. 276–278. Bradley. *Country housewife.* 1736. p. 88. R. Bayne-Powell. *Housekeeping in 18th century.* 1956 p. 61.

[7] Marshall. *Gloucester.* 1796. I. pp. 267, 273, II. pp. 158.

[8] *idem. Norfolk.* 1787. I. p. 328 II. p. 239.

[9] *idem. Midland counties.* 1790. I. p. 354 fn.

[10] Lawrence. *New farmers' calendar.* 1802. p. 510. Willich. *Domestic encyclo.* 1802. p. 525. Dickson. *Practical agric.* 1804. I. Plate XXII. Forsyth. *Prin. & pract.* 1804. II. p. 456. Garnett. *Westld. agric.* 1912. p. 137. *Abridgements of specifications A.D. 1777–1866.* Patent Office, and later volumes.

[11] Forsyth. *op. cit.* II. p. 449. Twamley. *Essays on dairy management.* 1816. pp. 22–26, 106, 107. Sir John Sinclair. *Code of agric.* 1817. pp. 118, 119. Lawson. *Modern farrier.* 1825. p. 383.

[12] Lawrence. *op. cit.* p. 507. *idem. General treatise on cattle.* 1805. p. 133. A farmer. *Rural recreations.* 1802. Sep. pp. 65, 66. Dickson. *op. cit.* II. pp. 976, 998. Forsyth. *op. cit.* II. p. 448. Young. *Farmer's calendar.* 1804. pp. 280, 281. *Communications to Board of Agriculture.* IV. (1805) p. 340. *Col. George Hanger to all sportsmen.* 1814. p. 162 cf. Robert Bloomfield. *Farmer's Boy.* 9th ed. 1806. p. 14 ff. Lawson. *op. cit.* p. 386. Ivy Pinchbeck. *Women workers in the Industrial Revolution, 1750–1850.* 1930. pp. 103, 109, 110.

[13] Holland. *Cheshire.* 1808. p. 100 Lawson. *op. cit.* pp. 390, 396 Young. *Essex.* 1805. II. p. 279. A Taylor. *Farmers' guide.* 1829. pp. 237, 238. Loudon. *Encyclo. of agric.* 1831. pp. 1035, 1039, 1040. Jackson. *Treatise on agric.* 1840. p. 107.

[14] *Report of Poor Law Commissioners on employment of women and children in agric.* 1843. pp. 5, 12, 125. c.f. Ivy Pinchbeck. *op. cit.*

[15] Jackson. *op. cit.* pp. 107, 108. Baxter's *Library.* 1836. p. 141. Low. *Pract. agric.* 1843. p. 641. Garnett. *op. cit.*


# NOTES TO CHAPTER IV (ii)

[1] A. J. Spencer & J. B. Passmore. *Agricultural implements and machinery.* Science Museum. 1930. p. 88.

[2] G. H. Andrews. *Modern husbandry.* 1853. pp. 386, 387.

[3] J. C. Morton. *Handbook of dairy husbandry.* 1860. pp. 60–62.

[3a] Ph. Pusey. *Report to H.R.H. the Prince Consort, the President of the Commission for the exhibition of works of industry of all nations.* J.R.A.S.E. 1851. pp. 637-8.

[4] Pringle & Murray. *Practical farming.* 1865. pt. ii. p. 52. Roland. *Farming for pleasure.* 1879. p. 62. Ward & Lock's *Book of farm management.* c. 1880. pp. 331, 353.

[5] *Report on trial of dairy implements at Bristol.* J.R.A.S.E. 1879. pp. 137–146.

[6] *British dairy farming.* 1885. p. 172 ff. *idem. Dairy farm* 1889. p. 20. J. P. Sheldon. *The farm and the dairy.* 1889. *idem. Dairy farming.* c. 1883. pp. 315–318. c.f. James Muir. *Manual of dairy work.* 1893. p. 53. Henry J. Webb. *Advanced agric.* 1894. pp. 609, 610.

[7] James Edwards. *Miscellaneous implements exhibited at Chester.* J.R.A.S.E. 1893. pp. 555, 556.

[8] Percy E. Crutchley. *Trials of churns at Cambridge.* J.R.A.S.E. 1894. pp. 487–497.

[9] J.R.A.S.E. 1872. p. 477: 1879. p. 154: 1881. p. 645.

[10] *idem.* 1875. p. 223: 1879. p. 702: 1881. p. 645 ff: 1880. p. 682. Pilley. *Elements of scientific agric.* 1881. p. 231. Sheldon. *Dairy farming.* p. 293 ff. Webb. *op. cit.* p. 609.

[11] See relative annual volumes of *J.R.A.S.E.* and *Bath and West Soc.* and of *Implement and Machinery Review.* Long in *Jour. B.D.F.A.* II. 2. 1886.

[12] J.R.A.S.E. 1879. pp. 147, 148: 1883. pp. 619, 620. Sheldon. pp. 310–313. Ward & Lock. p. 363. Muir. p. 54. Walker-Tisdale & Robinson. *Butter making on the farm.* 1903. p. 21.

[13] *J.R.A.S.E.* 1886. pp. 537, 538. Upton. *Profitable dairy farming.* 1888. Sheldon. *Farm & dairy.* 1889. p. 82. Long. *Dairy farm.* 1889. p. 21.

[14] John Holt. *Gen. view of Lancs.* 1795. p. 16 ff. Loudon. *Encyclo. of agric.* 1831. pp. 1039, 1040. Slight & Burn. *Book of farm implements and machines.* 1858. p. 511.

[15] Augustus Voelcker. *Milk.* J.R.A.S.E. 1863. pp. 313–317. Henry F. Moore. *Year's lessons in dairy implements and machinery.* Jour. Bath & West Soc. 3rd ser. XVI. 1885.

[16] *Idem. New method of testing milk.* J.R.A.S.E. 1880. pp. 583–592.

[17] Upton. *op. cit.* p. 139. W. Fleischmann. *Book of the dairy.* 1896. pp. 70, 71. tr. by Aikman & Wright.

[18] *J.R.A.S.E.* 1892. pp. 543, 544. 1893. pp. 563, 564, see also *Recent agricultural inventions* in both volumes. Ainsworth-Davis. (ed.) Fream's *Elements of agric.* 9th ed. 1914. p. 558.

[19] *Quarterly Jour. of Agric.* IV (1834) pp. 384, 385. Slight & Burn. op. cit. p. 512.

[20] *J.R.A.S.E.* 1865. pp. 401, 402.

[21] *Jour. Bath & West Soc.* II. 1854. pp. 223, 224. *ibid.* XI. pt. 2. 1863. p. 473. *J.R.A.S.E.* 1868. p. 308.

[22] J. Donaldson. *British agric.* 1860. III. pp. 692, 693. J. C. Morton. *Handbook.* 1860. p. 78.

[23] *Trial of dairy implements at Bristol.* J.R.A.S.E. 1879. p. 151.

[24] Morton. *Handbook.* 1860. p. 78. Stephens' *Book of the farm.* 1877. II. p. 257. *J.R.A.S.E.* 1879. p. 152.

[25] Hillyard. *Practical farming.* 1840. Stephens. p. 145 citing William Blurton. *Practical essays on milking.* 1839, a book I have not been able to trace.

[26] William E. Bear. *British farmer and his competitors.* 1888. W. J. Malden. *Recent changes in farm practice.* J.R.A.S.E. 1896. pp. 25–27. Herman Levy. *Large and small holdings.* 1911. pp. 176, 177.

# CHAPTER V

## *Butter and cheese making*

### (i). Butter making on the farm

'Of Milke', wrote Googe in the 1614 edition of his translation and expansion of Conradus Heresbachius, 'is made
Butter, whose Use (though it be chiefly at this Day among the
Flemings) is yet a good and profitable Foode in other Countries and much used by our old Fathers . . .The Commoditie
thereof, besides many other, is in the assuaging of Hunger and
the preserving of Strength'.

Butter and cheese were used in and exported from the
Low Countries from the thirteenth century, a trade that has
continued until the present day, and there are some very
optimistic estimates of the average yield of milk there. Large
quantities of milk were delivered to the city daily from the
countryside about Ghent in the fifteenth century. The Flemings liked to drink milk and to eat butter. The Bretons, too,
had a degree of preference for butter over cheese. This is not
to say that butter was not made and used in England and
Wales. As Googe was careful to point out it had long been
used. Careful calculations of the probable yield of milk, and
the proportion of butter and cheese that could be made from
it are supplied in the anonymous thirteenth century *Hosebon-
drie,* as well as the yield from ewe's milk. The equally anonymous *Seneschaucie* directed the provost of a manor not to
allow the dairymaids to carry away cheese, butter, milk or
curds from the dairy, and supplies rules for the office of dairymaid. Butter is, of course, very ancient, being known to the
Scythians and used in Biblical times as the familiar story of
Jael's gift of milk and butter in a lordly dish to Sisera shows.[1]

Though butter was made both from cow's and ewe's milk,

the writers of English didactic farming treatises whose work appeared in the sixteenth century did not discuss the processes involved in its manufacture. Tusser was emphatic enough about the conduct and cleanliness of the dairymaid, but only in relation to cheese making. In that masculine age this may have been a consequence of the work being almost wholly done by the women of the household, the wife and daughters of the farmer, and in large establishments by hired maids. It was most definitely the business of the farmer's wife to supervise most carefully the work of her daughters and dairymaids 'about the good ordering of the milke of her kine in the making of butter and cheese thereof'. This remained so throughout the following centuries until manufacture passed from the farmhouse to the factory.

The lady, whether wife or chief dairymaid, must not be too impatient to begin manufacture. The calf must have its due share of its mother's milk directly after it was born. This was no hardship because the first milk, excellent as it was for the calf, was no good for making butter or cheese. There was some difference of opinion about the treatment of the milk. Surflet advised that it should be set in a warm place immediately after milking to keep and grow thick. It was good practice to boil and stir vigorously before letting it rest, if it was not to be kept for three days or more, but in summer and other warm seasons it should not be kept more than one day as the heat would spoil it. Working up was therefore done as soon as possible at these times. Good milk was judged by its white colour, pleasant smell, sweet taste and reasonable thickness 'in such sort as being dropped upon one's nail it runneth not off presently'. The newest and fattest milk was reserved for butter making.

When making butter the Tudor and early Stuart dairymaid skimmed the cream of the morning milk at 5 p.m., and the evening milk at 5 a.m. on the following morning. She put the cream into a clean, well leaded earthenware pot, and covered it close, putting it in a cool place. If there were five or more producing cows in the herd, she did not keep the cream more than two days in summer, or four or five in winter. She

churned the butter at convenient times for use in the house
or for sale in the neighbouring market. Generally Tuesday
and Friday were devoted to this task because the butter could
then be sold at the Wednesday or Saturday market. The wise
dairymaid strained the cream through a cloth into the churn.
Care was taken to warm the churn in winter and cool it in
summer. Churning must be done with an even stroke, and
continued patiently until the butter came, sometimes a great
while, especially in hot weather. When the butter was come it
was slashed about with a knife every way to cleanse it of any
casual thing that may have happened to fall into it. Then it
was washed in clear, cold water, and worked by hand to remove the last drops of buttermilk. It could then be made into
pats, yards or whatever the local form was, or salted and
potted for sale in bulk. Butter making by this process was a
long, careful, and somewhat tedious job, and it is very evident
that the best practice was extremely careful and skilled, but
faking was not unknown. As early as 1476 a butterwife was
pilloried for selling a spurious imitation.[2]

Potting was either in earthenware pots, or in well-made
barrels (firkins). If stored in pots, they were scrupulously
cleaned and then a quantity of salt cast into the bottom. The
butter was then put in, and pressed down by hand. When
filled the whole was so thickly covered with salt that no butter
could be seen. If the daily quota of butter was not sufficient to
fill a pot, it was put in and covered with salt, more being
added and salted as it was continued to be made until the pot
was full. These variations must have caused large differences
in the saltiness of the butter, but were methods that continued in use for a very long time. The full pots were covered
'close', and stored where it was cold and safe. The barrels
were filled in the same way, and a brine made strong enough
to float an egg poured into holes made downwards through
the butter with a stick until it covered the butter. It was then
left to settle. Some added a sprig of rosemary to the barrel, a
practice Markham approved. He also thought May-butter, the
best of all, if stored in the sun for a month, 'exceeding

soveraign and medicinable for wounds, strains aches and such-like grievances'.

Butter was valued, too, as a symbol of prosperity, and the prosperous used it freely in cooking. After a wedding the nuptial pair were often given a pot of butter on their return home 'as presaging plenty and abundance of all good things'. Boiled beef, with its mixture of carrots, turnips and other herbs and roots was eaten well peppered and salted, and swimming in butter. Buttered ale was a favourite drink.[3] A commentary on dietetic habits was the belief of some Wilt-shire dairymen that the price of butter rose in the peas and beans season because of the large quantity used to garnish these vegetables. In these circumstances it is surprising that there is so little discussion of the best methods to be employed in making this well liked and apparently constantly consumed commodity. It must have been made in several different ways as it was in the late seventeenth and early eighteenth cen-turies.

Some people made it of whole milk, and a great housewife dwelling in the Isle of Ely assured Hartlib that the best butter was made without setting milk. She strained the milk as soon as it was taken from the cow, and churned it like cream. One pound of the resulting butter was worth $1\frac{1}{2}$ lb. of the best butter made of cream. The disadvantage of this process was that the excellent butter did not keep so well as that made of cream. Suffolk butter had maintained its good reputation throughout the seventeenth century, and was estimated by Houghton to exceed the northern butter in value by four shillings in the hundred, because the northern housewives failed to extract all the buttermilk. Good management was the secret of success as it was in cheese making.

Both Suffolk and Essex butter were renowned. Nowhere were there better dairies for butter or neater housewives— with a caveat 'if too many of them did not at the present time time (1710) smoke tobacco'. Their butter had a fragrance and flavour beyond anything to be met with elsewhere. By August it acquired firmness or hardness sufficient to make it fit for potting. The reason was supposed to be the number of cows kept and the small fields, so that they frequently had fresh pasture. Nevertheless it was recognised that the milk from different cows in the same pasture often varied and the reason given was the variation in the botanical composition of the feed, some herbs giving an odd, unfashionable taste to the product.

In Devon butter was made from scalded cream. The milk was heated in a brass pan, and when the cream wrinkled and rose in the middle it was taken off the fire, the cream skimmed and put in a tub. It had all the appearance of clouted cream. This cream was stirred by hand, the maid putting her arm into the pot and stirring it until the butter came. In hot weather when the hand was too warm a bottle was sometimes used. The result was very rich butter, but the process must have been long, tedious and wearing. This same method was common in Devon and Cornwall until the end of the nine-teenth century.

Farmer Elford of Chubbs, near Upcern, Dorset, (c.1700) did not agree with Markham and others that May butter was best. He thought the best was made after June. In May it was not so good because the cows did not recover from the winter hardship until the end of June. They must get into heart from the good spring feed before they could give abund-ance of milk. Chivers, previously mentioned in other connec-tions, believed in churning every day if enough milk was pro-duced. The cream was sweet when churned every day, and the butter made from it equally sweet and rich. The poor and small dairies where the maid churned only twice a week, doubtless the great majority, were obliged to use cream that was on the turn.[4]

The art of churning as practised in the early eighteenth century is minutely described in *Dictionarium Rusticum*. After the cream had been strained through a strong and clean cloth into the churn it was covered and set in the coolest place in the dairy in the summer, the warmest in winter. Cold water in summer, and hot in winter brought the churn to a proper temperature. It could also be put into a pail of warm or cold water for this purpose. Churning was done early in the morning or late evening in warm weather, at noon in cold. At first the strokes must be swift, and the operator mark the noise 'which will be solid, heavy and entire till you hear it alter and the sound is become light, sharp and more sprightly, afterwards you will see that the butter breaks.' Then the maid cleansed both the lid and the inside of the churn, and put all the butter together. She closed the churn again, and with easy strokes round and not to the bottom gathered the butter into one lump, being careful to leave no scraps separate. If she intended it for immediate use, she took it out and put it in a clean bowl or 'panshion', adding very clean water. She worked it by hand turning and tossing it to and fro until all the buttermilk was washed out. Next she scotched it about with a knife to remove hairs and any scraps of straining cloth and other particles and spread it in a shallow bowl, sprinkled it with salt, mingled it by hand, and made it up into dishes, pounds, or half pounds. Butter for potting was not washed with water, but only cleared of buttermilk by hand, as water might make it rusty or reese. It was weighed before salting, and the process continued as already described.[5]

At Over, Cambridgeshire and its neighbourhood, where much of the butter used in the Colleges was made, it was estimated that 12 quarts of milk a day was a good yield in April. Well skimmed this would give four pints of cream, from which about 2 lbs. of butter could be made. Some dairy farmers here used large barrel churns holding 22 gallons of cream when two-thirds full. A lusty man and maid could make this into butter in an hour, and it usually gave about 70 lb. One man at Denny, near Over, had 60 cows, and a churn that held a hogshead. The butter when not washed was drawn backwards and forwards with a fleeting (skimming) dish 'a little at a time to let out the buttermilk', and then salted at 1 quart salt to 30 lb., fleeted again, and weighed into pounds, made into long rolls, and hung in the well to keep until it was taken to market the next day.

Over butter did not keep as long as Suffolk butter, but one famous dairywoman made hers up into 30 or 40 lb. lumps, salted a trifle more than usual, and put it in the middle of a bin of flour where it would keep all the winter. Covering with brine in pots in the ordinary way was not so effective as this.

An elaborate system of butter making from new milk was practised in some places (unidentified) in 1726. The milk was conveyed in pipes from the cow to the churn where it was kept in constant motion by a horse until the butter came, when the buttermilk was drained off into another vessel for use in making cheese for domestic consumption. This butter had to be used at once as it did not keep.[6]

Ellis (1750) proposed various precautions to keep the cream sweet in summer. The most obvious was to stand the cream pot in cold water, changing the water every day. Another was to boil 'a wallop or two' of the first skimming or later, afterwards adding the next lot of raw cream to the boiled cream, and changing the mixture into a fresh glazed earthenware pot until wanted for churning. This was always done by one Vale farmer who had no cool cellar in which to store the cream. Near Bristol the dairywomen boiled their pans, and dried them before the fire in winter to raise more cream, and some skimmed the milk a second time six or seven hours after the first. He said that if two or three pewter spoons were put into a barrel churn in the summer it made the butter come quicker.

The public taste in the mid-eighteenth century was for yellow butter just as it is today. Ellis attributed the rich colour of summer butter to the cows eating the yellow flowers that decorated the pastures at this time of the year. To maintain this appearance in winter without artificial aid was impossible. Good housewives therefore stored marigold leaves against this contingency. A layer of flowers was put in an earthenware pot and covered with a layer of salt, alternate layers of flowers and salt being added till the pot was full. If covered close they would keep till winter. Then a few flowers were taken out, put in a wooden bowl, and the juice beaten out with an iron ball. A little skim milk was added, and the mixture strained and squeezed through a cloth into the cream. This gave the butter a summer-time bloom and colour.

The much praised Suffolk butter was made by an unusual process. Enough cream to make 6 lb. of butter was put in an upright churn, and set before the fire after six spoonfuls (a rather inexact measure) of rennet had been added. It was left there about one and a half hours without stirring. During that time the churn was turned so that all its sides were equally heated. Then it was churned with a mundle stick (a stick or slice commonly used in making puddings), and in about six minutes the butter would come. The rest of the work was done in the ordinary way. Ellis confessed that he had never tried it.

He also described the making of whey butter, a business that must have been very ancient. The whey drained out of the curd during cheesemaking was set for cream, and skimmed like milk. The cream was made into butter in the normal way, and used for family consumption. If a little milk cream was added it made butter only a trifle less valuable than that made from milk. The yield of butter was naturally much less than that from cream, and it would not keep so long, but if eaten when fresh was almost as good.[7] Whey butter was mainly made in the cheese districts—as is perhaps obvious.

One Essex lady removed her dairy to an underground vault in winter from which the external cold air was excluded. There the cream rose well, and the butter came easily. Too much heat, as long experience had shown, would prevent butter coming in some way. Essex butter, or as it was more usually called, Epping butter, enjoyed a very favourable reputation in London, where it found a ready sale. It was usually made in a barrel churn, though the old upright churn was still in use in 1834. The cream was allowed to go a trifle sour before churning. Some kept a little old cream to put in the churn, or used a little rennet, as Ellis had suggested. The butter here was thrown into clear water, and squeezed by hand in a bowl. It was salted slightly, the lump divided into pounds, again thrown into fresh water, squeezed and rolled by hand till about fourteen inches long, being then ready for sale. If not quite up to standard it was put up in $\frac{1}{2}$ lb. dishes. Willich (1802) thought so highly of it that the Essex methods were the only ones he troubled to describe, but he did not abide by this self-imposed restriction. The juice of carrots was used to colour the butter.[8]

When packed in firkins or pots the dairymen did their best to make the container airtight, but this must have been difficult with a wooden cask, or a pot with an open top fitted with a tied on lid. Twamley therefore suggested a chemical aid to the ordinary salt or brine. It was made up of one part each of sugar and nitre and two of salt, allowed to stand fourteen days in a barrel before use. When opened it must be used at once, and at the rate of 1 oz. to 16 oz. butter.

Such a precaution was all the more necessary towards the end of the eighteenth century because there was then great reason to believe that the milk of diseased cows was too often mixed with the rest, and made into butter and cheese. This practice was not new. It had been legislated against soon after Charles II's restoration. The Act of 1662 (Car. II c.26) recorded that bad and decayed butter was mixed and packed in firkins and pots with sound and good butter. Sometimes an excessive amount of salt was used. The Act forbade this, and ordered that no whey butter should be packed with that made of cream. Butter too suffered from the addition of saltpetre intended to nullify taints from unsuitable feeds and other causes. The penalty for such malpractices was to forfeit the value of all such butter so falsely packed. Another Act was passed in 1688 (3 & 4 William and Mary. c. 7), but if Adam's remark (1787) is correct it had not proved possible to enforce the regulations after the passage of a century.[9]

Young, who praised Suffolk butter highly, and in particular the methods of the famous Mrs. Chevallier of Aspall, and who was so voluminous on other subjects, paid little attention to dairy farming in 1804. 'The minutiae of dairy concerns', he wrote, 'would fill a book, and after all would not be useful to any extent'. Why he should have thought so I cannot imagine. The dairy industry was very substantial at the time he was writing as it had long been, not only in the West Midlands and Southwest, but also in his native Suffolk and the neighbouring county of Essex. Marshall was more detailed, and some of the writers of the county reports did not dismiss the subject so cavalierly. Two points Young did remark. Suffolk butter was often too heavily salted, the common rate being $3\frac{1}{2}$ to 4 pints of brine per firkin whereas 2 pints would have been ample. If the firkin could not be filled from one churning, the best dairymaids left the surface rough and broken so that the next lot would unite better. Again after the first skimming the milk was left in the pan for twelve hours and skimmed again to make a second butter that was sold cheaply to the poor. Something of the same sort was done in Hants. where more than one skimming was taken at intervals. The cream from each was kept separate, and churned separately to make butter of first and second quality. Here too it was the practice to take one-third of the cream, heat it almost to boiling point, mix it while hot with the remainder, stir and mix well to prevent souring. This was intended to give the butter a better keeping quality.[10]

Marshall found the normal methods from Norfolk through the Midlands. The only novelty he discovered was the Midland system of combatting rancidity in turnip butter and the bitterness of barley straw butter. Instead of putting the cream direct into the cream pot, the Midland dairymaids first poured it into hot water and let it stand till cool, when they skimmed it off the water. To Marshall this was a new idea and he thought it a most rational one though he had not proved it by his own experience. The great art in making good butter was, of course, to keep it free from rankness.

In Gloucestershire the methods varied little from those elsewhere except in some details. The milk was put into the cooler until its heat was reduced to about 80°F., and then put in skeels about one inch deep, and carefully kept level. It was skimmed with a skimming dish. The cream was put in earthenware jars, and stirred several times a day with the cream slice. The churn was warmed or cooled as necessary, and its mouth secured with butter pressed plasterwise into the joints, a process considered less troublesome than using a cloth. The autumn milk was coloured to produce a summer tint in the butter. Before washing the butter the maid scrubbed her hands with very hot water, rubbed them with salt, and plunged them into cold water. It sounds painful! When finished the butter was moulded into ½ lb. pats, four inches diameter and one and a half inches thick, and printed with the maker's pattern or mark. In Devonshire, Marshall, like everyone else, found the scalded cream method, where the cream, after standing some hours, was gently heated over the wood embers on an ordinary hearth, but sometimes on specially fitted charcoal stoves. The proper heat was indicated by the rising of blisters or pimples. Finally the butter was made by hand stirring. There was nothing new in this, unusual as it may have been to Marshall, and it went on long after his visit to this area. He thought it rather unhygienic, liable to boil over and to get soot and ashes in it, and to collect additional dirt and dust, while standing to cool, or even to being stolen by domestic animals. In East Devon and Dorset the more ordinary methods were general.[11]

The Lancashire system included some unusual details, and John Holt thought an account of them might be useful in other counties, a correct appreciation of the purpose for which he was instructed to undertake the survey of the county in 1795. Lancashire dairymaids divided the milk into two parts. The first drawn was kept for domestic use after being skimmed. The cream was stored and the whole milk of the second part mixed in and stirred. The mixture was kept according to the time of year exposed to the fire to promote fermentation and sourness. The vessels were occasionally rinsed with sour buttermilk to aid this process, which was said to produce more butter and of better quality than if the milk was churned in a sweet state.[12] Westmorland butter, made and packed in firkins for transport to distant markets, had a high reputation at the turn of the century: but as the holdings and herds were usually small, the cream was sometimes kept for rather longer than usual before churning.

During this time it 'was religiously stirred with a stick of the rowan tree to protect it from being witched'.[13] The famous Cheshire dairy farmers made a common practice of churning whole milk instead of setting it for cream. The milk was cooled as soon as it was brought to the dairy, and then put into four to six gallon jars, and left till 'carved' or clotted enough for churning. In winter the jars were placed in front of the fire. This method called for great skill in judging when it was ready for churning. The final product was made into lumps or dishes of 1½ lb. In Cheshire whey butter was commonly made, the churns being the upright plunge type. Some of these had a lever attached to make the work lighter, one farmer in 1808 even having a water wheel to drive his which could be regulated from 1 to 108 strokes a minute.[14]

Such were the practical methods of making butter on dairy farms at the end of the eighteenth century. The dairy farmers were probably satisfied to rely upon these methods, sanctified as they were by the traditional experience of centuries of this work, which had been taught by father to son and mother to daughter through so many generations. Theorists had however already begun to enquire into the general principles underlying the established methods, probably stimulated by the advances in chemistry which had been made in the last quarter of the eighteenth century.

Prominent amongst these was James Anderson, whose precepts were accepted and repeated in an exact or slightly garbled form by many later writers. It was generally recognised that the strokings were the richest part of the milk, and this had been confirmed by experiment. Several large teacups were filled at intervals during milking and weighed. The results invariably showed that the first drawn milk gave the least cream and the proportion increased as milking went on. Variation in quality was also caused by nearness to calving. As the flush of milk abated, it generally became thicker and more uniform in quality, but Anderson did not think any practical advantage could be taken of these conclusions, though the Scottish practice of allowing the calf to suck the first milk and then taking the rest for making up went some way towards it. One thing was possible. Milk carried a distance from the field to the dairy was so shaken up and partially cooled before being put in the setting pan that it did not yield so much cream as milk set immediately after milking. The cows should therefore be milked as near the dairy as possible, and to ensure this the principal pastures should be close to the buildings. Forsyth repeated all this, but both agreed that it was not the pastures but the skill of the dairymaids that was the foundation of the reputation of Cheshire cheese and Epping butter. Dickson complained that few experiments had yet been made in the best methods of raising cream, and that there had been no trials to decide the best material for making the vessels in which the cream was set. From the few experiments it seemed that the best temperature for raising cream in shallow trays was between 50° and 55°F. The proper time to leave the milk before skimming had not been determined. Various times had been suggested, but in practice it was left to the judgment of the maid. Epping cream was seldom kept three days, or at the most four. The largest Suffolk dairies churned the second or third day, but the cream was kept a day or two longer if the butter was to be salted. In cold weather it was sometimes kept six days. Some people thought it ought only to be kept one day, but Dickson did not approve of this as the cream did not become acid enough. Clearly opinion played a major part in deciding the point. The problem of determining the cream content of milk was simplified by the invention of the lactometer by Mr. Dicas of Liverpool, or would have been if the dairymen had used it. Parkinson dealt only with the practical aspect of butter making and potting, and his advice followed normal methods except in the matter of whey butter. He said that the whey should be boiled, and as it boiled some buttermilk should be added. The curds would then rise and could be skimmed, put into a vessel to sour and then churned. The resulting butter was nearly as good as that made from cream or milk, though it would not keep. It was excellent for pastry and other uses.[15]

Dairy farmers knew well enough by long experience that

their cows gave milk of varying degrees of richness as compared with each other, and at different times during the
lactation. It is a point that had been discusssed long before
Alexander Taylor advised that every cow's milk should be
kept separate until its quality was known. This was a simple
precaution to avoid mixing poor milk with rich. No milk
poor in cream ought to be made into butter. The farmer did
not in 1829 need to rely upon observation as he could use the
lactometer to determine the cream content. There were by
this time several types on the market. Taylor did not like the
common barrel churn, claiming that experiments had shown
that the upright churn gave the most butter. He did not
believe in washing the butter, but approved the use of colouring matter, carrot or marigold juice, to give an appetising
appearance to winter butter.[16] Baxter suggested a trifle of
annatto added to the cream would give the same effect.

The length of time the cream was kept before churning
was still determined by personal judgment or local tradition,
and varied between two and seven days. None of the writers
in the two decades, 1830-1850, did any more than remark
upon this, but most agreed that some degree of acidity was
desirable. Similarly many earlier advisers held the opinion
that the temperature of the churn was the most important
factor in successful butter making. The common practice, as
already said, was to warm the churn in winter and to cool it
in summer. The Highland and Agricultural Society promoted
some experiments to determine the proper temperature of
the cream for successful churning. Most writers thereafter
based their recommendations on the results, but they were in
fact so indefinite that the writers used a wide or narrow range
according to their own reading, or even pin-pointed a degree.
Loudon, for example, recommended a temperature of
between 50°-55°F. Baxter was more generous saying that the
best butter could only be produced at a certain temperature
between 45°-75°F. James Jackson repeated this, but David
Low twice stated that 56°F. was the correct heat, a degree to
which G. H. Andrews also subscribed. This may be regarded
as a measure of agreement, but certainly no more.

Salting was the most usual way of preserving butter in early Victorian days as it always had been. If the finest salt was used, 10 oz. to 14 lb. was adequate, well mixed in by hand, but other preservatives, very occasionally used in the eighteenth century, began to be more widely recommended and possibly used. One of these was Twamley's mixture of one part sugar, one part nitre, and two parts best Spanish salt finely powdered and mixed with the butter at 1 oz. to 1 lb. Covered with a saturated solution of salt, or with a syrup of sugar, the butter would however be safe enough; airtight casks were, of course, essential.[17]

The efforts of the chemists and the inventors had not had much influence on the practice of the dairymaid by 1850. For example, in Gloucestershire at that date almost every mistress of a dairy had some secret peculiarity or mystery, fancied or real, which was studiously kept from her equally clever neighbours. This was as it had always been. The result was a great variety of methods, but the differences must have been in trifling details rather than in general principles which were in the nature of things much alike.[18]

The Lancashire method again came in for some praise by Thomas Rowlandson in 1852. There the first drawn milk was set for cream, the last drawn mixed with it, and the whole churned, the heat during the operation being checked with a thermometer. The buttermilk was removed by manual kneading and several washings. In Dorset a smith sieved his milk, and cooled it in leads for twelve to thirty six hours, and then collected the cream in tin vessels until enough had accumulated to make churning worth while. Buckinghamshire dairymen did much the same, but occasionally let the skim milk stand a while longer, and took off a second lot of cream. In Oxfordshire, where Young had found that the farmers suckled calves for veal, the dairy farmers made more profit by making butter in 1854.[19]

All the advice given and processes used remained fairly static for the next few years: but in 1866 Samuel Copland optimistically declared that in all good dairies butter making

had been reduced strictly to a science which infallibly produced good butter. Obviously the process was better understood—as it must have been if this had been true—than when
difficulty in making it come was ascribed to a witch or fairy of
whom the dairymaid stood in wholesome fear. Nevertheless
authority continued to specify anything between 51°-65°F.
as the correct heat at which to churn in order to get the best
results. Hygiene was emphasised by everyone, and by 1872 it
was forbidden to use the human hand: wooden hands or
butter workers ought invariably to be used in the interests
of sanitary manufacture. A mixture of $\frac{1}{2}$ lb. salt, 4 oz. saltpetre,
and 4 oz. loaf sugar powdered together, kept a month to
mature, and used at the rate of 1 oz. to 1 lb. butter was a great
advance on previous advice. Unfortunately butter that had
become rancid could not be restored to its pristine condition,
but it could be immersed in clear spring water, kept over a
fire till the water boiled, allowed to cool and then skimmed.
Thus treated it would be good enough for pastry making as
the disagreeable acids are to some extent soluble in water,
and were evaporated or washed out.[20]

The large volume of scientific discussion in books, pamphlets and the more important agricultural periodicals, most of
which passed over the head of the ordinary dairy farmer,
clearly indicated the need for bringing it to his attention, and
persuading him to apply the newly discovered principles to
his practice. The gap between science and practice must be
bridged by education if it was to be bridged at all.

Very poor butter of irregular quality was made in Westmorland, and Lady Alice Kenlis, later Lady Bective, was so
concerned about this that in 1869 she began to offer prizes for
butter at the Kendal Agricultural Show. Her decision to do
this followed a time when butter made in the county was bad,
and consequently fetched low prices. She secured the services
of competent judges, and tried to raise the average quality.
Thirty years experience convinced her that the plan had not
succeeded for little improvement had resulted, and in 1898
she decided to discontinue her awards. Those who competed
for the prizes may have demonstrated that it was possible to

make butter superior to the average, but that was all. Fortunately other people, who were indignant at her decision, came forward to supply prizes, and the Society's awards were continued.[21]

The motto of the Royal Agricultural Society is 'Practice with Science', and many essays on dairy farming had appeared in its Journal in the sixties and seventies. One way of bringing the new ideas more forcibly to the farmer's notice, and to encourage him to apply scientific results in his practice was to show him the principles at work. The Society decided to set up a working dairy as a regular feature at its annual show. Experiments were made at the Bristol Show in 1878, and at Kilburn in 1879, and then the Aylesbury Dairy Company was asked to undertake the organisation of the working dairy at Carlisle. This was a successful arrangement, and the Company showed a wide range of plant. It was not however till 1888 that a butter making competition was included. This, and the working dairy shown every year by the Bath and West Society, must have influenced some dairy farmers, but others felt some doubt about their economic ability to provide the new apparatus and the technical knowledge required to use them successfully.[22]

The British Dairy Farmer's Association was at first doubtful about the value of technical dairy education, wondering if conditions in a school might be so different from those on a farm, that tuition there would be of little use when the pupil came home again. This was, of course, true, and was therefore a basic reason for schools, the purpose of which would be to inculcate new ideas for adoption by the novice, who would have to combat the obstinate preference for the older methods resulting from traditional experience. The Association preferred a system of visiting advisers. There were, however, already schools in Germany, France, Denmark and Sweden, and ten years later (1887) the Association established a dairy school and experiment station at Aylesbury. This institution, the National Institute for Research in Dairying, was later transferred to Reading, where it has had a long successful life, and continues to prosper.[23]

The Bath and West Society joined in the effort. There were few people fit to train teachers, but, with the aid of a government grant, the Society was able to undertake the organisation of short courses in 1888. The aid of local committees was sought to provide premises with a sufficient water supply. Two ten-day courses were held at Swindon in the autumn, and ended with a prize butter making competition. Evercreech Agricultural Society went one better with three courses at Shepton Mallet, and early in 1889 Chippenham held another three in succession. For the next few years this system was very successful in the south west. By 1895 the Society's schools had visited sixteen counties, and instructed 2,284 students. It claimed, not without reason, that it had shown the County Councils the way. Worcester County Council made a grant of £700 to establish a dairy school, and kept the instruction in its own hands. Westmorland started a migratory dairy school in 1889, and in 1896 joined with Cumberland in renting Newton Rigg as an experimental and dairy farm. Somerset County Council took over Mark House, Mark, near Highbridge, and boarded pupils. Kent and Surrey sent students to Wye for one month, and arranged for the best pupils to stay three months longer. The travelling butter school begun in Devon in 1893 was taken over by the County Council in 1897.[24] The effect of these and other efforts to educate the dairy farmer and dairymaid is not measurable, but the trained pupils who came back from the courses and schools must have adopted some of the principles on their farms, and, if successful, perhaps have been copied by their neighbours and friends. W. J. Malden said in 1896 that farmers had benefited by the help of science in the dairy; scientific investigations had shown why it is necessary to keep the dairy and all appertaining to it clean. This was no doubt an advantage, but everyone who had discussed dairying in the previous 400 years had insisted upon this necessity. Unrecorded persons had no doubt done so for much longer; but practice had never kept pace with precept so far as I can judge. Malden indeed admitted that science had helped the factories more than the farmer as only a minor proportion of small dairies had been materially affected. The new methods were too difficult and costly for these people to undertake and in the ordinary farm dairy, he thought there was little new, except the use of a thermometer.[25] The butter made on the farms at Blaxhall, Suffolk about 1900 was made in the traditional way, and the utensils were of ancient shape. Mrs. Pinmarsh, a farm wife in a Berkshire village, at the same date made her own butter, and took the profits. The churning was done by a maid, and during the hot weather the services of the cowman were called in to help as the butter was slow in coming. A neighbour, who had been to the classes, suggested regulating the temperature, but Mrs. Pinmarsh thought it unnecessary, being one of those new-fangled ideas. Cream was always contrary in hot weather, and not likely to be changed by putting a thermometer in it. The gentleman who kept a cow or two, maybe the suburban or some one new to country life, was advised to adopt the traditional way of setting milk, and churning cream into butter, and to use the mixture of salt, sugar and saltpetre which Anderson had recommended as a preservative a century before.[26]

The new scientific methods evidently spread very slowly. The old practices presented the same problems as always. Science and discussion went some way towards solving them, and suggesting improvements that would remove them from dairy practice: but as Maldon said the small dairy farmer could not cope with the novelties, and preferred to go on in his own way. Advice how to perfect this way was not wasted if acted upon, and the subjects that had been discussed for so long formed a substantial part of the textbooks published in these three decades. The question whether butter should be washed to help remove the buttermilk or not was one of these. Malden realised that washing was not a new practice. It had been done in Bedfordshire for at least fifty years, when a man was instructed in it by an elderly farm wife. It was in fact much more ancient than that. He approved of the constant exhortations to cleanliness, but did not think that altogether new either. The temperature of setting cream was restricted within narrower limits by these comparatively modern writers. It varied between 55°-58°F. in summer and 64°-66° or even 70°F. in winter. Throughout this time, too, several writers emphasised that setting for cream in shallow pans was the most common but not the best method. The Cooley and Swartz, and the Jersey and other creamers are mentioned, but everyone agreed that the mechanical separator was best. Emphasis, too, was laid upon the necessity for avoiding physical contact with the butter, Scotch hands being used in preference to human hands.[27]

It was advisable to watch the butterfat content of the milk, Pilley thought the average yield about 8 oz. from 1 quart of cream in 1881, but this was optimistic. Punchard, about ten years later, thought the average yield per cow was about 570 gallons of milk, and it took 3 gallons to produce 1 lb. of butter. James Long in 1889 admitted this fact, but thought that no cow that gave less than 1 lb. butter to 2½ gallons of milk should be kept.[28]

Butter making and cheese making on the farm occupied a prominent place in the dairy textbooks until the First World War. Invention had produced the separator, a great variety of churns and other implements for use on the farm. Science, particularly the work of Pasteur, had defined the reasons for the long recognised necessity for hygiene in the dairy. Education to teach the use of the new apparatus and the new methods had been arranged in most of the dairy counties by the turn of the century: but while all this was being done to bring farm butter making to perfection many causes were working together to bring it to an end. Not the least of these was the rapidly expanding trade in liquid milk, and the facilities that enabled it to be transported hundreds of miles, something that was to affect farm cheese making as well. Almost equally, if not more important, was the competition of overseas butter and cheese on the market, and the birth of a factory system in this country—factors to be discussed in the following chapter.

## (ii). Farmhouse cheese making

No more is to be found about cheese making in the six-teenth century than about butter making. Tusser's admoni-tions to Cisley, the sluttish dairymaid, warn her that careless-ness in her work will certainly appear in the result: but there is no more. Yet several different kinds of cheese were made. Some people however did not think the home produced as good as imported cheese. Googe, for example, thought Par-mesan cheese the finest; after that Dutch cheese (Edam was imported then just as it finds its way to our tables today); next Normandy and last English. Hartlib shared this opinion, but thought that Parmesan and Holland cheese might be made in England. The best of English cheeses came from Cheshire, Shropshire, Banbury, Suffolk, Essex and Hertford. The very worst was Kentish cheese, but the Suffolk must have run it very close. Hartlib slightly changed this order of selection. The best were made at Banbury, in Cheshire and the Cheddar district, but the last was 'seldom seen but at Noblemen's tables or rich Vintner's Sellars'. He preferred it to foreign cheese. John Heywood wrote 'I never saw Banbury cheese thicke enough, but I have seen Essex cheese quicke enough'.

Besides being named from the place where it was made cheese was described by the process employed in making it. There were one-meal cheeses (made from one milking); two meal cheeses; morning milk cheese; nettle cheese; skim or flet milk cheese; cheese made from the stroakings only, like Angelot; cream cheese like that of Padua; but in the six-teenth and seventeenth centuries the making of all of them was very similar. Details varied, but perhaps more in the mixture of milk, the use of cream, and the rennet than other-wise.[1]

In all this work the greatest care and cleanliness was essen-tial, and both Tusser and Surflet emphasised the need for the maidens to be cleanly. She must roll her sleeves well up. Some people preferred young children before the age of puberty to handle the curd from a superstition connected with men-struation. It is a commentary upon contemporary life that these young girls should not have 'scabbed or scurvie hands', nor of an intemperate heat. 'Such filthiness of hands hinders curding, and makes cheese full of eies'.

When these hygienic precautions had been taken the work could proceed. Perhaps the most general system of farmhouse cheese making in the sixteenth and seventeenth centuries was to make what was known as new milk cheese. It was a long and tedious business. 'Grosse and fat milk' was chosen.

The dairymaid took the morning's milk and 'syled' it into a clean tub. She added the cream of the previous evening's milk, straining it through a clean cloth into the tub. She then put in some boiling water to ensure that the mixture was not too rich and let the whole stand till cool. When it was no more than lukewarm she added the rennet at one spoonful to each gallon of milk, taking care that no curd went in. When the curd came she broke and mashed it by hand, a process in which the condition of the hands was obviously important as everyone agreed. Then she pressed it gently into the bottom of the tub with a thin dish, taking the whey off as clean as she could. After that she put the curd into a cheese vat, and pressed it down hard, and laid it on the cheese board, turning the cheese upon it. She laid the cloth in the vat and put the cheese in again. With a thin slice she thrust the cheese down close on every side, put a cloth on the top, and carried the whole to the great cheese press. She pressed it for half an hour, put on a dry cloth and pressed it again. She continued this process four or five times the first day. In the evening she left it in the press for twenty four hours till the following evening when she turned it for the last time, and put it into the vat without a cloth. When pressed sufficiently she laid it on a 'kimmel' (a powdering or salting tub), rubbed it all over with salt, and let it lie for a night. She rubbed it again in the morning, and turned it out on the brine which came from the salt for two or three days more according to size. Then she laid it on a clean scrubbed table, and kept turning it at intervals till thoroughly dry, and fit to go into the 'cheese heck', a cellar or some dark cool place.

Variations in the cheese were made by using only whole

milk, without any added cream; part whole milk and part skimmed; and wholly and drastically skimmed milk as in Suffolk. Flavouring, mostly of herbal origin, was added by some skilful dairymaids. Nettle cheese was made by placing a layer of nettles on the cheese in the vat. Floaten cheese is differently described. It may have been made of milk from which the cream had been 'floaten' or skimmed, or may have been made by heating some milk and adding it to the rest. Eddish or aftermath cheese, made when the cows were grazing the aftermath, was richer than spring cheese, because the milk was richest then or because of the difference in the temperature when it was made exactly in the same way as new milk cheese.

Careless work was easily discerned in the cheese itself. White and dry cheese was the result of too careful skimming. Argus eyes showed that the curd had not been properly worked. Hoven or blown cheese was caused in the same way. Tough cheese had been set too hot, or not worked up, and the curd broken at the proper time. Hairs in the cheese needed no explanation. Soft cheese had not had the whey properly pressed and drained out. Gentils came from fly blows, too much moisture or warmth. The dairymaid could not, in fact, disguise careless and slovenly work. Her cheese was her judge and jury.

She made her cheeselip bag or rennet of the stomach bag of a young suckling calf that had never had anything else but milk. She took out the curd and washed it clean of bits of grass and laid it on a clean cloth to drain. Next in another vessel she mixed the curd with a handful or two of salt. The bag she washed several times and then put in the curd and salt. She rubbed the bag with salt and closed up the mouth outside. For use the curd was taken out of the bag, and broken up with a wooden pestle in a stone mortar. She added the yolks of two or three eggs and $\frac{1}{2}$ pint of thick sweet cream, 1d. worth of saffron finely dried and beaten to powder, and a little cloves and mace, all mixed thoroughly together, and put it in the bag again. She boiled a very strong brine with a handful of saxifrage, and when it was cold, cleared it into an earthen vessel and mixed half a dozen 'pompols' and a few walnut tree leaves. She took out a few spoonfuls of the former curd and mixed it with this brine. After this she closed up the bag and hung it. The rennet was ready for use in a fortnight, and 4 spoonfuls were enough for at least 12 gallons of milk. Other materials that could be used, and were in some places, were the rennet of lamb, kid or hare, the juice of figs or ginger, and the seed of the wild thistle (*Carduus benedictus*), but in England the calves' vell was the most usual. Surflet condemned the use of vinegar as it prevented the curd coming.[2]

The writer of *Tusser Redivivus*, 1710, only amended the remarks on the dairy made by Thomas Tusser in 1577, by pointing out that milking ewes was then little done in southern England, and not so much in the north as formerly. Thomas had estimated that the milk of five ewes was equal to that of one cow, but if they were no longer milked it made no odds as his reviver thought this milk only fit for cheese. It was used in some parts of Wales and the north for the family table until quite recent times. John Mortimer, who lived in Essex, did not think butter and cheese making worth discussing because most good housewives were acquainted with the way of it. Some land, he thought, made unsound cheese, perhaps a reflection of Hartlib's idea that 'It were against all reason and experience to think that the notable difference between Suffolk and Cheshire cheese comes only from different ways of making it . . .' Mortimer advised that if cheese began to go rotten the bad piece should be cut out and the hole filled with powdered chalk covered in with butter. The chalk would stop the progress of the rot by drying up the moisture 'that causeth it to corrupt'. If mites began to breed the cheese must be rubbed over with oil or oak ashes once in three months and this would kill them.[3]

Thomas Tusser had believed that hoven or blown cheese resulted from inadequate working of the curd; others, like Mortimer, blamed the land, or the season of the year. Wiltshire dairymen found that when hay was fed to cows feeding on the early spring grass, cheese made from their milk was apt to heave and was stronger than that made later in the year. This cheese must be kept a year to ripen properly. Stephens, a tenant farmer at Pomeroy, Wiltshire, subscribed to the belief that the feed affected the cheese. For example, the farmers of East Lydford, near Somerton, Somerset, could not make yellow coated cheese like that made in North Wilt-shire. The fault was partly in the housewives whose standards were lower, but more in the grazing. The grass of the low rich pastures of Somerset were 'less spirituous and less con-cocted and digested, more gross and gnash', and consequently the cheese lacked the virtues of the North Wiltshire where the grass grew more slowly 'yet the watery juices are more rectified and qualified'. Some dairywomen had a prejudice against broad clover, Mrs. Bissy of Holt amongst them. Cheese made from it was not good and tasted strong and bitter. North Wiltshire cheese at the end of the seventeenth century was classified according to the season when it was made: hay cheese made for some time after the cow's calving; spring grass cheese made in May and June; and aftermath cheese. The last was the best if kept long enough as the cow's milk then had the most cream.

Hartlib thought Cheddar cheese far better than foreign, indeed preferable to any in the world; Stephens that it was often too dry because it was made too large. Also the farmers there kept their milk collecting too long. They had long been in the habit of putting their milk together to make cheese larger than ordinary, weighing from 30 to 100 lb.[4] The system in the early eighteenth century was an example of well-organised co-operation. All the people who lived in the village were cow-keepers. Each brought his milk daily to a common room or depot where the quantity was recorded. The whole of the day's milk was put together, and every meal's milk made into one cheese, so that the cheese was bigger or smaller as the milk yield varied. This method was intended to preserve the goodness and reputation of the cheese, which Defoe (1724) praised as highly as Hartlib had seventy five years before.[5]

The eighteenth century method of making Somerset or Cheddar cheese differed from others largely by the addition of heated whey mixed with water to the curd that had been broken and strained, and then breaking again. After a proper quantity of rennet had been put into the milk, the Somerset dairymaids broke the curd slowly into small pieces, and then dripped out the whey. With the whey they mixed as much water and heated it between warm and scalding. When it was at the proper heat they strained it on the dry curd in a tub and worked it round by hand, afterwards leaving it for half an hour until the whey creamed over. Then they dripped the whey out, and again kneaded and broke the curd, wrapped it in a cloth, and pressed it in the vat for an hour, removed it, washed the cloth, and replaced it till evening. They took it out again, salted it on both sides, and pressed it again until the next morning, when it was taken out, put in a dry cloth and left till evening, the cloth then removed and the cheese left to stand naked all night. The next morning it was put upon a shelf to cure. How many times it was turned while curing is not stated, but it must be done often. The whey and water was a precaution against hoving.

A rather fuller description makes the cheese sound much richer in content, though it was said in 1772 that it was seldom made having formerly been more in fashion than it was then. This is not very credible. The milk of at least 12 cows was required for the purpose, and if one man had not enough two or more neighbours joined together—a modification of the co-operation of the whole village described by Defoe. To the morning milk of the twelve cows the cream from the previous evening's milk was added with about 3 spoonfuls of rennet. When the curd came it was broken and whey'd, broken again. At this point 3 lb. of fresh butter was worked in, and the mixture put in the press, where it was turned frequently for an hour or more. The cloths were changed as often and washed each time. Wet cloths were used at first but finally two or three dry ones. After this it was left in the press for thirty to forty hours, taken out, washed in whey, and laid on a dry cloth till dry. It was then ready for storing and curing, but must of course be turned often. An old Somerset rhyme made this clear:

> If you will have a good cheese and have'n old
> You must turn'n seven times before he is cold.

No mention of salt is made here, but this may be either an accidental or intentional omission.[6]

The process of making Cheddar cheese was evidently not standardised in the eighteenth century, there being regional differences with other parts of the county not doing quite the same as the inhabitants of Cheddar village itself. Possibly butter may have only been added when a very rich cheese was being made. Billingsley made no mention of it in 1797.

Cheddar cheese was then made in Mere and Cheddar, and was much admired by persons of taste. Cleanliness, sweet rennet, and care in breaking the curd were the principal requisites in making it successfully. He omitted the addition of the previous evening's cream to the morning milk, simply saying that when the milk was brought home it was strained into a tub and three tablespoonfuls of rennet added, if sufficient to make a 28 lb. cheese. It was then left for two hours, and the process continued as above. No butter was added, but salt was when the curd was taken out of the vat the first morning, and it was salted once a day for twelve days after it finally left the press. Some skimmed milk cheese was made in other parts of Somerset.[7]

By 1851 all the Somerset farmers south of the Mendips were devoted to cheese making, the finest of their product being known as Cheddar. The area stretched from Axbridge to Wells and from Shepton to Glastonbury. The herds here were usually from thirty to sixty cows, and modern appliances were already beginning to be used, some attention being given to temperature by the use of the thermometer. Unfortunately the cheese turners introduced in the Midlands were not used here, and the farmer's wives and daughters were still compelled to do this heavy work manually.[8]

The later nineteenth century process, assisted by the new utensils, was slightly modified. It was regulated by the clock and the thermometer. The morning's milk was mixed with previous evening's at a temperature of about 80°F., the rennet added and an hour allowed for the curd to form. It was carefully broken up and slip scalded i.e. the scalding whey was added to the curd while it was still in a pulpy state before it had time to subside and get hard, and the mass of curd and whey heated to 100°F. If Cockey's apparatus was used hot water run into the container below the vat did this; if not hot whey was poured into the mass. The whole was well stirred until the desired heat was reached. The curd was then allowed to subside, the whey drained off, and the dry curd passed through the curd mill, salt then being added at 1 lb. to 56 lb. The salted curd was next put into the vat and press and left three days, after which it was taken to the cheese room. The cloths were changed as the cheese was turned in the press, but this was done twice only. Some added annatto to colour the cheese, but the best makers deplored this. The smell was unpleasant and the taste filthy. Cheese making as a science was still not understood, complained Joseph Harding, whose wife was so renowned that she had been invited to Ayrshire to lecture on the subject.[9]

The process remained essentially the same until modern times, when only a few farmhouse cheese makers exist in the Cheddar area, but already by 1878 proprietary brands of essence of rennet were being used in place of vells prepared by the dairymaid. Ten years later half a dozen makers were selling this product, and it was being generally used by Cheddar dairymaids.[10] The early Cheddar with its addition of cream and butter must have been very rich, and have well deserved its fame as a gourmet's choice. Today it is made in only a few farmhouses in Somerset, Wiltshire and Dorset, but it is a factory product made in many parts of the world and known to almost every table in this country.[11]

Using purchased rennet was not, of course, confined to the Somerset dairies in the later years of the nineteenth century. It was adopted by dairymaids all over the country. Before that time rennet was always made on the farm, and in general the methods of manufacture were alike. Minor variations were practised in the different dairy districts, and some dairymaids followed more complicated methods than others.

THE THISTLE MILKING MACHINE

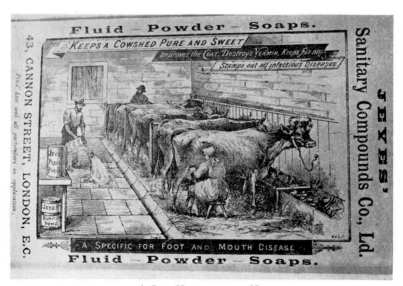

A COW HOUSE ABOUT 1889

Lawrence's Refrigerator

John Laurence (1726) theorised a little. To make a good keeping cheese, the curd must be made very firm. Therefore an acid, sour thing must be put into the milk, such as the flowers of thistles, or artichokes or rather chardons. The maw of a suckling calf was most common. Some used this maw after it was dry, by snipping off a small piece at a time, and putting it in a little fair water or sack for twelve hours. Some pickled it and dried it in the smoke 'and put the Cheese together while the Milk continues warm, or heat a Part and mingle it warm with the rest'. The maw itself must not go into the milk. Laurence commended the Spanish way of using dried flowers of Chardons, as it ought to be the English, because it was the cleanliest and best way of turning milk into curd. His method of making rennet was very simple. Take the curd out of the calf's bag, wash and pick it well from hairs and stones, season it well with salt. Wipe the bag, and salt it both inside and out. Replace the curd, and let the whole lie in salt for three or four days, and then hang it up.[12] The Essex and Hertfordshire dairymaids made rennet in this way, and sometimes hung it up in a corner of the kitchen chimney, as apparently they did in Durham; but the former preferred to close the refilled bag with a skewer, put it in an earthenware crock, and cover it up tightly. It would then keep a year. For use they boiled a quart of water, salted it to a density to float an egg, and allowed it to cool. This brine they poured into the bag, and then pricked it full of holes, laying it in a clean pan. With rennet prepared in this way a spoonful of the fresh liquor was sufficient to turn or set about 16 to 20 gallons of milk, and it kept its virtue for about a month. Its temperature was important. When put in the milk it must be as warm as it would have been in the living calf's bag, but not hotter, or the cheese would be hard. An artificial rennet could be made from the plant known as Rennet Wort boiled with some tops of Sweet Briar. Indeed Bradley (1736) thought that the presence of Goose Grass, Clivers or Rennet Wort, and some other weeds in the pasture to some extent the equivalent of rennet, and that consequently not so much was necessary to cause the curd to form. It is not clear whether he meant in the composition of the milk used, or in its effect upon the curd in the calves' bag formed from its mother's milk. He does suggest that one reason for the hardness of Suffolk cheese was the badness of the local rennet because the feed of the cows was not so good,[13] an opinion that is open to question.

Ellis shared Bradley's theory that good grass made a good rennet bag. A good one could be made still better if the calf sucked about six hours before it was killed because the curd was then newer. It must be got away as soon as possible. Otherwise he described the procedure in almost the same words as Bradley.[14] John Mills dismissed the subject quite cursorily, but Marshall treated it in detail. His receipt was along the established lines with some additions that had possibly accrued from local experience, and remained a standard practice, perhaps with individual divergences dictated by personal taste, until the adoption of the chemists' essence of rennet.

All that Mills had to say in 1776 was that the clods of curdled milk found in the third or fourth stomach of a suckling calf are, after being dried in the air, the rennet made use of for curdling milk. The longer it is kept the better it is; and a very little of it was sufficient to turn a large quantity of milk, as is well known to all who keep dairies.[15] Marshall, when in Norfolk, had a small dairy, and prepared his rennet with the care that might be expected of him. He removed the curd from the calf's bag, maw or stomach, washed it clean, salted it thoroughly inside and out, leaving a white coat of salt over every part of it. He then put it in an earthen jar to stand for three or four days, in which time it formed the salt and its own natural juices into a pickle. Next he took it out and hung it up for two or three days to let the pickle drain from it, resalted it and placed it again in a jar, which he covered tight with paper pierced with a large pin. So it was kept till it was wanted for use. It is noteworthy that he does not say that he replaced the curd in the bag after cleansing it as earlier writers advised, and he does not make it clear whether the jar in which the resalted vell was stored was a clean one, or that in which the first pickle remained. The detail of drying after the first treatment and resalting is also new.

Marshall did this, but the average Norfolk dairymaid was much less particular. She used the curd that happened to be contained in the stomach of the calf when butchered together with the hairs and dirt inseparable from it—apparently in its natural state. 'Hence probably', remarked Marshall reasonably, 'the rancid flavour of the Norfolk cheese'.

In preparing for use the rennet he had made Marshall introduced more herbs than usual, a practice he may have learned in Gloucestershire. He took a handful each of the leaves of sweet briar, dog-rose and bramble, boiled them in a gallon of water with three or four handfuls of salt for about fifteen minutes. He then strained off the liquor and let it stand till cool when he put it in an earthen vessel with the prepared maw, and added a sound good lemon stuck round with about $\frac{1}{4}$ oz. of cloves to give the rennet an agreeable flavour. The longer left the stronger the rennet would be, and consequently its use called for some judgment. The bag could be taken out, dried, resalted, and put in again several times until its virtue was exhausted. Additional bags put in would make the rennet stronger.

Marshall thought the leaves and spice had no other effect than overpowering the tang inseparable from the maw however well cleaned. Wiltshire dairywomen had a different idea. A rank pasture caused a quality in the milk that produced hoven or blown cheese. The herbs in the rennet corrected this, and some of them pretended to so much skill in their use that they could make up different prescriptions to correct the different pastures. Marshall would have none of this. So small a proportion of vegetable juices as passed with the rennet into so much milk could not have much effect, but he felt that a course of judicious chemical experiments would lead to the discovery of a vegetable or mineral preparation 'adequate to this valuable purpose'.[16]

The dairywomen of the Vale of Gloucester did not pretend to any such skill as did their neighbours in Wiltshire. They differed in one important respect from some others. There

was, of course, a local supply of calves' vells, but large numbers were brought from London and Ireland pickled in casks,
and sold by grocers and other shopkeepers. English vells cost
6d.; Irish about 4d. apiece being smaller and sometimes
suspiciously like lamb's vells. There was no standard method
of treating these vells to make rennet, but the prevailing
system was to salt some whey until it would bear an egg (the
magic density), and leave it to stand all night 'to purge itself'.
In the morning it was skimmed, and racked off clear. An
equal quantity of water brine was added, and into the mixture some sweet briar, thyme, hyssop and other 'sweet herbs'
with a little black pepper and saltpetre. The herbs were tied
in bunches and left in the brine for a few days. Then either
4 English vells or enough Irish to equal them were put into
about 6 quarts of the liquor for three or four days, and the
rennet was ready to use. Many dairymaids did not bother to
take so much trouble. All they did was to steep the vells in
cold salt and water.[17]

Marshall's Norfolk system of making vells was long quoted.
Lawson and Loudon confined themselves to this method using
a close approximation to Marshall's own words.[18] Youatt
quoted him in 1837, but also gave Hazard's prescription
(1785), and Holland's from his *General View of Cheshire*,
1808. All these were quoted again about 1880 in Ward and
Lock's *Book of Farm Management*.

Hazard lived at Stoney-Littleton, Somerset, and his method
was to procure a perfectly sweet vell (if slightly tainted the
cheese would fail). In 2 quarts of clean, soft water some salt
was dissolved and sweet briar, rose leaves and flowers, cinna-
mon, mace, cloves, in short almost every sort of spice and aro-
matic that could be got, boiled up until the liquor was reduced to three pints, when it was strained clear from the
spices. It was allowed to cool until it was not warmer than
milk from the cow, and then poured over the vell. A lemon
could be sliced into the container if desired, and the whole
left a day or two, after which it might be strained and bottled.
Prepared in this way and well corked, rennet would last

twelve months or more. The vell could be salted, dried for a week or so near the fire, and used again.[19]

The Cheshire method was to take a lien on the maw-skin (bag) when they sold a calf to the butcher. Those who lived near a butcher watched the slaughter of calves, and chose those they thought the best. There were imported vells sold in the county too, but these were often mixed with the vells of lambs and kids, which were not so effective in use.

The Cheshire dairymaid removed all the curd, washed the maw-skin very carefully, filled it nearly full of salt, and laid it in the bottom of a mug kept for the purpose, and designed to hold three skins. She put the first in on a layer of salt and covered each with salt as added. Finally she filled up the mug with salt, covered it with a dish or slate, and put it into a cool place until the approach of the cheese making season in the following year. She then took the skins out and laid them to drain the brine away. When dry she spread them on a table, powdered each side with fine salt, and rolled it smooth with a paste roller to press in the salt. After that she stuck a thin piece of wood across each to keep it extended while hung up to dry.

The steep or rennet for use the Cheshire dairymaids commonly made by cutting off a piece of dried maw-skin in the evening and soaking overnight in a solution of as much salt as would cover a shilling in lukewarm water. In the morning the infusion, from which the piece of skin had been removed, was put in the cheese tub. This was a rather hit or miss method because the quality and strength of the infusion must have varied greatly. An improved system was followed by some of the more advanced workers, and this Holland believed to have been the only important change in making Cheshire cheese for centuries. All the skins provided for the season, pickled and dried as before, were put into an open vessel, or more than one if required. For each skin three pints of pure spring water was added, and allowed to stand for twenty four hours. The skins were then taken out and put into other vessels with a pint of spring water for each to stand for another twenty four hours. They were taken out the second time and gently stroked down with the hand into the infusion. The skins were then done with. The two infusions were mixed together, and passed through a fine linen sieve. Sufficient salt was added to saturate the water, and leave a trifle undissolved at the bottom. Through the summer the scum that rose to the surface was carefully skimmed, and fresh salt added so that some always remained undissolved. Somewhat less than a wine half pint of this preparation was thought enough for 60 lb. of cheese. The liquid must be well stirred every time some was taken out.[20]

The practice of putting the curd back into the bag while curing it, as was done earlier in the 18th century, thus appears to have been pretty well abandoned by the end of that century. It was sometimes done in 1837, but the more usual practice was to use only the salted and dried skins, because most dairymaids believed the curd would give a harsh taste to the cheese. Judging the strength of the rennet and the quantity to use was a matter of great nicety, and it must have been very easy to make a serious mistake with material prepared in this way. Not only was the chemical composition of the different maw-skins, and the different parts of each a variant, but the treatment to which it was subjected lacked uniformity, a character then impossible to maintain, and so probably introduced further chemical variation. This was unfortunate because the quality of the cheese depended very largely upon the proper application of the right amount and strength of rennet. If too new or too strong the cheese was apt to heave and swell and to become full of eyes and holes.[21]

Though Ward and Lock's *Book of Farm Management* adds nothing to the methods of making rennet, it enlivens the subject by introducing a touch of Victorian refinement. The use of the contents of the bag, where it persisted, had become repugnant to many, and the writer called the process a somewhat nauseous idea. Slightly ridiculous! A more reasonable view was held by Coleman, and by Donaldson. The best agent for coagulating the curd was the one provided by nature, the gastric juices found in the fourth stomach of a milk fed calf. Other acids could be used, but were less appropriate.

'The value of rennet is not its mere capacity to curdle milk, for this phenomenon will result from the use of any powerful acid. It is in the fact that it is a digestive agent converting the raw curd into a mellow and deliciously flavoured cheese'.

This was known in the time of Dioscorides and remains true today, but great care was necessary in using it—as so many people said. Even the ready made rennet which began to be used in the last quarter of the nineteenth century varied in strength. Coleman suggested that each farmer should experiment to find the exact quantity of any given supply that was necessary to bring the curd from a given volume of milk in a given time. Half a dozen makers were offering supplies of essence of rennet by 1889, and this relieved the cheese maker from making his own, but apparently it did not supply him with a product of uniform strength any more than his own rather haphazard methods.[23] The small bottles of rennet sold by the grocers for use in making junket and other dairy products vary in just the same way.

Cheddar was a gourmet's cheese, or so it was said. It has not proved possible to retain its high reputation, nor to restrict its manufacture to its native place. Cheshire cheese has done both these things, and the Cheshire dairy farms still produce more of their local cheese than those of any other dairy area in the country. It has always been thought that the fine peculiar quality of Cheshire cheese owed so much to the pastures on which the cows grazed—some of the early writers praised the early growing and prolific weeds (herbs)—and that attempts to make it elsewhere were therefore bound to fail.

This cheese was made and is still made on the general system of a new milk or two meal cheese already described. The earliest account of the process I know is that of John Laurence. It is obviously defective, or so I judge. I have been unable to find an earlier recipe, but one or more may come to light among the county archives as they are examined.

According to him, at Nantwich the milk was strained into

a cheese tub as warm as possible from the cow, about 6 spoonfuls of strong rennet added and stirred well with a fleeting dish. Then a fitting wooden cover was placed on the tub, the curd coming in forty-five minutes or less. This could very well be done with the morning milk but hardly with the evening, or the maid would have been working all night: nor does it indicate the quantity of milk to which 6 spoonfuls of rennet were added. The only conclusion is that the evenings milk was heated, possibly skimmed, before being put in the cheese tub as described in later records. The process continued in the same way as it had done, possibly for centuries. The curd was broken very small with a dish and gently stirred by hand, pressed down with dish and hand until all the whey was expressed, and then broken very small into a vat and heaped up to the highest pitch. This was squeezed manually and heaped up again about two inches above the level of the top of the vat. Every drop of whey possible must be got out, or the cheese would be sour and full of holes and eyes. The curd was next wrapped in a cloth and pressed by a weight of about 4 cwt. from 9 a.m. to 2 p.m., removed, rewrapped in a dry cloth, and pressed again till 6 p.m. when it was taken out and salted all over. It was put into the vat again for the night, presumably under pressure, though that is not stated. The following morning it was salted again, and placed on a dresser where it was turned every day for four days. Next it was washed in cold water, wiped with a dry cloth, being careful to see that all traces of salt were removed, and taken to the cheese loft. It must be turned every day while stored and as the quantity increased this must have been an exhausting task. Ellis, who in 1750 described this as the old way of making Cheshire cheese, suggested the quantity of milk used as six quarts a meal from sixty cows.[24]

The modern way of making Cheshire cheese was twofold then. Some used all new milk; others half skimmed and half new which made it a two meal cheese. All heated the milk till it was as warm as when it came from the cow, and put in three or four spoonfuls of rennet to make a 1 cwt. cheese. If so large it was usual to make it wholly of new milk. The rest of the process is the same as Laurence's except that after breaking the curd the first time about $\frac{1}{2}$ lb. of salt for every 50 lb. cheese was worked into the curd. Instead of being salted on the outside the cheese was placed in a tub of strong brine after pressing and left completely immersed for six days, but turned once a day in the tub. After this it must be laid on green rushes for two or three weeks, turned daily and wiped with a hair cloth. Finally it was stood on the floor or a shelf, being turned and rubbed once or twice a week till hard, when it was rubbed all over with $\frac{1}{2}$ lb. butter to give it a yellow colour. Some great Cheshire dairymen made two cheeses of 1 cwt. each daily until Michaelmas, and then a poorer sort for local consumption ending up with butter to pot for their own use. Ellis had known Cheshire cheese to be kept in a wine vault on a pipe of sack, or fed with sack in a hole in the cheese which gave it a surprising degree of richness. A Bedfordshire gentleman he knew tried to make Cheshire cheese on his estate in that county, but failed although he imported Cheshire hands.[25]

With only minor variations this method of making Cheshire cheese was general throughout the nineteenth century, and is the same today on the farms where cheese is made.[26] By 1792 annatto was used for colouring if necessary. Spanish annatto was the best, but some very adulterated kinds were on the market. The weight of a guinea and a half was enough for 60 lb. cheese. Some tied up the necessary quantity in a linen bag, dipped it in milk, and rubbed it on a smooth stone until the milk became a deep red. This infusion was added to the milk in the cheese vat. Others put it into half a pint of warm water overnight and into the milk in the morning, rubbing it against the palm of the hand as long as any colour came out. Skewers were run through the cheese by holes in the vat, and withdrawn to help drain off the whey. A circle of tin an inch or so wide was placed at the top of the vat, and the curd piled high above it. Both tin ring and curd were forced down into the vat by hand pressing.

There was no guide to the proper way to do these things. So early as 1808 Henry Holland complained that everything in the Cheshire dairies was done by guesswork. It was really necessary to establish a dairy school in the county where the correct management of details could be decided by experiment, said this far-seeing man. The dairymaids all pretended to esoteric knowledge, but this was mainly fantasy. The heat of the milk was tested by the fingertips; the cream or cream and milk heated in a conical tin in the copper or boiler was used when the maid estimated that it was right. Everybody used some rennet and annatto, but only experience decided the amount to be used. The same complaints were repeated during the following 150 years.[27]

Baxter advised that the milk should be heated to 85°-90°F. before adding the annatto and rennet, but whether anyone ever used a thermometer to test it is doubtful. At that heat the curd took about two hours to come. Henry White recommended 80°-85°F. in 1845, the time when the pole press was giving place to the screw press. G. H. Andrews preferred the higher temperature of 90°F. Curd breakers had been in use for a decade or so by 1853, but the Cheshire dairymaids did not like them and preferred hand work, though breakers were used in some dairies. Olmstead believed that annatto was mixed with tumeric and soft soap.[28]

Besides the ordinary large cheese some dairymaids produced small cheeses of novel shape, no doubt to tempt a higher price. Some were in the shape of pineapples, for example, but apparently this project did not attract very much attention.[29] Otherwise the work went on as it always had. Most people agreed on 90°F. as the proper temperature in the second half of the nineteenth century, and some added a little saltpetre in summer to take away the bitter taste of the buttercups. Cluett's curd breaker was coming into general use in 1888. If there was virtue in the Cheshire cheese it does not seem to have been because the manufacture was scientific, or in any way reduced to a system. The main outline of the process was always the same, and guesswork played a large part in its making: so it may have been to the pastures— it certainly was not in the choice of their cows—that the cheese owed its peculiar quality. In the past this may have been due to the centuries old practice of marling, later of boning and so on. But of course the cheese may have owed much to the maligned dairymaid who would use no thermometer, nor measure her materials other than salt. Cheshire cheese was also made successfully in the neighbouring counties of Stafford and Shropshire. The hard cheese made in Derbyshire differed from Cheshire chiefly in the method of salting.[30] In the Cheshire and the Cheddar systems the salt was mixed in the curd immediately the latter was ground; in the Derbyshire system it was applied the following morning or evening as appropriate, and only to the outside of the cheese. The Derbyshire dairy farmers had not been backward in adopting new appliances. In the 1850's their utensils were few and primitive. Thirty years later it would have been impossible to see a maid kneel on a board placed on the curd, which was carefully balanced on the 'cheese kettle' in order to express the whey. Curd breakers of one kind or another were used. The press developed from the pole press, through the screw press to the lever press, and the first cheese factories were established in this county, but the manufacturing of milk was already on the decline. It was certainly easier and perhaps more profitable to sell liquid milk from the 1880's onwards. Nevertheless this cheese is still made in spite of being less a connoisseur than a utilitarian product.[31]

Gloucester cheese is not, so far as I am at present informed, remarked by any seventeenth century writer. It was praised by Morden and more emphatically by Defoe, and must have been well established long before this time.[32] William Marshall (1796) certainly thought so. Both in the upper and lower Vale of Gloucester there were shades of difference in practice, and Marshall was convinced that the prime necessity was some degree of scientific knowledge of the processes involved to secure the desired and desirable uniformity. The lower Vale dairymen sometimes used the milk 'neat from the cow', but this was probably unusual. The ordinary plan was to make a one-meal or two-meal cheese. Here as elsewhere the evening's milk was set for cream and skimmed. A part of the skimmed milk was heated and the whole added to the morning's milk. Some took some cream from this before using it to make cheese. The use of annatto was well established. It was criminal in Marshall's opinion. The curd was broken and stirred with the curd knife and when broken up as small as peas hot water or whey or a mixture of the two was poured on. The scalding liquor was ladled off, and the curd crumbled into the vat which was placed on a cheese ladder resting on a pail or other receptacle. The curd was squeezed by hand, and the vat tipped to let the whey run off. The vat filled and rounded high in the middle was covered in a cloth, and the curd turned out into it. The vat was washed or dipped into the whey. The curd, still in the cloth, was replaced in the vat, any angles or rough edges pared off and the cloth tucked in. The vat was then put in the press. Any spare curd was made into small cheeses for sale locally. The cheese was pressed for about three hours, turned and pressed again till the evening, when it was taken out again and salted by rubbing all over with handfuls of salt, leaving as much on it as would cling. It was then put into the bare vat and pressed, turned morning and evening for a day or two, taken out and put on the dairy shelf. The whole time of pressing was about forty eight hours. For ten days the cheeses were turned at intervals determined by the judgment of the dairyman. After this they were soaked in a large tub of whey for an hour or so, and scraped smooth with a blunt case-knife, 'to a polished neatness'. Next the cheese was rinsed in the whey, wiped with a cloth and stored in the cheese chamber.[33]

The Vale of Berkeley dairy farmers who made thin cheeses (single) from April to November and thick (double) in May, June and the beginning of July, often took some cream for making butter before running the milk for cheese. This was harmless here because the high feeding in the Vale gave a very rich milk, and the skimmed milk lowered the temperature of the new milk from the cow. It is difficult to collate this with Marshall's statement that the cheese was invariably new milk—one meal—best making. He had his information from Mrs. Wade of Maberley near Berkeley, an hereditary dairywoman, and Mr. Bigland of Frocester, a factor and owner of more than 50 cows. The new milk was considered too warm to run, and was cooled to the appropriate temperature by the addition of cold water, the rennet then being added. The curd was broken with the curd knife or by hand, and the whey ladled off as separated. The curd was next put in a naked vat, rounded up in the middle as usual and pressed well in manually. A loose cloth was thrown over and tucked in, and the vat put in the press. After ten or fifteen minutes it was turned out, broken up by hand and with the double knife. It was then scalded with a pailful of mixed water and whey thrown upon the crumbled curd, and the whole stirred briskly till evenly mixed. It stood a few minutes, and then the liquor was ladled off. The curd was squeezed by hand, and put into a vat until the receptacle was half full. About 1 oz. of salt was sprinkled on it and worked in, and the vat filled, the contents being turned two or three times. It was finally turned out into a cloth and treated further as in the Vale of Gloucester. Apart from reducing the temperature and consistency of the milk by the addition of cold water before beginning to process it the method was the same in both Vales.

The identification of Gloucester cheeses was made easy for the wholesale buyer and the consumer by the practice of external painting. It had only been recently adopted when Marshall was making his enquiries, and he could not discover how it originated. He suspected fraud, but in fact it was a kind of trade mark. Unfortunately the art of painting had begun to migrate as well as the use of annatto for colouring. The result was that the Gloucestershire dairy was then suffering through its own artifice, and ought in all reason to abandon these two practices, resting the reputation of their cheese upon its natural colour.[34] Marshall's protests had no effect and Gloucester cheese continued to be coloured and painted.[35]

The adjoining dairy district of North Wiltshire and the Vale of White Horse both made thin and thick cheese, which were sold as single and double Gloucester. Much of this was thin or single Gloucester, which Marshall attributed to the quality of the grazing. In Wiltshire a loaf cheese known as

North Wiltshire cheese was made, and had become very fashionable, fetching a higher than average price. Unfortunately only a portion of the grazing was good enough to produce it and more skill as well as more trouble was involved in making it. In general the Wiltshire dairymen used whole milk for cheese making, and continued the manufacture the year round. If the winter cheese proved scurfy and white coated, it was kept longer and painted. The milk was run as it came from the cow, or reduced in temperature by the addition of a little skimmed milk. No one bothered to use a thermometer, and Marshall discovered a variation ranging between 86° and 91°F. The principal difference in making the three types of cheese was in the degree of fineness in breaking the curd after the first draining of the whey. For thin cheese it was broken into fine particles; for thick into still finer; for loaf cheese into atoms. This is illustrative if not precise. Another detail was the cutting of the curd with a long knife two or three times into slices, and pressing it manually, ladling off the whey between each cutting, and thus obtaining a curd perfectly free from whey. Again the North Wiltshire cheese was salted before it was scalded 'to keep the fat in the cheese'. After scalding, too, the pieces of curd were put into the vats and pressed down 'as hot as the hand would bear'. As soon as two or three vats were filled, they were placed in a shallow tub, and a loaded vat put upon them 'to close the curd while warm'. Marshall thought this admirable, in theory likely to be possible, and among the last things he had expected in practice. The rest of the process was the same as in Gloucestershire.

By this time Marshall had collected a good deal of experience of cheese making in many parts of the country. They varied, but mostly fell into two categories, one of a loose texture and rough austere flavour, the other milder in taste and of a close, waxlike texture. The former was sold as Cheshire, and was made there, in North Wales, Stafford and Salop: the latter was known as Gloucester cheese, or Warwickshire, but was in fact produced in several counties. The cheeses made in Somerset, Wiltshire, Berkshire, Oxford,

Gloucester, Worcester, Warwick, Leicester, Stafford, Derby and Yorkshire were very similar, but all so different from Cheshire as if made of different material.[36] This is a reasonable conclusion in the light of the similarity in the processes of manufacture disclosed by the contemporary writers who described them.

The claim that Cheshire cheese could and can only be made in that county or its neighbourhood may be substantial. The same certainly cannot be said of the single and double Gloucester. It was made in Lanarkshire by James Bell of Woodhouselee, and by Mr. Nicholl of Easton House, North Wiltshire in a competition organised by the Highland and Agricultural Society. Their methods of manufacture were exactly those described by Marshall and repeated by Lawson, Loudon and others.[37]

The earlier writers said that the difference between single and double Gloucester was caused by the removal of some of the cream from the milk used to make the thin cheese. Some dairymaids certainly did skim the evening milk, and used part of the cream for making butter. Some went so far as to take a little cream from the morning milk as well, but most returned at least half the evening milk cream to the cheese tub. Indeed some of the best makers made cheese twice a day, and so the cheese was always a whole milk one meal cheese. By the 1880's Sheldon had reluctantly to confess that Gloucester cheese was no longer so famous as it had once been. This was not because of any change in making it, but largely the result of heavy importation of foreign cheese, and the expanding trade in liquid milk for London and other large cities. Double Gloucester was by then rarely made, but single was in a good many farmhouses. The only difference between these was in thickness. There was nothing in the idea that it was caused by the abstraction of some of the cream. The single was between two and three inches thick and about 15 lb. weight; the double was four or five inches thick, and 24 lb. weight. Both were about sixteen inches diameter and were of equal quality with perhaps a slight balance in favour of the single. The thinner cheese ripened

more speedily than the thick. Sheldon thought, correctly as
it turned out, that the Gloucester system would

> 'gradually be displaced by improved methods which in-
> volve less expenditure of time and labour for the cheese
> of the county does not really possess any special features
> or qualities which will render it proof against the march
> of modern improvements.'[38]

Sheldon admired Stilton cheese, as who would not. It was
unique in shape, in flavour and in quality, and was prized by
epicures everywhere: yet it was, he said, one of the most
modern of English cheeses, barely one hundred years old. For
this assertion he depends upon Marshall's well-known story
about Mrs. Pauler of Wymondham, the first maker of Stilton
cheese, who supplied Cooper Thornhill, at the Bell Inn, Stilton, with cream cheese. He used it on his customer's table,
and sold it at half a crown a pound. Mrs. Paulet was still
living in 1780,[39] but Stilton was already famous when Defoe
wrote his 'Tour' in 1724, and was called the English Par-
mesan, being

> 'brought to table with the mites or maggots round it so
> thick that they bring a spoon with them for you to eat
> the mites with as you do the cheese'.

Richard Bradley at about the same time found Stilton cheese
not so good as it used to be. He did not know why, unless it
was because some unscrupulous salesmen there, depending
upon the established reputation of the cheese, bought from
other places where nothing was known of the proper way of
making this cheese, but the shape. He was able to buy an excellent one at the Blue Bell Inn during or before 1728, where
they could be ordered by anyone who wanted one. Mrs.
Paulet may, of course, have been a very young woman then,
but it seems hardly likely. Bradley did not supply a recipe in
his *Country Housewife* because it had

> 'already fallen into a good number of hands with my
> former Pieces, and has been thought good enough to
> be copied from me, with many other articles and pub-
> lished by Mr. Laurence'.

Laurence, whose *New System of Agriculture* is dated 1726,

THE DANISH SEPARATOR

DAIRY SUPPLY CO.'S STERILISING PLANT

POCOCK'S PATENT MILK CAN WASHER

said that Stilton had then recently become famous, and consequently thought it would be as well to publish a receipt from Bradley's monthly Papers. He hoped it was more accurate than Bradley's geography, which placed Stilton in Lincolnshire, whereas it was in Huntingdon. John Nichols, as quoted by André L. Simon, tells yet another story. This cheese first made by Mrs. Orton at Little Dalby about 1730, its quality being supposed to be due to the rich milk of cows which fed in one particular close, called Orton's Close at the end of the eighteenth century. This proved incorrect, even though in 1756 it was made by three persons; Nichols must have been misinformed on this point as was Guy Paget, who attributed its invention to a Mrs. Stilton, dairymaid to the fifth Duchess of Rutland in 1800.[40]

The receipt which Bradley claimed to have had from a reliable friend, and which was quoted by Laurence, was,

'Take Ten Gallons of Morning Milk and Five Gallons of Sweet Cream, and beat them together; Then put in as much Boiling Water as will make it warmer than Milk from the Cow. When this is done put in Rennet made strong with large Mace, and when it is *come* (or the Milk is set in Curd) break it as small as you would do for Cheese-Cakes; after that salt it, and put it in the Vat, and press it for two Hours. Then boil the Whey, and when you have taken off the Curds, put the Cheese into the whey, and let it stand half an hour. Then put it in the Press, and when you take it out, bind it up for the first fortnight in Linnen Rollers, and turn it upon Boards for the first Month twice a day'.[41]

In Marshall's day Stilton was made in a large number of Leicestershire villages, and in Rutland and Huntingdon, but for him 'Cream cheese is an article of luxury only and a species of produce that cannot become of general utility to agriculture'. The art of making it did not he felt come within the scope of his work, and he did not supply details.

The idea that Stilton owed much to the pastures on which the cows grazed persisted long after Orton's Close had been forgotten. Mr. Jubal Webb of Kensington, who supplied

Sheldon with details of the current way of making Stilton about 1880, was convinced that the first thing was to find suitable land on which to graze the cows. It must be rich old pasture

'such as will keep them strong, full of milk and healthy without extraneous help in the form of cake, corn, grains or roots, all of which tend to spoil either the flavour or the quality of the cheese.'

Nearly a century before Joseph Hazard was very doubtful about this. From the nicest observation he could find nothing in the Leicestershire pastures 'in any respect superior to that of other counties'. If other people adopted the Stilton plan they would be able to make Stilton cheese, a pronouncement which has since been fully justified. The process then remained the same as in Bradley's and Laurence's day. A cheese was made every morning, and to the morning milk they added the cream taken from that milked the night before. This and the age of the cheese was the secret of its virtue. Hazard added that excellent cream cheeses were made in Lincolnshire by the same process, being pressed gently two or three times, turned for a few days, and eaten while new with radishes and salad, but this was not, of course, Stilton.[42]

The process seems to have been slightly changed in the early nineteenth century. After the cream and milk had been mixed, the rennet added and the curd come, it was not broken but taken out whole and put in a sieve to drain, while draining it was pressed till firm and dry, and then put into a hooped chessart (vat) as it was 'so rich that it would otherwise disintegrate'. The outer coat was first salted and the cheese wrapped in a clean cloth. If it shrunk in drying, it was put in a smaller vat. When firm enough to be taken out of this vat, the cheese was placed on a dry board, tightly bound in a cloth, changed daily, to prevent any cracks in the skin. In due time, when well coated and sufficiently firm, the cloths were no longer necessary, but the cheese must be turned and brushed, some said daily, others frequently, for two or three months. This cheese was not considered fully ripe until it had been kept two years.[43]

Jubal Webb used a different system. It was the old one of Laurence and Bradley. As soon as the curd was come he broke it up very little, left it to stand ten minutes, and then put it into 'leads covered with cloth strainers to allow the whey to drain away gradually'. As it drained he brought the ends of the strainer cloth together, and tied it closer and closer until the curd became tolerably firm and dry. He then put it in a large tin strainer, and cut it into square pieces. He left it so until he thought it fit to be put into the hoops. The rest of his method was that generally followed. Sheldon said that Stilton was being made in many counties in 1889, and even in Canada. Muir said it was made at this time without pressing, but this can hardly be correct.[44]

By 1912 the majority of Leicestershire farmers were producing little winter milk from the natural pastures; nor was there any great attempt to produce it in Derbyshire. In both counties, aside from the factories, cheese makers had become specialists taking the milk from many, up to fifty or sixty farms, besides using their own production. The other reason for sticking closely to summer milk production was that the Stilton cheese makers only bought in that season. In Derbyshire a hard curd type of large flat cheese was made, but the really important product was Stilton. This movement had begun more than forty years before.[45]

The Cotherstone cheese, made in Yorkshire, and similar to the Stilton, was not mentioned by Marshall in his *Rural Economy of Yorkshire*. It was indeed a neighbour and relative of Wensleydale cheese and that made in Swaledale. Little or none of these cheeses came on the consumer market. They were domestic cheese made of the summer flush of milk, and bartered to local dealers. By 1880 it could be said that little Wensleydale was made, and that its chief peculiarity was that after being treated much like any other two meal cheese it was pressed for twenty four hours, and then pickled in brine for three days just as cheese was in Lancashire. The farms were scattered in the Dales, and each dairymaid used her own judgment in processing the cheese. The lack of uniformity in the result was not therefore very surprising, but outside the Dales the taste for those cheeses was perhaps limited to the cognoscenti. By the end of the nineteenth century the large percentage of poor cheese produced in the Dales had done its reputation little good, and combined with the better market for liquid milk to further reduce the output.[46]

Another cheese like Stilton used to be made at Cottenham and neighbourhood in Cambridgeshire, and enjoyed a fine reputation. It was thicker than Stilton, and its superior delicacy and flavour were attributed to the rich herbage of the commons on which the cows were pastured: according to Professor Martyn (Professor of Botany at Cambridge) specifically to the presence of *Poa acquatica* and *Poa pratensis.*[47]

Skim or flet milk cheese was made all over the country, mainly for local or domestic consumption, but some of it achieved a greater reputation, enviable or not. So much has been written about the hardness of Suffolk cheese that a repetition of it all would be monotonous. On the other side of the country, Dorset Blue Vinney, perhaps not quite so hard, was rather sought after.

Bradley, as already mentioned, believed the hardness of Suffolk cheese to be caused by poor rennet derived ultimately from poor feed. If rennet was obtained from a short grass country this cheese might be improved. Another of his reasons was that the cream of Suffolk milk rose so quickly and substantially that it left no fat in the skim of which the cheese was made. Forsyth said that it was much used at sea being less affected by climate than other kinds, a sufficiently ambiguous remark. The method of manufacture both in Norfolk and Suffolk was simple in Loudon's description, but Marshall made the former county's process rather more complicated.

After the curd was come it was put in a basket to drain before being broken up by hand into separate vessels. Salt was scattered over the curd while this was being done. When mixed the curd was put in a cloth, and the vat filled to a height of one inch over the brim. A round board was pressed down upon it, and the whey squeezed out. The whole was then put in a press for two hours. Next it was soaked in hot whey for an hour or two, dried and pressed again for six or eight hours, turned a second time, taken to the salting room, rubbed and wrapped, and pressed again for twelve to fourteen hours. The edges were pared, and the cheese laid on a dry board and turned every day. Skim cheese required to be kept warm when young, and cool afterwards. Little art was necessary, but there was often a great difference in the quality of skim milk cheese owing solely to the care, or lack of it, with which it was made.[48]

Marshall thought the Norfolk dairymaids were too impetuous. As soon as the curd was come, part of the whey was ladled off, and the rest, with the curd, poured into a cloth. After the whey had drained through it, the curd was shaken in the cloth, kneaded down into a vat, and put under a light press or a stone. The cloth was changed once, the whole turned, 'and lo! a Norfolk cheese appears'. On his own farm Marshall had a Wiltshire dairymaid who followed her own customary methods. Wiltshire cheese was sometimes afflicted with a white scurfy coat, and that was why it was painted. The Norfolk maids only salted in an earthen platter by covering as in curing bacon.

'Being in a manner compressed; never cleaned and but seldom turned; it is no wonder that in a short time the white scurfy coat gets full possession of it'.

It looked more like a sugared plum cake than cheese. If not sold unripe it was attacked by the maggot from a small black shining fly like a winged ant which was very difficult to get rid of. In the area of Harleston and Diss and generally on the Suffolk side of the county skim milk cheese was made as in Suffolk.[49]

In Dorset much more palatable, and not quite so hard, skim milk cheese, the famous Blue Vinney, was made. Little or no whole milk cheese was made in the county. Usually the cream was taken about twenty four hours after the milk was set, thirty six hours in winter, or only twelve in the heat of summer. Only a part of this cheese developed the streaks of blue mould. Mr. Otten of Wooten Fitzpaine said in 1815 that it was produced by breaking and sprinkling the curd with flour after it had been pressed. Another suggestion that was current a half a century ago was that copper wire was run through the cheese, and the blue was nothing more than verdigris. The same was supposed to be done to Stilton. Others supposed it due to the soil or management; whatever caused it the colour was highly esteemed. Dorset farmers in 1788

> 'take all the cream from their cheese yet think it equally delicious to the rich kinds made in Somerset where it is thought high treason to take any'.[50]

Burritt in 1868 found that a two meal cheese was being made in the Blakemore Vale. It was generally made in the common way of the night and morning milk, the first set for cream twelve hours, skimmed and mixed with the morning milk. 'Thus the largest part was laid under contribution to butter on its way to the cheese tub.' This was the best. None was made of whole milk any more than it had been in the past. Some of what Burritt called old-fashioned skim milk cheese, similar to that well known in New England and called there white oak cheese, was made. Possibly part of this was Blue Vinney. 'Softer missiles', said Burritt 'have been fired with great effect from cannon', so this cheese was evidently hard like Suffolk. At a wayside inn on his road from Shaftesbury to Bridport Burritt was minutely instructed in butter and cheese making by a small girl of nine years old.[51]

Besides all these there were many other ways of making cheese, which were modified both in time and place. Cheeses called by the same name were not always made in the same way by everybody nor at all times. This must be apparent from what has already been said. A good example is what was known as slipcoat cheese.

Just after the Restoration Sir Kenelm Digby recorded one method. It was to take 3 quarts of the last strokings of all the cows in the herd, and keep it covered so that it remained warm. To this a skimming dish of spring water was added and 2 spoonfuls of rennet. Then let it stand till it be hard come. The curd was taken up by degrees, but not broken, put in the vat and a fine cloth worked in at the sides with a knife. A board was laid over the vat for half an hour, a $\frac{1}{2}$ lb. stone added and left for two hours. It was turned, re-clothed, and pressed again for two hours, turned again on a dry cloth, and pressed till the following morning with a 2 lb. weight. After that it was taken out, and turned on a dry board for three days. If it began 'to run abroad' it was set up with wedges. Finally when stiff enough it was laid on and covered with rushes. It was fit to eat in about eight days.[52]

Bradley knew this cheese as slipcoat, and said it was called cream cheese. Ellis and later writers repeated the name. Laurence called the cheese made by Digby's process water cheese. Bradley's instructions for making it, which Ellis followed, were not identical with Digby's, but were concise and to the point. Take 6 quarts of new milk and a pint of cream and add a spoonful of rennet just warm, and let it stand till the curd is come. No water is mentioned. Lay a cloth in the cheese vat, cut out the curd with a skimming dish, and fill the vat, turning the cloth over it. Add more as the curd settles. When the whey is drained out turn the cheese into a dry cloth and lay a pound weight upon it. At night turn into another dry cloth, and next morning salt it a little. No salt is mentioned by Digby, and he recommends more frequent turning. Then make a bed of nettles or ash leaves to lay it on and cover it, shifting them twice a day till the cheese is fit to eat in about ten days. 'This cheese is approved to be the best of its kind in the whole Country, and may be made the whole Summer'.[53]

Hale described a nettle cheese which was merely a thin new milk (morning's milk) cheese to which rennet was added immediately it was put in the tub just as it came from the cow. A better cheese which he called a 'running cheese' was partly like slipcoat, and partly what came to be called 'scalded'. Equal parts of strokings and of rich cream were heated by putting the pot containing them in a pan of water filled to the level of the cream and milk. This was placed on the fire till the whole was as warm as milk from the cow. The pot was taken out of the pan, and the rennet added to the mixture. The curd was pressed down, and the whey taken off and heated separately. When hot it was thrown on the curd. The curd was next taken up by hand, if possible without breaking it, and laid in the vat. It was pressed first by a small weight, and later by one slightly heavier, but never in a screw press. When the whey was finally expressed, the cheese was taken out, salted a little and laid on a bed of nettles.[54] Later slip-coat cheese was made from new milk to which one-third of warm water had been added before the rennet was put in, but all these variants may have been practised during the whole period.[55]

Cream cheese, which had been frowned upon by Marshall, was generally only made for immediate use. Some may have been a merchantable commodity, but most of it must have been used in the house. Ellis provided two recipes, both of which included strokings as well as cream, but in one 2 quarts of cream were heated to boiling point; 4 quarts of strokings warm from the cows were stirred in to reduce the heat somewhat, and then 2 spoonfuls of quick rennet were added. When the curd came it was turned into a cloth, and the whey queezed out, vatted, pressed with a 10 lb. weight, turned every hour or so till no more whey remained. It was then salted to taste, allowed to lie a day or two, finally put between two pewter dishes turned daily for three weeks, removed from the dishes, and kept four or five days before eating it. The other (Montgomery) method was to mix 6 quarts of strokings or new milk with 1 quart of cream, put 1 quart of boiling water on it, add a spoonful of rennet, and treat much as before, but keeping the finished product in grass near the fire with flannels over and under it.

Youatt, following Twamley, considered cream cheese little but thick sweet cream, dried by being put in a small perforated cheese vat about $1\frac{1}{2}$ inches deep. It was covered with rushes or maize stalks, so that it could be turned without being touched, and was only pressed gently between cloths by hand. Cream cheese must be kept warm to sweat and ripen but not too hot, and must never be allowed to get chilled or touched by frost. This, written in 1836, and taken from Twamley whose work first appeared in 1784, was repeated in Ward and Lock's *Book of Farm Management* of about 1880. Clearly it was a method that had been used for at least a century then. Morton's receipt of 1878 was a variant. A pint of new milk was mixed with a quart of cream, and warmed in hot water to about 90°F. To this a tablespoonful of ordinary rennet was added, and the whole let stand till it thickened. It was then broken with a spoon and placed in a frame eight inches square by four deep, lined with a fine canvas cloth. In this it was slightly pressed with a weight for twelve hours. Then it was lifted out and replaced in a finer cloth over which a little salt had been powdered. This type was fit for use in a day or two, but was 'a mere household delicacy'.[56] Oddly enough, considering the reputation of Suffolk cheese in general some cream cheese was at one time made at Blaxhall, but this was made from whole milk straight from the cow, or warmed if it had got cold in transit. The process as described is, however, rather that of a soft curd one meal cheese.[57]

Cheese was made all over the country during the period. Many makers confined themselves to the general outline of the process followed in their locality contemporarily, but for one reason or another, or possibly for no reason except their own choice, often introduced some slight amendment of their own. Consequently there was a great number of locally named cheeses besides the two or three well known makes. Some indication of these has been given. There were also Lancashire, Lincolnshire, Worcestershire and other cheese as well as cheese coloured with sage and other herbs, but the principal stages of manufacture have necessarily remained the same at all times and in all places. Coagulation was caused by adding rennet to the milk fresh or mixed with additional cream. The whey must be expressed by cutting the curd into pieces of varying sizes according to the type of cheese being made, the curd heated or 'cooked' for hard but not for soft cheese, the whey drained off, the curd broken into small pieces, and put in a vat or mould of the shape desired. The final detail was pressing the curd in the vat, which was done more or less, for longer and shorter times, and with various turnings, according to the usage of the time and place. Many of the general treatises on farming as well as those specifically on dairying, which began to appear towards the end of the eighteenth century, set this out in unmistakeable style, and indeed the chemistry of cheese making enforces it. Unfortunately farmhouse cheese making, like farmhouse butter making, suffered serious setbacks in the second half of the nineteenth century, and has almost disappeared since the two World Wars.

### NOTES TO CHAPTER V (i)

[1] Googe. *Whole art and trade of husbandry.* 1614. f. 138v. E. Parmalee Prentice. *American dairy cattle.* 1942. pp. 99, 105. *Walter of Henley's Husbandry, etc.* Ed. by Lamond and Cunningham. 1890. pp. 72, 74, 88, 100, 116. Judges V. 25. c.f. Thorold Rogers. *Six centuries of work & wages.* 1906. pp. 93, 94.

[2] Surflet. *Countrey ferme.* 1600. pp. 89, 90. Markham *English housewife.* 1653 (1615) pp. 145–148. Garnier. *Annals of the British peasantry.* 1895. p. 389.

[3] Christina Hole. *English housewife in the 17th cent.* 1953. pp. 17, 18, 54, 55, 58, citing T. Muffitt. *Health's improvement.* 1655 and Misson.

[4] Hartlib's *Legacie.* p. 263. R. Bayne-Powell. *Housekeeping in the 18th cent.* 1956, p. 62. Lisle. *Observations.* pp. 301, 304, 305. *Tusser redivivus.* 1710. April. pp. 12–14. Garnier. *op. cit.* p. 208 A. K. Hamilton-Jenkin. *Cornwall and its people.* 1945. pp. 401, 402.

[5] *Dictionarium rusticum.* 2nd ed. 1717. arts. *Churning & Butter.*

[6] Laurence. *New system.* 1726. pp. 136–138. Country Gentleman. *Complete grazier.* 1767. pp. 79, 82–84.

[7] Ellis. *Mod. husb.* 1750 II May, pp. 128–137. III July, pp. 76–78. VII. p.. 91 Ellis' *Husb. abridg'd* 1772. II. pp. 273–275. cf. Seebohm. *Evolution of English farm.* p. 273.

[8] Country Gentleman. *op. cit.* p. 81. Twamley. *Essays.* 1816. (1784). Hazard in *Letters & papers. Bath & West Soc.* III (1788) pp. 140–145. Young. *Gen. View. Essex.* 1807. II. p. 279. Willich. *Dom. encyclo.* 1802. art Butter. Young. *Farmers' calendar.* 1804. p. 282. Jefferys Taylor. *The farm.* 1834. p. 99.

[9] James Adam. *Practical essays.* 1787. II. p. 456. Willich. p. 407. Frederick A. Filby. *History of food adulteration and analysis.* 1934. pp. 52, 237.

[10] Young. *Farmers' calendar.* 1804. Jan. pp. 17, 18. Vancouver *Gen. view. Hants.* 1813. pp. 358–360.

[11] Marshall. *Norfolk.* 1787. II. p. 240. *Midlands.* 1790. I. p. 351. *Gloucester* 1796. I. pp. 276–278. *West of England.* 1796. I. pp. 249–253.

[12] John Holt. *Gen. view. Lancashire.* 1795. p. 155. Willich. p. 404.

[13] Garnett. *Westmorland agric.* 1912. p. 137.

[14] *Annals of agric.* XXVIII (1797). p. 12. Holland. *Gen. view. Cheshire.* 1808. p. 259. This account is copied verbatim from Wedge's report of 1794.

[15] James Anderson. *Rural recreations.* 1800. III. pp. 322–333. Forsyth. *Principles.* 1804. II. pp. 454–461 (quotes Anderson) Lawrence. *New farmers' calendar.* 1802. pp. 509, 510. Dickson. *Pract. agric.* 1804. pp. 1000–1008. Holt. *Lancs.* 1795. p. 160 ff. Parkinson. *Treatise on livestock.* 1810. pp. 40–47.

[16] Alex. Taylor. *Farmers' guide*. 1829. pp. 236–244.

[17] Loudon. *Encyclo*. 1831. pp. 1041. 1042. Baxters *Library*. 1836. pp. 152, 153. James Jackson. *Treatise on agric*. 1840. p. 109. Low. *Pract. agric*. 1843. pp. 644, 645. *idem. Domesticated animals*. 1845. pp. 281–284. G. H. Andrews. *Mod. husb*. 1853. p. 385. John Sherer. *Rural life*. c. 1850. pp. 678, 679.

[18] John Bravender. *Farming of Gloucester*. J.R.A.S.E. 1850. p. 153.

[19] Rowlandson. *On the production of butter*. J.R.A.S.E. 1852. pp. 30–43. Ruegg. *ibid*. 1853. pp. 68, 69. Read. *Farming of Oxford. ibid*. 1854. p. 226.

[20] Donaldson. *British agric*. 1860. III. pp. 689, 690. Morton. *Handbook*. 1860. pp. 55–63. Pringle & Murray. *Pract. farming*. Stock. 1865. pt. ii. pp. 63–69. Copland. *Agric*. 1866. I. pp. 753–756. II. pp. 150, 188, 189. Charles A. Cameron. *Chemistry of food of livestock*. 1868. pp. 138–146. Macdonald. *Cattle, sheep & deer*. 1872. pp. 121, 130–148. Stephens' *Book of the farm*. 1877. II. pp. 238–246.

[21] Garnett. *Westmorland agric. 1800–1900*. 1912. p. 139.

[22] J. A. Scott Watson. *History of the Royal Agricultural Society of England, 1839–1939*. 1939. pp. 176, 177. Herbert J. Little. *Report on working dairy at Derby show*. J.R.A.S.E. 1881, and subsequent reports.

[23] John Oliver. *Dairy schools*. Journ. B.D.F.A. I. (1876). pt. 2. James Long. *Technical education in dairy farming. ibid*. IV (1888) pt. i. *British dairy institute. ibid*.

[24] Thos. F. Plowman. *The Society's dairy schools*. Jour. Bath & West Soc. 3rd ser. XX (1888–9) pp. 81–95. cf. p. 73. Story Maskelyne. *ibid. ibid*. XXI (1889–90) p. 94. Plowman (1891). pp. 132–137 *id*. 1898 and subsequent volumes. F. J. Lloyd. *Dairy schools and their influence in promoting the dairy industry*. Jour. Farmers Club. Nov. 1895. Gaut. *Worcester agric*. 1939. pp. 373, 374, 377. Garnett. *Westmorland*. pp. 139, 239. Plowman as before, 4th ser. XIII (1903). p. 156 ff. Henry H. Howman. *Development of dairy education*. Journ. B.D.F.A. VII (1892) p. 54 ff.

[25] W. J. Malden. *Recent changes in dairy practice*. J.R.A.S.E. 1896. pp. 25, 26.

[26] G. E. Evans. *Ask the fellows who cut the hay*. 1956. p. 70. E. G. Haydon *Travels round our village*. 1905. p. 102. Mrs. Rundell's *Home Cookery*. c. 1900. II. p. 112.

[27] Roland. *Farming for pleasure*. 1879. pp. 70–73. Ward & Locks' *Book*. c. 1880. pp. 342–363. Long. *British dairy farming*. 1885. pp. 116–126. Col. J. F. Curtis-Hayward. *Butter making*. Jour. Bath & West Soc. 3rd ser. XIX (1887–8) pp. 281–283. Long. *id*. XX (1888–9). Scott Burn. *Outlines*. 6th ed. 1888. pt. iv *The dairy*. pp. 48–57. Upton. *Profitable dairy farming*. 1888. pp. 65–84. James Muir. *Manual of dairy work*. 1893. pp. 36–63. Webb. *Advanced agric*. 1894. pp. 610–619. Tisdale & Robinson. *Butter making on the farm*. 1913. (1903) pp. 33–51. Freer-Thonger. *Some essentials of successful dairy farming*. Jour. B. & W. Soc. 4th ser. XIII (1903) pp. 83–96.

[28] Pilley. *Scientific agric*. 1881. p. 233 Punchard in Jour. B.D.F.A. 1892. Long. *Dairy farm*. 1889. p. 19.

## NOTES TO CHAPTER V (ii)

[1] Googe. *Whole art*. 1614. f. 139 v. Hartlib's *Legacie*. 1655. p. 129. Garnier. *Annals of the British peasantry*. 1885. p. 209. Ernle. English farming. 1961. pp. 109 fn. 136, 193.

[2] Tusser. *Five hundred points*, 1577. eg. Mavor. 1812. pp. 142–144. Surflet. *Countrey ferme*. 1600. pp. 91, 92. Markham. *English housewife*. 1653 (1615). pp. 142–151.

[3] Mortimer. *Whole art of husbandry*. 4th ed. 1716. I. pp. 228, 229.

[4] Lisle. *Observations*. 1757. pp. 302–304. John Laurence. *New system*. 1726. p. 140.

[5] Defoe's *Tour*. 1724. Everyman ed. I. p. 278.

[6] Ellis. *Mod. husb.* 1750. II. May. p. 121. Mrs. E. Smith. *Compleat Housewife* cited in Andre L. Simon. *Cheeses of the world.* 1956. p. 34. Ellis' *Husb. abridg'd.* 1772. II. pp. 291, 292.

[7] Billingsley. *Somerset.* 1797. pp. 247 fn. 248 fn.

[8] T. D. Acland & William Sturge. *Farming of Somersetshire.* 1851. pp. 53, 134. A. W. Coysh & others. *The Mendips.* 1954. p. 192.

[9] *Report on cheesemaking by Ayrshire Association of Agriculture.* Jour. B. & W. Soc. V (1857). p. 164. Joseph Harding. *Recent improvements in dairy practice.* J.R.A.S.E. 1860. pp. 89, 90. Morton. *Handbook.* 1860. p. 75. *idem. Dairy farming.* J.R.A.S.E. 1878. p. 673. Harding. *Cheese making in small dairies.* Jour. B. & W. Soc. XV (1867) p. 250. Thomas Jackson. *Report on systems of cheese making.* J.R.A.S.E. 1879. p. 37 ff. Buckmaster & Willis *Elementary principles of scientific agriculture.* c. 1883. p. 174 ff. Long. *British dairy farming.* 1885. p. 135.

[10] J. P. Sheldon. *The farm and the dairy.* 1889. p. 94. G. Gibbons. *Practice of Cheddar cheese making.* J.R.A.S.E. 1889. p. 419 ff. & in Jour. B. & W Soc. 3rd ser. XXL (1890). Edith J. Cannan & F. J. Lloyd. *Manufacture of Cheddar cheese.* id. 4th ser. 1892. p. 136 ff. James Muir. *Manual of dairy work.* 1893. p. 64. Henry J. Webb *Advanced agric.* 1894. p. 620.

[11] Simon. *Cheeses of the world.* 1956. pp. 35–37.

[12] John Laurence. *op. cit.* pp. 139, 140.

[13] Richard Bradley. *Country housewife.* 6th ed. 1736. pp. 71–76.

[14] Ellis. *Mod. husb.* II. May. pp. 112, 113.

[15] John Mills. *Treatise on cattle.* 1776. pp. 314, 315.

[16] Marshall. *Norfolk.* 1795. II. pp. 208–211.

[17] *idem. Gloucester.* 2nd ed. 1796. I. pp. 293–295.

[18] A. Lawson. *Modern farrier.* 1825. p. 387. Loudon. *Encyclo. of agric.* 1831. p. 1043.

[19] Jos. Hazard. *On making butter and cheese.* Letters & papers. Bath & West Soc. 2nd. ed. III (1788). pp. 150, 151.

[20] Henry Holland. *Cheshire.* 1808. pp. 264, 265, 268, 269: this is all quoted from the earlier report by Thomas Wedge. 1794.

[21] W. Youatt. *British husbandry.* 1837. II. p. 420.

[22] Ward & Lock's *Book.* p. 376.

[23] Donaldson. *British husb.* 1860. p. 691. Coleman. *Cattle of Great Britain.* 1887. pp. 100, 101.

[24] John Laurence. *op. cit.* p. 140. Ellis. *Mod. husb.* II. May. p. 124.

[25] Ellis. *ibid.* May. pp. 124. 116. June, pp. 171, 172. cf. Ellis *Husb. abridg'd.* 1772. II. 286–290.

[26] See Andre L. Simon. *op. cit.* pp. 31, 32.

[27] *Annals of agric.* XVII 1792. pp. 47–50. Holland. *Cheshire.* 1808. pp. 266–286. Lawson. *op. cit.* pp. 390, 391 Loudon. *op. cit.* p. 1045.

[28] Baxter's *Library.* 1836. p. 154. Henry White. *A detailed account of making Cheshire cheese.* J.R.A.S.E. 1845 p. 103 ff. G. H. Andrews. *Mod. husb.* 1853. pp. 388–390. Olmstead. *Walks & talks.* 1852. pp. 169, 172.

[29] Leonce de Lavergne. *Rural economy of England.* 1855. p. 242.

[30] H. Evershed. *Agric. of Staffordshire.* J.R.A.S.E. 1869. Morton. *Handbook.* p. 71. idem. *Dairy farming.* J.R.A.S.E. 1878. pp. 675, 676 Roland. *Farming for pleasure.* 1879. p. 79. Long. *British dairy farming.* 1885. p. 131 ff. Sheldon. *Farm & dairy.* 1885. p. 97. Muir. *Manual.* 1893. p. 90. Stella Davies. *The Cheshire dairy.* Cheshire Historian No. 6. 1956. pp. 1–8.

[31] Sheldon. *Dairy farming.* c. 1883. pp. 233–238 idem. *Farm & dairy.* 1889. pp. 99–101. Simon. *op. cit.* pp. 43, 44.

[32] Robert Morden. *New description and state of England.* 1704. Defoe. *Tour.* Everyman ed. I. pp. 283, 284.

[33] Marshall. *Gloucester.* 1796. I. pp. 295–313. Thomas Rudge. *Gloucester.* 1807. pp. 289–295.

[34] Marshall. *ibid.* II. pp. 115–130.

[35] *Ayrshire Association of Agric. Report* as Note 9. p. 161. Sheldon. *Dairy farming.* c. 1883. p. 240.

[36] Marshall. *ibid.* pp. 155–179, 183–185. c.f. Morton. *Dairy farming.* J.R.A.S.E. 1878. pp. 678, 679. William Mavor. *Berkshire.* 1813. pp. 374–376.

[37] Baxters' *Library.* 1836. p. 136, 137. Lawson. *op. cit.* p. 389. Loudon. *op. cit.* p. 1046. Little. *Farming of Wilts.* J.R.A.S.E. 1845. p. 175. Lavergne. *op. cit.* p. 245. *Ayrshire report*—note 35—pp. 159–162. Morton. *Handbook.* 1860. p. 69. etc. etc.

[38] Sheldon. *Dairy farming.* pp. 239, 240. c.f. Miss A. Colnett. *Cheeses of Great Britain. 12.* Gloucester. Dairy Engineering. Nov. 1955. p. 339 ff.

[39] Ernle. *English farming.* 1961. p. 187 fn. based on Marshall. *Midlands* 1790. I. p. 355.

[40] Simon. *op. cit.* pp. 38, 39.

[41] Laurence. 1726. pp. 142, 143.

[42] *Letters etc.* Bath & West Soc. III (1788). pp. 153, 154. c.f. Willich. *Dom. encyclo.* 1802. art. *cheese.* p. 496.

[43] Willich. *ibid.* Lawson. *op. cit.* p. 392. Loudon. p. 1047. Youatt. *British husb.* 1837. II. p. 431. Baxter's *Library.* 1836. p. 158. Morton. *Handbook.* 1860. p. 77. Copland. *Agric.* 1866. I. pp. 752, 753. Roland. *Farming.* 1879. p. 86.

[44] Sheldon. *Dairy farming.* c. 1883. p. 243. *idem. Farm & dairy.* 1889. p. 104. Muir. *Manual.* 1893. p. 82. see. Simon. p. 40.

[45] A. D. Hall. *Pilgrimage of English farming.* 1913. pp. 421, 408. George Gibbons. *Report on cheese making in Derby.* J.R.A.S.E. 1881. pp. 533, 534.

[46] R. Parkinson. *Treatise on livestock.* 1810. p. 63. Sheldon. *Farm & dairy.* 1889. p. 105. Richmond Commission. *Mr. Coleman's Report.* 1880. p. 136. L. Jebb. *The small holdings of England.* 1907. pp. 36, 37.

[47] Willich. *op. cit.* 1802. p. 496. Parkinson. *Livestock.* p. 55. Simon. p. 43.

[48] Bradley. *Country housewife.* 1736. p. 74. Loudon. pp. 1044, 1045. Twamley. *Essays on the management of the dairy.* 1816. p. 162.

[49] Marshall. *Norfolk.* 1787. II. pp. 208–235.

[50] Stevenson. *Dorset.* 1815. pp. 384, 385. Thomas Davis. *On superior advantages of dairy to arable farms.* Letters. B. & W. Soc. III. (1785) p. 75. Parkinson. *Livestock.* 1810. p. 56.

[51] Elihu Burritt. *Walk from London.* 1868. pp. 126, 129.

[52] *The closet of Sir Kenelm Digby Knight opened.* (1669), quoted in Simon pp. 54, 55.

[53] Bradley. *Country housewife.* 1736. pp. 83, 84. Laurence. *op. cit.* p. 141. Ellis. *Mod. husb.* 1750. II May. pp. 117, 118. Ellis's *Husb. abridg'd.* 1772. II. p. 292. Parkinson. *Livestock.* 1810. p. 62. Twamley. *op. cit.* 1816. p. 159.

[54] Thomas Hale. *Compleat body of husb.* 1756. pp. 577, 581.

[55] Youatt. *Brit. husb.* 1836. II. p. 456. Roland. *Farming for pleasure.* 1879. p. 90.

[56] Ellis. *Mod. husb.* II. May. p. 118. Youatt. *op. cit.* p. 435. Morton. *Dairy Farming.* J.R.A.S.E. 1878. p. 686. Sheldon. *Farm & dairy.* 1889. p. 86.

[57] G. E. Evans. *Ask the fellows who cut the hay.* 1956. p. 68.

# CHAPTER VI

## *The Trade in Dairy Products*

### (i). Butter and Cheese

The limiting factor in the trade of dairy produce in Tudor times was the slowness and cost of transport. Liquid milk could not be carried any great distance to market if it was to arrive in saleable condition, though butter and cheese were less perishable, and could be taken to comparatively distant markets on the roads or by sea. The relation between production and consumption is more difficult to assess.

Although there can hardly have been more than $4\frac{1}{2}$ million persons in the kingdom[1] the traffic for their maintenance was increasing beyond what it had been. During the sixteenth century an urban market where people employed on other business bought most of their food was developing. London was the largest, but there were food buyers in the larger provincial towns, in the embryonic Black Country, the Tyneside mining area, the textile districts of Yorkshire, East Anglia and the West.[2] The supply of these markets developed at a time when the statutory labour on the roads was becoming less efficient, so that inland mobility was becoming less flexible than perhaps it had been.[3] Roads were quite unmade and the increase of heavy wheeled traffic, waggons and coaches, and the greater number of beasts of burden and beasts for meat which traversed these dirt tracks made them steadily worse. Still in spite of all exordiums upon the vileness of such roads[4] any pack or meat animal could walk along them, provided it did not get submerged in mud and water. The great wide wheeled, slow moving waggons could be dragged along by huge teams and main force.

In such elementary conditions of development recourse to water transport wherever possible is usual, and a great deal of heavy goods were carried coastwise or along such rivers as could be navigated. This business was not, of course, in the hands of primary producers. A great deal of emphasis has been laid upon the isolation and self-sufficiency of the farmers, perhaps too much. No tiller of the soil, and especially no grazier, shepherd or dairyman, can supply all his own needs. There are many things he requires for his business that he must buy. He can grow his own food, breed his own meat, clip his own wool, and tan his own leather, while the woods will supply him with the material for part of his tools, and even for a dwelling,[5] but he needs iron and many other things that must be brought to him.

The ready exchange of farm produce and farm require-ments was provided for by the weekly market in most towns, and the annual or half-yearly fair, and this made it unneces-sary for the farmer to journey far to sell his produce, or to buy his needs,[6] but the merchants, factors and peddlers, who attended these markets and fairs must have possessed a much greater mobility. Some fairs were definitely cheese fairs, and it was at these, as well as at more general fairs that the factors representing cheesemongers from the centres of population attended to buy up the local output of cheese and butter. They may also have lived in the districts all the year round, and visited farms to make purchases. Details of the system emerge more clearly as records become more precise in later times. This kind of system was essential in the stage of economic development when goods are produced in small lots by domestic producers and small farmers, and must be sold to distant consumers in small lots,[7] conditions that continue to apply to the trade in dairy produce. Already in the reign of Henry VIII government regulation of this business had proved necessary. It was then forbidden to buy butter and cheese to sell again 'in gross', upon pain of forfeiture of double the value of the goods. All stocks bought for resale must be sold in open shop, fair or market. John Hovell, who evidently had a sizeable stock of butter and cheese in his Suffolk house in 1554 was ordered by the Justices to put it on the market because supplies were scarce. When he failed to do so, they seized it and sold it, and offered the money to Hovell.[8]

The bulking and transport of butter and cheese had however to be arranged. The producing centres were almost all relatively far away from the consuming public in days of horse and ox transport. London was, of course, the largest consumer market. For liquid milk the inhabitants were dependant upon cow-keepers in the immediate vicinity or in the city itself. Middlesex farmer's wives came to town two or three times weekly with supplies of milk, butter and cheese amongst other things.[9] Supplies of butter and cheese were sent from many of the Home Counties. Sussex farmers sent both, but Surrey men butter only, their cheese being robbed to enable the butter to be sent to London. Suffolk farmers did the same, but their butter, like that made in Surrey, was good at the expense of the cheese. The Suffolk trade to London was perhaps the largest. One Suffolk haven is said to have supplied 900 loads in an ordinary year. Essex also sent fair quantities, and increasing amounts were shipped from the north-east coast, Lincolnshire and Norfolk.[10]

Large quantities were exported. One fortunate monopolist got a licence for 21 years, from 1629, to transport 3,200 barrels of butter yearly 'to be bought within the counties of Norfolk, Lincoln and York' with the proviso that he was not to export when the price was more than 4d. a lb.[11] The barrel was a reputed firkin of 56 lb. In 1626 Glamorgan farmers were unable to pay their rents because Turkish pirates had taken their ships trading to France and Ireland with butter. Piracy was also a menace in the English Channel. Welsh butter and cheese sent across the Severn to Bristol and other ports on the south coast of the Bristol Channel travelled with less risk. Cardiff was one of the ports for this trade, and Pembroke another. A licence was granted in 1634 to transport out of Wales and Monmouth 3,000 barrels of butter yearly on the same terms as a previous licence i.e. that no export should take place when the price was above 3d. a lb. in summer, and 4d. in winter.[12] A few years later it was said that 5,742 firkins had been unlawfully exported from Hull, and measures were taken to prevent this trade.[13] In 1630 the situation of the country was so bad that enemy craft on the Norfolk, Suffolk and Essex coast prevented sailings from Yarmouth and the Thames, so that cargoes of cheese, butter and fish for London were delayed and likely to decay if a convoy were not speedily provided for the shipping. Apparently there was some combination or co-operation between the merchants for the petition is from the cheesemongers of London.[14] Some of the West Midland counties, including Derby, sent their butter and cheese to great markets, already well established in the seventeenth century, such as Uttoxeter, where the London cheesemongers had set up factories. The butter was sent to these factories packed in coarse, unglazed butter pots of Staffordshire ware.[15]

Though Bristol and other Somerset ports were partly supplied by the cross Channel trade from Wales and Monmouth, the inland Somerset farmers exported locally overland. Yeovil was a great market. Large quantities of both butter and cheese were sent to Hampshire and Wiltshire from here.[16] Devon farmers were not happy about their cheese, but their butter was good. They exported very little, except a few who lived on the borders of Somerset and Dorset, and they must have eaten their clotted cream themselves. A licence granted in 1607 to a badger to buy butter and cheese in Somerset to sell at any fair in Wiltshire, Hampshire and Devon confirms this. At a later date most of the cheese sold at the great Weyhill Fair came from Cheddar and Frome, Hampshire not being so great a cheese country.[17]

So much of the trade in butter was commonly seaborne that it was easy to divert the traffic to foreign countries if the home market was not favourable, and the government kept a close eye upon it, so that the home consumers should not suffer. There was doubtless some illegal trade, but the export licence already mentioned, and another to export 5,000 barrels annually for twenty one years may indicate that the average supply was in excess of the demand.[18]

S

Regulations about packing were issued both in 1634 and 1637, and ordered that the old esteemed methods should not be changed. 'Time out of mind', the Proclamation ran, 'every firkin used to be 56 lb.' and the cask might only weigh 8 lb. Some casks were then being used that weighed 12 or 14 lb, and when filled 58 to 62 lb., an evil practice only equalled by that of mixing corrupt butter with best cream butter.[19]

There is no means of estimating the total volume of the trade in butter and cheese, nor the proportion of the trade that went to different markets, but the volume of trade in these products was relatively large in proportion to the human and animal population. It was possibly growing too, as output may have been. The length of the lactation, and consequently the total yield of milk per cow had been expanded since medieval times. Tusser's dairy season extended from the beginning of April to the end of November. In earlier times it had been from May to Michaelmas only, but the cows that yielded the milk were not very big. One that weighed 600 lb. was considered a good average; doubtless some were larger, but many may easily have been a good deal smaller.[20]

Milk yields were corresponding. A gallon at a meal was not to be despised, a gallon and a half good; two gallons rare and extraordinary. Robert Loder, a practical farmer, was not as optimistic as Markham. He established a milking herd in 1618, and estimated that the cows would give 12 pints at a meal all the year round, the equivalent of Markham's good yield, but this proved impossible. When calculating profits for his future guidance, his twelve cows had only given $\frac{1}{2}$ a gallon a meal from Whitsun to Michaelmas, possibly the ordinary output of the time. His estimate of $1\frac{1}{2}$ gallons at a meal was, if restricted to a lactation of 129 days, not, perhaps, over optimistic, but if the lactation was 200 days would be an almost modern yield of 600 gallons. These estimates were not greatly exceeded in West Cornwall twenty years ago, and a good farmer there in 1912 expected only 400 gallons.[21]

Besides the slow growth of population dwelling in urban or semi-urban centres, the demand for butter and cheese must have been affected favourably by the need for provisioning the ships going on long voyages, and the new naval stations.[22] In 1542 a commission was issued to Mawbye and Bryde to purchase no less than 1,000 way of cheese at the King's price, and for carts and carriages for conveying it to Berwick. Amongst other things butter and cheese were sent to Guisnes in 1550. Norfolk and Suffolk butter and cheese were ordered to be bought for Ireland in 1573-4 if it could be done without raising the price, and in 1574-5 supplies were obtained from Wales, Worcester and Salop with carriage by water or land, and enquiries were made in 1574 about the supplies in Essex, Suffolk and Norfolk, because the goods were being shipped abroad under pretence of being required for Ireland. This was an easy deception to practise because supplies from these counties were constantly required both for Ireland and for the Navy. Some cheese that was intended for Sluys in 1581 had to be sold at a loss because it was too new. In 1597 some 65 barrels of butter and 110 ways of cheese were in the hands of Thomas Sawell, cheesemonger for the Navy, and 11 other London cheesemongers offered Suffolk butter and cheese, but this was not purchased. A Yarmouth merchant offered Friesland cheese and butter for delivery in the river Thames evidently for the Navy, so the home producer was already confronted with some foreign competition. Joseph Andrews, customer at Bristol, too, was ordered to buy Welsh and Monmouth supplies for the Army in Ireland, the produce to be shipped to Bristol and thence to Ireland. Other supplies went from London.[23]

Similar government orders continued to be given throughout the troubled years of the first half of the seventeenth century. The ordinary rations of a seaman or a soldier of that time were on a scale that had been in operation in the reign of Elizabeth I and probably before, a daily ration including a bottle of beer, 3 cakes of biscuit—1 lb.; $\frac{1}{4}$ lb. butter and $\frac{1}{2}$ lb. cheese which together cost 6d. In 1628 an Order in Council restored the two flesh days a week of former times. This daily consumption of butter and cheese by the armed forces formed a substantial market.[24] For example, on

10 April, 1620 the farmers of the Customs were instructed to give orders for the free transport of '12 thousand weight of cheese and 100 firkins of butter unto the port of Leith' for the supply of troops to be raised in Scotland.[25]

The business became more complicated later. When war threatened with the Scots over the Covenant in 1639 and 1640 Charles I assembled an army at York. It had to be provisioned. An order was made forbidding the export of butter and cheese and other victuals, and these were all to be sent to Hull with the greatest possible expedition. So much was sent that by September, 1640, Denis Gawden, possibly a London cheesemonger, bought 450 barrels of butter returned from the army in the north, and sought permission to export it because it was no longer fit for the King's lieges. Butter and cheese was then once again allowed to be sent to London from Essex, Suffolk and Norfolk. It seems unlikely that this trade had been wholly interdicted, but that is what the terms of the petition indicate. The following January 3,300 firkins of butter, part of a great quantity sent to Hull, was returned as unserviceable 'being near two years old and much decayed'. It was sold for export.[26]

Something over 1,000 firkins of butter was seized at Scarborough by the Parliament forces in 1648, and afterwards paid for because the owners were well affected to that side of the dispute. Cromwell, too, had to purchase supplies for the army in Scotland and the forces in Ireland in 1649. Some cheese was imported from Holland, including 200 tons from 'Yminghem' for this purpose. Denis Gawden had a finger in this remunerative pie, and in supplying Scotland. He was paid no less than £3,243.16.6 in 1651. Robert Baynes was ordered to sail to the Tees to convoy some vessels laden with 6,000 firkins of butter for the fleet at Gravesend early in 1650.[27]

All this activity was due to war, external or internal, and does no more than indicate that the Tudor and early Stuart cheesemongers were able to move these comparatively bulky goods with unexpected facility. Thousands of firkins of butter weighing 60 lb. or more apiece and hundreds of tons of cheese were transported to distant points of consumption, but these supplies for military purposes can have been only a fraction of what went by normal routes to the inhabitants in general. When the diet of the seaman and the soldier included $\frac{1}{4}$ lb. butter and $\frac{1}{2}$ lb. cheese a day it is perhaps permissible to assume that these articles formed a major part of ordinary diet. The rations of the forces are, however, notoriously better than those of the civilian population, in bulk if nothing else, and it is reasonable to think that the civilians ate less of these things. However, their requirements were, in total, much greater, and the transport facilities required to move them proportionately larger.

This is emphasised by the theory recently advanced that there was a species of industrial revolution between 1575 and 1620 when many new or virtually new industries were established, the personnel employed forming a new food market that offered expanding opportunities to agricultural, including dairy, production, and to the middlemen who bulked the goods and redistributed them.[28]

Little wonder therefore can be felt at the intense preoccupation of advanced minds with the possibility of improving river courses and making water transport more general. John Taylor, the water poet, suggested joining the Thames and the Avon in the early years of the seventeenth century. He found the Thames so blocked in some parts that he had to wade and haul the boat, but this did not dissuade him. He tried the Salisbury Avon for possibilities of tapping the corn country of that neighbourhood.[29]

Actual projects were not wanting. In the time of Charles I Sir Richard Weston canalised the Wey; in 1661 Sir Richard Sandys obtained powers to cut channels and build locks on the Wye and the Lugg. In 1665 Francis Mathew published a book on the 'Opening of Rivers for Navigation', and propounded to Cromwell a scheme for connecting London and Bristol by a canal to join the Thames and Avon. About the same time Yarranton proposed to connect Banbury with the Thames and the Severn by making the Cherwell navigable from Oxford to Banbury, and by cutting a new channel from

Banbury to Shipton-on-Stour, whence goods could be carried by the Avon into the Severn below Tewkesbury. The famous Lynn navigation, tapping much of the eastern counties, was the subject of careful discussion, both in relation to the drainage of the Fens, and to its carrying capacity for goods.[30]

The export business continued during the remainder of the century with an occasional protest when supplies were scanty as, for example, in 1654, when the City of London petitioned Parliament to prohibit export unless the price at home was less than 4d. a lb. The quantity that could be sent to the Channel Islands was regulated in 1652. Some was even consigned to Bilbao, but the coastwise trade of the eastern and north eastern counties was hampered by the Dutch wars.[31]

It is a little odd that amongst all the references to the provision of cheese for Ireland there is, if I am not mistaken, only one reference to the purchase of Cheshire cheese for this purpose—by Charles Walley, who bought 15 tons in 1650. This was a small amount compared with the total shipments of Lancashire and Cheshire cheese. Some 612 tons were sent out of Chester in 1674 by thirteen merchants. The largest shipper in that year was George Paston with 80 tons. This year may have been a good one. Only five merchants shipped in 1691 a total amount of 253 tons. One of them transported 157 tons of this. The other four dividing the balance between them. Somewhat similar quantities were exported from Liverpool at this time. In 1674 some 640 tons were shipped and in 1690 four merchants shipped 234 tons. It seems that coastwise shipping of Cheshire and Lancashire cheese only attained these dimensions after the Restoration as negligible quantities were sent by this route before the Commonwealth. The fame of the cheese however suggests that quantities were carried to London from these and neighbouring counties. Can it have been by land carriage? This is a question that cannot at present be answered.

The seventeenth century trade in butter and cheese from the Eastern counties was of somewhat the same order. Between Christmas, 1637 and Christmas, 1638 some 525 loads of butter and cheese were shipped out of Ipswich, then probably the chief port of Suffolk. The quantity rose to 6,335 firkins and 1 hamper of pots of butter by 1684-5. Larger quantities were sent out of Hull, 11 tons of butter and cheese for London in 1628, and in 1684 no less than 23,231 firkins of butter. Scarborough dispatched 2,665 firkins in the same year.[31]

When a business attains these dimensions there are often abuses. Indeed it had been necessary to issue regulations long before, and it proved necessary once again in the fourteenth year of Charles II's reign (13 & 14 Car. 2. c. 26). This Act ordered that the weight of the firkin must be plainly marked and pots also. The kilderkin of butter must contain 112 lb., and the firkin 56 lb. besides the tare of the cask, and every pot 14 lb. or more besides the weight of the pot. The farmer's name must be branded on the barrels with an iron brand. Butter must not be repacked. Heavy penalties for infringement were provided. Whether any officer was appointed to see that these things were done is not clear, although Charles II had appointed 'one Reade to such an office before the Act was passed.' Ten years later two men petitioned to be appointed to gauge all empty butter casks and pots and to search all butter put into them.[33]

Other Acts (32 Car. 2. c. 2. and 4 William and Mary c. 7.) having the same objects and some others were afterwards passed. In addition to requiring that the name of the factor or buyer must be set on the cask, and that there must be no mixture of defective butter, these Acts provided that after a factor or buyer had bought the commodity and approved it, the seller was absolved from all penalties of an Act for reforming abuses in the weight and false packing of butter. The London cheesemongers (as a corporate body or in temporary association) objected to this. They could not carry their own weights about the country nor immediately take away such quantities of cheese and butter as they bought. They had to rely on the honesty of the seller, but if they purchased and approved butter and left it in the seller's house, there was nothing to prevent the seller changing it. None but an eye-witness could convict of such cheats. Not unreasonably they also objected to the powers of entry and search that these Acts conferred, but their objections are open to suspicion of poor motives.[34] These Acts were passed, and were very much in the consumer's interest if properly enforced.

Overlookers were appointed whose duty it was to see that short weight was not consigned, but they did not supervise the business of the London cheesemongers 'who send their own vessels to Chester for their own goods'. The trade and its methods were already stabilised by the end of the seventeenth century, and the procedure remained the same during the whole of the eighteenth.[35] In 1692 the cheesemongers became involved in a dispute with the town of Liverpool. A good deal of cheese was shipped from that port, and the town authorities demanded from the shippers the town dues on their wares, but the shippers claimed exemption under charter. The dispute lasted until 1700 when arbitrators were appointed, with what result is doubtful. Throughout the earlier documents the defendants (if so they may be called) are cited as 'the Cheesemongers of London' as if they were a guild or other corporate body, and this reading seems to have been accepted by Westerfield, but the document of 1700 cited them as 'Nathl. and others, Cheesemongers of London', which may be taken to show that they were not then a combine, but were cited as individuals.

That the cheesemongers may have lost the decision is suggested by their action in 1709 when they opposed a Bill for building a dock at Liverpool, because they would not be able to use it. The Bill passed in spite of their opposition, and a loan of £6,000 was authorised. This attempt has been used to support the belief that they were a combine: it certainly shows that upon occasion they were capable of concerted action.[36] Butter and cheese formed a higher proportion of ordinary diet at that time than they do today as the quantities supplied to the forces show. This continued to the end of the eighteenth century, but the part played by these commodities declined after about 1850.[37] Cheese formed a solid part of the diet of eighteenth century workhouses, and the aged pensioners of Greenwich Hospital ate $2\frac{1}{4}$ lb. each a week in 1802.[38] This being so the quantities dealt in by the 'mongers', factors, etc., must have been very large. Contemporary estimates of the volume of trade, however, are undoubtedly exaggerated. In the early years of the century Defoe generously put it that the 'County of Chester and its adjacent land' sent 'near 30,000 tons of cheese to *London* and all other places'. This is sufficient to supply $1\frac{1}{4}$ million adults with 1 lb. a head weekly for a year, and the saving grace of the statement is 'and all other places'.[39]

The total supply of cheese and butter for London was drawn from many other places besides Cheshire and its environs. Maitland classified the sources for the year ending 25 March, 1730 as follows:—

*Butter*

| | | |
|---|---|---|
| From York, Hull, Scarborough and Stockton | 114,937 | firkins |
| „ Newcastle-on-Tyne | 15,705 | „ |
| „ Suffolk | 56,703 | „ |
| All this was brought by sea. | | |
| From Cambridge (year: Christmas, 1731-32) | 74,918 | „ |
| „ other parts | 30,000 | „ |
| | 292,263 | „ |

*Cheese*

| | | |
|---|---|---|
| From Cheshire | 5,756 | tons |
| „ Hull and Gainsborough | 1,407 | „ |
| „ Suffolk | 985 | „ |
| „ Newbury, Abingdon, etc., by barge | 2,375 | „ |
| | 10,573 | „ |

The figures for the Cheshire cheese are derived from the Receiver's Account of Freight, and should therefore be accurate. These figures look as if they were a reasonable approximation on the basis of the probable consumption at the very substantial rates of the time. This quantity of butter would provide rather more than $\frac{1}{2}$ lb. a week each for half a million people, and the cheese about 1 lb. a week, but some doubt is cast upon them by the Port Books evidence.[40]

In the mid-century the Cheesemongers themselves represented their dealings as of the following order:—

Butter made in Norfolk, Isle of Ely and parts of Lincolnshire, sent to Cambridge by water, thence by land to London weekly is 90,000 firkins approximately 2,250 tons.

Quantities of cheese annually brought to London from Warwick, Leicester, Derby, and Stafford by land carriage is about 500 tons; from Gloucester, Berkshire and Wiltshire by land annually 2,000 tons.

It may be interpolated here that Ernle says, with what authority he does not state, the 'Gloucestershire cheesemakers sent their cheese to London down the Thames from Lechlade'. The statement is probably based upon Defoe.

Essex, Hertford, part of Sussex, part of Kent, Bedford and Buckingham are supplied from London with 2,000 tons annually (of cheese and salt butter).[41]

These figures are contained in a petition of the several traders . . . being dealers in butter and cheese within the cities of London and Westminster against the provisions of a Bill, then pending in the House, for limiting the number of horses that might be harnessed to waggons, a measure that passed into law, with only slight modifications, in spite of the wealth and power of the cheesemongers.

This petition, showing once again joint action by the cheesemongers, has been accepted as further evidence that they had formed a combine, or 'club' as it was called, controlled the better part of the supplies and arranged prices. An explicit statement to this effect was made by Mr. Wimpey, writer on agricultural subjects, in 1770. It is in relation to the supplies obtained from Cheshire that he makes the accusation, and clearly the figures given to the House, which omitted this source for obvious reasons, did not cover the whole consumption of London. The 90,000 firkins of butter would only have supplied approximately 180,000 adults with 1 lb. a week each, and the cheese about 200,000 with $\frac{1}{2}$ lb. each.

Wimpey wrote

'The most considerable cheesemongers in London have formed themselves into a club. They are owners of about 16 ships, which are employed between London, Chester and Liverpool. They employ these ships chiefly in bringing up cheese to London. They have factors in Cheshire who buy up the cheese for them, and lodge it in their warehouses at Chester. At their weekly meetings they settle what Quantities each shall have brought up to Market. By this means the Market is fed in such a Manner, that they command whatever price they please'.[42]

Another grievance was that the Club would not suffer individual action, 'intimidating', by means readily envisaged, such rash persons as dared it, and, of course, because they went north light, the ships could carry freight that way at cut rates, thus further consolidating their monopoly, which was, in the opinion of the day, a scandal and a wicked means of oppressing the consumer. The system, however, which was described two years later in the same words, probably secured a more regular supply than would otherwise have been available.[43]

Defoe's estimate of the Cheshire cheese was much to high. It was elaborated by some of the topographers, who were busily employed in writing treatises about the geography, antiquities and trade of the country during the eighteenth century, but none of them puts the output at so vast a figure as Defoe. They take no account of increase or decrease in the trade over fairly long periods. According to these estimates 14,000 tons of Cheshire cheese were sent annually to London, 8,000 tons down the Severn and Trent to Bristol and York, besides great quantities shipped at both Chester and Liverpool to Ireland and Scotland.[44] The amount said to have been sent to London would have provided over 600,000 people with 1 lb. a week each for a year, without taking into account supplies from other places: more the quantities shipped in the mid-century from Liverpool and Chester to London were 952 tons and 798 tons respectively, but the Port Books quoted by Willan may have been incomplete. It is indeed difficult to make anything of such widely divergent figures.

Factors were employed by the London cheesemongers in almost all the districts which exported cheese. The Cheshire farmers delivered the cheese either at Chester, whence it was shipped direct to London or elsewhere, or at Frodsham, whence it was taken to Liverpool for shipment. At the end of the century some went up the new Staffordshire canal to the inland counties, and the factors also supplied the local markets of Stockport and Manchester, which in turn supplied the increasing population of South Lancashire and West Yorkshire. Bridgnorth was a collecting centre for cheese for the three counties of Stafford, Salop and Cheshire, and there were factories for cheese at Tarvin. Derby produced butter and cheese and the chief trade of Ashbourn was in these commodities. The county was thought to export nearly 2,000 tons to London, and several seaports on the east coast, another apparent exaggeration. The business in cheese was all in the hands of factors at the end of the century and was well organised, although perhaps not always to the advantage of the farmers. It was brought to London by land carriage.[45]

Marshall estimated that the total supply of factor's cheese produced in the Midlands was nearly equal to that from Gloucester and North Wiltshire. He seems to have had Warwick and Stafford in mind. The Staffordshire dairies of the Moorlands supplied quantities of butter and cheese to Uttoxeter market, where the market had been established since the Middle Ages. On the borders of Needwood Forest this town was affected by practically no other traffic. No stage coach passed through it till 1830. Butter from Salop went to the manufacturing towns. Besides this there was Stilton cheese produced in Leicestershire.[46]

Cumberland and Westmorland both produced surplus butter and cheese, the latter not being greatly esteemed however; but the former was brought 'for many places' as Kalm relates he was told. The butter was either sold in the neighbouring market towns in Cumberland, or put up in firkins and sold to dealers. At the end of the century this trade was valued at £30,000 yearly. Westmorland also found that the export of butter paid, except near Kendal, were fresh milk sold at a ½d. a quart was more profitable. Skim milk was sold at one-third of that rate, used in the family, or made into cheese.[47]

The coasting trade from the eastern and north-eastern counties continued, but the famous Epping butter was sent to London by road. Epping and Woodford were centres of the dairy business there. There was a weekly market at Waltham on Tuesdays as well as at Epping on Fridays. Some of the product was sold to higglers and at fairs, but the larger dairies usually had an arrangement with a Clare Market dairyman for the whole stock.[48] Tusser referred to Sturbridge Fair where butter and cheese were sold by farmers in the sixteenth century. In the eighteenth century those of Norfolk, Suffolk and Essex continued to do so, and purchased clothes and other household requisites there. It is probable too that this fair was frequented by sellers from more distant places. The best cheese was bought up by the factors, and cheese from Cheshire, Wiltshire, and Gloucester by gentry, farmers and dealers from Suffolk, Norfolk and the adjacent counties. Large quantities of Cottenham cheese were offered for sale by farmers once, but this fair had sunk into practical oblivion by 1882.[49]

The Suffolk dairies made more impression on Defoe. 'High Suffolk' was 'famous for the best Butter and perhaps the worst Cheese, in England'. It was shipped from Dunwich (? by sea), Framlingham, Halstead, and other places (? by road) and went to London and overseas to Holland. The cheese was, of course, skim milk cheese, and some of this type from other counties was apparently called Suffolk cheese on the London market. The business was largely in the hands of the London cheesemongers.[50]

Young was informed in 1786 that the quantities of butter annually sent to London from three counties were:—

| | | |
|---|---|---|
| Yorkshire | 100,000 | firkins |
| Cambridge | 70,000 | firkins |
| Suffolk | 40,000 | firkins |

But, as the cheesemongers had already reported to the House of Commons the Cambridge figure included a good deal from Norfolk, and some probably from Lincoln as the shipping point was Denver Sluice near Downham. Butter boats also sailed from Lynn. Butter from West Norfolk was given the trade name of Cambridge to increase saleability. When he wrote his report on Suffolk in 1797 he did not see any reason to alter the figure for that county. Similarly that made at St. Neots and on the Duke of Grafton's estate was sold to London as Epping. The Cambridge colleges obtained their supplies of butter locally. It was made up in rolls a yard long by 2 inches circumference. The quality was nowhere excelled was the modest claim in the locality. Some of the export in the earlier year was carried by the veal carts that went regularly to London, and this product was sold in the Metropolis as 'hay butter'. It was the larger dairies in West Norfolk from which the butter, joining that of Cambridge, went to London; that from the smaller dairies in the east of the county, as well as the cheese produced, was largely disposed of in the 'Ped' market at Norwich, to which it was carried and sold retail by the farmer's wife or daughter. Their customers were not selective: they bought rank butter and rancid cheese.[51]

One of the primary objects of the enclosed Vale of Pickering was butter, the better quality being sent to London, but the inferior sorts to the manufacturing towns of the West Riding. In Marshall's day the London cheesemongers were well established here, having agents scattered about the county who watched their interests and controlled the direction taken by each quality. The searchers divided the product into three classes and grease. First and second quality only went to London. So early as 1778 the export of butter from Newcastle-on-Tyne was estimated as seldom less than 30,000 firkins, and in addition 40,000 firkins of tallow left this port.[52] Most of these figures are impossible to substantiate. They are indicative only of the importance of the trade, and perhaps of its growth during the eighteenth century.

Besides all this the dairy district of Bedford and Buckingham and all the counties along the Thames valley added their quotas to the supply. The principal towns in Bedford from which London drew supplies were Ampthill and Woburn; the Vale of Aylesbury was the source in Buckingham. The butter was made up in 2 lb. lumps, packed flat in ozier baskets, which were the property of the carrier. From 3 to 10 dozen of butter was packed in a flat. The dairyman had to carry it to the nearest point the carrier passed, but the London dealer who had contracted for the supply paid the carriage. The average yield was about 200 lb. on forty weeks. These arrangements were stabilised by 1794. How long they had been in operation cannot easily be determined, but Purefoy refused to pay carriage for a customer in 1738 'as nobody does here'.[53] There was also some local retail trade both direct between producer and customer and at the local markets.

At the end of the eighteenth century a wharf had been erected on the Thames at Buscot, Berkshire, by Mr. Liveden, and warehouses built 'for the reception of cheese'. These were rented by the ubiquitous cheesemongers of London, and it was estimated that not less than 2,000 or 3,000 tons of 'single Gloucester' cheese (a wide range) were annually sent down the Thames. About 1,000 tons were believed to be made in Berkshire. From the grazing lands of North Oxfordshire and the neighbouring similar land in Northampton waggons carried butter to London. They were chiefly loaded between Bicester and Wheatley. Large quantities were sent from the Brackley neighbourhood, and indeed from the whole district of Whittlemore Forest. There was also a supply of cheese at Burford fair, which was on the border of Gloucester in the west of Oxford.[54]

Chipping Sodbury in the same area was named by Defoe (1724) as the greatest cheese market in England, but there was at least one competitor for this honour—Atherston-on-Stour in Warwick. Defoe also tells us that some of the cheese of Warwick and Gloucester was taken to Bristol down the Avon, so this area had two outlets for its surplus.

A large proportion of Gloucester cheese was consumed in Bath and Bristol, and Bristol exported some to the West Indies. Another large part of the output continued to be taken to Lechlade and Cricklade and carried down the Thames to London. Warwickshire cheese was sent by land, and the London cheesemongers re-distributed supplies of both by sea and river navigation into Essex, Suffolk, Norfolk, Kent, Surrey and Sussex, or else to Stourbridge Fair. The supplies made in the Upper Vale of Gloucester were sold three times annually July, Michaelmas and in the spring, to cheese factors who lived in or near the district. The same factor frequently had the same dairy year after year often without seeing it or making a bargain. Almost the whole produce of the Vale of Berkeley passed through the hands of two men, Mr. Bigland of Frocester and Mr. Hicks of Berkeley, each of whom had his particular dairies. There were butter markets at Gloucester, Cheltenham. Tewkesbury and Evesham. The butter was packed in baskets shaped like a long cube that held 12 or 18 lb., with two lids hinging on a liece under the bow. These were put in a wallet with a smaller basket or counterpoise at the opposite end, and this was tightly strapped to the saddle 'judiciously made on purpose' with the heavy end on the off-side. The maid dexterously mounted, and preserved the balance with her own weight. The basket was lashed on so as to ride level, and preserve the prints. In summer the butter was packed in the leaves of garden orache sown in the gardens every year for the purpose. The supply was estimated at 1,000 —1,200 tons yearly. The total output may have been of the order Marshall estimated, because an anonymous writer then suggested that the Vale produced 7,500 tons, and other parts 500, and Warner, who visited the county a little later, that the quantity was between 7,000 and 8,000 tons annually.[55]

Bristol drew some supplies from Glamorgan as it had done since the sixteenth century. Welsh butter was sold in Bath. Pembroke sent salt butter and cheese to Bristol and to London, both by sea.[56]

A good deal of the cheese sold in London as Double

Gloucester was produced in Wiltshire, that made in Gloucester being sent to Bristol. The Wiltshire was no doubt that
referred to by Twamley as Marlborough cheese, which was
sold at Newbury, Andover and Weyhill and Reading by the
Marlborough factors. Wimpey complains that it was formerly
sent direct to market possibly in hired waggons.[57] The business
seems to have been completely in the factor's hands in both
counties. The Wiltshire product was in two classes, 'young'
and 'old'. The former went to London by land carriage for
quick sale, the latter by sea as it was more mature and would
keep longer. The product of North Wiltshire was estimated
by Marshall at 5,000 tons a year.

Not all the Cheddar and other Somerset cheese was sent to
London. Some was offered at Bridgwater, many waggons
being brought here for the supply of Devonshire in 1751. At
the end of the century it was mainly purchased by jobbers,
and sent through the medium of Weyhill, Giles Hill, Reading, and other fairs to the London market, where it was sold
under the name of double Gloucester. In Devon, like other
counties, the local inhabitants were satisfied with skim milk
cheese. The butter produced in the Vale of Exeter went to
swell the supply of London. For example, there was no butter
to be had in Axminster except on market day, all the large
dairies being under contract to London dealers. The adjoining parts of West Dorset, which Marshall called a natural
cheese district, had turned to making butter for London by
the end of the century, but Weymouth, steadily becoming a
more and more fashionable watering place, made growing
demands upon the county output. Butter made in the Isle of
Wight, like that on the low chalk pastures of Eastern Dorset,
the Isle of Purbeck, and some coastal districts, went to supply
Portsmouth.[58]

In Kent the waggons that took the hops to London brought
back Irish butter and cheese, the latter probably of the skim
milk type. Here milk and fresh butter were the portion of the
higher classes only, the poor having to be content with Irish
butter and the London cheese. In Surrey the Farnham hops
were sold at Weyhill, and carried to London. The Farnham

T

waggons brought back cheeses from that fair. The Weald of Sussex farmers made butter, but it was all sold in the local markets, and consumed locally.[59]

There is no way of collating all these estimates, remarks and repetitions about the trade in butter and cheese in the eighteenth century: but, of course, London was still the largest unit of population in the country, and its demands dominated the market. There were by 1800 other large units which also had to be supplied. The embryo centres of population that existed in the late Tudor and early Stuart times had grown steadily larger, and their demands for food, including butter and cheese, had led to heavy cross country traffic in these commodities. It was made possible only by the improved main roads that were everywhere being built under the inspiration of such amateur but successful engineers as Blind Jack of Knaresborough, Telford and Macadam. The rage for canal construction and improving rivers that developed assisted this as it did the transit of other heavy goods: but there was no official way of judging its total size nor the proportions that went here and there about the kingdom. Contemporaries were as puzzled as we are likely to remain.

Another estimate of the butter consumed in London at the end of the century is probably exaggerated. 'London' it runs 'is said to consume 50,000 tons annually'. Of this amount Cambridge and Suffolk were supposed to supply 50,000 firkins, but none of the butter brought in equalled that of Epping (? in quantity). The enormous amount of 50,000 tons represents 2 million firkins, and even if each person in the city consumed 1 firkin per annum, more than 1 lb. a week each, this would have provided for two million people—more than double the population in 1801. Some of that received in London was sent out again, but allowing for that, this estimate is too high. The consumption of the country as a whole was however outstripping the production. At the turn of the century fairly large supplies were being obtained from Ireland, and smaller quantities from Holland, Germany and France. In the five years from 1806 to 1810 Irish butter amounted to:—

Butter exported from Ireland to Great Britain.

| Year | Cwts. |
|---|---|
| 1806 | 258,407 |
| 1807 | 286,071 |
| 1808 | 311,311 |
| 1809 | 330,155 |
| 1810 | 337,070½ |

This did not all go to London. In the year Christmas, 1799 to Christmas, 1800 that city received 182,072 cwts. approximately, and therefore a fairly large proportion of Irish butter went elsewhere.[60] It was not a new trade, but had been substantial for at least half a century, though before then it was negligible. In 1759-60 43,421 cwts. entered London; in 1779-80, 169,027 cwts. Irish cheese imports were small. Indeed only small quantities of cheese were imported until after 1780. The actual figures for both commodities are as follows:—

*Imports of butter into London*

| | | Holland cwts. | Germany cwts. | Ireland cwts. | France cwts. | Total cwts. |
|---|---|---|---|---|---|---|
| Xmas, | 1759 | | | 43,421 | | 43,421 |
| ,, | 1760 | | 5 barrels | | | & 5½ |
| ,, | 1779 | | | | | barrels |
| ,, | 1780 | 338 | | 169,026 | | 169,613 |
| ,, | 1799 | | | | | |
| ,, | 1800 | 67,884 | 24,776 | 182,072 | 13,788 | 289,507 |

*Imports of Cheese into London, 1800*

| | cwts. | | cwts. | | cwts. |
|---|---|---|---|---|---|
| Holland | 87,902 | Germany | 15,222 | | |
| Flanders | 640 | Italy | 441 | Total | 104,480 |

Small quantities of cheese had been imported from most West European countries before 1800, but can only have been to meet a luxury demand, the amounts being negligible in comparison to the total consumption.[61] From these small beginnings a vast importation developed in the nineteenth century.

The demand for foodstuffs had risen in proportion to the population in the eighteenth century, and was about double at the end of the century of what it had been at the beginning. A much larger proportion of the people too were non-food producers at the end of the century than ever before. It was remarkable in the conditions of the time that the dairy farmers of the country should have been able to go so far towards meeting the unprecedented demand, and should have needed what was then comparatively little help from imports. There was undoubtedly some increase in the yield from each cow, but it was nothing remarkable and the variations between breeds and districts were wide: it could not have amounted to very much on the average. The increased output was, I think, derived from a larger number of cows, but there is no means of testing this assumption.

Sir William Petty's estimate of the produce of an Irish cow was accepted as applicable to England, and quoted with approval by Bradley, Ellis and later writers, as was Markham's. Petty's figure was 384 gallons of milk equal to $2\frac{1}{2}$ cwt. of raw milk cheese, and 1 cwt. whey butter with whey for pigs. Two gallons a day is said to have produced 4 lb. of butter a week in the Isle of Wight, and from June to Michaelmas a cow produced 70 lb. of butter. The yield of course varied through the lactation. The large Shorthorn gave more than the smaller breeds, and so on. The Suffolk Red Poll gave a high yield: but all the evidence suggests that 400 gallons was about the national average in or about 1800. In the butter dairy anything between 1 and 4 firkins was produced in a lactation: in the cheese dairy the range was from $2\frac{1}{2}$ to 4 cwt, and here and there a little more. There was, of course, always the exceptional and outstanding cow that reached as much as 1,000 gallons but she must have been very rare.[62] Most of the dairy farms were small or smallish, but on the whole it may perhaps be said that their produce was mainly sent to distant and central markets through the medium of the factors, who overcame the difficulties of transport as best they could.[63]

The business methods of the factor's employers, the

London cheesemongers, were condemned by Wimpey and others, but the fact of the matter was that during the eighteenth century the cost of living was rising, and, since the reasons were not too well understood, complaints were rife. All sorts of improbable people were accused of combination for the purpose of bleeding the consumer, amongst whom the farmers, then quite unorganised, figure prominently, as well as the graziers and others. Since the business of dealing in butter and cheese had developed into a routine, there was every reason why the cheesemongers should be blamed: but there is no clear evidence that they were in fact a combination, although they, or some of them, were members of a club. One at least was in business in a very substantial way. In 1733 Abraham Daking sold 40,566 firkins of butter and about the same amount of cheese. He was reputed the greatest dealer in the kingdom, and probably in the world at that time. Such a man would, of course, be able to exercise some influence of his own strength. However the organisation of the trade may have affected the farmer, it probably enabled the rapidly growing population of London (1700—674,350; 1801—900,000; 1811—1,050,000)[64] to obtain its supplies of butter and cheese with regularity or with little other fluctuation in price than the increase which was affecting all commodities.

In those days of free competition there was no price control, but the government continued its efforts to prevent false weight and adulteration. By 36 Geo. III. c. 18 and 38 Geo. III c. 73 the regulations made by earlier legislation were reaffirmed. The weight of the tub and firkin was regulated, and the thickness of the timber used for top and bottom specified. The cooper must brand his name and address on the bottom with the exact weight or tare. Every person packing must brand his name on the bottom within and top without, and imprint his name on the top of the butter within the vessel; he must state the weight of butter. No old or corrupt or whey butter to be used, and only fine ground salt. Any fraud with regard to vessel or butter was subject to a penalty of £30 for each offence. No butter might be repacked for sale, and foreign butter must be plainly marked as such if repacked.

A prison sentence of one to three months could be given if the appropriate fine could not be paid under distress.

It has been suggested that one of the results of the large scale enclosure that took place between 1750 and 1850 was to reduce the number of dairy farms, that the large scale farming it involved was almost exclusively directed to corn growing and stock feeding, known as mixed farming. No doubt there was a good deal of misguided ploughing up of grassland during the French Wars, but this was corrected again in the depression that followed them when land reverted to grass again, especially where of the marginal type. There is reason to believe, too, that some dairy land was enclosed without legislation and remained dairy land. The growth of population and the comparatively small proportion of imports indicate that the home dairy industry, so far from decreasing, must have expanded to a quite notable degree. Unfortunately this is another problem to which no exact or arithmetical answer can be given. Again much play has been made with the change in social circumstances of the farmer, and the consequent dislike of his wife for milking and dairy work, which she refused to do any longer. What proportion of farmers was affected has not however been determined, and it is certain that the farmer's wife and daughters on a great many dairy farms continued to do this work until the end of the nineteenth century. It is unlikely to have been the reason for the practice of letting dairies in the south western counties; it was indeed much older.[65] In the Suffolk dairy district however rather less butter and cheese than would supply local needs was produced in 1846, instead of the large quantities formerly sent to London and Northern England, yet few but Suffolk Red milch cows were bred.[66]

Since the business went on, the butter had to be packed and transported, and the majority of farmers were doubtless careful to maintain their reputation and value of their produce by doing this well. Others were less scrupulous. Sometimes butter was 'packed hollow, with water between or bad butter placed within and good just at the ends of the firkin'. The more scrupulous seasoned the firkins by exposing them to the air after frequent washing, and then filled them to within an inch or less of the top. The space left was for salt. After a few days the contents shrank a trifle, and the barrel was then filled up with brine 'strong enough to float an egg', and headed up. Cheese was not so liable to adulteration and disguise as butter except for stray impurities that might have crept in during manufacture. Occasionally metallic poisons were introduced with the annatto, or in the paint with which the outside was coloured. The annatto may have been coloured with Venetian red, and that stain itself with red lead. Tumeric was also used, and flour sometimes to cause blueing so that it is not surprising that these materials were sometimes found in cheese by analysts in the mid-nineteenth century. The use of vitriol or sulphate of zinc to prevent heaving had caused cheese poisoning in Germany since 1820, but this was difficult to detect. The legislation of three centuries had so far been ineffective.[67]

The construction of canals had partly solved the problem of cheap and easy transport of heavy goods. The coming of the railways did much more. By 1848 some 5,000 miles of railway had been laid in this kingdom, and steam power had been applied to ocean going ships. The railways were a boon to the traders in butter and cheese, and later proved so to the milk producer, but the more rapid ocean going steam ships introduced a new factor of competition by conveying foreign butter and cheese to this country in large quantities.

There is no discussion of the internal trade of the country in the nineteenth century comparable to the large body of topographical and pamphlet literature of the eighteenth century, possibly because the national prosperity then depended upon a rapidly expanding export trade. The production of butter and cheese must however have increased during the nineteenth century in spite of the imports, not only because the population became rapidly greater, but also because, with some setbacks, there was a rise both in monetary and real wages, there were more mouths to fill and greater economic capacity to provide for them. The population in 1851 was 17,927,609; in 1901 32,527,843. The general structure of the trade in butter and cheese did not change greatly though I have met with no suggestion that the wholesalers had maintained the eighteenth century combine, if one did indeed exist then. The butter and cheese made in North Wilts was said to be sold locally in 1850, but that means perhaps that it continued to be sold to factors at fairs like Marlborough, or by personal arrangement as formerly. The butter produced in Oxford and Buckingham were still taken by carriers to London, but by rail instead of along the Thames or by road. The carrier found the hampers and cloths for packing the butter. The farmer's wives too continued to carry their produce, butter and eggs, to the local weekly market for sale.[68] The butter for market was made up in 1 lb. lumps or other sizes, laid on or covered with dock leaves, and the whole made dainty with a spotless white cloth laid over it. Macdonald in 1872 preferred firkins to be made of white oak, but they must be well cleansed before the butter was put in. Butter was sometimes packed in new boxes then, presumably for transport by rail, or by post. The new wood was liable to taint this butter or to give it an unpleasant flavour. This could be prevented if a lb. of bicarbonate of soda was put into each 32 lb. box, and boiling water poured on it. The solution was left overnight, and then it was safe to use the box.

In London, Manchester and Rochdale the Irish butter formerly so popular was, Macdonald said, being ousted by French, but this was an impression gained from the increasing quantity of French butter on the market, a growing market that was capable of absorbing both the Irish and French imports as well as others. Imports from France into the United Kingdom had in fact risen from practically nothing in the 1820's to some thousands of cwts. in the 1850's, and then rapidly to nearly ½ million cwts. annually in the 1860's, which could very easily have given rise to Macdonald's impression. Amounts ranging between 300,000 and 500,000 cwts. continued to come in until the end of the century.

Butter was made on Sussex farms, but usually only for home consumption, the Sussex cows not being great milk producers. One farmer Mr. Bull of West Town, Hurstpierpoint, who kept a herd of Alderneys, made between 400 and 500 lb. a week, and sent it to London on contract by rail. He received a good price as can easily be believed.[69] Not all the English butter offered for sale came up to his standard. Farm butter making was 'at a low ebb'. There was little uniformity in the product, and at the International competition of 1879, promoted by the Royal Agricultural Society, the native product was 'beaten by sheer force of knowledge and skill'. Too much of the making was now left to servants, complained Henry Chester in familiar words, 'the farmer's wives and daughters being above the manual operations of the dairy', an old complaint by then, and one that could only have been true in a limited degree. More attention to details would be the way to defeat the butter makers of Holland and Normandy. It was not, of course, only the competition of foreign butter the farmers had to fear, but also the growth of the demand for liquid milk, which was an easier way of selling it now that railway transport enabled it to be carried long distances. It is unlikely moreover that the home product could have met the whole demand by any possible effort. So early as 1867 it was suggested that the factory system might well be applied to the making of butter as well as cheese, a subject to be discussed later.

The variable quality of home produced butter had, it is said, been exaggerated by adulteration. At one time 'no article of food was so largely adulterated as butter'. Melted fat bought from the butchers as suet underwent treatment and was mixed with butter. Lard too was used for this purpose, but the series of Acts dealing with the adulteration of food and drugs, beginning with that of 1860, effectively put a stop to these practices, which were probably rather more rare than was suspected at the time: but in spite of the increased consumption, and the economic and climatic conditions that forced the farmers to turn to dairy farming there was still little uniformity in home produced butter at the end of the century. Bad flavours were imparted by feed, and dirty and unventilated housing gave a cowhouse flavour to the milk, which was perceptible in the butter made from it. Packing was poorly done, although if it were efficient, neat and pleasing to the eye, it added to the market value. 'Vegetable parchment paper and boxes of wood perfectly free from smell and flavour' were recommended as the best materials for packing butter for sale in 1894. Bradford's small wooden butter boxes, manufactured specially for this trade, were excellent. The print was preserved and the butter did not get soft: but these boxes were heavy and added to the cost of postage.[71] The existence of a specially manufactured butter box seems to indicate a direct trade from the farm to the consumer, but this may have been of small dimensions; or the boxes may have been used for sending butter from the home farm to the town houses of landed proprietors. Equally, of course, the boxes may have been used for sending farmhouse butter by rail to wholesalers or to shops. I have been unable to find any evidence about this.

The competition of imported butter was complicated by the introduction of 'butterine' put up in tub form and looking like genuine butter. Some of this actually contained 50% of butter. By 1879 some 15,000 tons were said to be imported, and this was in addition to the output of factories set up in this country. The Dutch government—most of the margarine was then made in that country—required plain branding, but some of it was sold as butter when it got here. In the main it was then made of body fat of steers, but some makers added 'earth nut oil', or olive oil, and about 10% of milk. The Bermondsey factory used beef and veal suet with other ingredients, salt and chemicals. The import had increased to 886,573 cwts. in 1886; to $1\frac{1}{4}$ million in 1887. In that year a factory at Southampton was said to produce 20,000 tons per annum. Bear thought it was freely sold as butter in spite of the Margarine Act of 1887 (50 & 51 Vict. c. 29), which required all imitation butter to be plainly marked. Later legislation and the tests devised by analytical chemists facilitated the detection of margarine in butter, and other 'methods of sophistication', and combined with the inspection of samples etc., to make it difficult, if not impossible, to sell margarine as anything but what it was.[72]

Even more foreign cheese was imported after the middle of the nineteenth century than butter. A substantial quantity had been imported from continental countries since 1800, but this did not reach a total of much more than 200,000 cwts. until after the 1840's when the U.S.A. began to export. By the 1860s these imports had reached almost $\frac{1}{2}$ million cwts. per annum, and for a few years in the 70's well over 1 million, after which they declined slightly, but maintained a standard of approximately $\frac{3}{4}$ million till the end of the century. The total imports from all countries into the United Kingdom touched 1 million cwts. in 1870, and rose steadily until the end of the century, when nearly $2\frac{3}{4}$ million cwts. were brought in. A small percentage of both butter and cheese were re-exported.

During this time the per capita consumption of cheese declined slightly, and that of butter rose. The poorest class of the community in respect of money wages, and therefore purchasing power were the farm workers. From 1863 they reduced their weekly consumption of cheese from 0.4 lb. to 0.3 lb. in 1902. At this level it remained till 1912. Their butter consumption rose from 0.4 lb. to 0.5 lb. in the same time.[73] There must have been many people in the towns whose consumption was no more, though the well-to-do classes probably ate more of both. To estimate at the maximum however the imports of cheese in the 1870's would have provided at $\frac{1}{2}$ lb. a week each for four million people, and at 1900 for eleven million at that rate. Similarly the butter imports rose from 1 million cwts. annually in the 1860's to 3.4 million in 1900, and the same sort of calculation makes this roughly sufficient for four million people at the earlier date, and 13.6 at the later. The supply most likely did not fully satisfy so many, but at both dates there was a much larger population to be supplied from home sources than there had been in the days before there was any substantial importation. The inference is that the home production was increasing to meet the demands of the new markets. For example, the Wensleydale cheese in 1879 was sold at fairs at Yarm, and went to Northumberland and Durham. That made in Cheshire and

Salop went mainly to Manchester and Liverpool in 1910. very little going to London, its former destination.[74] Consequently there was no need for the farmers' fears of this competition, especially if they had taken some precautions to see that their own produce was as uniform in quality and as attractively packed as the imported goods.

## (ii). Cheese factories and the farmer

American cheese had been imported for some two decades when the outbreaks of cattle disease afflicted our dairy and stock farmers in the 1860's. The quantity, though increasing, had only been more than 100,000 cwts. in the three years before then, but during that decade it very quickly rose to almost, and sometimes quite, $\frac{1}{2}$ million cwts. per annum. The Americans studied our market, and did everything possible to make their product acceptable. They were able to sell at prices few English dairies could command, or so it is said. The fact was, I imagine, that the American cheese was a factory product, and therefore not subject to the variations in quality that were then so marked in the individually manufactured English cheese and butter.

The first American cheese factory was organised by Jesse Williams, a farmer living near Rome, Onieda County, New York, quite unintentionally if the story current about him is credible. He had made a name for himself as a cheese maker. In 1851 one of his sons became a farmer on his own account, and Jesse undertook to sell the cheese of both farms at a good price. But the son was doubtful about his ability to make such good cheese as his father. They arranged for the son's milk to be made up at the father's farm. From that simple beginning grew factory cheese making. It was successful, and very soon spread over a wide area of the U.S. and Canada, several farmers being associated in each undertaking. By

1866 there were no less than five hundred factories in New York State.

An earlier attempt to introduce factory cheese making was based on a mistaken principle. In 1848 some persons or farmers in Ohio put up suitable buildings for cheese manufacture, and proceeded to accept the curds produced by their neighbours. They also undertook the collection and transport of the curds to the factory and paid a set price per lb. What seems now an obvious weakness of this scheme led to its failure. The curds made by so many different people were of various standards instead of all being the same. Consequently it was impossible to produce a prime standard type of cheese.

The visible success of the other system and the large quantities of American cheese to be seen in our shops convinced the dairy farmers that they would speedily be ousted from the market—a fear that was quite exaggerated but was very real. As usual in such crises then—before the National Farmers Union had been founded—the Royal Agricultural Society stepped in. Lord Vernon of Sudbury Hall, near Derby, moved an enquiry into the American factory system in 1868, and a report was published in 1870 though it was not the first information on the subject to be made public.

In the autumn of 1869 the Derbyshire Agricultural Society and the Midland Agricultural Society were both concerned about the economic situation of English dairy farmers and their future. The former in February 1870 decided to organise limited factory production in that county as an experiment. This decision was made for five sound reasons. First, they hoped to obtain greater uniformity in the product; second, to improve the cheese of dairies then turning out a poor grade; third, to reduce the hard work of home dairies, especially for the farmer's wives and daughters; fourth, to improve land values; fifth, to achieve a uniform system with better plant, skill, and organisation.

To induce strong support by the farmers a guarantee fund of £5,000 was collected, and it was agreed that 6½d. a gallon should be paid for milk delivered at the factory, payment being made on the last Friday of each month during the manufacturing season. At first only one factory was proposed, but Mr. Roe of Derby, placed a building, orginally a cheese warehouse, at the disposal of the Society rent free for one year, and this made it possible to open two factories, one in urban and the other in rural surroundings. The second was on the estate of the Hon. E. W. K. Coke of Longford. It was thought desirable to open in a situation where there were not less than 400 cows within a radius of three miles of the building. This would have been quite easy to achieve because there would have been enough cows in an area of that size to supply several large factories.

The Longford site had a stream beside it, but the water supply from it was so uncertain that pipes were laid for over a mile to tap a never failing source. The building was constructed of wood, partly because it was planned on American advice, and partly because a timber building was cheaper and more rapidly erected. Operations began at Derby on 8 April, 1870 with milk from seventeen farms aggregating 300 cows. An equal number were refused from a sense of the Managing Committee's inexperience in spite of having engaged an American expert, Cornelius Schermerhorn, to manage the factory. They very sensibly wanted to walk first. The Longford factory commenced work at about the same date, and since it was found impracticable for one man to supervise both Schermerhorn's brother was brought over to control one.

Mr. Gilbert Murray displayed a model of the Derby factory at the Royal Show at Oxford in 1870, and was awarded a silver medal for it. An ingenious can was provided for the milk suppliers for conveying the milk to the factory. It was cylindrical in shape, and the lid fitted like a piston, being pushed down on top of the milk to prevent waste or undue agitation.

On arrival at the factory the evening's milk was delivered into a tinned receptacle and weighed, duplicate tickets being made out, one for record and one for receipt. A valve in the bottom of the tin allowed the milk to run by gravity direct into vats in the making room. These vats consisted of a strong wooden frame supporting a shallow tin with a hollow beneath it that could be filled with cold water to reduce the temperature of the milk. The water flowed through the system of vats, and turned a small overshot wheel when it finally ran out. This wheel gently agitated a series of wooden rakes that floated on the top of the milk, and kept the cream from rising. When the morning's milk arrived it was added to that in the vats, the cold water drained away, and steam heating applied by means of a pipe running round the inside of the vat. Perforations in the pipe ensured an equal distribution of the steam.

At the proper temperature, 82°–86°F. according to the weather, rennet and annatto were added, and the curd allowed to form. The curd was then cut with specially designed knives, and the temperature slowly raised until the whey was sufficiently acid. It was then syphoned off and the curd tipped into the dry vat, being well stirred by hand. The temperature was reduced by exposure to the atmosphere. A whey vat four feet deep and six wide had been dug at one end of the factory; it was lined with blue bricks set in cement.

The curd, when salted, was put in hoops (vats), and these placed in presses. Mr. Murray's special press, giving 3 to 5 tons pressure, could deal with several cheeses at the same time. After ten or twelve hours the cheeses were stored in a loft, and turned daily until fit for market.

Parallel to the enthusiasm that started these factories was a strong undercurrent of opposition from the factors who were following the centuries old system of buying up cheese made on the farm. This opposition, with the mistakes that are at first inevitable in any new enterprise, was rapidly overcome.

The cheese made under the supervision of the Schermerhorn brothers was too much like American cheese, and had its defects as well as its merits. Its texture was not compact; it had a peculiar taste and smell; and lacked fine flavour. Consequently it fetched only a comparatively low price. This was altogether changed by a change in method. At first acidity had been wholly developed in the curd and whey together, but later it was only started together, and completed in the curd alone.

The milk suppliers received an unexpected increment of the 1870 profits. They had been paid by the gallon on the basis of 10 lb. to a gallon, whereas the average English gallon weighed 10 lb. 4 oz. so they were overpaid the first year. This was not their fault, and they had been astonishingly faithful in sending the whole of their milk unskimmed, except for their home needs, to the factories. One or two black sheep had kept some milk for making butter, or sent skimmed milk, or even watered milk, but proper precautions were taking care of this difficulty. It would have been quite extraordinary if nothing of the sort had happened.

By 1872 these two factories were firmly established, and the farmers sending the milk felt that they could release the guarantors from any further responsibility. They formed themselves into local and independent committees, and became dairy associations on a co-operative basis. Owing to outbreaks of Foot and Mouth Disease 1872 was a difficult year, but the Longford factory sold 82 tons of cheese (1640 cwt.), 1 lb. a week for 3,300 people, and the Derby factory 49 tons (the same for 2,000 people). Slightly over $6\frac{3}{4}$d. a gallon was paid for the milk. In the following year the farmers bought the plant from the guarantors.[2]

The experiment aroused intense interest all over the country and even abroad. Visitors to the factories were encouraged, and shown everything they wished to see unless there was some great obstacle. Most of the visitors were farmers, and many of them must have been greatly impressed because the number of factories steadily increased.

By 1874 there were at least six in Derbyshire. One of these —Holms Cheese Factory—had been started by a group of tenant farmers without any help from the landowners. It was built by Mr. Shirley of Rewlack at his own cost, and on his own land. It had sufficient capacity to deal with the milk of 300 cows, and cost Mr. Shirley £360. Several others were described in 1875, but whether the list given by J. Chalmers Morton is complete is uncertain—he was not at all definite about it himself. In Derbyshire, besides the two original factories at Longford and Derby, others were working at the

following places: Mickleover with twelve contributors sending 570 gallons daily from 250 cows; Holms with eighteen
suppliers; Windley Hall, also with eighteen milk suppliers;
Alstonfield with 17. There were six other Derbyshire factories which dealt with the milk of 2,700 cows. At Tattenhall
in Cheshire milk from two large farms was dealt with on the
factory system. Fifteen Staffordshire farmers sent milk as far
as four miles to a factory at Lichfield. The incidence of Foot
and Mouth Disease was disastrous that year, and the milk
suppliers dropped to ten, owning between them 150 cows.
Gloucester and Somerset farmers followed this good example.
Mr. Wilkins of Nethercore, near Bourton-on-the-Water, had
his own factory, and bought the milk from 167 cows at 6d. a
gallon, in addition to using that of his own herd of 25. Two
farmers, who lived at Rooksbridge, near Weston-super-Mare,
built a factory to which ten others sent their milk, leaving
the whey as payment for the labour, fuel and materials. Morton, who compared home and factory cheese making in 1875,
had visited all three. Two Cheshire factories at Balderton and
Alford, were the largest of all at this date. Each received the
milk from 800 cows. There was a small factory at Worle,
Somerset, and one dealing with the milk of 300 cows at Beedy
near Melton, Leicestershire. Morton, not unreasonably, felt
that it was plain that the factory system was developing.

One serious difficulty prevented any more rapid rise in the
number of factories. There was a dearth of skilled managers.
The best place for a young man to learn, indeed the only
place, was in one of the well established Derbyshire factories.
J. P. Sheldon, one of the originators of the Derby and Longford schemes, thought that the committees of proposed cheese
factories ought to have the prospective managers trained
there. The system adopted at the new establishments was
almost the same as that at Derby. Morton was nevertheless
emphatically in favour of factory cheese making, a conclusion
that is not altogether surprising. The Derby committee,
according to Sheldon, found it had five great advantages: (1)
more curd in proportion was produced than under the home
system; (2) there was a saving in labour; (3) the purchase of

U

materials in bulk was advantageous; (4) there was less loss and waste of curd than in small dairies; (5) no loss by cheese cracking occurred.[3]

Prospects were excellent in 1875 for a large extension of small scale co-operative factory production of cheese by the dairy farmers. Unforseen events prevented this. Already in 1874 the Derby factory which had eighteen suppliers was sending liquid milk to London customers. This was a sad falling away from the original project, but was perhaps inevitable. After 1875, too, the price of cheese declined until by 1879 it had dropped some £25 a ton. Another factor was that the initial high standard of cheese produced was not maintained. Nevertheless Voelcker said that there were some twenty factories in five different counties in 1878, and that they made cheese from the milk of 6,000 cows. He thought, too, that they were a success and well adapted for making Cheddar cheese. In the previous year Mr. G. M. Allender, managing director of the Aylesbury Dairy Co., had emphasised the necessity for establishing butter factories, and his company did establish a cheese factory and piggery at Swindon, which was worked in combination with the supply of liquid milk to London.[4]

The drop in price was partly due to increased imports of cheap American cheese, or so it was argued, and partly due to a general trade depression that was no fault of the producers, but which no doubt reduced consumption and demand. In 1880 these conditions worsened. The cheese produced was poor. Only half the output was equal to that made by the enthusiastic originators of the scheme. There was a grievous decline in the attitude of the personnel towards the job. It was no longer a novelty, just a job. Some of the managers were slovenly and careless, even dirty. They ought, according to Sheldon, to have met at some central point to discuss their problems anxieties and achievements. By this means their interest would have been stimulated, and their enthusiasm retained.

Meanwhile they were inclined to hurry the process too much, thus making inferior cheese. The utensils were not

kept scrupulously clean, and the buildings were often neglected. Again the cheese was often not properly attended to
after it was made. A worse category of faults could hardly
have been found with the poorest farm cheese dairy. Some of
the milk suppliers were not blameless. They tried to gain a
paltry advantage by sending skimmed or sour milk. Farmers
who sent skim made butter to the value of a few shillings
weekly; others sent sour, often the result of their own neglect,
so as to be paid for it. Some failed to keep the vessels used
scrupulously sweet and clean. These were stupid, self-
applied brakes on success.

Another deterrent was in effect a superstition, though it is
not yet finally disposed of in other connexions. Artificial
fertilisers were being increasingly used on the pastures and
meadows as well as on arable land and ley. Many farmers
thought that these new fertilisers communicated something
to the milk that made it difficult to make a satisfactory cheese
or butter from it. This may have been a good excuse for their
own shortcomings, for often they failed to cool the milk properly before it left the farm. This was disastrous—warm milk
in closely lidded cans, jolted a mile or two over rough country
roads, often very rough, in a springless farm cart and half
churned in the process, was in no fit state to be made into
cheese.[5]

Economic developments were rapidly taking place that
these small cheese factories could neither control nor compete with. Already in 1875, as I have said, the Derby factory
was sending liquid milk to London in the height of summer.
Holms factory was using some for making butter at the same
date. Ten years before W. H. Heywood had pointed out that
selling liquid milk was the most profitable way for the farmer
to dispose of it. On a farm of 200 acres in North Cheshire he
estimated the annual profit from cheese or butter making at
£189, grazing stock at £215 15s. od. and milk selling at £304.
This was the impetus towards liquid milk selling that was to
prove too much for these factories. Ward and Lock's *Book*
agreed that cheese making was more a factory business which,
to be carried out successfully, required a considerable amount

of technical knowledge and experience combined with previous practice.

'The English cheesemaker has also to enter into competition with cheese produced in America and on the Continent where it is made on a very large scale and by thoroughly routine systems. It will not be found to answer as well (save in very exceptional cases) as disposing of the produce in the form of butter or milk'.

The advantages of factories in this writer's opinion were the uniform product, the better bargaining power and the relief of drudgery on the farm. Less labour was employed than when each farmer did the work separately. What difficulties there had been in sending milk to the factory had been overcome by the enterprise of the owners of 'milk teams' who collected and delivered the milk all the season for a small payment.[7]

In spite of all the disadvantages and criticisms factories, run by private enterprise on a commercial basis, were a necessary development. Carrick's Cumberland Dairy, Low Row, Carlisle was established in 1881. Butter was the main object, but there was some cheesemaking to use up the separated milk. This undertaking obtained its supplies from sixty to seventy farms within a diameter of thirty to fifty miles in the stock raising district about Carlisle. It had a retail business in Newcastle-on-Tyne and expected to open more. A large quantity of separated milk was sold daily through agents to the working population far and near, and some was used for calf rearing. An ingenious type of mechanical churn of large capacity had been designed. Some 400,000 gallons of new milk had been received in 1885, and a large quantity of butter and skim milk produced.

None of the writers on the subject ever gave a complete list of dairy factories. James Long considered the Duke of Westminster's Aldfold Cheese Factory and Lord Vernon's Sudbury, Derbyshire Factory the two best known in 1885. The second was then mainly employed in making butter. Other factories operating at that time were:—Hailwood's, Broughton Park, Manchester; King's, Bromley, Lichfield;

Plymouth Dairy Co.; Aylesbury Co., London and presumably, Swindon; Kings' Head Dairy, Gloucester. In April, 1883 a factory had been opened at Berkeley, Gloucester.[8]

Some factories had a very short life. The first one in Westmorland was started by Messrs. Hollins in the autumn of 1886 at Barbon. It was adequately equipped, and power was derived from a 4 h.p. steam engine. It was worked by the Lunedale Co-operative Dairy Co. The butter, sold at a higher price than farmhouse butter could be bought at local markets. The following year it closed down because of the low price of butter. Apparently it could not produce so cheaply as the farms could. The Culgaith Dairy Factory was opened in 1887 in spite of this warning. It was managed by the directors of the Vale of Eden Dairy Co., and leased to J. Hills. It was modestly successful though the price of Westmorland butter was very low. J. Cropper and J. Wakefield wished to open a factory at Kendal in 1891, but the farmers could not be persuaded to send their milk and the project fell through.[9]

Viscount Hampden also started a butter factory at Glynde in Sussex, and obtained a manager who had been trained in Lord Vernon' factory. He equipped the place with the latest machinery worked by steam. The separated milk was sold at 3d. a gallon, and a jug cream trade was being started in 1888. Other butter factories were established in Cornwall, notably the Catchall Dairy in the Penzance district, by 1899. One result of the establishment of all these factories, whether they individually had a long or short life, was that the monopoly formerly enjoyed by the butter and cheese factors was broken up, and this ought to have enabled the farmers to get better prices. It is, however, not very certain that they did.[10]

By the end of the century, too, several condensed milk factories had been built, but these were not, as they might have been, farmer's co-operatives. Indeed Sir Daniel Hall remarked severely in 1913 that the production of milk remained primitive and uncombined, deriving no help from modern knowledge or modern methods. The co-operative butter and cheese factories did not prove so successful as those run by private enterprise, perhaps because the farmers had little experience of mutual organisation before the first World War.[11]


## (iii). Liquid Milk


It is probably safe to say that our Tudor ancestors did not drink much, if any, milk. They preferred it in the form of butter and cheese. There was no coffee, tea or cocoa on their menu, and no need of milk to dilute these beverages. It was however used in cooking, and for making junkets and sylla-bubs, and for other purposes. The demand for liquid milk as a commodity to be purchased cannot have been very large. Long after in 1865 when dietetic habits were greatly changed, and milk was used in the customary beverages Morton esti-mated that only 1/5th of a pint each was used daily by the population.[1] It was perhaps fortunate that the Tudor con-sumption was so low because yields were small, and problems of transport, except for a few miles between the farm and the consumer, were insoluble. No doubt milk was an article of consumption in rural England, especially in the dairy dis-tricts, where the population lived largely on 'white meats'. Most villages and small towns must have been self-supporting in milk, and indeed most farmers and cottagers would have had their own supply. Only in large towns like London and the slowly developing industrial areas was there a consumer demand.

This was met by the producer-retailer, who either lived in the town or its immediate neighbourhood. About London there were many fields and commons. Tothill Fields were fields. Lincolns Inn Fields, and the district north to Hamp-stead and Highgate, to Islington and east of Aldgate were rural. Across the river there were few houses, so there could have been no difficulty in keeping enough cows, either actu-ally in the town or close to it, of a sufficient number to provide what was wanted. The other small aggregations of population were placed in an even more rustic situation, and supplies could have been on their doorstep. But this is pure speculation based on conditions that existed at the end of the eighteenth century, which must have developed with the growth of population from arrangements of the same sort.[2] The cowkeepers of Moorfields, for example, were already in 1700 conducting their business on the same lines as were so vividly described a century later. The cows were heavily fed all the time they were milked, but on 'such foul or rank food, that it rots them in the space of two years or at most two years and a half'. The astute owners sold them off fat then 'lest they should be found dead on a sudden'. The feed was grains, cabbage leaves and bean shells of which last the milk tasted strongly during the season.[3]

There must have been a sizeable trade in liquid milk in London by this time because the town milkmaids had a customary May Day celebration that was apparently already well established.

> 'On the first of May' wrote a Dutch visitor, 'and the first five or six days following, all the young and pretty peasant girls, who are accustomed to bear about milk for sale in the city, dress themselves very orderly and carry about them a number of vases and silver vessels, of which they make a pyramid adorned with ribbons and flowers. This pyramid they bear on their heads instead of the ordinary milk pail, and accompanied by certain of their comrades and the music of a fiddle, they go dancing from door to door surrounded by young men and children, who follow them in crowds; and everywhere they are made some little present'.

Some of these girls must have worked for retail shops. The Nell Gwynn Dairy, New Exchange Court, Strand was established in 1666. The premises were acquired by Mr. Robert Barham in 1850. He was the father of the founder of the Express Country Milk Co. Ltd. (now the Express Dairy Co., Ltd.). The building was pulled down when the Strand was improved in 1900. It can hardly have been the only retail dairy in Restoration London.[4]

The pail was rarely carried on the head. More usually the maid carried two pails, open to the high heavens and all that might drop from them and lesser heights, on a yoke on her shoulders. The milkmaids May Day dance and gathering of her annual luckpenny was in its hey day when the Dutchman saw it.[5] A hundred years later this pleasantly simple ceremony had become over-elaborated, and soon after was dropped altogether.

The milk produced and sold in London was not of a very high quality, nor was it free from impurities so long as it was carried about the streets in open topped pails. Ellis complained in 1750 that it was thin and watery. Weston confirmed this and added that it was insipid compared with the country product. The land where the cows fed was good, and the animals large, fine and well fed so that they ought to have produced fine milk, but London milk was rarely well tasted, nor did it contain thick rich cream. Feeding with brewers' grains was assumed to be one cause of watery milk;[6] skimming the cream and adding water were two certain reasons.

In 1760 milk was carried to Liverpool and Manchester from farms not more than about ten miles distant on horseback, and sold to consumers direct. By 1795 the milk was transported in wooden vessels carried in carts. Fewer cows were kept in Manchester than in Liverpool, only 6 as against 500-600. The former town drew its supplies from farms along the Duke's (Bridgwater) Canal, whereas Liverpool had the sea on one side, and therefore less surroundings. The Liverpool cow-keepers worked on much the same system as those in London, buying at calving and selling to the butcher as soon as the yield dropped to less than 6 quarts a day. The cows were grazed in fields near the town during the day and housed at night. Only a few years ago there were still forty three cow-keepers in Liverpool, so this business has continued longer than in most cities.[7]

The towns were well supplied with milk, or at least supplied in a degree that met the effective demand, but only in counties like Lancashire and Westmorland were the villages supplied. This was because of the large proportion of small farmers there who kept cows and were willing themselves to retail the milk. It was sold at 1d. a quart in these two counties at about 1800, but in the industrial areas of Cumberland and Durham there was shortage. Generally over the whole country there was tendency between 1780 and 1813 for the milk producers, who did not make cheese and butter, to enter into contracts with town dealers, some of them wholesalers, rather than to supply their neighbours. The difficulty of purchasing small quantities of milk became more pronounced as the nineteenth century progressed. Some attempts were made to overcome it. At the end of the eighteenth century some Staffordshire tradesmen undertook to keep cows for supplying milk to the poor, and at Stockton, Durham, it was made a condition of a lease that 15 cows should be kept whose milk should be sold locally at $\frac{1}{2}$d. a pint. J. C. Curwen planned milk production on his Schoose Farm to supply cheap milk to the inhabitants of Workington. Even in London, he said, milk was used principally as a luxury. It formed no part of the necessities of life to the mass of the people. Under his plan the people of Workington were better off, and Lord Dundas proposed to follow his example at his great 'allom' works in Yorkshire. Dr. Beddoes hoped to see it established at Bristol, but what was the outcome of the last two hopes and proposals I do not know.[8]

Towards the end of the eighteenth century several writers concerned themselves with the London milk supply. Thomas Baird in 1793 estimated that 6,000 cows were necessary to provide for London and the suburbs, but after obtaining data from fifty cowkeepers raised the number to 8,750. The yield was 5 gallons in summer and 4 in winter, though some believed it higher. The Liverpool average was estimated at 9 quarts a day all the year round. Some of the cowkeepers had very big herds. Mr. West of Islington had 'near a thousand' on different farms there. Cows were kept all about the town. Five years later Middleton set out the total number of 8,500 as follows:

| Middlesex | | | Kent | |
|---|---|---|---|---|
| Tothill Fields | } | 205 | Deptford | |
| Knightsbridge | | | Rotherhithe | |
| | | | Greenland Dock | |
| Edgware Road | | 550 | New Cross | |
| | | | Bermondsey | 681 |
| Paddington | | | Surrey | |
| Tottenham Court Road | | | Lambeth | |
| Battle Bridge | } | 3950 | South Lambeth | |
| Grays Inn Lane | | | Kennington Bridge | |
| Bagnigge Wells | | | Coldharbour | |
| Islington | | | Peckham | |
| | | | Peckham Rye | |
| Hoxton | | 150 | Newington | |
| Ratcliff | | 205 | Camberwell | 619 |
| Mile End | | 406 | | ———— |
| Limehouse | | 180 | | 8,500 |
| Poplar | | 70 | | |
| Bethnal Green | | 200 | | |
| Hackney | | 600 | | |
| Bromley | | 160 | | |
| Bow | | 100 | | |
| Shoreditch | } | 200 | | |
| Kingsland | | | | |
| Odd cows | | 224 | | |
| | | ———— | | |
| | | 7,200 | | |

The system was for the retail dealers to call at the cowsheds where each milked the number of cows necessary to supply the quantity of milk he wished to buy. Clearly therefore Middleton correctly said that the milk was given to them 'in its genuine state'. The retailers were greatly condemned. They were accused of the grossest malpractices 'The famous black cow' to which they openly resorted in the milk rooms was the highest yielder of all. It was the pump which was used to 'pump water into the milk vessels at their discretion'.

If there was no pump they were not above dipping their pails in a common horse trough. The milk too was often impregnated with worse ingredients, best left to the imagination. These men were anathematised as 'the refuse of other employments, possessing neither character, decency of manners, nor cleanliness'. A system of annual licences issued by a magistrate on the production of a certificate of good conduct signed by the cowkeeper and a number of customers was proposed, subject to the man being sworn to sell the milk pure and unadulterated.[9] This came to nothing as might have been expected in the contemporary state of the social conscience.

Ellis, as I have said, did not think the average yield was much higher, if any, in 1750 than it had been a century before; in the Vale of Aylesbury it was then about 400 gallons, but some cows gave as much as 16-18 quarts a day. Most of the records are, however, stated in terms of butter and cheese production, and it would be somewhat chancy to interpret these in terms of liquid milk. Lawrence in 1805 suggested 3-5 gallons a day, but this fell to about half in the winter months. A small West country herd of 8 cows gave 16 quarts a day for 48 weeks at that date. The cows belonging to the famous breeder, Princep, of Croxhall, averaged 16 quarts, a yield equal only to the estimate made so long before by Markham, but some Staffordshire cows ranged from 16 to 24 quarts a day. Two farmers, whose addresses are not supplied, keeping 400 or more cows, averaged the same in 1810 but Strickland claimed that some very large Holderness cows gave so much as 8 gallons, rather more than those kept by the London cowkeepers. These statements are so confusing that no real approximation can be more than guessed at, but it is doubtful whether the national average exceeded, if it reached, 450 gallons per lactation at that time.[10]

Already by the turn of the century the small farmers of Salop had recognised that the most profitable way of disposing of their milk, if they were near centres of population, was direct to the consumer, especially in winter.[11] The dairymen of Westmorland, who did this, were suspect and very justly.

An inspection of their measures in 1836 discovered seventy-one out of seventy-nine to be short. A meeting of consumers was held, and the price fixed at 2d. a quart for new milk, 1d. for skimmed, delivered out of stamped measures. Even this was considered too high, and in 1842 prices were fixed at 1½d. for a quart of new milk and the same for 2 quarts skimmed.[12] Since the people of Appleby and Kendal were so conscious of their interests, they were probably careful to see that the milk they bought was not diluted or otherwise adulterated.

Londoners were not so lucky. Their consumption was estimated at 60 quarts per head per annum in 1829, or some 70 million quarts a year. This individual consumption was apparently more or less static for many decades: but the milk continued to be diluted often by so much as 4 pints of water to 10 or 11 of milk. Poor quality owing to the feeding was thus further reduced. Little was gained by having the cow brought to the house and milked at the door, but at least milk from the cow was bought and not water. The milkmen, said Taylor, have neither intellect nor capital. Their nefarious practices continued. They skimmed the cream, which they sold separately in short measures, mixed in water, boiled the skim milk, and sold it warm from the fire instead of warm from the cow. This was partly the consumer's own fault. There was a demand for warm milk. This was the limit of their chicane. Before 1820 no preservatives were added. The milk was only diluted, though sometimes dirty water was used. Accidental impurities from want of precautions in milking and transport and distribution must have been usual. Contamination by street dust and worse could not have been avoided. By the middle of the century they were accused of adding treacle to sweeten, salt to bring out the flavour, and annatto to colour the milk. Professor Queckett had observed sheep's brains in milk, but who he was I do not know; chalk and starch, tumeric to colour, gum to thicken, and even soda to prevent sourness were other knaveries. Voelcker vehemently denied this. These contaminations existed only in the imagination of the credulous and half informed men of science, who repeated the errors of their predecessors. Whatever may have been the truth, the Adulteration of Food Acts were effective deterrents from 1860 onwards.[13]

In 1830 John Claudius Loudon, that far-seeing man, anticipated that when the railway came, London would get its milk from distant counties, because railway trains could travel at no less than thirty miles an hour. Even then a good many little country dairies from five to twenty-five miles outside the city were sending milk to town in closed containers carried by fast trotting ponies. Milburn perhaps twenty years later claimed to have brought milk twenty miles in less time and with less injury than often happened between milkman and customer. But the greater part of London's milk supply was produced in the city and suburbs at least until the cattle disease of the 1860's and even after that. The last town dairy in Stepney closed down in the 1950's.

About 1830 two of the largest London producers were Mr. Laycock and Mr. Rhodes at Islington. A third large dairy in Edgware Road had also belonged to Rhodes, but he sold it at some date between 1822 and 1828 when there was a good deal of bubble speculation by joint stock companies in London dairies. By 1830 nearly all these had burst. None remained worth notice except the Metropolitan Dairy, the property of Mr. Wilberforce.

Rhodes carried the bell as London's premier cowkeeper. His family had long been established as farmers at Islington, having been referred to by Dr. Brocklesby in 1746. About 400 cows were normally milked, but sometimes the number was very much larger, even up to 1,000. A large part of the milk produced was sold under contract, direct to public hospitals and other institutions, though what the others were I am at a loss to understand. They may have been poorhouses, of course. There was no similar direct sale to the housewife, only to the retailer in the way already long established. If the cows allotted to one of the dealers gave more milk than he could sell, Rhodes kept the surplus; if less, he made up the required quantity from other cows. The arrangement sounds complicated, but no doubt it was simple enough in practice. There was an efficient system of accounting, checking milk out and feeding stuffs in.

Laycock's Islington Dairy was about the same size as Rhodes'. The number of cows kept fluctuated between 400 and 700. A subsidiary undertaking was providing overnight accommodation for cattle driven to Islington for sale in the market. Laycock's sheds could accommodate 8,000—9,000 head. The Metropolitan Dairy in Edgware Road was managed by Mr. Wilberforce on the same lines as Mr. Rhodes had done before he sold it. Some 360 cows were kept. Laycock occupied other farms at Enfield and Clapton where dry in-calf cows were kept. He also had some original ideas about cleanliness. He clipped the hair on his cows' tails in order to keep dirt from dropping into the milk. Sometimes his cows were curry-combed. Both practices were rare in those days.

The greatest defects of the average London dairy were dirt and lack of ventilation, more especially, of course, in the cellars and backyard sheds where some cows were kept by men who had only one or two. Mr. Rhodes had shown how these defects could be overcome in the larger enterprises. A gutter between the two rows of standing cows and a lane along which the dung could be carted away got rid of the manure; windows and adjustable shutters in the roofs could provide light and ventilation: but Loudon, with a Scotsman's partiality, compared these London dairies with Harley's famous one in Glasgow—much to their disadvantage. They were behind the Dutch and German dairies in these qualities too.

The Liverpool system of cowkeeping where Mr. Wakefield had a large enterprise, and Mr. Littledale of Liscard produced big supplies was more like farming. The cows went out to fields in the day, but were tied up at night. The Littledale business was rather smaller than Rhodes, but was managed almost like Harley's, who had, said Milburn with some justice, remodelled the whole dairy system of towns.[14] This was only true to a limited extent. Harley had erected very large buildings specially designed for their purpose, and had demonstrated their efficiency to men of large capital and enterprise, but the numerous cowkeepers, with only a cow or two could not make any large investment in buildings. They kept their cows where they could.

This was one reason for the prevalence of contagious diseases amongst town cows. Pleuro-pneumonia and foot and mouth disease were almost endemic from about 1840, and in 1865, 1866 and 1867 there was a bad outbreak of rinderpest amongst the 24,000 cows then estimated to be kept in and about London. By the Cattle Diseases Prevention Act of February, 1866, the slaughter of diseased animals was made compulsory, so the contagion was finally controlled. Some opinion held that the cattle plague (rinderpest) was introduced into the London herds by the importation of cattle from Holland.[15] This import fluctuated, but in 1864 and 1865 about 20,000 animals were landed in the United Kingdom. Comparatively large numbers of cows also came from Germany. Whatever truth there may have been in this suspicion, the outbreak and its control policy had a marked effect on the town dairymen and their trade. There was a sudden increase in the quantity sent to London by rail, and this drew attention to problems that became more acute as the volume of milk handled grew larger.

The turnover of cows kept by the town cowkeepers was very rapid, as already emphasised, but by 1865 they made replacements by buying double or treble the number they did twenty-five years before. In a few months the new intakes got pleuro-pneumonia, and had once again to be replaced. Despite this there were thought to be many advantages to an adequate town dairy supply of milk. It was sold just as it came from the cow, with the addition of some water, if sold direct to the consumer. The London retailer preferred to pay 2¾d. a quart for milk supplied by a neighbouring dairyman rather than 2d. for country milk. The last was not so fresh because the country producer kept his morning milk till afternoon dispatch, and his evening milk till the next morning, so that he could skim some cream for making butter. Nevertheless the supply of country milk was already reducing the number of town cowkeepers.[16]

The rapid development of the railway network placed the question of profitable disposal squarely before the rural dairy farmer—was it better to manufacture or to sell liquid milk. The length of line open for traffic doubled between 1854 and 1873 from 8,053 miles to 16,082 and still further to 20,646 miles in 1893 so more farmers had to find the answer as time went on. It was almost obvious. Others had decided it before, but J. P. Sheldon brought the weight of his authority to bear in 1880, though many farmers had found the practical answer before. The milk trade properly conducted would, he said, outprofit cheesemaking anywhere if only a railway is handy enough.[18]

The immediate problem was to draw enough supplies of liquid milk from the country to compensate for the loss of production from slaughtered town cows. Part of the solution was the large increase in the quantity of liquid milk carried by the Great Western Railway between 1865 and 1867, though there were some monthly fluctuations. Significant figures are:—

|  |  | No. of cans | Gallons |
|---|---|---|---|
| January, | 1865 | 1,051 | 8,954 |
| ,, | 1866 | 12,611 | 143,600 |
| May, | 1866 | 16,706 | 285,918 |
| June, | 1866 | 16,000 | 221,851 |
| January, | 1867 | 12,539 | 143,588 |

During 1867 the quantity shipped remained fairly stationary. Most of it came from Swindon, Purton and Cricklade, a distance of seventy or a hundred miles from London, though the supply began in the long valley of Berkshire below Reading, 'all the grass country to below Swindon'. The G.W.R. had not allocated special trains for milk, but the Deputy Chairman thought that might prove necessary if the traffic developed sufficiently—as of course it did. Meanwhile the milk was carried from the receiving station by slow passenger trains. No special trucks were used. A number of old second class carriages had been converted into milk vans.

The dairy farmers delivered the milk to the stations in

cans (churns) of their own providing, and they or their men helped to load it. The cans were consequently not of uniform design, but generally held about 17 Imperial gallons, and when full weighed nearly 200 lb. They were then too heavy and awkward for one man to handle. The closure of these churns was not always satisfactory, and the milk was shaken up a good deal in transit. A perforated top, sometimes with a cloth round it, was occasionally used, and often this cloth was none too clean. One great fault was that the milk was put into the cans 'hot', though some farmers put 'full cans into a stream to cool'.

The organisation of the trade was that the dairy farmer consigned his milk to one of several wholesale dealers in London. On its arrival the wholesaler's representative received it, and immediately sold it to retailers, who took away what they wanted in their own conveyance, and mainly in their own cans. Most, if not all, of the farmer's cans were emptied without being taken away from the station, and were sent at once to the other side of the line for return. The business was completely in the hands of the wholesalers. There was no competition between them. They agreed the price and the whole quantity of milk was consigned to them. It was not exactly a milk market since there was not room enough. Each salesman had his regular customers every day. There were about ten dealers, and on arrival about thirty or forty retailer's carts were waiting to take the milk away. This was as speedy a method of distribution as then seemed possible.

The London and North Western Railway carried about the same volume of milk: 490,320 gallons in 1865 and 1,209,284 in 1866: by April, 1867, the trade had levelled out to about 54,000 gallons a month. There was a marked increase in this traffic in August, 1865, when disease first broke out in the herds of Lord Granville and Miss Coutts, kept in the northern outskirts of London. Two special milk trains were run daily in the busiest times by this company, one arriving at 11.45 a.m. and the other about 8.30 p.m. The cans supplied by the senders were packed in open carriage trucks, no special mode of stowage being adopted. The milk came from Aylesbury and district, north through Dunstable and to as far away as Rugby. The charges were 1½d. a gallon for less than one hundred miles and 2d. for greater distances. In the time of the greatest drop in town supplies milk had been brought from as far as Huddersfield, Macclesfield, etc., but in April, 1867 it did not travel more than ninety five miles on the average.

The Company's officials did not think the milk carriage trucks could be improved. The trade was carried on in the same way as that on the G.W.R., the dealer's men assisting in unloading at the terminus. There was not much room in the station so they occupied the neighbouring streets until the police stopped them. They needed a market place. Not all of them were honest; occasionally cans were stolen, and porters had been seen to tilt the churn and fill jugs.[19] The other railways, the N.E., S.W., and G.E.R. also carried large quantities of milk.

The milk did not always arrive in very good condition, and at the time of the greatest scarcity an experiment was made in sending small cans of milk suspended in the truck from Carlisle, but it spoiled and this method was at once abandoned. The railway companies were inclined to blame the large churn favoured by the farmer; the farmers to blame the railway companies for not carrying the milk in a special train built for the purpose.

Both sides referred to the better arrangements made for the transport of milk to Paris. A standard can was used. This was only about half the size of the English churn, and was easily handled by one man. It was closed by a stopper that went right down into the milk, and was kept in place by a screw. The milk was tightly fixed, and there was no churning as there was so often in the less tightly closed English can. The French cans, too, were cylindrical, not tapering in shape, and could therefore be packed in a railway truck with greater economy of space. The French railways provided specially designed trucks; these had two floors, one above the other, forming two tiers on which a large number of cans could be packed, but allowing a good circulation of air round them. The cans were slightly heavier in proportion to the milk they carried than the English type, but had various advantages to counterbalance this. Though the Paris end of the business does not seem to have been organised by the railway companies or anyone else, it had become regular. From these stations the milk was collected in a uniform type of van, and the empty cans returned. Every owner of a milk walk had his own van. The English railways, could not however induce our farmers to use the French can, and were not apparently willing to introduce the French type of truck.[20]

In hot weather the French producers covered the cans with a loose linen cloth soaked in water to keep the temperature evenly low during the journey. The practice perhaps originated in 1859 with a process worked out by M. Chartier, a veterinary surgeon. He caused the milk, immediately it was drawn, to be put into long tubes, which were plunged into fresh cold water. By this means the temperature was reduced to 12° or 13°C. It was then quickly decanted into the can, and this was covered with a woollen cloth well soaked in water. The milk travelled about 100 miles to Paris without changing temperature.[21]

The French methods were so evidently better than ours that they might well have been adopted, but for two obstacles. The railway companies thought that the traffic in liquid milk to London would fall off as the number of town kept cows rose to normal again. They were therefore not disposed to invest in specially designed trucks. The farmers were charged at a rate per can for returning empty churns and if they had adopted the smaller French churn this charge would have been higher in proportion to the milk sold.

The producer's dislike of any but the churn they used did not deter the Royal Society of Arts from offering a premium for a design of an improved churn for carrying milk by rail. The prize was won by the Aylesbury Dairy Company in 1868.[22]

In the same year Harry Chester declared that the transit of milk by rail demanded instant attention. A very short journey damaged it and lowered the price, but a little combination

amongst the producers in any dairy district would be sufficient to compel the railway companies to improve their
arrangements. Action of this kind was of course completely
foreign to the farmers of the time who were the individualists
*par excellence* of an individualistic age. Chester thought the
supply of milk inadequate to real requirements especially of
children. The milk sold to the rich was not much diluted,
but the cream was retailed in measure 25% short of the
proper amount—as an established practice of the trade. The
trade amongst the poor was in the hands of such very small
men, who sold so little that they could not make a living without recourse 'to the cow with the iron tail'. The milk was
the subject of the grossest frauds (of an unspecified nature),
and so diluted that it was no wonder that the poor did not
like it. These small men could not contract with a country
farmer for milk, but were entirely in the hands (I had almost
written at the mercy of) the wholesalers. The country milk
was often somewhat diluted because the price paid to
the farmers was so low. The police, said Chester, ought to be
empowered to test with a lactometer milk offered for sale in
the London streets as they were in France and Belgium.[23]

One great obstacle to the sale of pure milk even to the
wealthy was the domestic servant's demand for a percentage
on all orders placed and bills paid. They expected 5% on the
gross, which Morton estimated was about the net profit on an
honestly conducted West End business. If the retailer
declined to pay the commission he lost the business.

An ambitious reformer, Mr. Hope, founded a Dairy Re-
form Company. This company proposed to sell pure milk.
It had a depot in the West End and transported the milk
from about 300 cows from (I think) Barking Farm in its own
vans to prevent tampering. A small quantity of new milk was
sold to the poor in Whitechapel, and a branch was established
in Westminster. Hope looked forward to setting up branches
in all parts of London. Naturally his efforts were strongly
opposed by the local dealers, especially in Whitechapel.
Having failed to bribe the company's agent to leave it, they
employed what the films have taught us to call 'strong arm

men' to molest the customers until the police put a stop to this. They then placed a man in front of the shop with a can of milk to sell as the company's. The opposition sold watered milk at 1d. a pint cheaper. All the features of a trade war were present. Contracts to supply workhouses were placed at such low rates that only skimmed milk could be supplied, and that diluted. One man sold milk to such an institution at 2d. a gallon less than he paid for it. As he did not apparently go out of business the conclusion is obvious. Dilution was estimated in general at 30 to 40%, and if it were prohibited by legislation about 50% more cows were calculated to be necessary to supply London in 1854.[24]

The deficit was, in spite of the railway companies' doubts, made up from the countryside. The rail traffic in liquid milk continued to increase as the towns grew steadily larger. So did the local traffic on the roads. In the 1860's for example some Sussex downland farms began sending liquid milk daily into Brighton. Only when they did this were they able to get a daily paper regularly. There was another struggle between local suppliers and customers in Westmorland in 1873 when a committee of consumers at Orton organised a supply from outside the district, and brought the dealer's price down. Broderick was surprised that the continuous rise in the price of milk in the decades before 1880 had not stimulated a greater increase in dairy farming. The Midland dairy farmers could, he said, well afford to deliver milk carriage paid at a London terminus for 8d. or 9d. a gallon in summer, and 10d. or 11d. in winter. This being so they were unwilling to sell their milk to their country neighbours even at a greater profit, so that at last the demand has died out 'to the great injury of the rising generation'. Even on farmhouse tables tins of Swiss condensed milk were often seen.[25]

The farmer's churns were not much improved as a result of the Royal Society of Arts' premium design. In 1879 the Royal Agricultural Society therefore carried out a test on several milk churns entered for a prize they had offered. The churns were filled and loaded on a lorry which was drawn 'at a high speed' by a traction engine over rough ground. After this searching test the prize was awarded to Messrs. Alway, whose churn was considered best for railway transport. It tapered from the bottom upwards, and was made of strong material. There were no outside hoops and casings, and it was free from inside angles and projections. The top was of malleable cast iron, and there was an inner and an outer lid. The inner was liable to get lost, but if the two were made in one like a bottle stopper this practical fault would be met. Fifteen cans were entered for this competition by 8 makers, but some were unsuitable for rail transport because they were mounted on wheels. One made by Cluett was of uniform width throughout. It had a lid floating inside on the milk. The judges thought this beautiful in theory, but unsound in practice—a little rough usage would speedily prevent the lid from working. Vipan and Headley entered an elaborate churn of 'strongly tinned charcoal iron', mounted on two wheels, and divided into two compartments fitted with a locking cover and a ventilating pipe.[26]

The last firm built carts for the milk trade. They used English oak and ash for the bodies, and secured a low body by fitting a cranked axle. Strong springs prevented undue jolting. A removable framework allowed two swinging cans to be carried from which the milk was drawn by taps. A trough underneath prevented waste, but what was done with the spilt milk is not disclosed. For filling the cans the shafts could be raised, bringing the cans to a proper level and making it unnecessary to lift them when full. The cans could be locked to avoid shaking. The cart was provided with two adjustable seats and a box for account books. It would have been, it seems, ideal for collecting milk from the stations and delivering it to customers. It was also recommended for carrying milk from the farm to the railway, when four cans could be carried easily, six at a pinch.[27]

Improved churns were exhibited by Vipan and Headley at the Royal Show at Reading in 1882. The Reading Ironworks won the Society's silver medal in that year for a machine for washing milk cans. The machine was driven mechanically or by horse power through a belt and pulley at 140 rpm. It was optimistically estimated by the makers that two men could wash two hundred cans per hour with it, though the actual work of lifting them into the tank and out again would have had to be done very quickly and dexterously to maintain such a rate. The two side brushes could be thrown out of gear and a small circular brush attached to the end of the middle one when cleaning lids.[28]

By 1878 it was estimated that one-third of all the milk produced in the country was sold as liquid milk, and this was still much the same in 1894, if both estimates are correct.[29] All this was taken in the producer's carts to a railway station, to a depot or creamery for redistribution, or to one of the great consuming centres for sale to wholesalers or by retail if the dairy farm was near enough. The first regulation governing the conditions of milk production was made in that year. Milk was then travelling to London from Derbyshire, Stafford, Nottingham, Leicester, Wiltshire, Hampshire, Gloucester, Somerset and many other counties. There were as yet no special milk trains but a milk van was attached to most of the fast long-distance morning and evening trains. A lot of milk was however always carried in the guard's van, and not specially treated in any way. One train mainly loaded with milk ran from the Cheshire district to Liverpool. This was not far, but it then seemed a significant example, and likely to be followed for longer journeys.[30]

Much of this trade was undoubtedly encouraged by the railway facilities that were steadily growing more general, but it could not have expanded as it did had it not been for the invention of the so-called refrigerator. The importance of cooling the milk immediately it was taken from the cow, and before it was put in the churn for transport was quickly realised. The judges at the Cardiff Royal Show in 1872 recommended the use of Lawrence and Co's 'Patent Capillary Refrigerator' for the purpose (see p. 178). Ten years later it was in pretty general use.

J. P. Sheldon approved the prize winning Alway churn as the best. It was made of two pieces only so as to have the minimum of seams; the bottom hoop was double the ordinary strength, and was put inside instead of outside the body. The cover or lid too was made of one piece only. This construction had obvious advantages, for churns were treated without tenderness by the railway employees. Their carelessness was soon imitated by the farm hands, particularly in handling the returned empties, the full ones being so heavy that they could not easily be moved even by two men. The empty cans were pitched here and there, lids and rims were smashed, side crushed in, and the paint knocked off. After six months use they looked folorn indeed. This was hard on the farmer who provided the churns.

The Alway churn had plenty of competition. A good many patents were taken out during the next thirty years, some embodying rather overwhelming ideas. Baldwin and Amies showed a new design in 1879 in which a ring of vulcanised rubber formed an airtight seal for the lid. The Aylesbury Dairy Co. tried to get the same result with the lid slightly tapered to fit closely into the churn. A bead on this lid fitted into an inclined groove in the can, so that when the lid was turned round it was firmly closed. This was considered easier to clean than the rubber joint, but was liable to jam. These cans were tested by being filled with water, and rolled along the ground, presumably to find out if they leaked.

There were two different schools of thought about churns, the one believing that they should be tightly closed or sealed and locked; the other that it was necessary for the milk to be ventilated. A pure refinement was the churn with an ice-box attached to the lid, designed to keep the milk cool on the journey. It is doubtful if this was ever extensively used. Most of the numerous patent churns put out between 1880 and 1910 were on very similar lines, the patent being granted for some trifling detail of construction or shape. Some makers put various sizes of churns on the market, but most of the smaller must have been used by retailers or producer-retailers. Farmers were stubbornly attached to the 8 barn gallon churn that held 17 Imperial gallons. Despite the awkwardness of handling such a clumsy weight, the 8 barn gallon churn remained in use for railway transport until at least 1914.[31]

The price received by the farmer varied as between summer and winter milk but the cost of transport, usually 1½d. or 2d. a gallon, was deducted. From the Midland counties this charge included the free return of empties, but return was charged for by some railway companies. From the farmer's point of view, no less than the city retailer, the business was fraught with risks. Often the farmer contracted bad debts with the city salesman. When the trade began to expand so rapidly many men of straw and speculators entered it. The demand too fluctuated with the weather, and the retailers then had milk on their hand that must be wasted. When they saw this happening they at once telegraphed to the farmer to hold back one or two meals' milk. Some encouraged this by keeping the empty cans so that the farmer could not send milk even if he wanted to. He must immediately turn to making butter or cheese; or feed the milk to livestock. Coupled with bad debts this often caused heavy loss to the milk producer.

This was not the worst difficulty. Pure fraud was sometimes practiced on the farmers. For example, George Pearce and Charles Headon pretended to be milk dealers at various addresses in Liverpool and Manchester. They advertised for supplies and answered advertisements of milk for sale. They did not pay for what they received, and were eventually discovered, tried and sentenced to twelve months imprisonment with hard labour. How they disposed of the milk does not appear. Henry Brunsden of Coate, Wiltshire, who had nursed the infant Richard Jefferies, was the victim of a similar swindle. A London firm contracted with him for 260 barn gallons a day, and when he had become deeply indebted to all the farmers around, whose supplies he took to make up this large quantity, he discovered the firm was bogus. He was ruined. The whole of this area, formerly mixed arable, had turned to milk production after 1879.[32]

These may have been isolated events, but that seems unlikely. Sheldon thought the trade honest and trustworthy at that time. It was certainly growing very large. He estimated that there were 10,000 cows kept in London by 895 cow-keepers; the animals lived in 1,100 sheds. Estimating the national average yield at 500 gallons he calculated that 84,000 cows were necessary to provide London, that the average herd was 28 (a figure I feel is too large) so that the whole was owned by some 3,000 farmers, and at 10 to a man milked by nearly 9,000 men. These are impressive figures, and when to them is added the 12,000 shops in London selling milk, the 4,000 horses and men engaged in delivering milk, and the workers in the London cowsheds, a massive business is formulated. He thought it probable that no town in the world was so well supplied with milk as London. He was nevertheless a trifle optimistic about the national average yield. George Gibbons of Tunley Farm, near Bath estimated that of Somerset with over 450,000 cows at 450 gallons, but this subject I must return to.[33]

It must not be forgotten that milk was being carried by rail to other places in the 1880's. For example Mr. Charles Miles of Tatenhill Farm, near Burton-on-Trent was sending milk from Baron and Warton Station, three miles from his farm, to Birmingham in large quantities, about 17,000 gallons in 1882 and about 19,000 in 1883. He sold some milk at home, and made some into butter and cheese. His must have been a large enterprise, but the total volume of the whole milk business directed to all the great and growing centres must have been very great. The textbooks do not make any attempt to calculate it as they do the requirements and supply of London.[34]

Milk transport had become very important to the railways. Their charges and arrangements were sometimes not very satisfactory to the farmers. By the end of the 1880's a protracted discussion on railway rates for carrying milk, and the conditions in which it was conveyed began. For example the milk produced by the extensive Suffolk area of dairy farms was by 1888 being sent by rail to London, or to the new condensed milk factory set up at Colchester. The Great Eastern Railway Company obviously had a monopoly of this traffic, and had initiated a porterage charge of 1/- a week to every farmer sending milk. The only competition the railway had was the parcel post by which packets of butter and cream cheese could be sent, but this amounted to no competition at all. The railway charge for cream was double that for milk. The Ipswich provision market had fallen into disrepair, and this was an additional handicap to the dairy farmer.[35]

The discussion of rates arose out of the provisions of the Railway and Canal Traffic Act, 1888, under which the railway companies tried to raise the rates for the steadily increasing traffic. By this time there were milk trains that carried only milk, and were treated like passenger trains. As Sheldon had said a few years before the empty cans were usually returned free, but the railways felt that a regular charge should be made. The distances the milk was carried were getting longer as facilities were extended and the trade developed. This meant that it was more costly to bring milk to town, and the farmers naturally did not want to pay higher freight rates. One complained of a difficulty that must often have arisen in districts from which there was no regular milk train—his men loaded the full churns and unloaded the empties; if there was a train it was put on, if not, it waited.

This was more or less usual. The loading was done at the dispatching station by a porter assisted by the farmer's man. Otherwise the farmer would have had to send two men with every load. Since much of the milk arrived at the terminus in different passenger trains, it was impossible for the consignees to send men to meet it and difficult for them to keep men at the station all day to unload as they had done when the trade was first begun. Consequently the railway companies wanted to make a terminal charge for the use of the station. The farmers opposed the proposal. They rightly said that milk had been carried for about fifty years without any such charge. Perhaps they forgot that in the early days the terminal station had been more or less a market used by the wholesale buyers and the retailers they supplied. The discussion of rates became very complicated, and was heard by a committee of the Board of Trade in 1890, the authority to which the railway companies had to submit their proposed charges for approval.

Several groups of farmers had formed local associations by this date. The Derby Dairy Farmers' Association members owned 12,000 cows, and produced nearly $7\frac{1}{4}$ million gallons a year. Of this three-fourths went to London, and the rest to Birmingham, Manchester, Sheffield, and Middlesbrough. The Buckinghamshire Dairy Farmers' Association were mainly milk sellers sending to London. The Nottingham Dairy Farmers' Club declared that if the rates were charged per can, no more milk would be sent from Derby and Nottingham. Mr., afterwards Sir George Barham, managing director of the Express Dairy Co., founded in 1850 by his father, and of the Dairy Supply Co., Museum Street, took a prominent part in this controversy.[36] The complaints were at least a decade old, and it is clear that the rates were irregular. The charge from Hazel Grove and Disley to Stockport was double as much as from Buxton—twice the distance. Joseph Hampson, of Lostock Hall, Poynton complained in 1881 that the charges were 1/- then against 6d. when the railway was first opened 30 years before.[37]

Methods of handling varied. Milk was sent from Chelford to Manchester by rail, a distance of sixteen and a half miles. About ninety cans were lifted into trucks by farmers twice daily. The trucks were not specially designed for the traffic. Both the London and Brighton Railway and the Great Eastern demanded help from senders in loading and from consignees in unloading milk. The South Western Railway unloaded all milk at the terminus. At Lime St. Station, Liverpool, 3,349 churns arrived every week in trucks. The dealers provided three men who unloaded the full churns and loaded the empties, and their men took the milk away.

At some country stations the facilities were very poor. William Wadman of Firle, Sussex dispatched about 150 gallons of milk daily from Glynde, but here there was practically no station and no help. The single porter labelled the churns and checked the quantity. Most of his time was taken up with passenger traffic, and the farmers were obliged to load the churns themselves or there would have been great delay. The milk went to Norwood Junction. Lord Hampden had recently established a creamery at Glynde. Occasionally the milk was left behind because the farmer's men were not at the station to load it. This happened at Tattenhall Station with milk for Liverpool, but the Liverpool milk sellers complained that if the farmers had more milk than necessary to meet their contracts they would keep the overplus and send it with the next consignment. The result was that the milk always arrived sour: so all parties were fallible. If only one porter was employed at a wayside station he could not be expected to lift the heavy 17 gallon cans into the train. Their weight was acknowledged to be too much for one man.[38]

Sometimes the churns were left standing in the station in the sun or in other unpropitious places. Duncan Kelly of Coombe Farm, Kingston-on-Thames told the Farmers' Club in 1908 that he knew of a station where ten or fifteen churns stood every day summer and winter for hours under the window of a public convenience. Milk was also taken out of churns and used by people who frequented the platform. This was bad, but at the other end of the journey the consumer had little discretion. On the same occasion James Sadler, once a retailer in Manchester said that he had had almost every domestic utensil, except one, handed to him over the counter or at the door to receive milk.[39]

Manchester was a very big city at the end of the century with some 900,000 effective milk consumers. A century before it had depended upon supplies brought along the Bridgwater canal, by cart or produced within the city. Its consumption in 1897 was about 14·7 million gallons per annum, only about 16 gallons a head or under 2·46 pints a week. The supply was mainly composed of milk brought by rail from Cheshire, Derby, Stafford, Lancashire and Salop, and delivered to stations in and within a 4 mile radius of the city amounting to 10·36 million gallons annually. Cows kept in the same area produced 2·8 million gallons, and a further supply of 1·5 million was brought in by cart from a radius of about eight miles. Inspection showed that the milk was comparatively pure. Of the samples taken in 1875 some 33·33% were adulterated: in 1897 only 2·01%, whereas for the whole country the figure was 11·1%. A large quantity of condensed milk was brought into the city, 32,220 cwt. by the ship canal alone in 1896.[40]

The high percentage of adulteration and the condition in which the milk arrived at the consumer's door had already begun to exercise the government as well as those engaged in the trade. The invention of refrigeration enabled milk to be sent distances of two hundred miles, and the disappearance of the town kept cow was imminent at the turn of the century. The cows which had for so long been a feature of St. James Park, well over a century, to provide a fresh milk drink for fashionable children and others, were ordered away in September, 1885. Consequently better facilities at the railway stations were essential to cope with a traffic that was increasing so rapidly. The heaviest load was carried by the Great Western Railway. In 1892 it carried 1,049,511 cans, 757,793 to London: 1904 figures were 2,141,778, 1,026,616 to London. Large amounts were transported by the London and South Western Railway from the western counties. The L. and N.W.R. carried 1,054,802 cans in 1892: 1,499,712 in 1904. The line ran to London, Liverpool and Manchester. The Great Eastern carried 392,000 cans in 1894; 520,000 in 1904, some 30% of which went to Liverpool Street, and the balance to suburban stations before the terminus. The North Eastern Railway carried 29,000 cans in 1904, only 9,000 in 1900. This company had built a depot at Northallerton Station to serve as a collecting centre for the newly formed Wensleydale Pure Milk Society, which bought milk from local farmers, cooled it and bottled it, boxed the bottles and put them in a refrigerator pending consignment. This was intended for Newcastle-on-Tyne. Milk from the Eden Valley also went there and to Shields. From Kirby Stephen district it went to Liverpool and London. The Great Northern Railway tapped supplies from North Stafford and Nottingham, Leicester, Derby and Huntingdon. The Midland Railway carried milk to London, Birmingham, Manchester, Nottingham, Sheffield, Leeds and Bradford.[41]

The stations, especially the country stations where the milk was put on the train, were not at all convenient. Access to the platform from the road was extremely difficult in many places. This was resented, and there was a strong feeling among farmers that the companies ought to arrange for the farmer's carts to have easy access by a different gate from that used by passengers. The milk should be loaded by railway porters, and unloaded at a special platform at the terminus. Properly constructed vans were necessary, built for convenience in loading, well ventilated and light, and used solely for the milk traffic. Frequent cleaning and inspection were essential. Neither fish nor poultry should travel with the milk. Empties ought to be returned promptly and handled carefully by the railway employees—not just thrown out of the trucks.[42] This was a counsel of perfection, but the complaints were partly met by some companies. Special milk vans were provided for some of the traffic, and unloading facilities at some termini were good, notably Euston and Paddington.

The same complaints were nevertheless generally applicable in 1909. Only on some main lines were there milk trains with special trucks: milk churns were frequently carried in the guard's van with other miscellaneous luggage and goods. The local traffic along the branch lines took its chance. It was still a condition of the farmer's contract that his men should help in loading the churns. This was more frequently done on the branch line stations, but not on all. Often the churns stood on a wayside station for some hours before being loaded on a slow train. Occasionally one meal was twenty-four hours old before dispatch.[43] It was no wonder that much of it was tainted when distributed.

The government intervened in an attempt to improve conditions of production. The Dairy and Cowshed Order of 1885, and Amending Order of 1889 required a minimum standard of accommodation in dairy and cowshed on the farm. The Order was supplemented by good advice. Every dairy farmer was told that it was essential to cool his milk before dispatch. This he must do immediately after milking. Full buckets should not be left in the byre, but carried at once to the cooling house. There was no difficulty in reducing the temperature to 54°-56° F. with a good cooler. The best dairy farms had been equipped with this apparatus for a good many years, but there are always some laggards.[44]

The Board of Agriculture felt so strongly about this problem that it sent a circular to churn makers. It advised that (1) the tare weight of the churn should be stamped on; (2) the lid should be made easy to seal; (3) the churn be constructed to prevent the removal of milk or addition of water while it is sealed; (4) the churn must be dirt and dust proof.[45]

The dangers to which milk might be exposed in transit so impressed some people that they suggested all milk should be bottled on the farm, a somewhat tall order especially for the smaller enterprises. Bottling machines had been available for some time. The Dairy Supply Co. Ltd., won a silver medal at the Royal Show at Leicester in 1896 for a sterilising plant comprising a milk receiver, a patent filter composed of bags of swansdown, and a self-contained sterilising chamber with an automatic device for closing the bottles while in the sterile vapour. A bottle washing tub with a brush and rinser and a supply of bottles were supplied with it. The milk was heated to 214° F. kept at boiling point for twenty minutes, cooled and bottled. The bottles were fitted with stoppers made of porcelain with a wire loop through the top attached to another loop round the neck of the bottle. This stopper could be levered home, and the two loops held it fast. The closure was made airtight by an india rubber washer in the neck of the bottle.[46]

Another method of closing bottles was by a fibre disc pressed in by hand. This looked excellent, but in practice the milk bottles could be filled from a churn in a delivery cart, and the lids put in them so there was no guarantee of any hygienic precautions. I recently saw bottles closed in this way standing outside a cottage door in the remote countryside. The "Dan" bottle with the patent aluminium "Crown" closure was also on the market, but was not widely used by retailers, though by 1900 Vipan and Headley were advertising hand barrows for the delivery of milk in bottles. J. and E. Hall had supplied over one hundred machine refrigerating rooms to dairies in England and the Colonies. Macewen thought them very desirable.

Many retailers thought glass bottles a failure almost before they had really been tried: but often they were not properly washed and sterilised on return and the next lot of milk went sour. So before 1914, and indeed until 1930, in large towns like Bristol and Derby, a great deal of milk was delivered to customers in cans that were filled from a churn transported in a pony cart, or from a milk pail that was all shiny with brass bands outside, but opened at the top for use. The milk was dipped out with a long handled measure.[47] I have seen a hand cart carrying a churn and metal measures used in Sudbury, Suffolk, a few years ago: but in the days of horse transport milk so exposed was even more likely to contamination than it would be today.

The dangers to which milk sent to the big cities was exposed were many, and when to these dangers was added the fact that much of it came from tubercular cows it is really remarkable that anyone used it at all. The consumer was used to the sort of milk he was supplied with, and it was in all respects better at the end of the century than ever before, though far from perfect.

It was not the fashion to drink milk as a beverage by itself before 1914: but Leonce de Lavergne had been struck by the enormous consumption of milk and milk products he had found usual all over England in 1855. Cooking was done with butter rather than with fat and oil, and cheese was eaten at every main meal. He must have had the privileged classes in view. The actual per capita consumption of liquid milk remained at a low level, and most authorities agreed that it was no more at the end of the century than in the middle years. J. A. Clarke put it at 1/5th of a pint or 9 gallons a year in 1878, but 15 gallons a year or 1/3rd of a pint a day were generally accepted throughout the period. It was no more in 1919. Bristol people used 0·35 pint in 1927; Derby rather more at

0·53 pint in 1928.[48] The farm labourers consumed 0·5 pints a week per head in 1863, 1·2 pints fresh or 2·3 pints skimmed in 1902 and the same in 1912. Macclesfield silk weavers 41·5 fluid oz. (20 fluid oz. equals 1 pint) per head per week in 1862; Coventry weavers 11 fluid oz.; Spitalfields 7·6 oz. and Bethnal Green only 1·6 oz.

The demand was much larger because the population had so greatly increased between 1871 and 1901, and production followed it. There are few estimates of probable total output; what there are vary widely and are based on guesses at the average yield; nor do they deal with the same area. Some apply to England only; others to the United Kingdom or to Great Britain. It is difficult therefore to accept any without profound reservations. For what they are worth they are:—

| | | |
|---|---|---|
| Clarke, J.R.A.S.E. | 1878 p.486 | 650 million gallons England |
| Morton, J.R.A.S.E. | 1878 p.647 | 1,000 million gallons G.B. |
| Rew. J.R.Stat.Soc. | 1892 p.259 | 570 million gallons U.K. |
| Rew. J.R.A.S.E. | 1895. | 576 million gallons U.K. |
| Rew. J.R.A.S.E. | 1903 p.120 | 630 million gallons U.K. |

The last three estimates are of liquid milk only. The large supplies of butter and cheese then made, would, if converted into milk units, add considerably to these figures to make up total production at these dates. Apart from other considerations the number of cows and heifers in milk or in calf was substantially larger at the end of the century than in 1870:— England only:—

| | | | |
|---|---|---|---|
| 1871 | 1,460,693 | 1881 | 1,621,249 |
| 1891 | 1,917,078 | 1901 | 1,887,414 |
| 1911 | 2,108,500 | | |

These cows too were doubtless producing more milk on the average per capita, but there is really no satisfactory means of determining how much the average yield was greater. Anderson had suggested that the milk from each cow should be examined for quantity and quality so long before as 1800, but few people had done this or kept any records. If they had there was no central organisation where the figures could be collected and collated.

One or two enterprising people did so—probably more than I know of. Edward Lakin of Beauchamp Court, Worcester was one of these but his 'registry of Milk' kept before 1846 is not printed in Gaut's *Worcestershire Agriculture* of 1939, where it is mentioned. Another was J. Thornhill Harrison of Frocester Court, Gloucestershire, a place that had a succession of farseeing occupiers. Harrison hung up in his cowshed graphs showing the daily produce of a cow taken once a week, and a larger one showing the weekly produce of the herd, in saleable milk. The maximum yield of a cow was nearly 20 quarts, but it varied with feeding and Foot and Mouth Disease, dropping to just over 5 quarts then. The maximum is high, but Harrison himself said that 21 of his cows averaged 642 gallons in 1855. Yields here varied between 317 and 708 gallons but Morton thought that if the poor cows were culled the average would range between 650 and 700 gallons.[49]

David Low estimated the annual average at 600 to 800 gallons at about the time Lakin was making his record, but that is optimistic. The average of 3 Wiltshire Shorthorn cows in 1860 was 625 gallons, and even higher yields were obtained in Surrey from the same breed. Twenty years later in 1865 Pringle and Murray guessed between 500 and 700 gallons, but Carrington, a real practical Staffordshire farmer with some years of experience of milk production, to which he had turned from grazing beef, put it at 400—600 gallons then.[50]

Morton recast his ideas in 1878 when he estimated the national average at 440 gallons of which one-sixth was taken by the calf. Murray at the same time suggested 600 as the yield of an ordinary Shorthorn. Pilley went further and gave Holderness as 29 quarts a day, Alderney 19, Devon 17, and Ayrshire 20. Buckmaster and Willis put the general average at 500-550 gallons; Long at 472, the measured average of nearly 200 cows. Coleman said a well managed cow should yield 550-650 gallons—some Yorkshire Shorthorns had given

1,100 Ayrshires 850, but these were exceptional. Primrose McConnell's Ayrshire herd in Essex gave 600 gallons in 1888: Sheldon's Staffordshire Shorthorns 750: Gooderham of Monewden's Suffolk Red Polls 804: Hall of Erdleigh Court, Reading's Jerseys 600. In 1879 Sheldon thought the national average for England about 480: ten years later he was inclined to raise it 20 gallons, because there had been a great improvement in the milking quality of cows in the interval. Sir Daniel Hall thought it might be 600 gallons in Cheshire in 1910 and the Census of Production for 1908 gave 550 gallons.[51]

The result that can be gathered from all these figures is that in rather more than two centuries the average yield of the national herd had risen from Petty's 384 gallons to 550, an increase of some 43%. In addition the number of cows in the national herd was larger, but there is no possible measure of this. The early estimates are no more than guesses, intelligent guesses though some of them may be, and are usually of total cattle, not considering cows separately. King's estimate was $4\frac{1}{2}$ million cattle in 1696; Young $3\frac{1}{2}$ million in 1779 and Mulhall 5,200,000 in the United Kingdom in 1830.[52] I should not like to hazard a guess at the sex distribution of these, supposing the numbers to have been anywhere near the truth.

Milk production became a more important branch of farming in the second half of the nineteenth century, and especially in the last quarter, than ever before. The farmer's natural interest in the 'economic' cow, or rather in the best yield for the least food led not only to this interest in the average yield, but also to an interest in the yield of his own cows. He was encouraged to take records for his own benefit, and competitions began to be organised to stimulate recording. In October 1881, Thomas Higgins of Liverpool proposed to give a £50 challenge cup for the best kept record giving the number of calves dropped, the quantity and quality of milk produced and the final value of the cow for the butcher when it was culled. Lord Braybrooke offered a prize in 1882 for records including a weekly summary of produce. The milk from each cow had to be measured into a gauged pail at every milking, and noted on a tablet in front of her standing. This was afterwards copied into a book. Many other details were included, and six competitors entered that year. Mr. R. E. Turnbull of Twyers Wood and East Park Farm Burton Constable had a fine system of recording each cow daily in 1883. He had a retail dairy in Hull. Charles Hobbs of Fairford, Gloucestershire, kept records. At the milking trials at the London Dairy Show particulars of the yields were taken. Bear emphasised that proper recording would enable farmers to cull their uneconomic animals and so did Upton, Long and Muir. Some of the Herd Societies included such records in their 'Books' from the 1890's.[53] Unfortunately none of this activity produced evidence to enable better estimates of the volume of production to be made than those of Rew in the 1890's already mentioned, but it is clear that great progress had been made although there is no adequate measure of it.

One thing the dairy farmers had in the main failed to do. As Curwen had found in the beginning of the nineteenth century local supplies of liquid milk were scarce in the villages. They were no more plentiful at the end of the century. Many people had made plans for the labourers to keep a cow by means of cow clubs and similar philanthropic plans, but these had not amounted to very much Skim milk was cheap in the dairy district of Gloucester in 1880, but in Derbyshire the labourers could not buy milk. In many rural districts of Berkshire milk could not be purchased by retail in 1906; Sir John Russell, when a boy went on a walking tour through Essex, and had great difficulty in getting milk. In those parts of the country where there were small holdings milk was sold in the villages, and in Durham, at Stocksfield, the milk was nearly all retailed to private customers.[54]

Tins of condensed milk took the place of fresh milk, and were even seen on the farmer's table. It had first been introduced by the Anglo-Swiss Milk Co. in 1867 and by 1900 a total of nearly 1 million cwts. was being imported annually from several countries. In addition there were several factories making it here. Much of it was consumed in the large industrial towns and cities, but it was also sold extensively in the village shops. The factories here formed another outlet for the farmer's milk.

Many of the cheese factories of the last quarter of the nineteenth century had been run on co-operative lines by the farmers providing the milk. Towards the end of the century several co-operative societies were formed in different parts of the country for handling liquid milk. The society usually collected the milk from the farms, cooled it, and sent it to the consumer co-operative societies in the towns. Private enterprise established collecting depots or creameries in the dairy farming districts, like that of the Aylesbury Dairy Co. at Swindon, which was followed by other companies, local or based in the cities—but this is not the place to discuss the development of the milk distributive business: here I pretend to no more than the story of the English dairy farmer and his business during the four centuries immediately prior to the first World War. In that time he was translated from a producer of raw material which he manufactured in his home into a seller of the raw material itself with but the slightest of processing. But, at the end of the time he was supplying the effective demand for liquid milk of ten times the population, and at the same time producing a great deal of their requirements in butter and cheese. Such is the measure of his achievement. It cannot be stated with arithmetical precision, but it is none the less highly impressive.

## NOTES TO CHAPTER VI. (i)

[1] Julius Beloch. *Die Bevölkerung Europas zur Zeit der Renaissance*. Zeitschrift für Sozialwissenschaft. III (1900). pp. 765–786.

[2] F. J. Fisher. *The development of the London food market*. Econ. Hist. Rev. V (April, 1935) pp. 46, 56.

[3] J. W. Gregory. *The story of the road*. 1930. pp. 197–216.

[4] Henry Martyn Dexter & Morton Dexter. *The England and the Holland of the Pilgrims*. 1905. p. 10. Eleanor Trotter. *Seventeenth century life in a country parish*. 1919. p. 124.

[5] R. E. Prothero (Lord Ernle). Agriculture and gardening in Sir Sidney Lee (ed.) *Shakespeare's England*. 1916. I. p. 357.

6 *Harrison's description of England in Shakespeare's youth*. ed. by F. J. Furnivall. 1877. I. p. 294.

7 R. B. Westerfield. *Middleman in English business, particularly between 1660 & 1760*. 1915. p. 127.

8 32 Henry VIII. cap. XXI. Acts of Privy Council, 1554. see also:— 3 & 4 Ed. 6. c. 21; 5 & 6 Ed. 6. *c*. 14; 5 Eliz. c. 12.

9 John Norden. *Speculum Britannica—Middlesex*. 1593. p. 12.

10 *Idem. Surveyors' Dialogue*. 1607. p. 216. John Aubrey. *Natural History of Surrey*. 1719. p. 326. Robert Reyce. *Suffolk in the 17th cent. 1618*. 1902. p. 38. Norden. *Speculum—Essex*. Camden Soc. IX. 1840. Fisher. *op. cit.* p. 48 Table II.

11 C.S.P.D.S. Chas. I (1629–31). pp. 56, 555.

12 *Ibid.* (1626) p. 213; (1634–5) p. 197: (1637) p. 522. Acts of the Privy Council, 1576. D. J. Davies. *Econ. hist. of South Wales prior to 1800*. 1933. pp. 59, 60.

13 C.S.P., D.S., (1635–6) pp. 32, 162, 163.

14 *Ibid.* (1629–31) p. 206.

15 Francis Redfern. *History and antiquities of Uttoxeter*, 1886. p. 362. ff. citing Robert Plot. *Natural history of Staffordshire*. 1686. pp. 107–8.

16 Davies. *op. cit.* pp. 59, 60. C.S.P., D.S. (1634–5) p. 197: (1637) p. 522. Thomas Gerard of Trent. *Particular description of the county of Somerset*. ed. by E. H. Bates. 1900. p. 172.

17 William Chapple. *Review of Risdon's Survey of Devon*. 1785. pp. 26–28. R. H. Tawney & Eileen Power. *Tudor economic documents*. 1924. I. p. 167. R. M. Heanley. *History of Weyhill, Hants., and its ancient fair*. 1922. p. 36.

18 C.S.P., D.S. (1628–9) p. 215.

19 *Ibid.* (1634–5) p. 290: (1637). p. 313.

20 Seebohm. *Evolution of English farm*. 1952. p. 204. *Letters and papers of the Verney family to . . . 1639*. Camden Soc. LVI. 1833. p. 87. A. H. A. Hamilton. *Quarter Sessions from Queen Elizabeth to Queen Anne*. 1878. p. 9. G. C. Brodrick. *English land and English landlords*. 1881. p. 49 n.

21 Markham. *English housewife*. 1637. p. 192. *Robert Loder's farm accounts, 1610–1620*. Camden Soc. 3rd ser. LIII 1936. pp. xxii, 156. see Trow-Smith. *British livestock husbandry to 1700*. 1957 for a discussion of Loder. Robert Boutflour. *Need for a sincere standard of excellence in dairy cattle*. Jour. Farmers' Club. April, 1934. p. 42. W. H. Long and N. F. McCann. *Study of foods fed to livestock in West Cornwall*. Farmers Report Sec. III. No. 5. 1933 (Seale Hayne Agric. College). A. D. Hall. *Pilgrimage*. 1913. p. 350. For modern yields see E. R. Cochrane. *Milch cow in England*. 1946. pp. 19, 20. M. McG. Cooper. *Competitive farming*. 1956 pp. 32, 118.

22 H. C. Darby. *Historical geography of England before 1800*. 1936. p. 365. L. Dudley Stamp. *Man and the land*. 1955. p. 67.

23 Acts of the Privy Council. 1542, 1550, 1551, 1573–5, 1576–7, 1587, 1591, 1596–7. C.S.P., D.S. 1587 Oct. 2., 1594., Jan. 31., 1597, April 5, 8, 9, 22, June 30, July 9, 10, 11, Sep. 2.

24 Acts of Privy Council, 1627, 1628. C.S.P., D.S. 1628 cvi. p. 144. cvii. p. 162.

25 Acts of P.C. 10 April, 1620.

26 C.S.P., D.S. Sep. 3, 9, 30, Oct. 9, 11, 1640; Jan. 31, 1640/1; April, 25, 1641.

27 *Ibid.* Feb. 13, May 7, June 27, 30, July 2, 10, 18, Sep. 22, Oct. 23, Dec. 25, 1649; Jan. 4, 11, March 12, April 4, 16, 25, July 16, Oct. 18, Dec. 9, 1650; Jan. 27, 1651.

[28] Mildred Campbell. *English yeoman*. 1942. pp. 197, 204, 248. Wallace Notestein. *The English people on the eve of colonization*. 1954. p. 20.

[29] John Taylor. *Last voyage and adventure*. 1641. Idem. *New discovery by sea with a wherry from London to Salisbury*. 1623. pp. 23–26 in Charles Hindley. *The old book collectors miscellany*. 1873. vol. 3.

[30] Benaiah W. Adkin. *Land drainage in Britain*. 1933. p. 91 see also John Lloyd jun. *Papers relating to the history and navigation of the rivers Wye and Lugg*. 1873. pp. 2–12. Andrew Yarranton. *England's improvement by sea and land*. 1677. I. p. 116. Cornelius Vermuijden. *Discourse touching the drayning of the Great Fennes* 1642. William Dugdale. *History of imbanking and drayning of divers fenns and marshes*. 1662.

[31] M. P. Ashley. *Financial and commercial policy under the Cromwellian protectorate*. 1934. p. 31. C.S.P., D.S. July 29, Nov. 12, 1952; Feb. 16, Apl. 2, 19, 25, 1654; Apl. 25, May 29, June 7, July 5, 1655; Jan. 2, Nov. 27, 1656; May 11, Nov. 16, 19, 28, 1666; March 28, 1674; July, 1677; Feb. 23, 1678.

[32] *Ibid*. April 16, 1650. T. S. Willan. *The English coasting trade, 1600–1750*. 1938. pp. 48, 85.

[33] C.S.P., D.S. July 29, 1684.

[34] *Ibid*. Dec. 1692.

[35] *Annals of Agric*. XVII (1792) p. 47 ff. Holland. *Cheshire*. 1808. p. 315.

[36] J. A. Picton. *Selections from the municipal archives and records of Liverpool*. I. p. 300. ff. II. p. 48.

[37] See G. E. Fussell. *Change in farm labourer's diet in two centuries*. Econ. Hist. no. 2. May, 1927.

[38] Clergyman. *Useful and practical observations in agric*. 1783. p. 217. Anon. *Considerations on the present state of Great Britain*. 1773. p. 49. Sir John Sinclair, Bt., *Essays on misc. subjects*. 1802. p. 467. Rev. Jas. Willis. *On the poor laws of England*. 1808.

[39] Defoe. *Compleat English tradesman*. 2nd (?) ed. 1727. II. pt. ii. p. 31.

[40] Maitland. *History of . . . London*. 1756. pp. 758–9. Willan. *op. cit.* pp. 48, 84–86.

[41] Ernle. *English farming*. p. 276. *Journal of the House of Commons*. XXVI. 31 May, 1751. p. 273.

[42] Westerfield. *Middleman*. p. 208. Wimpey. *Thoughts on interesting subjects*. 1770. pp. 39, 40 and in *Letters . . . Bath and West Soc*. IV. (1788) pp. 155–158.

[43] *A view of real grievances with remedies*. 1772. p. 274 ff.

[44] Samuel Simpson. *The agreeable historian*. 1746. p. 114. Anon. *Present state of England*. 1750. I. p. 52. Benjamin Martin. *Natural history of England*. 1759. II. p. 242. Anon. *Description of England and Wales*. 1769. II. p. 2 ff. etc. These figures are derived from Defoe. *Tour*. 1724. II. letter III. p. 108.

[45] Holland. *Cheshire*. 1808. pp. 315, 316. R. Whitworth. *Advantages of inland navigation*. 1766. p. 60. J. Baker. *Imperial guide*. 1802. p. 8. Rev. Edmund Butcher. *An excursion from Sidmouth to Chester*. 1805. p. 294. John Aikin. *Description of the country . . . round Manchester*. 1795. p. 69. John Farey. *Derby*. 1815. III. pp. 30, 61–63.

[46] Benjamin Martin. *op. cit.* II. p. 183. E. Bowen. *Complete system of geography*. 1747, *Staffordshire; Bishton. Salop*. 1794. p. 10. Amice Lee. *Laurels and rosemary: the life of William and Mary Howitt*. 1955. pp. 20, 21.

[47] *Kalm's account of his visit to England . . . in 1748*. tr. by Joseph Lucas. 1892. John Housman. *Topographical description of Cumberland, Westld., Lancs., etc.* 1800.

pp. 55, 60, 99. Andrew Pringle. *Westmorland*. 1794. p. 24. Bailey and Culley. *Cumberland*. 1794. p. 19.

[48] Kalm. p. 172. *Annals of Agric*. XI (1789). p. 129. Young. *Essex*. 1805. II. p. 279.

[49] *Tusser redivivus*. 1710. Aug. pp. 14, 15. Cornelius Walford. *Fairs past and present*. 1883. pp. 150, 151, 157, 158.

[50] *Tour*. 1724. I. letter I. pp. 78–81. cf. topographers. Simpson. *op. cit*. III. p. 928. Bowen. *op. cit. Suffolk*. Twamley. *Dairying exemplified*. 1784. p. 56.

[51] *Annals of agric*. V (1786). pp. 199, 214; XVI (1791). p. 488. Gooch. *Cambridge*. 1813. p. 268. Naomi Riches. *Agricultural revolution in Norfolk*. 1937. pp. 99, 106. Marshall. *Norfolk*. 1787. I. p. 330 II pp. 328–9. Ivy Pinchbeck. *Women workers in the Industrial Revolution 1750–1850*. 1930. pp. 9, 11.

[52] Marshall. *Yorkshire*. 1788. I. p. 293. II. p. 196. Seebohm. *op. cit*. p. 273. W. Hutchinson. *View of Northumberland*. 1778. p. 416.

[53] T. Stone. *Bedford*. 1794. p. 28. Thos. Batchelor. *ibid*. 1808. pp. 445, 526. William James and James Malcolm. *Buckinghamshire*. 1794. p. 15. St. John Priest. *ibid*. 1813. pp. 298, 299. G. Eland. *The Purefoy letters*. 1931. I. p. 159–161, 190. II. p. 232.

[54] Mavor. *Berkshire*. 1808. p. 375. T(homas) Q(uincey). *Tour in the Midland Counties ...in... 1772*. 1775. p. 411. Young. *Oxford*. 1809. p. 278. M. Sturge Henderson. *Three centuries of North Oxfordshire*. 1920. p. 108. Audrey M. Lambert. *Agric. of Oxfordshire at the end of the 18th cent*. Agric. Hist. v. 29. (Jan. 1955). pp. 36, 37.

[55] *Tour*. 1724. II. Letter. III. p. 60. Postlethwayt. *Universal dictionary of trade and commerce*. 1751. pp. 63, 64, 835. Marshall *Gloucester*. 1796. I. pp. 105, 109, 262, 283, 284, 313, 314. II. pp. 130, 132, 161, 163, 179, 182. Twamley. *Essays*. 1816. pp. 93, 94. Anon. *Tour to Cheltenham Spa*. 1783. p. 86. Rev. Richard Warner. *Tour through the Northern Counties*. 1802. I. p. 23. Westerfield. *Middleman*. p. 205.

[56] Defoe. *Tour*. 1724. II. Letter. III. p. 82. J. Mathews. p. 11.

[57] Bowen. *op. cit. Gloucester*. Simpson. *op. cit*. II. p. 3. Rev. Clement Cruttwell. *Tour through Great Britain*. 1801. p. clxxxix. Joseph Wimpey in *Letters . . . B. & W. Soc*. IV (1788). pp. 157, 158.

[58] Postlethwayt. *op. cit*. II. p. 743. Billingsley. *Somerset*. 1798. p. 247 fn. Marshall. *Western counties*. 1796. pp. 120, 148, Wimpey. *op. cit*. p. 156. Stevenson. *Dorset*. 1812. p. 383. Marshall. *Southern counties*. 1798. II. pp. 283, 309.

[59] Hubert H. Parker. *The hop industry*. 1934. Marshall. *Southern counties*. 1798. I. pp. 279, 322. II. pp. 76, 146.

[60] Willich. *Domestic encyclo*. 1802. I. p. 402. *Census*. 1801. App. p. 199—900,000. *Accounts & papers* XXIII (1826). p. 293.

[61] These figures are derived from the Port Books. The Milk Marketing Board kindly collected them.

[62] Confirming details will be found in my, *Milk production in the 18th cent*. Home Farmer, and the references cited therein July, 1936. cf. Seebohm. *Evolution*. p. 271. F. H. Garner. *Cattle of Britain*. 1944. p. 17.

[63] Hermann Levy. *Large and small holdings*. 1911. pp. 7–17.

[64] *Census*. 1811. app. p. 199.

[65] Pinchbeck. *Women workers*. 1930. pp. 40–42. T. S. Ashton. *Economic history of England: the 18th cent*. 1955. pp. 31, 39. Levy. *op. cit*. pp. 61–64.

[66] William and Hugh Raynbird. *Agric. of Suffolk*. 1849. pp. 97, 118.

[67] Taylor. *The farm*. 1834. p. 99. Lawson. *op. cit*. 1825. pp. 298, 400. Fredk. A. Filby. *History of food adulteration*. 1934. p. 52 citing Fredk. Accum. *Treatise on*

*adulteration of food.* 1820 and p. 198 citing A. H. Hassell. *Food and its adulteration.* 1855. Voelcker. *On poisonous cheese.* J.R.A.S.E. 1862. Copland. *Agric.* II. pp. 189, 190.

68 Bravender. *Farming of Gloucester.* J.R.A.S.E. 1850. p. 152. Read. *Oxfordshire. ibid.* 1854. pp. 224, 225. *idem. Buckingham. ibid.* 1855. p. 299. J. W. Robertson-Scott. *The day before yesterday.* 1951. pp. 29, 185.

69 Macdonald. *Cattle.* 1872. pp. 130, 133, 134. Maude Robinson. *Southdown farm in the sixties.* 1947. p. 26.

70 Chester. *Food of the people.* J.R.A.S.E. 1867. p. 119. Baldwin. *Report on butter and cheese at Kilburn. ibid.* 1879. pp. 669, 672. Ward & Lock's *Book.* c. 1880. p. 282. Scott Burn. *Directory.* 1881. p. 48.

71 Ward & Lock's *Book.* p. 359. Filby. *op. cit.* p. 201. Pilley. *op. cit.* 1881. p. 234. Upton. *op. cit.* 1889. pp. 84, 85. Webb. *op. cit.* 1894. pp. 616–619.

72 Ward & Lock's *Book.* p. 359. Long. *British dairy farmer.* 1885. pp. 90–97. James Howard. *Butterine legislation.* Jour. B.D.F.A. III. 2. (1887). pp. 96, 97. William E. Bear. *Failure of the Margarine Act. ibid.* VII (1892) pp. 27–40. Idem. *The British farmer and his competitors.* 1888. p. 102. Filby. *op. cit.* pp. 201, 247.

73 See my *Change in farm labourer's diet.* Econ. Hist. No. 2. May, 1927. p. 273.

74 W. Livesey. *Wensleydale and its dairy farming.* Jour. B.D.F.A. I. 2. (1879). p. 49. Hall. *Pilgrimage.* 1913. p. 213.

## NOTES TO CHAPTER VI. (ii)

1 H. M. Jenkins. *Report on the American cheese factory system and its adaptation to English dairy districts.* J.R.A.S.E. 1870. pp. 173–203. see also idem. *On cheese factories.* Jour. Roy. Soc. Arts. 1870. George Jackson Tattenhall, Cheshire, *On cheese factories.* Lecture to Farmers' Club. 1868.

2 Gilbert Murray, Elvaston, Derby. *The origin and progress of the factory system of cheese making in Derbyshire.* J.R.A.S.E. 1871. J. Coleman, Park Nook, Quornden, Derby. *English cheese factories, how to establish and manage them.* Lecture to Farmers' Club, 1871.

3 J. C. Morton. *On cheese making in home dairies and in factories.* J.R.A.S.E. 1875.

4 Voelcker. *Influence of chemistry on the progress of English agric.* J.R.A.S.E. 1878. pp. 845, 846. G. M. Allender. *Manufacture and management of butter.* Jour. B. & W. Soc. 3rd ser. IX 1877. p. 187.

5 J. P. Sheldon. *Dairy farming.* 1881. pp. 257–280.

6 W. H. Haywood. *Comparative profits from making of cheese and butter, and selling milk or grazing.* J.R.A.S.E. 1865. pp. 338–343. W. T. Carrington. *On dairy farming. ibid.* pp. 344–354.

7 Ward & Lock's *Book.* pp. 277, 364.

8 Long. *British dairy farming.* 1885. p. 268. Rev. Canon Bagot. *Handbook on dairy factories.* 1886. pp. 38–41, 45.

9 Garnett. *Westmorland agric.* p. 138.

10 William E. Bear. *British farmer & his competitors.* 1888. pp. 107–109. Sheldon. *Cheese and butter factories, shall we adopt them.* Jour. B.D.F.A. II. 2. (1886) p. 127 ff. *Report on farm prize competition in Notts, Lincoln etc.* J.R.A.S.E. 1889. p. 43. James McCreath. *Dairying in Cornwall.* Jour. B. & W. Soc. 4th ser. IX (1899). p. 127.

11 Hall. *Pilgrimage.* p. 413. Levy. *op. cit.* pp. 193–197. Margaret Digby. *Agricultural co-operation in Great Britain.* 1949. p. 53.

## NOTES ON CHAPTER VI (iii)

[1] J. C. Morton. *Town milk.* J.R.A.S.E. 1868. p. 95. *idem. Dairy farming. ibid.* 1878. p. 670.

[2] Frank H. Garner. *British dairying.* 1948. p. 10.

[3] Lisle. *Observations.* 1757. pp. 276, 277.

[4] Information provided by Mr. Ashworth of the Express Dairy Co. Ltd.

[5] H. M. de V. *Memoires et observations faites par un voyageur en Angleterre.* ed. by F. M. Misson. 1698.

[6] Ellis *Mod. husb.* 1750. III July. p. 61. R. Weston. *Tracts on practical agric.* 1773. pp. 270, 271. cf. Matthew Bramble's remarks in Smollett's *Humphrey Clinker.*

[7] Holt. *Lancashire.* 1795. pp. 149–151. L. W. Moffitt. *England on the eve of the Industrial Revolution.* 1925. pp. 69, 70, 120. H. Hill. *Liverpool—last stronghold of town cowkeepers.* Dairy Engineering. April, 1956. pp. 107–110.

[8] J. L. & Barbara Hammond. *The village labourer.* 1920. pp. 105, 106. G. C. Broderick. *English land and English landlords.* 1881. p. 63. Levy. *op. cit.* pp. 5, 6. Garnett. *op. cit.* p. 140. Ernle. *English farming.* 1961. p. 312. J. C. Curwen. *Hints on agricultural subjects.* 1809. pp. 82–84.

[9] *Annals of agric.* XXI (1793). pp. 112–116, 526, 532. Baird. *Middlesex.* 1793. Foote. *ibid.* 1794. Middleton. *ibid.* 1798. pp. 327–338. James Malcolm. *Compendium of modern husb.* 1805. I. p. 349.

[10] Ellis. *Mod. husb.* II. May. p. 137. June. p. 144. III. July. p. 62. John Lawrence. *General treatise on cattle.* 1805. p. 144. *Communications to the Board of Agriculture.* 1805. IV p. 213. Pitt. *Staffordshire.* 1808. pp. 175, 176. Parkinson. *Treatise on livestock.* 1810. p. 89. Strickland. *E. R. Yorks.* 1812. p. 222.

[11] Plymley. *Shropshire.* 1803. p. 257.

[12] Garnett. *op. cit.* p. 140.

[13] Taylor. *Farmer's guide.* 1829. pp. 225, 226. Milburn. *The cow.* c. 1851. p. 70. Morton. *Handbook.* 1860. p. 51. Voelcker. *Milk.* J.R.A.S.E. 1863. pp. 312, 313. Stephens' *Book of the farm.* 1877. II. p. 262. Ward & Lock's *Book.* p. 346. Filby. *op. cit.* pp. 50, 199.

[14] Richard Brocklesby, M.D. *Essay . . . mortality . . . horned cattle.* 1746. Loudon *Encyclo.* 1831. pp. 1027–1029, 1038. Youatt. *Cattle.* 1834. pp. 261–265. Milburn. *op. cit.* pp. 69, 70, 72.

[15] Ernle. p. 372.

[16] *Quarterly Jour. of Agric. N.S.* July, 1865–April, 1866. p. 121.

[17] Sheldon. *Dairy farming.* p. 270.

[18] R. H. Rew *Railway rates.* J.R.A.S.E. 1895. p. 289.

[19] *Jour. Roy. Soc. of Arts.* 15. (1867) pp. 321–324, 357.

[20] *Ibid.* p. 525. cf. H. M. Jenkin. *Report on dairy farming . . . N.W. France.* J.R.A.S.E.. 1879. pp. 293–296.

[21] *Quarterly Jour. of Agric.* N.S. 1859. p. 161.

[22] Derek Hudson & Kenneth W. Luckhurst. *The Royal Society of Arts, 1754–1954.* 1954. p. 302.

[23] Henry Chester. *Food of the people.* J.R.A.S.E. 1868. pp. 116, 117. Morton. *Town milk. ibid.* pp. 71, 72.

[24] Morton. *ibid. Jour. Roy. Soc. Arts.* 1867. pp. 356, 357.

[25] Robinson. *Southdown farm.* 1947. p. 30. Garnett. *op. cit.* p. 141. Broderick *English land.* 1881. pp. 295, 296, 396. Levy. *op. cit.* pp. 64, 79.

[26] *Report on trial of dairy implements at Bristol, 1879.* J.R.A.S.E. 1879. p. 136.

[27] *Report on miscellaneous implement awards at Derby, 1881. ibid.* 1881. pp. 630, 631.

[28] *Report on cream separators. ibid.* 1882. p. 622.

[29] Morton. *Dairy farming.* J.R.A.S.E. 1878. p. 670. Garner. *op. cit.* p. 11. Nigel Harvey. *Farming kingdom.* 1955. p. 57. Edwin A. Pratt. *Transition in agriculture.* 1906. p. 10.

[30] *Report on the marketing of dairy produce Pt. I.* Economic Series No. 22. Ministry of Agriculture. 1930.

[31] *J.R.A.S.E.* 1879. pp. 137–142; 1885. p. 716. Sheldon. *Dairy farming.* 1880. pp. 342, 343. *Farm & Home.* 1882. v. 1. Hugh A. Macewen. *The public milk supply.* 1910. pp. 62—64. C. Fream. *Elements of agric.* 9th ed. 1914. p. 562.

[32] Alfred Williams. *Villages of the White Horse.* 1913. pp. 122, 123.

[33] Sheldon. *Farm & dairy.* 1889. *Jour. B.D.F.A.* VI. i. 1890. p. 203.

[34] *J.R.A.S.E.* 1884. p. 587; 1881, p. 535. Richmond Commission. *Preliminary report.* (C. 2778) 1881. p. 30.

[35] J. A. Smith. *Distribution of dairy produce.* Jour. B.D.F.A. (IV). pp. 43–45.

[36] George Barham. *Railway rates for dairy produce. ibid.* VI. i. (1890). pp. 89–204. *ibid.* (1891). p. 9 ff.

[37] Richmond Commission. *Assistant Commissioner's Reports: Coleman on Cheshire.* pp. 54, 70, 71.

[38] Barham as Note 36.

[39] Christopher Middleton. *Present and future aspect of dairy regulations.* Jour. Farmers' Club. Feb. 1908. pp. 682, 686.

[40] William E. Bear. *Food supply of Manchester. II Animal produce.* J.R.A.S.E. 1879. pp. 508–510.

[41] C. E. Vulliamy. *Polderoy papers.* 1943. p. 271. E. A. Pratt. *op. cit.* pp. 11–17. L. Jebb. *Small holdings of England.* 1907. p. 43. Garnett. *op. cit.* p. 141.

[42] Chas. B. Davies. *Supply of milk to large centres.* Jour. B.D.F.A. XVI (1909). p.30–33.

[43] J. T. Horner. *The milk supply from the distributor's point of view. ibid.* XXIII (1909). p. 38.

[44] *ibid.* p. 47. Macewen. *op. cit.* p. 62.

[45] Macewen. pp. 63, 64.

[46] J.R.A.S.E. 1896. p. 454.

[47] Macewen. p. 66. F. J. Prewett. *Survey of milk marketing (Bristol).* 1928. p. 29. *idem. ibid.* (Derbyshire). 1930. p. 61.

[48] Lavergne. *Rural econ. of England.* 1855. p. 53. Morton in J.R.A.S.E. 1878. p. 647. Clarke. *ibid.* p. 486. Sheldon. *Farm & dairy.* 1889. p. 57. Rew. *Jour. Roy. Statl. Soc.* 55 (1892). p. 59. *idem. Farm revenue and capital.* J.R.A.S.E. 1895 and *Food production and British farms. ibid.* 1903. p. 120. Prewett as note 47.

[49] *J.R.A.S.E.* 1878. p. 699. J. Thornhill Harrison. *Dairy statistics.* Jour. B. & W. Soc. XII (1864). p. 29. Morton. *Town milk* as above. p. 90.

[50] Low. *Pract. agric.* 1843. p. 651. Morton. *Handbook.* 1860. p. 3. Pringle & Muray., *op. cit.* c. 1865. p. 23. W. T. Carrington. *Dairy farming.* J.R.A.S.E. 1865. p. 345.

[51] Morton. *J.R.A.S.E.* 1878. p. 647. Murray. *Notes.* n.d.p. 5. Pilley. *Scientific agric.* c. 1883. p. 174. Long. *British dairy farming.* 1885. p. 19. Coleman. *Cattle.* 1887. p. 90. Bear. *British farmer.* 1888. p. 124. Sheldon. *Farm & dairy.* 1889. p. 57. Hall. *Pilgrimage.* 1913. p. 213. Venn. *Foundations of agricultural economics.* 1923. p. 149.

[52] see my *Size of English cattle in the 18th cent.* Agric. Hist. (U.S.A.) III (Oct. 1929). pp. 160–181.

[53] *Jour. B.D.F.A.* II. i. (1885). p. 137. *J.R.A.S.E.* 1883. p. 534. *Jour B. & W. Soc.*

3rd ser. XV (1883–4). pp. 108, 117. Bear. *op. cit.* p. 128. Upton. p. 112. Long. *Dairy farm.* 1889. pp. 17, 70. Punchard. *Dairy farming of Cumberland and Westmorland.* Jour. B.D.F.A. VII. (1892). p. 106. Muir. *Jour. B. & W. Soc.* 4th ser. V (1895). p. 61. C. Bryner Jones. *Livestock of the farm.* 1920. I. p. 129.
[54] Henry Evershed. *Supply of milk to labourers.* J.R.A.S.E. 1880. pp. 103, 104. J. E. Vincent. *Highways and byways in Berkshire.* 1906. p. 188. Sir John Russell. *The land called me.* 1956. p. 38. Levy. *op. cit.* p. 174. *Report . . . prize farms.* J.R.A.S.E. 1887.

# BIBLIOGRAPHY

*Official publications*
1. Calendar of State Papers; Domestic Series.
2. Census of Population.
3. Accounts and Papers.
4. Acts of Parliament: 32 Henry VIII. c. xxi; 3 & 4 Edw. VI. c. xxi; 5 & 6 Edw. VI. c. xiv; 5 Eliz. I. c. xii.
5. Acts of Privy Council. 1542, 1550, 1554, 1557, 1576 etc.
6. Patent Office: Abridgements of Specifications 1777–1866 et seq.
7. Poor Law Commissioners. Report on the employment of women and children in agriculture. 1843.
8. Royal Commission on Agriculture, 1880 et seq. Reports of Assistant Commissioners. Minutes of Evidence, etc.
9. House of Commons Journal 1764.
10. Select Committee of House of Commons. Report relating to the Corn Laws, 1814.

*Publications of Societies etc.*
1. Archaelogia Cantiana.
2. Letters and communications to the Bath and West of England Society, 1788–1829.
3. Journal of the Bath and West Society. 2nd to 5th ser. 1853–1917.
4. Publications of the Bedfordshire Historical Records Society.
5. Board of Agriculture. General View of the agriculture of . . . (each county) published in two editions between 1793 & 1816.
6. Idem. Communications to the . . . 6 v. 1797–1811.
7. Journal of the British Dairy Farmers' Association.
8. Publications of the Cambridge Antiquarian Society.
9. Derbyshire Archaeological Journal.
10. Economic History Review. 1st and 2nd ser.
11. Journal of the Farmers' Club.
12. Transactions Leicester Archaelogical Society.
13. Journal of the Royal Agricultural Society of England, 1839 et seq.
14. Journal of the Royal Society of Arts.
15. Shropshire Archaelogical Society Transactions.
16. Surrey Archaeological Collections.
17. Surtees Society Publications.
18. Sussex Archaeological Collections.

N.B. The names of the authors and the titles of the separate papers quoted are given in the notes. To have stated them individually would have occupied an extravagant amount of space here. If only one or two articles have been quoted particulars will be found in the general list of authors below.

# BIBLIOGRAPHY

*Periodicals*

1. Agriculture: formerly the Journal of the Board, later Ministry, of Agriculture.
2. Annals of Agriculture. 1783 et seq.
3. Farm and Home. 1882.
4. Farmers Magazine. 1800–1811, 1820—1825, 1837–1847.
5. Quarterly Journal of Agriculture. 1828–1843.
6. Land Agents Record. 31 July, 1943.
7. Museum Rusticum et Commerciale. 1763 et seq.
8. The Plough. Jan. 1846–June, 1847.

*Books, pamphlets, etc.*

1. Accum, Frederick. *Treatise on adulteration of food.* 1820.
2. Acland, Thomas Dyke. *The farming of Somersetshire.* 1851.
3. Adam, James. *Practical essays on agriculture.* 2 v. 1787.
4. Adkin, Benaiah W. *Land drainage in Britain.* 1933.
5. Aikin, John. *Descriptions of the country . . . round Manchester.* 1795.
6. Ainsworth-Davis (ed.) *Fream's Elements of agriculture.* 9th ed. 1914.
7. Anderson, James. *Essays relating to agriculture and rural affairs.* 6 v. 4th ed. 1797.
8. Anderson, James. *Practical essays on agriculture.* 3 v. 1787.
9. Andrews, G. H. *Rudimentary treatise on agricultural engineering.* 1852–3.
10. Andrews, G. H. *Modern husbandry.* 1853.
11. Anon. *Considerations on the present state of Great Britain . . .* 1773.
12. Anon. *Description of England and Wales.* 1769.
13. Anon. *Dictionarium rusticum.* 1717.
14. Anon. *Ellis' Husbandry abridged.* 2 v. 1772.
15. Anon. *Present state of England.* 2 v. 1750.
16. Anon. *A tour to Cheltenham Spa.* 1783.
17. Anon. *Tusser redivivus.* 1710.
18. Anon. *A view of real grievances with remedies.* 1772.
19. Armstrong, S. F. *British grasses and their employment in agriculture.* 1937.
20. Ashley, M. P. *Financial and commercial policy under the Cromwellian Protectorate.* 1934.
21. Ashton, T. S. *Economic history of England: the 18th century.* 1955.
22. Astell, P. F. *Grazing in the Midlands.* Bull. No. 10. Imperial Bureau of Plant Genetics. Herbage Plants. 1933.
23. Atwel, George. *The faithfull surveyor.* 1662.
24. Aubrey, John. *Natural history of Surrey.* 1719.
25. Aubrey, John. *Memoires of naturall remarques in the county of Wilts.* ed. by John Britton. 1849.

26. Badcock, H. *Practical observations on husbandry of East Cornwall.* 1845.
27. Bagot, Rev. Canon. *Handbook of dairy factories.* 1886.
28. Baker, J. *Imperial guide.* 1802.
29. Balston, Thomas. *Housekeeping book of Susan Whatman. 1776–1800.* 1956.
30. Baxters' *Library of agricultural and horticultural knowledge.* 3rd ed. 1836.
31. Bayne-Powell, Rosamund. *Housekeeping in the 18th century.* 1956.
32. Bear, William E. *The British farmer and his competitors.* 1888.
33. Beddowes, A. R. *The rye grasses in British agriculture.* Bull. H. 17. Welsh Plant Breeding Station. 1953.

34. Beloch, Julius. 'Die Bevölkerung Europas zur Zeit der Renaissance'. *Zeitschrift für Sozialwissenschaft*. v. III. 1900.
35. Benese, J. F. *Anglo-Dutch relations from the earliest times to the death of William III*. 1925.
36. Billing, Robert. *An account of the culture of carrots*. 1765.
37. *The Bible*. Judges V. 25.
38. Bingley, William. *Memoirs of British quadrupeds*. 1809.
39. B[lagrave], J[oseph]. *The epitome of the whole art of husbandry*. 1675.
40. B[lagrave], J[oseph]. *New additions to the . . . art of husbandry*. 1675.
41. Blome, Richard. *The gentleman's recreation*. 1686.
42. Bloomfield, Robert. *The farmer's boy*. 9th ed. 1806.
43. Blundell, Margaret. (ed.) *Blundell's diary and letter book, 1702–1728*. 1952.
44. Blurton, William. *Practical essays on milking*. 1839. (cited in Stephens' *Book of the farm*, but untraceable).
45. Bowen, E. *Complete system of geography*. 1747.
46. Bradley, Richard. *A general treatise of husbandry*. 1726.
47. Bradley, Richard. *The gentleman's and farmer's guide*. 1729.
48. Bradley, Richard. *The country housewife*. 1736.
49. Brocklesby, Richard. *An essay concerning the mortality now prevailing amongst the horned cattle about London*. 1746.
50. Broderick, G. C. *English land and English landlords*. 1881.
51. Brown, Robert. *The compleat farmer*. 1759.
52. Brown, Robert. *Treatise of rural affairs*. 2 v. 1811.
53. Browne, Chas. A. *A source book of agricultural chemistry*. 1944.
54. Buckmaster, J. C. & Willis. J. J. *Elementary principles of scientific agriculture*. n.d., c. 1883.
55. Burn, R. Scott. *Directory for the improvement of landed property*. 1881.
56. Burn, R. Scott. *Outlines of modern farming*. 6th ed. 1888.
57. Burritt, Elihu. *Walks in the Black Country and its green borderland*. 1869.
58. Burritt, Elihu. *A walk from London to Land's End and back*. 1868.
59. Butcher, Rev. Edmund. *An excursion from Sidmouth to Chester*. 1802.

60. Cameron, Charles A. *Chemistry of food and livestock*. 1868.
61. Campbell, Mildred. *The English yeoman under Elizabeth and the early Stuarts*. 1942.
62. Carrier, E. H. *The pastoral heritage of Britain*. 1936.
63. Chapple, William. *Review of Risdon's Survey of Devon*. 1785.
64. Clergyman, *Useful and practical observations on agriculture*. 1783.
65. Cochrane, E. R. *The milch cow in England*. 1946.
66. Coleman, John. *Cattle, sheep and pigs of Great Britain*. 2nd ed. 1887.
67. Colnett, Miss A. 'Cheeses of Great Britain. 12. Gloucester'. *Dairy Engineering*. Nov. 1955.
68. Comber, Thomas. *Rural improvements in agriculture*. 1772.
69. Cooper, M. McG. *Competitive farming*. 1956.
70. Copland, Samuel. *Agriculture; ancient and modern*. 2 v. 1866.
71. Country Gentleman. *The complete grazier*. 1767.
72. Coysh, A. W. & others. *The Mendips*. 1954.
73. Cruttwell, Rev. Clement. *Tour through Great Britain*. 1801.
74. Culley, George. *Observations on livestock*. 1786.
75. Cunningham, W. 'Common rights at Cottenham and Stretham in Cambridgeshire'. *Camden Miscellany*. 3rd ser. XVIII. 1910.

76. Curtis, William. *Practical observations on the British grasses.* 1790.
77. Curtler, W. H. R. *A short history of English agriculture.* 1909.
78. Curwen, J. C. *Hints on agricultural subjects.* 1809.

79. Darby, H. C. *Historical geography of England before 1800.* 1936.
80. Darby, H. C. *The drainage of the fens.* 1940.
81. Davies, D. J. *Economic history of South Wales prior to 1800.* 1933.
82. Davies, J. Llefelys. *Grass farming in the Welland valley.* 1926.
83. Davies, Maude F. *Life in an English village.* 1909.
84. Davies, Stella. 'The Cheshire dairy'. *Cheshire Historian.* No. 6. 1956.
85. Davies, William. 'A grassland survey of Kent'. *Kent Farmers' Journal.* v. 54. April, 1942.
86. Davies, William. *The grass crop.* 1952.
87. Defoe, Daniel. *A tour through England and Wales.* 1724. Everyman's ed.
88. Defoe, Daniel. *Compleat English tradesman.* 2nd ed. (?). 2 v. 1727.
89. Dexter, Henry Martyn & Morton. *The England and Holland of the Pilgrims.* 1905.
90. ..., R. W. *Practical agriculture.* 2 v. 1804.
91. ..., Sir Kenelm. *The closet of Sir Kenelm Digby opened.* 1669.
92. Digby, Margaret. *Agricultural co-operation in Great Britain.* 1949.
93. Donaldson, John. *A treatise on manures.* 1842.
94. Donaldson, John. *British agriculture.* 3 v. 1860.
95. Dugdale, William. *History of imbanking and drayning of divers fens and marshes.* 1662.

96. Eland, G. (ed.) *The Purefoy letters, 1735–1753.* 2 v. 1931.
97. Ellis, William. *Practical farmer.* 2nd ed. 1732.
98. Ellis, William. *Modern husbandry.* 8 v. 1750.
99. Epstein, H. 'Domestication features in animals as functions of human society'. *Agric. Hist. U.S.A.* 29 (1955). 4.
100. Ernle, Lord. *English farming past and present.* 6th ed. 1961.
101. Evans, George Ewart. *Ask the fellows who cut the hay.* 1956.

102. A Farmer. *Rural recreations.* 1802.
103. Filby, Frederick A. *History of food adulteration and analysis.* 1934.
104. Fitzherbert. *Husbandry* 1523. reprinted in *Certain Antient Tracts.* 1767.
105. Fitzherbert. *Surveying.* 1523. reprinted in *Certain Antient Tracts.* 1767.
106. Fleishmann, W. *The book of the dairy.* tr. by Aikman & Wright. 1896.
107. Flemyng, Malcolm. *A proposal in order to diminish the progress of the distemper amongst the horned cattle.* 1754.
108. Folkingham, W. *Feudigraphia.* 1610.
109. Forbes, Francis. *Modern improvements in agriculture.* 1784.
110. Forsyth, Robert. *Principles and practice of agriculture.* 2. v. 1804.
111. Franklin, T. Bedford. *British grasslands.* 1953.
112. Fuller, Thomas. *History of the worthies of England.* 1662. new ed. ed. by G. P. Austin Nuttall. 3 v. 1840.
113. Furnivall, Frederick J. (ed.) *Harrison's Description of England in Shakespeare's youth.* 1877.
114. Fussell, G. E. 'Change in farm labourer's diet during two centuries'. *Economic History* No. 2. May, 1927.

X

115. Fussell, G. E. 'John Wynn Baker: an improver in 18th century Ireland'. *Agric. Hist.* U.S.A. V. Oct. 1931.
116. Fussell, G. E. 'Size of English cattle in the 18th century'. *Ibid.* III. Oct. 1929.
117. Fussell, G. E. 'Milk production in the 18th century'. *Home Farmer.* July, 1936.
118. Fussell, G. E. (ed.) 'Robert Loder's farm accounts, 1610–1620'. Camden Soc. 3rd ser. v. 53. 1936.
119. Fussell, G. E. 'Animal Husbandry in 18th century England'. *Agric. Hist.* XI. Apl. & July, 1937.
120. Fussell, G. E. 'Benjamin Stillingfleet'. *Notes & Queries.* 29 May, 1948.
121. Fussell, G. E. *The farmers' tools, 1500–1900.* 1952.
122. Fussell, G. E. 'Four centuries of Cheshire farming systems'. *Trans. Hist. Soc. of Lancs. & Ches.* v. 106. 1954.
123. Fussell, G. E. 'History of cole (Brassica sp.) *Nature.* 9 July 1955.
124. Fussell, G. E. & Atwater. V. G. B. 'Farmers' goods and chattels, 1500–1900'. *History.* XX. Dec. 1935.
125. Fussell, G. E. & Compton. Maurice. 'Agricultural adjustments after the Napoleonic wars'. *Economic History.* Feb. 1939.

126. Gamgee, John. *Dairy stock.* 1861.
127. Garner, F. H. *The cattle of Britain.* 1944.
128. Garner, F. H. *British dairying.* 1948.
129. Garnett, Frank W. *Westmorland agriculture, 1800–1900.* 1912.
130. Garnier, Russell M. *History of English landed interest.* 2. v. 1893.
131. Garnier, Russell M. *Annals of the British peasantry.* 1895.
132. Garrad, G. H. *A survey of the agriculture of Kent.* 1954.
133. Garrard, George. *A description of the different varieties of oxen common in the British Isles.* 1800.
134. Gaut, R. G. *History of Worcestershire agriculture.* 1939.
135. Gerard of Trent, Thomas. *Particular description of the county of Somerset.* (ed. by E. H. Bates). 1900.
136. Gilbey, Sir Walter. *Farm stock 100 years ago.* 1910.
137. Gonner, E. C. K. *Common land and inclosure.* 1912.
138. Googe, Barnaby. *Four books of husbandry.* 1577.
139. Gregory, J. W. *The story of the road.* 1930.
140. Guenon, François. *Traité des vaches latières.* 1839.

141. Hale, Thomas. *Compleat body of husbandry.* 1756.
142. Hall, A. D. *A pilgrimage of British farming.* 1913.
143. Hall, Hubert. *Society in the Elizabethan age.* 1887.
144. Hamilton, A. H. A. *Quarter sessions from Queen Elizabeth to Queen Anne.* 1878.
145. Hammond, J. L. & Barbara. *The village labourer.* 1920.
146. Hanger, Col. George. *to all Sportsmen. . . .* 1814.
147. Hardy, B. Cozens. (ed.) *The diary of Sylas Neville, 1767–1788.* 1950.
148. Harrison, Gustavus. *Agriculture delineated.* 1775.
149. Hartlib, Samuel. *Legacie.* 1655.
150. Harvey, Nigel. *The farming kingdom.* 1955.
151. Hassell, A. H. *Food and its adulteration.* 1855.
152. Haydon, E. G. *Travels round our village.* 1905.
153. Head, Sir George. *A home tour in 1835.* 1836.
154. Heanley, R. M. *History of Weyhill, Hants., and its ancient fair.* 1922.

BIBLIOGRAPHY

155. Hearnshaw, F. J. C. 'Leet jurisdiction in England'. *Southampton Record Soc.* 1908.
156. Hecht, J. Jean. *Domestic servant class in 18th century England.* 1956.
157. Henderson, M. Sturge. *Three centuries of North Oxfordshire.* 1920.
158. Hewitt, H. J. *Medieval Cheshire.* 1929.
159. Hill, H. 'Liverpool—last stronghold of the town cow-keepers'. *Dairy Engineering.* Apl. 1956.
160. Hillyard, C. *Practical farming and grazing.* 3rd ed. 1840.
161. Hiscock, W. G. *John Evelyn and his family circle.* 1955.
162. Hole, Christine. *English housewife in the 17th century.* 1953.
163. Houghton, John. *A collection of letters for the improvement of husbandry and trade.* 1681–3.
164. Housman, John. *Topographical description of Cumberland and Westmorland, Lancs. etc.* 1800.
165. Hudson, Derek & Luckhurst. Kenneth W. *The Royal Society of Arts, 1754–1954.* 1954.
166. Hughes, Edward. *North country life in the 18th century.* 1952.
167. Hutchinson, W. *View of Northumberland.* 1778.

168. Impey, F. *My small dairy farm.* App. to C. W. Stubbs. *The land and the labourer.* 1885.

169. Jackson, James. *A treatise of agriculture and dairy husbandry.* 1840.
170. Jacob, Giles. *The country gentleman's vade mecum.* 1717.
171. Jebb, L. *The small holdings of England.* 1907.
172. Jenkin, A. K. Hamilton. *Cornwall and its people.* 1945.
173. Johnson, C. W. *The modern dairy and cowkeeper.* 1850.
174. Jones, C. Bryner. *Livestock of the farm.* 1920.

175. Kalm, Pehr. *Kalm's account of his visit to England . . . in 1748.* tr. by Joseph Lucas. 1748.
176. Kent, Nathaniel. *Hints to gentlemen of landed property.* 1776.
177. Knapp, J. L. *Gramina pascua, or representations of the British grasses.* 1804.

178. Lambert, Audrey M. 'Agriculture of Oxfordshire at the end of the 18th century'. *Agric. Hist.* 29. Jan. 1955.
179. Lamond, Elizabeth & Cunningham. W. *Walter of Henley's husbandry,* etc. 1890.
180. Laurence, John. *New system of agriculture.* 1726.
181. Lawrence, John. *New farmers' calendar.* 4th ed. 1802.
182. Lawrence, John. *A general treatise on cattle.* 1805.
183. Lawson, A. *The modern farrier.* 8th ed. 1825.
184. Lawson, William. 'Reflections on milk production'. *Sussex Agricultural Jour.* Nov.–Jan. 1955–6.
185. Lavergne, Leonce de. *Rural economy of England.* 1855.
186. Layard, D. P. *An essay on the nature of the contagious distemper among the horned cattle in these kingdoms.* 1757.
187. Leconfield, Lord. *Petworth manor in the 17th century.* 1953.
188. Lee, Amice. *Laurels and rosemary: the life of William and Mary Howitt.* 1955.
189. Levy, Hermann. *Large and small holdings.* 1911.
190. Lindemans, P. (ed.) *Sir Richard Weston; Verhandeling over de landbouw in Vlanderen en Brabant, 1644–5.* 1950.

345

191. Lindemans, P. *Geschiedenis van de landbouw in België*. 2. v. 1952.
192. Lisle, Edward. *Observations in husbandry*. 1757. (relates to period 1690–1712).
193. Lloyd, John jr. *Pepers relating to the history and navigation of the rivers Wye nad Lugg*. 1873.
194. Lodge, Eleanor C. (ed.) *An account book of a Kentish estate, 1616–1704*. 1927
195. Lodge, Thomas & Greene, Robert. *A looking glass for London and England.*. 1594. Reprinted in J. Churton Collins. *The plays and poems of Robert Greene*. 2 v. 1905.
196. Long, James. *The dairy farm*. 1889.
197. Long, James. *British dairy farming* 1885.
198. Long, W. H. & McCann. N. F. *Study of foods fed to livestock in West Cornwall*. Seale Hayne Agric. College. Farmers' Report Sec. III. No. 5. 1933.
199. Loudon, J. C. *Encyclopaedia of agriculture*. 1825. 2nd ed. 1831.
200. Low, David. *Practical agriculture*. 4th ed. 1843.
201. Low, David. *Domesticated animals of the British Isles*. 1845.
202. Lowe, E. J. *A natural history of British grasses*. 1862.

203. Macdonald, D. G. F. *Cattle, sheep and deer*. 2nd ed. 1872.
204. Macewen, Hugh A. *The public milk supply*. 1910.
205. Magne, J. H. *How to choose a good dairy cow*. 1853.
206. Maitland, *History of London*. 1756.
207. Malcolm, James. *Compendium of modern husbandry*. 3 v. 1805.
208. Malden, W. J. *Farm buildings*. 1896.
209. Manley, Gordon. *Climate and the British scene*. 1953.
210. Markham, Gervase. *Cheape and good husbandry*. (1614) 8th ed. 1653.
211. Markham, Gervase. *The English housewife*. (1614) 8th ed. 1653.
212. Markham, Gervase. *Inrichment of the Weald of Kent*. 1620.
213. Marshall, William. *Rural economy of Norfolk*. 2 v. 1787.
214. Marshall, William. *Rural economy of Yorkshire*. 2 v. 1788.
215. Marshall, William. *Rural economy of the Midland Counties*. 2 v. 1790.
216. Marshall, William. *Rural economy of West of England*. 2 v. 1796.
217. Mershall, William. *Rural economy of Gloucester*. 2 v. 1796.
218. Marshall, William. *Rural economy of Southern Counties*. 2 v. 1798.
219. Martin, Benjamin. *Natural history of England*. 1759.
220. Mascall, Leonard. *The government of cattle*. 1627.
221. Mathews, Ernest. *Economics of dairy farming*. 1903.
222. Milburn, M. M. *The cow: dairy husbandry and cattle breeding*. c. 1851.
223. Mills, John. *A treatise on cattle*. 1776.
224. Minchinton, W. E. *British tinplate industry*. 1957.
225. Misson, F. M. (ed.) *H. M. de V. Memoires et observations faites par un voyageur en Angleterre*. 1698.
226. Moffitt, L. W. *England on the eve of the Industrial Revolution, 1740–1760*. 1925.
226ᵃ. Moore, H. I. *The science and practice of grassland farming*. 1949.
227. Morden, Robert. *A new description and state of England*. 1704.
228. Mortimer, John. *Whole art of husbandry*. 4th ed. 1716.
229. Morton, J. C. *Handbook of dairy farming*. 1860.
230. Morton, J. C. *The Prince Consort's farms*. 1863.
231. Muffitt, T. *Health's Improvement*. 1655.
232. Muir, James. *Manual of dairy work*. 1893.
233. Murray, Gilbert. *Notes on dairy farming*. n.d., c. 1880.

# BIBLIOGRAPHY

234. Needham, Ronald T. *Modern farm dairy equipment.* 1952.
235. Nicholls, George. *The farmer.* 1844.
236. Norden, John. *Speculum Britannia—Middlesex.* 1593.
237. Norden, John. *Speculum Britannia—Essex.* 1594. Camden Soc. IX. 1840.
238. Norden, John. *Surveyor's dialogue.* (1607) 3rd ed. 1618.
239. (North, Roger.) *A person of honour in the county of Norfolk. The gentleman farmer.* 1726.
240. North, Richard. *An account of the different kinds of grasses propagated in England.* 1759.
241. Notestein, Wallace. *The English people on the eve of colonization.* 1954.
242. Nourse, Tim. *Campania foelix.* 1700.

243. Olmstead, Fred Law. *Walks and talks of an American farmer in England.* 1852.
244. Orwin, C. S. & C. S. *The open fields.* 2nd ed. 1954.
245. Osborn, E. F. D. (ed.) *Political and social letters of a lady of the 18th century, 1721–1727.* 1891.

246. Parker, Hubert H. *The Hop Industry.* 1934.
247. Parkinson, Richard. *Experienced farmer.* 2 v. 1807.
248. Parkinson, Richard. *Treatise on the breeding and management of livestock.* 1810.
249. Peters, Matthew. *Winter riches* . . . 1771.
250. Picton, J. A. *Selections from the manuscript archives and records of Liverpool.*
251. Pilling, John J. *Scientific agriculture.* 1881.
252. Pinchbeck, Ivy. *Women workers in the Industrial Revolution, 1750–1850.* 1930.
253. Plot, Robert. *Natural history of Oxfordshire.* 1676.
254. Plot, Robert. *Natural history of Staffordshire.* 1686.
255. Plumb, J. H. *Studies in social history.* 1955.
256. Postlethwayt. *Universal dictionary of trade and commerce.* 2 v. 1757.
257. Powell. *A view of real grievances; with remedies proposed for redressing them.* 1772.
258. Practical farmer. (David Henry). *The complete English farmer.* 1772.
259. Pratt, Edwin A. *Transition in agriculture.* 1906.
260. Prentice, E. Parmalee. *American dairy cattle.* 1942.
261. Prewett, F. J. *Survey of milk marketing (Bristol).* 1928.
262. Prewett, F. J. *Survey of milk marketing (Derbyshire).* 1930.
263. Pringle R. O. & Murray. Prof. *Practical farming: stock* n.d., c. 1865. This book is based on J. H. Magne. *Choise des vaches laitières* & P. A. Thier. *La laitérie.*
264. Prothero, R. E. (Lord Ernle). 'Agriculture and gardening' in *Shakespeare's England.* v. 1. 1916. (ed. by Sir Sidney Lee).

265. Q[uincey]. T[homas]. *Tour in the Midland Counties in 1772 and 1775.* 1775.

266. Randall, John. *The semi-Virgilian husbandry.* 1764.
267. Raven, C. E. *English naturalists from Neckham to Ray.* 1947.
268. Rawstone, L. *Some remarks on Lancashire farming.* 1843.
269. Raynbird, William & Hugh. *On the agriculture of Suffolk.* 1849.
270. Redfern, Francis. *History and antiquities of Uttoxeter.* 1886.
271. Reeve, Gabriel. *Directions left by a gentleman to his sons for the improvement of heathy and barren lands in England and Wales.* 1670.
272. Reyce, Robert. *Suffolk in the 17th century.* 1618. With notes by Lord Francis Hervey. 1902.
273. Riches, Naomi. *The agricultural revolution in Norfolk.* 1937.

274. Ringsted, Josiah. *The farmer*. n.d., c. 1796.
275. ———. *Riplingham Grange, 1839–1874. Mss. account book*.
276. Roberts, George. *Social history of the Southern Counties of England*. 1856.
277. Robinson, Maude. *A Southdown farm in the sixties*. 1947.
278. Rogers, Thorold. *Six centuries of work and wages*. 1906.
279. Rhode, E. S. *The story of the garden*. 1933.
280. Rohde, E. S. *Shakespeare's wild flowers*. 1935.
281. Roland, Arthur. *Farming for pleasure and profit: dairy farming*. 1879.
282. Rowse, A. L. *The England of Elizabeth*. 1950.
283. Rundell, Mrs. *Home cookery*. 1900.
284. Russell, Sir John. *The land called me*. 1956.

285. Scott, J. W. Robertson. *The day before yesterday*. 1951.
286. Seebohm, M. E. *The evolution of the English farm*. 1952.
287. Shakespeare. *Midsummer night's dream*.
288. Shakespeare. *Love's labour lost*.
289. Sharp, Mary. 'Beenham, Berks'. *Berks. Bucks. and Oxon. Archaeological Jour.* XXII. 1916.
290. Sheldon, J. P. *Dairy farming*. n.d., c. 1883.
291. Sheldon, J. P. *The farm and the dairy*. 1889.
292. Sherer, John. *Rural life*. n.d., c. 1850.
293. Simon, André L. *Cheeses of the world*. 1956.
294. Simpson, Samuel. *The agreeable historian*. . . . 1746.
295. Sinclair, Sir John. *Essays on miscellaneous subjects*. 1802.
296. Sinclair, Sir John. *Code of agriculture*. 1817.
297. Sinclair, George. *Hortus gramineus Woburniensis*. 1816.
298. Slight & Burn. *Book of farm implements and machines*. 1858.
299. Smith, Mrs. E. *Compleat housewife*. 1724.
300. Smith, Gent. John. *England's improvement reviv'd*. 1670.
301. Smollett, Tobias. *Humphrey Clinker*. 1770.
302. Society of Gentlemen. *The complete farmer*. 4th ed. 1793.
303. Speed, Adam. *Adam out of Eden*. 1659.
304. S., Gent. A. (Adolphus Speed). *The husbandman, farmer and grazier's complete instructor*. 1697.
305. Spencer, A. J. & Passmore. J. B. *Agricultural implements and machinery*. Science Museum. 1930.
306. Stamp, L. Dudley. *Man and the land*. 1955.
307. Stapledon, R. G. *The land, today and tomorrow*. 1942.
308. Steer, Francis W. *Farm and cottage inventories of mid-Essex, 1635–1749*. 1950.
309. Stephens, Henry. *Book of the farm*. 2. v. 3rd ed. 1877.
310. Stevenson, Matthew. *The twelve moneths*. 1661.
311. Stocks, Helena. (ed.) *Records of the borough of Leicester, 1603–1688*. 1923.
312. Surflet, Richard. *The countrey ferme*. tr. fr. French of Estienne and Liebault. 1600.
313. Sutton, Martin J. *Permanent and temporary pastures*. 5th ed. 1895.
314. Swayne, Rev. G. *Gramina pascua*. 1790.
315. Switzer, Stephen. *Ichnographia rustica*. 3 v. 1718.

316. Tawney; R. H. & Power. Eileen. *Tudor economic documents*. 1924.
317. Taylor, Alexander. *A farmer's guide*. 1829.
318. Taylor, Jefferys. *The farm*. 1834.

319. Taylor, John. *A new discovery by sea with a wherry from London to Salisbury.* 1623.
320. Taylor, John. *Last voyage and adventure.* 1641. Both in Charles Hindley. *The old Book-collector's miscellany.* 1873.
321. Thomason, A. G. *The small dairy farm.* 1955.
322. Trotter, Eleanor. *Seventeenth century life in a country parish.* 1919.
323. Trowell, Samuel. *New treatise of husbandry.* 1739.
324. Trow-Smith, Robert. *British livestock husbandry to 1700.* 1967.
325. Tusser, Thomas. *Five hunared points . . . 1577* (ed. Mavor) 1812.
326. Twamley. *Essays in management of dairy.* 1816.
327. Tyler, Cyril. 'The development of feeding standards for livestock'. *Agric. Hist. Rev.* IV. 1956.

328. Upton, H. M. *Profitable dairy farming.* 1888.

329. Varlo, Charles. *A new system of husbandry.* 3 v. 1774.
330. Venn, J. A. *Foundations of agricultural economics.* 1923.
331. Vermuijden, Cornelius. *Discourse touching the drayning of the Great Fennes.* 1642.
332. Verney family. Letters and papers of . . . to 1639. *Camden Soc.* LVI. 1833.
333. Vincent, J. E. *Highways and byways in Berkshire.* 1906.
334. Vulliamy, C. E. *Polderoy papers.* 1943.

335. Walford, Cornelius. *Fairs past and present.* 1883.
336. Walker, John. *The cow and calf.* 1886.
337. Walker, John. *Farming to profit in moaern times.* 1888.
338. Walker-Tisdale. C. W. & Robinson, Theodore R. *Butter making on the farm.* 1903.
339. Wallace, Robert. *The livestock of Great Britain.* 1889.
340. Wallace, Robert & Watson. J. A. Scott. *Farm livestock of Great Britain.* 5th ed. 1923.
341. Walton, Isaac. *The complete angler.* 1653.
342. Ward & Lock. *Book of farm management.* n.d., c. 1880.
343. Warner, Rev. Richard. *Tour through the Northern Counties.* 1802.
344. Watson, J. A. Scott. *History of the Royal Agricultural Society of England, 1839–1939.* 1939.
345. Webb, Henry J. *Advanced agriculture.* 1894.
346. Westerfield, R. B. *Middleman in English business, particularly between 1660 and 1760.* 1915.
347. Weston, Richard. *Tracts on practical agriculture.* 1773.
348. Whishaw, James. *A history of the Whishaw family,* 1935.
349. Whitworth, R. *Advantages of inland navigation.* 1766.
350. Willan, T. S. *River navigation in England, 1600–1750.* 1936.
351. Willan, T. S. *The English coastal trade, 1600–1750.* 1938.
352. Williams, Alfred. *Villages of the White Horse.* 1913.
353. Williams, Myrddin. *Milk and money from grass.* 1952.
354. Willich, A. F. M. *Domestic encyclopaedia.* 1802.
355. Willis, Rev. James. *On the Poor Laws of England.* 1808.
356. Wimpey, Joseph. *Thoughts on interesting subjects.* 1770.
357. Winchester, Barbara. *Tudor family portrait.* 1955.
358. Worlidge, John. *Systema agriculturae.* 1666.

359. Yarranton, Andrew. *The improvement improved by a second edition of the great improvement of lands by clover.* 1663.

360. Yarranton, Andrew. *England's improvement by sea and land.* 1677.
361. Youatt, William. *Cattle.* 1834.
362. Youatt, William. *British husbandry.* 3 v. 1837.
363. Young, Arthur. *Six weeks tour.* 1769.
364. Young, Arthur. *Six months tour through the North of England.* 4 v. 2nd ed. 1771.
365. Young, Arthur. *Farmers' calendar.* new ed. 1804.

*Note.* There are many methods of preparing bibliographies. Here I have chosen to arrange the books consulted alphabetically by author's names irrespective of date or subject. It would have been possible to distinguish between contemporary and modern writers, but it seemed difficult to choose a date to separate them. Another arrangement could have been by subject, but overlapping would have been inevitable, and repetition of titles is obviously undesirable. Comments on the relative value of the sources might have been added, but considerations of space excluded them.

# INDEX